AF599020

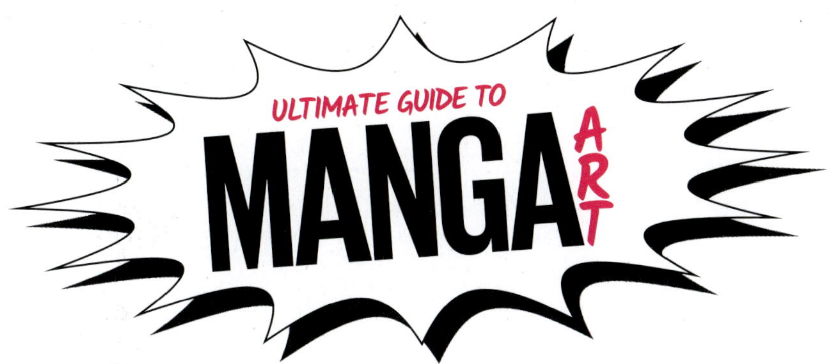
ULTIMATE GUIDE TO
MANGA
ART

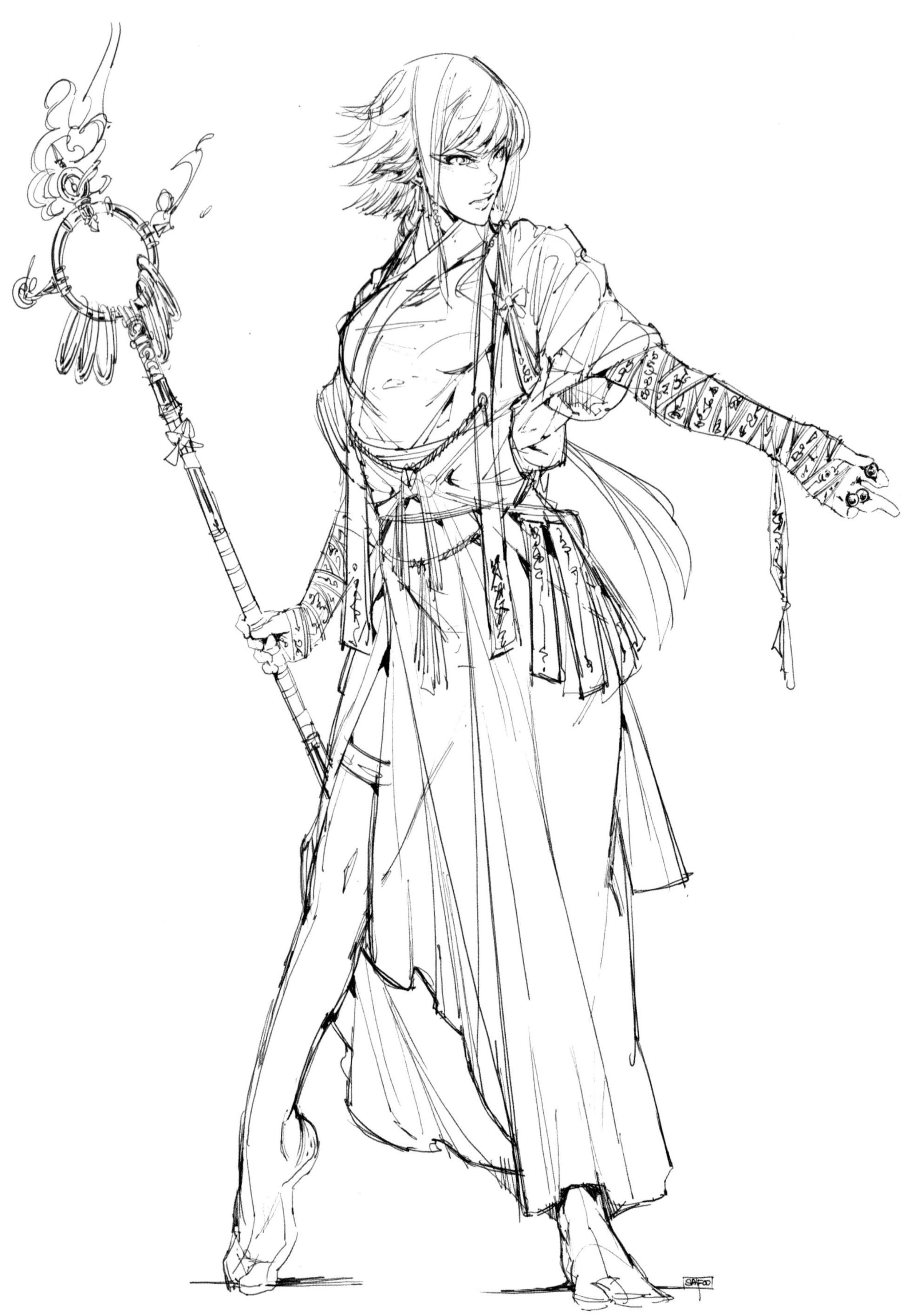

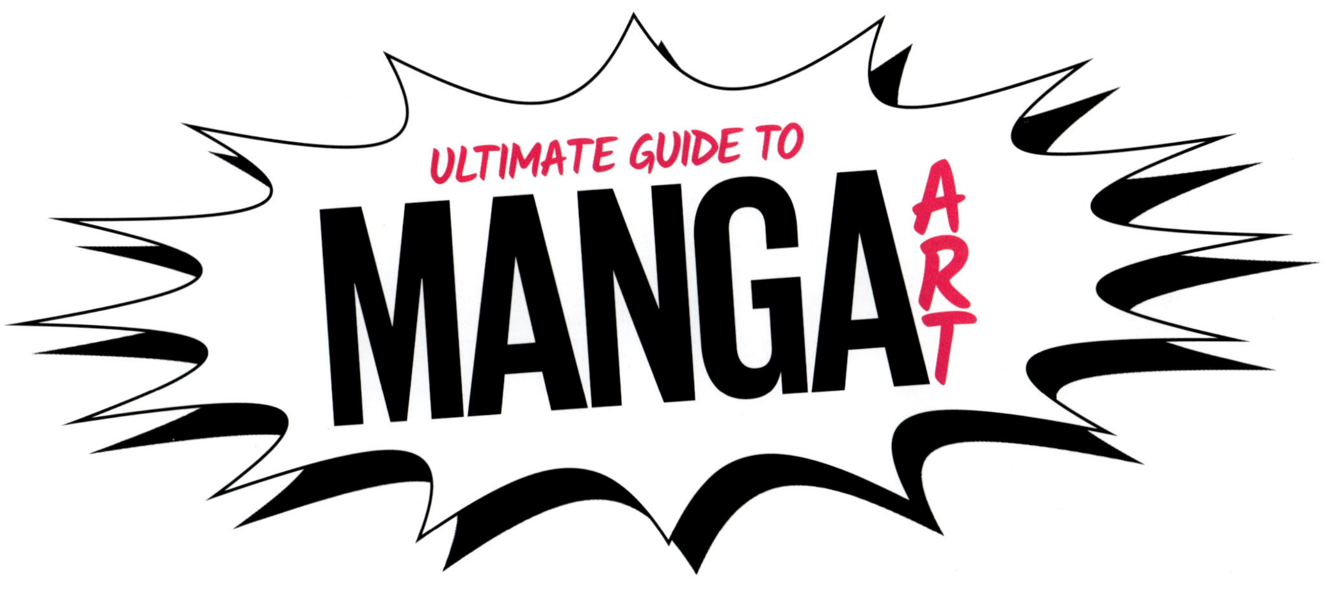

Contributors:

April Madden, Ilya Kuvshinov, Heikala,
Asia Ladowska, Djamila Knopf

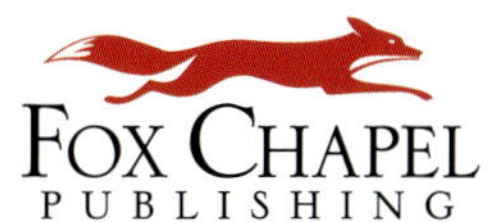

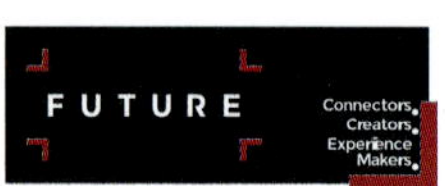

For more information about the Future plc group, go to **http://www.futureplc.com**.

ISBN *978-1-4972-0685-4*

The Catalog-in-Publication Data is on file with the Library of Congress.

To learn more about the other great books from Fox Chapel Publishing, or to find a retailer near you, call toll-free 800-457-9112 or visit us at *www.FoxChapelPublishing.com*.

We are always looking for talented authors. To submit an idea, please send a brief inquiry to acquisitions@foxchapelpublishing.com.

Printed in China
First printing

INTRODUCTION

Welcome to the marvelous world of manga! Whether you're a seasoned fan or new to the style, the tips, techniques, and tutorials from professional artists in these pages will help you develop your style. Go beyond the comic-book monotones of traditional manga and delve into the wider world of this evocative Japanese-influenced art style. Learn how to draw figures and faces with the unique manga look, then develop them into action poses with anime-style backdrops. Explore how to deploy vibrant color palettes and line effects to create atmosphere and movement, and how to use specialist tools like Paint Tool SAI, Clip Studio Paint, and Manga Studio alongside Photoshop to achieve the effects you want. Let's get started!

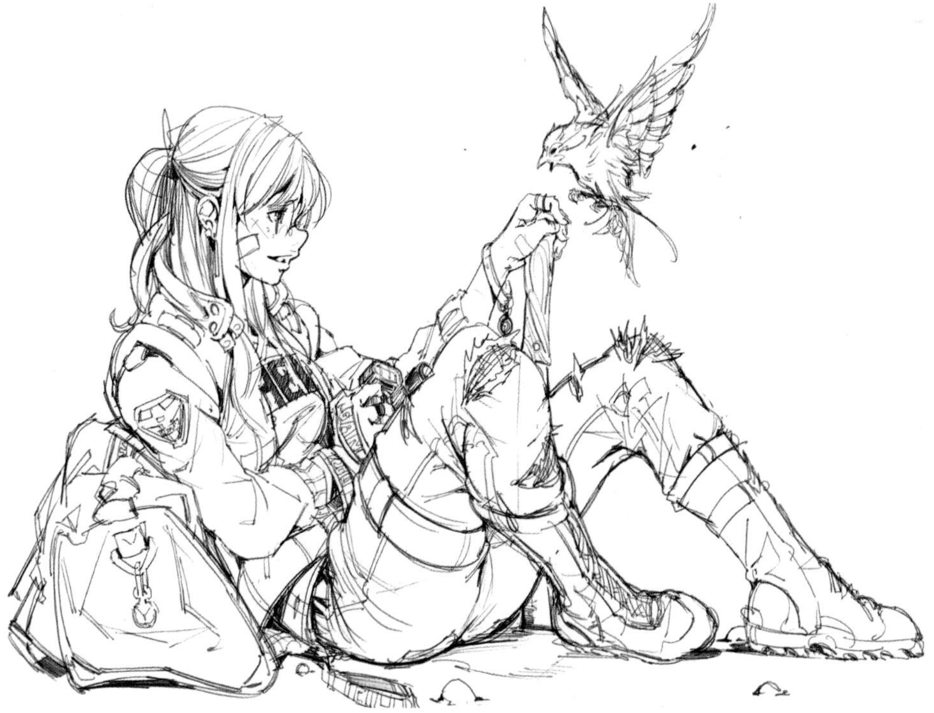

CONTENTS

8

17

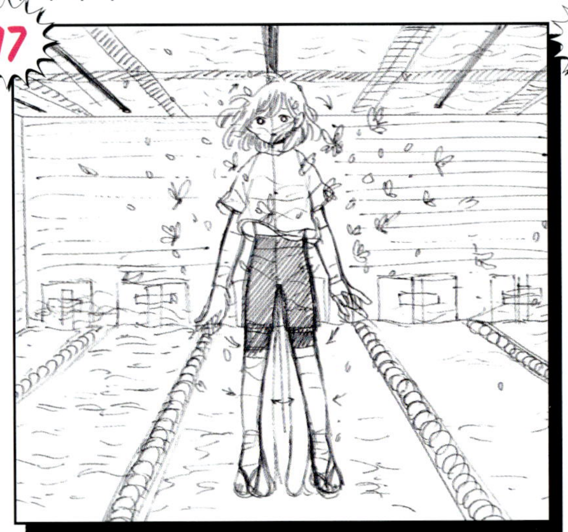

30

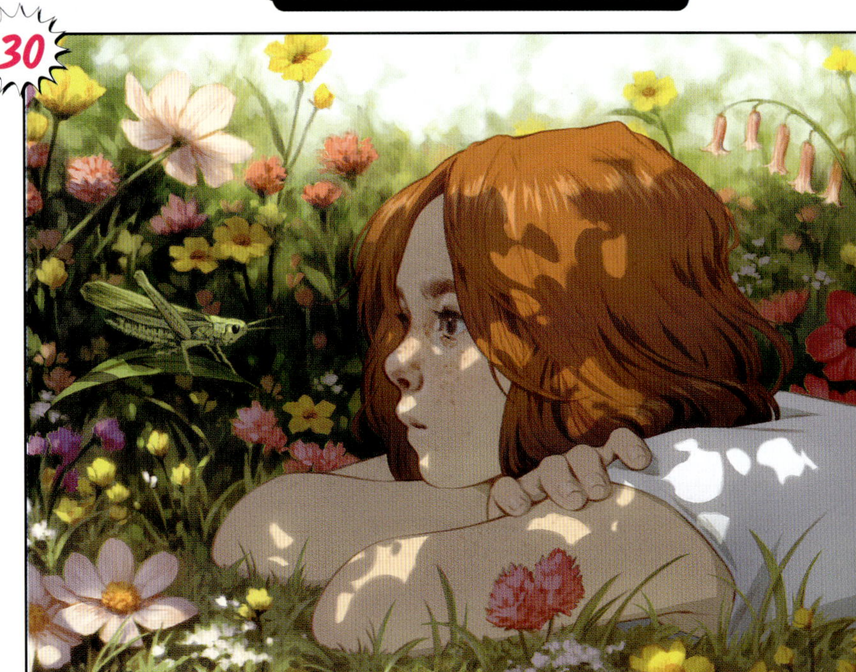

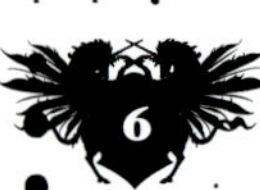

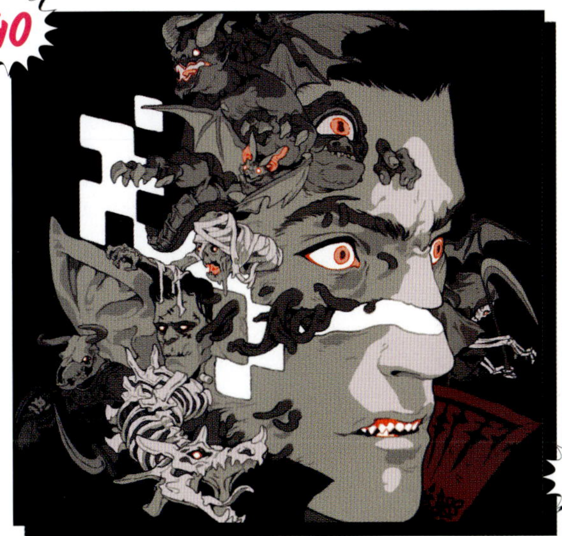
40

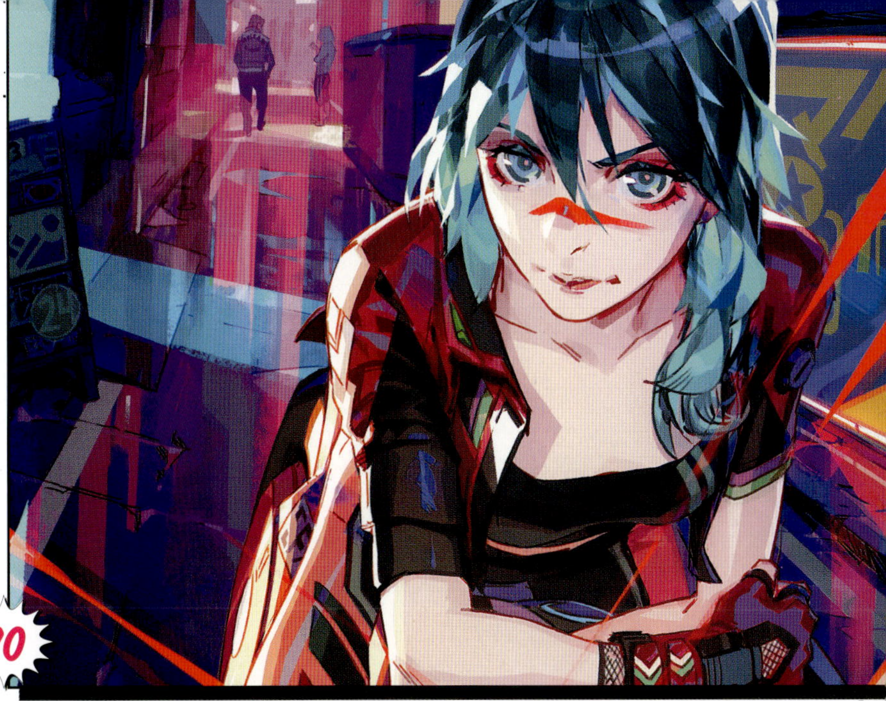
70

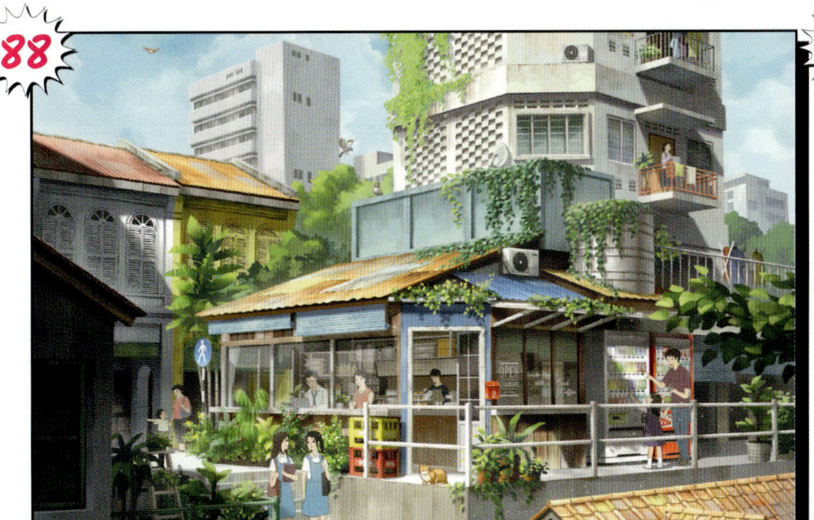
88

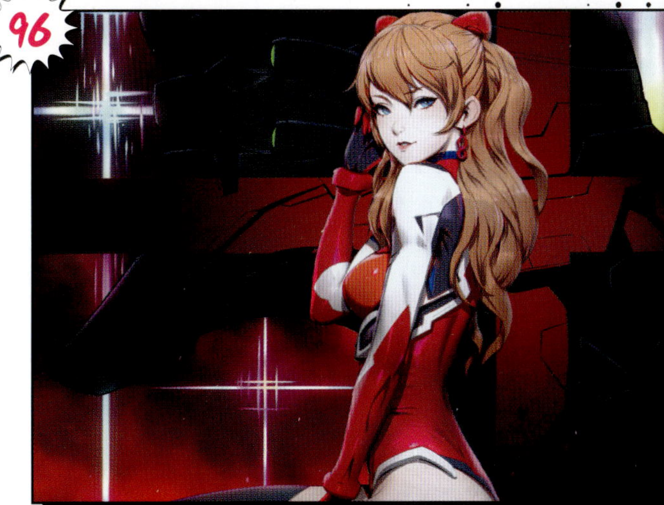
96

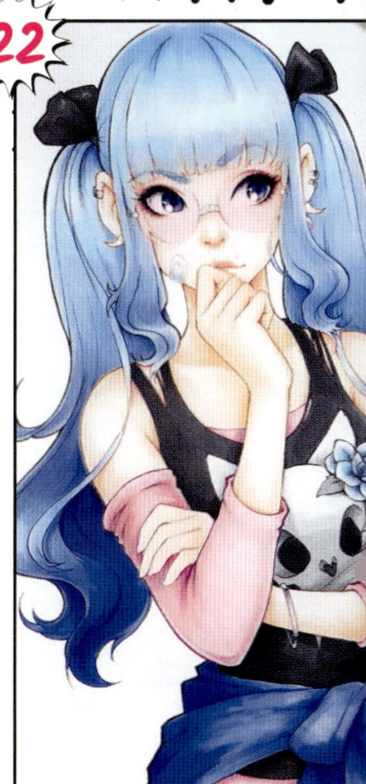
122

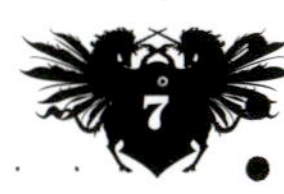

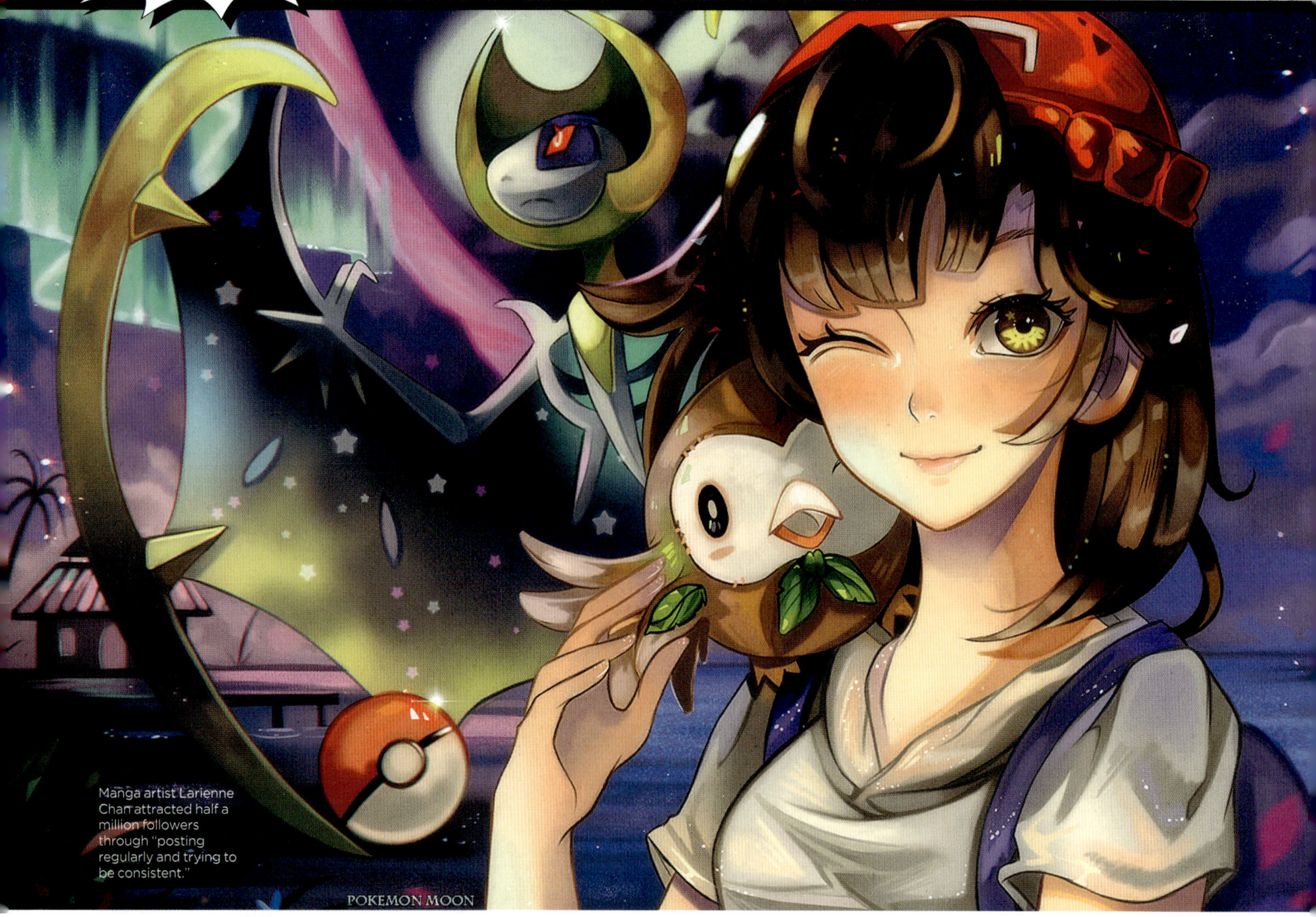

Manga artist Larienne Chan attracted half a million followers through "posting regularly and trying to be consistent."

POKEMON MOON

How to Be a Manga Superstar

Fame Game: Pro artists at the top of their game tell **Tom May** how they've been able to attract global acclaim for their manga artwork.

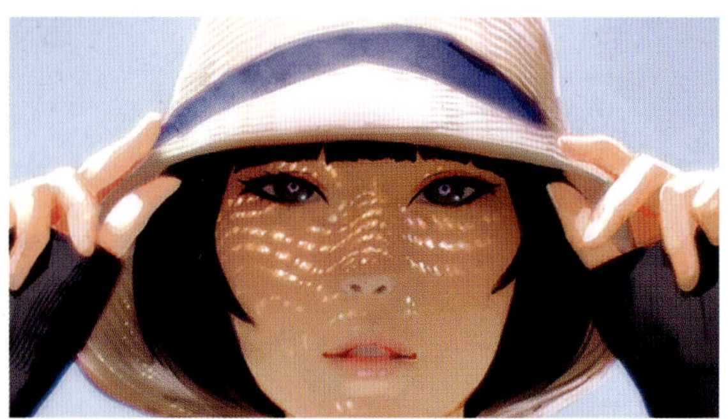

Manga is rising in popularity, and if you paint it, you're in good company. It's now possible for manga artists to amass hundreds of thousands of social media followers, get crowdfunded via sites like Patreon, sell their art commercially, and even go and live and work in Japan itself.

But how do you go about it? Here, four artists who have found success share their advice on how to follow in their footsteps.

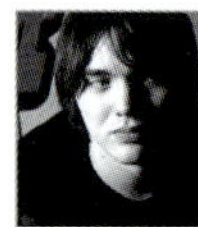

The first, and perhaps most obvious, point is that you need to get your art in front of people. "If you create a lot of illustrations but don't post them anywhere, nothing's going to happen," says **Ilya Kuvshinov**, a Russian artist based in Tokyo with 1.9 million Instagram followers (**@kuvshinov_ilya**). "It can be scary to expose your work publicly, but there'll be people who love it—trust me!"

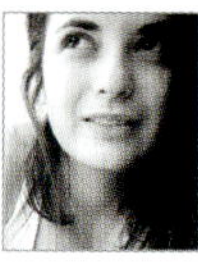

Just posting in one place, though, may not be enough, says **Larienne Chan**. Better known as Lärienne or Princess Lärienne, the Polish illustrator has made a huge impact on the DeviantArt community, which honored her with its Deviousness Award in 2016. But she's also built strong bases on Instagram (**@lariennechan**), Tumblr, and the online Japanese art community, Pixiv. ➤➤

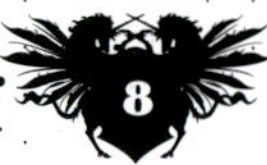

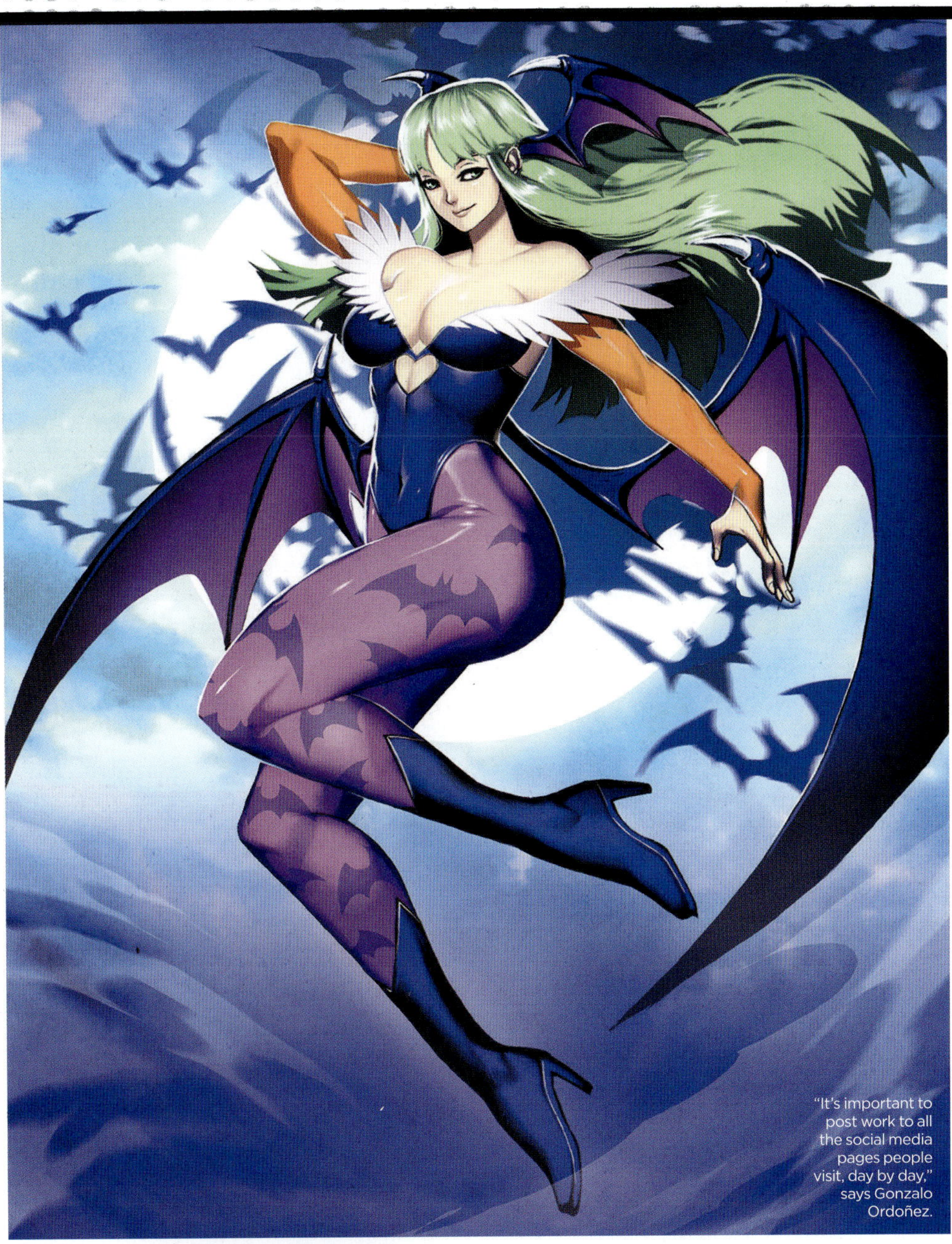

"It's important to post work to all the social media pages people visit, day by day," says Gonzalo Ordoñez.

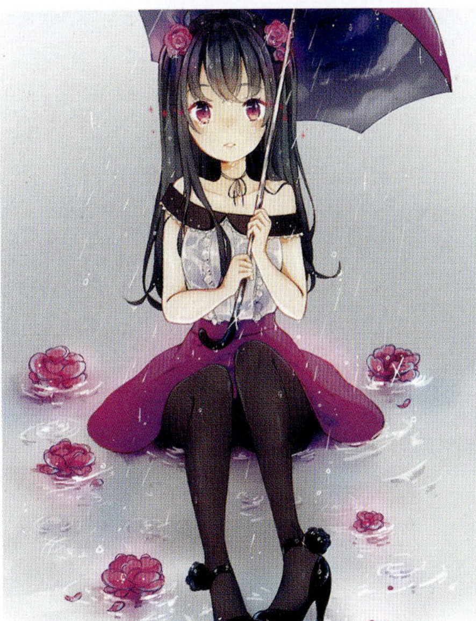

"Aiming to give my art a different feel to other manga has helped it stand out," says Aleksandra Spryszynska.

> **"If you create a lot of illustrations but don't post them anywhere, nothing's going to happen."**
> **—Ilya Kuvshinov**

INDUSTRY INSIGHT:

ILYA KUVSHINOV

Discover how this Russian manga artist gained followers and fame.

How did you first get started?
I created a short, visual-novel game. I did the script, the art, and coding myself, and sent it to a Russian gaming magazine. After that, I began working as a freelance illustrator and concept artist for a video game development company. I did a lot of illustrations for practice, and uploaded them to social networks. After some time, I've gained quite a following.

Which social media channels do you think manga artists should focus on?
It depends on your target group. For example, Instagram and Facebook aren't as popular as Twitter in Japan. Pixiv is for Asia, DeviantArt is for English-speaking countries. If you know who you're creating for, you'll know where and when to post.

How did you get more than a million Instagram followers?
By posting every day. The way Instagram's algorithm works, if someone likes your post, then there's a chance your account will be recommended to the friends of this person.

Why do you think your work is so popular?
I try to concentrate on the little things—details such as gestures or expressions that make you feel the uniqueness of every moment, bring you closer to the character. I'm not trying to stand out from other artists, though. I'm just doing what I'm interested in.

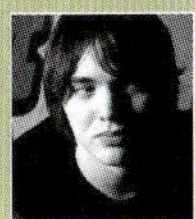

To further promote his illustrative work, Ilya published Momentary: The Art of Ilya Kuvshinov *last year.*

http://ifxm.ag/ilyak

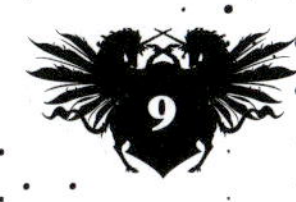

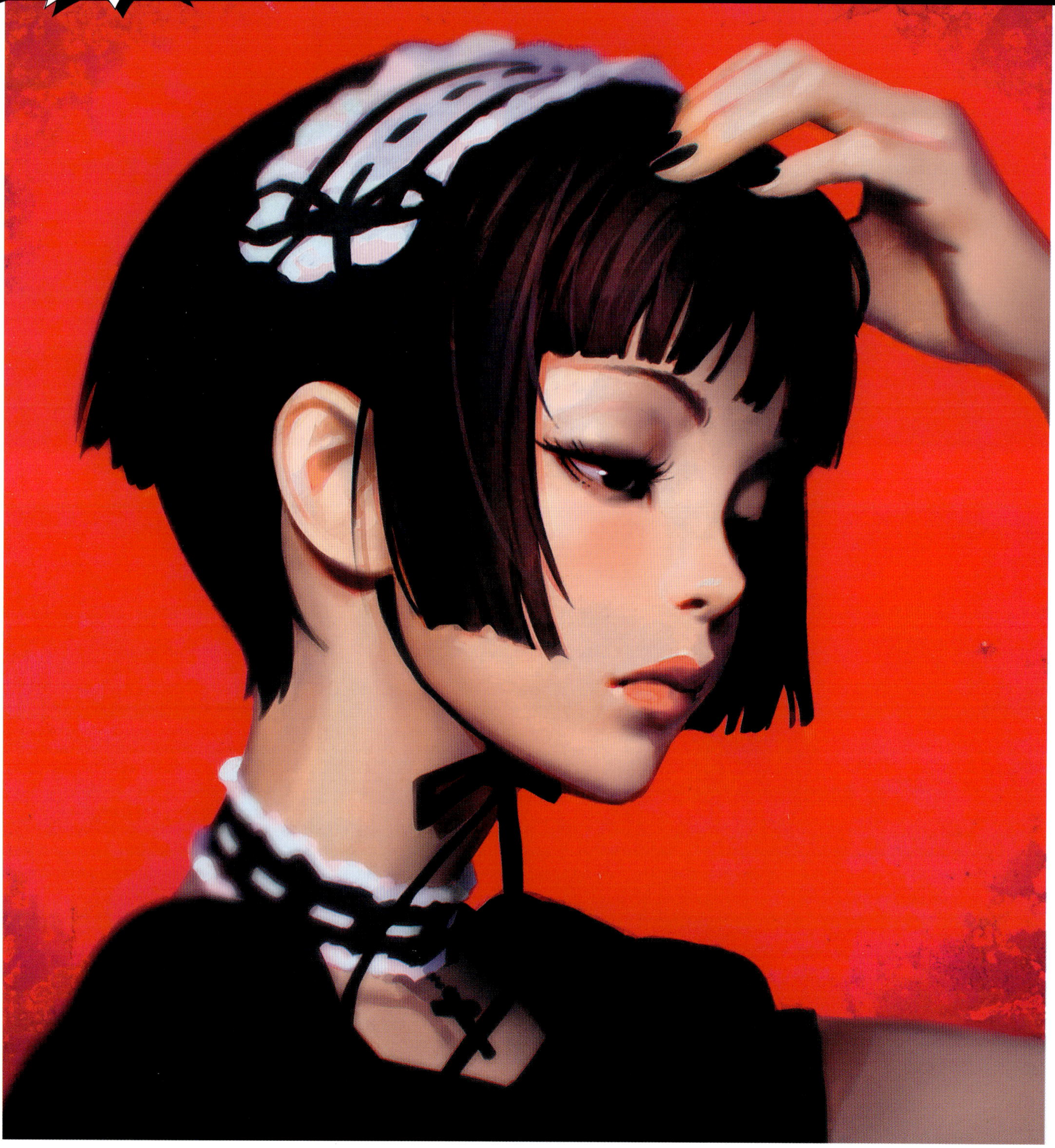

▲ One of the illustrations from Ilya's book, *Momentary: The Art of Ilya Kuvshinov.*

FIERCE COMPETITION

"Some people think just being good is enough, but unfortunately that's no longer true," Larienne says. "In these times of constantly changing algorithms and fierce competition, you never know where clients or fans are coming from, so you need to be in as many places as possible."

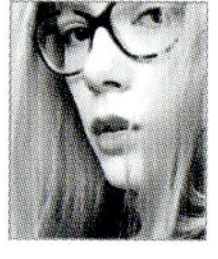

It's also important to post often, says Aleksandra Spryszynska, a Polish art student who's attracted almost a quarter of a million followers on Instagram as Yenko

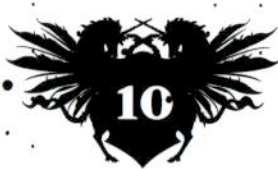

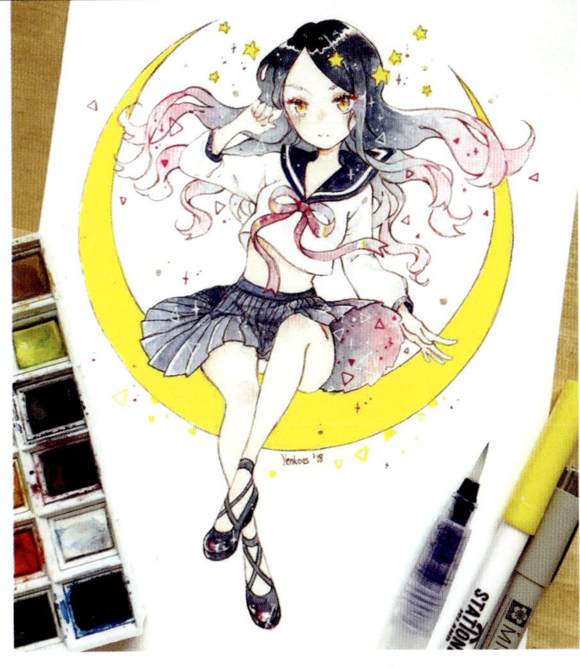

▲ "My Instagram posts have been my best promotional tool so far," says Aleksandra Spryszynska.

(@**Yenkoes**). "Being consistent is key," **Aleksandra** stresses. "You need to keep posting new things, come up with new ideas all the time, so that people don't forget you and will introduce you to their friends."

Aleksandra's own Instagram feed is a great mixture of photography, sketches, and full artwork, which makes it feel much more personal than just a straightforward gallery. "People would rather see a photo of your artwork than a clean scan of it," she stresses. "They like to see behind the scenes, the workspace. It's also a great way to show the tools you've used."

▶ "You have to produce work that people can recognize as yours, rather than replicating another artist's style," says Gonzalo Ordoñez.

Ilya Kuvshinov uses this illustration as his avatar on his social media pages. ▼

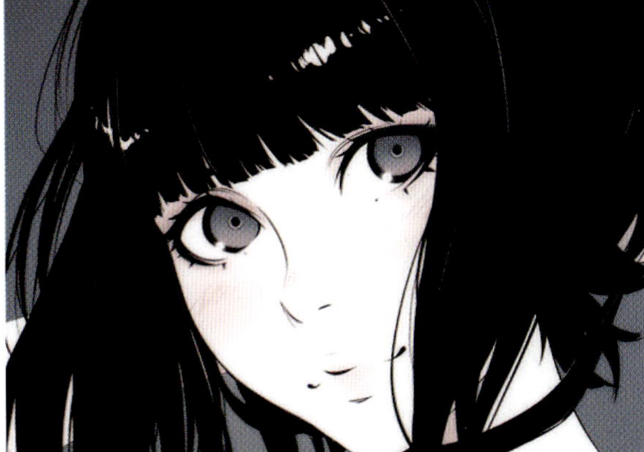

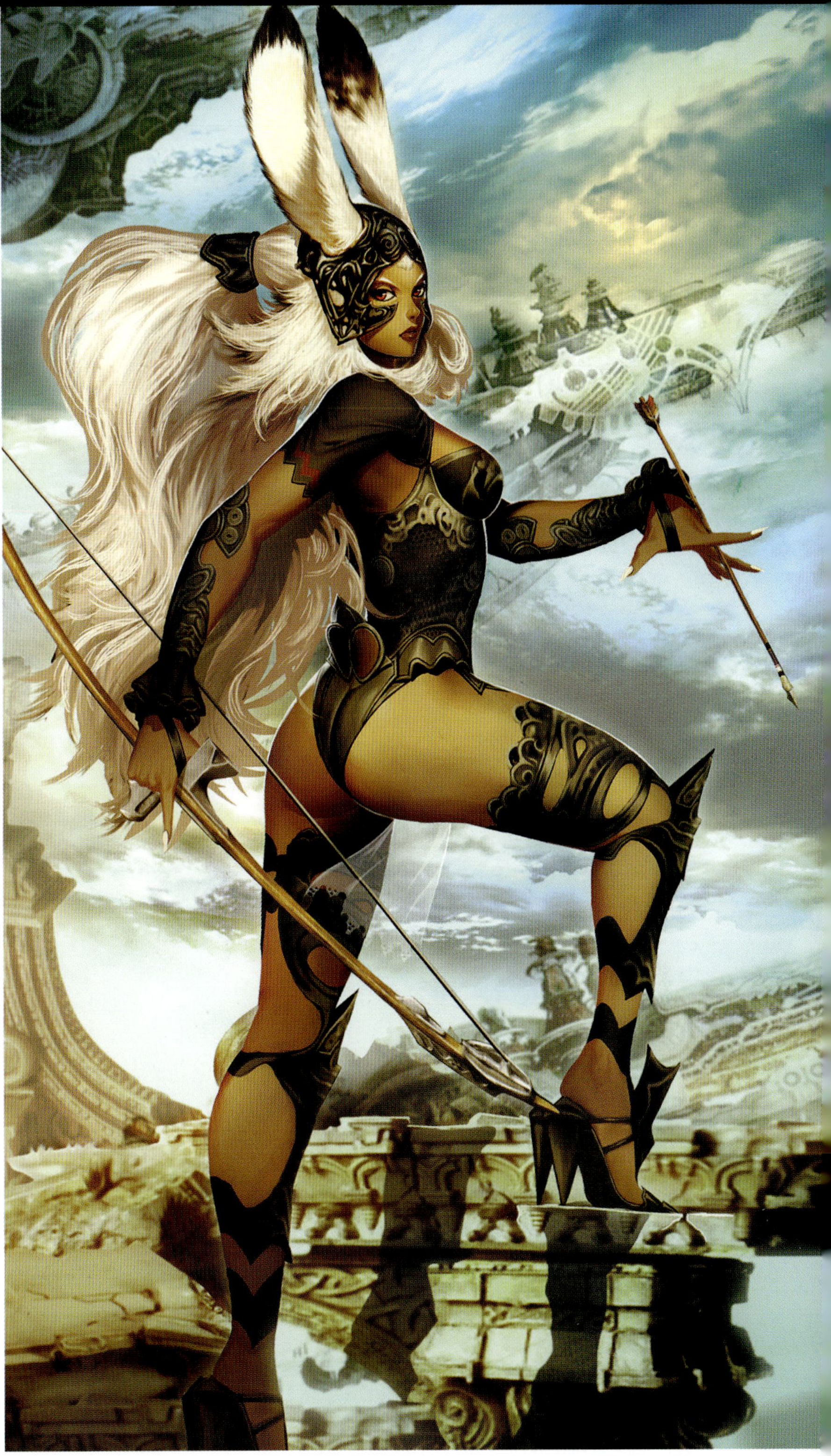

> "When you do nothing but fan art, people might start to see you more in those terms than as a creator."
>
> —Gonzalo Ordoñez

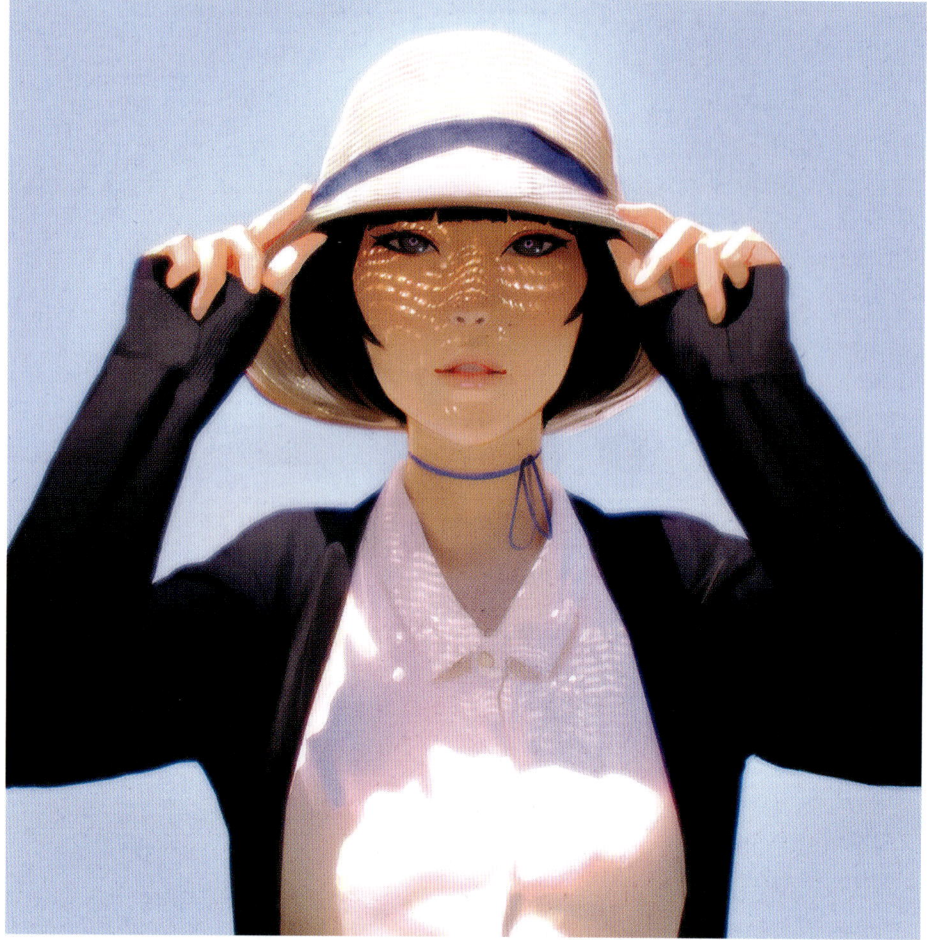

"When it comes to promoting my art, 99% takes place on the internet," says Ilya Kuvshinov.

STAY TRUE TO YOUR VISION

Given that other manga artists will be doing all that as well, though, how do you ensure your work stands out? Aleksandra believes it's essentially about being true to your vision. "Just like in other types of art, we all have our own style, and other things that make our work unique," she says. "Concentrate on what interests you, and others will follow."

That said, some have found that posting fan art can be an effective way of getting extra attention and boosting their audience. "My own 'big break' came when I shared fan art of Mathilda from the film *Léon* on Instagram," says Ilya. "Suddenly I found myself with a huge number of followers."

It was a similar story for Larienne. "My real breakthrough came with applying my personal style to fan art of western cartoons," she says.

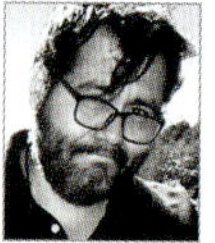

Yet for every fan artwork that goes viral, a thousand more get ignored, and it's not something you should rely on, believes **Gonzalo Ordoñez**, aka the popular Genzoman (**@mrgenzoman**). "When you do nothing but fan art, people might start to see you more in those terms than as a creator," he says. "So I think a better strategy is to combine your own ideas and concepts with fan art, not just one thing or the other."

Aleksandra adds that if you're

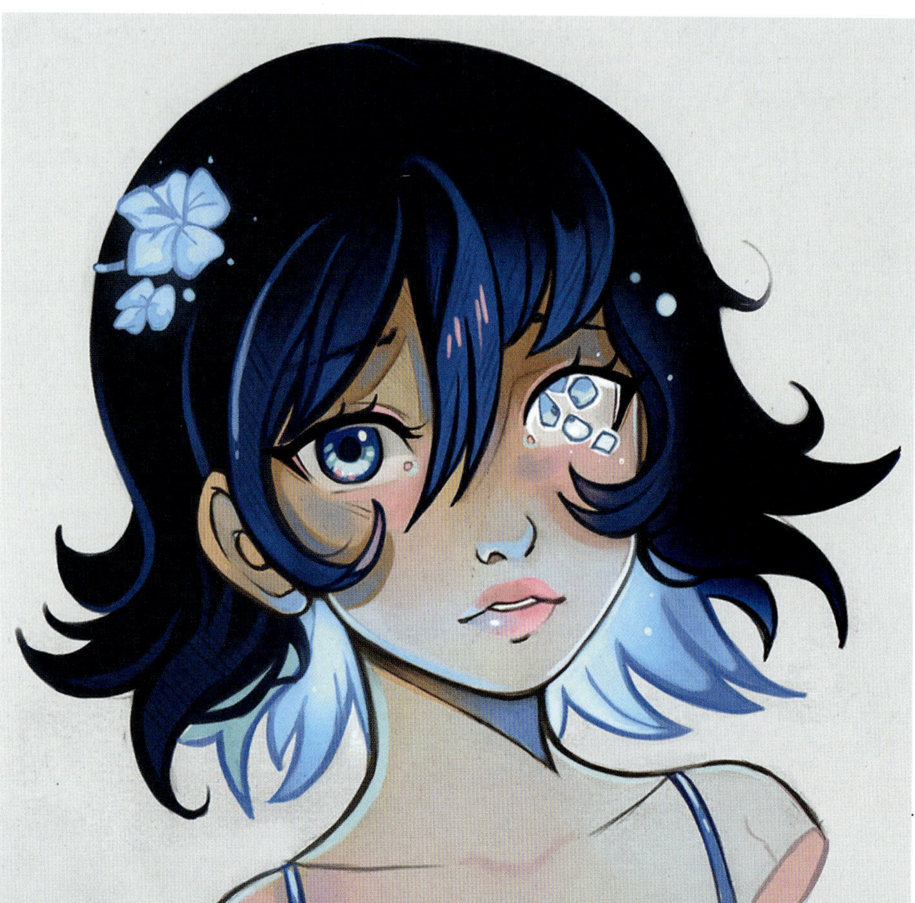

"With so many talented people around, your artwork needs to be unique to stand out," says Larienne Chan.

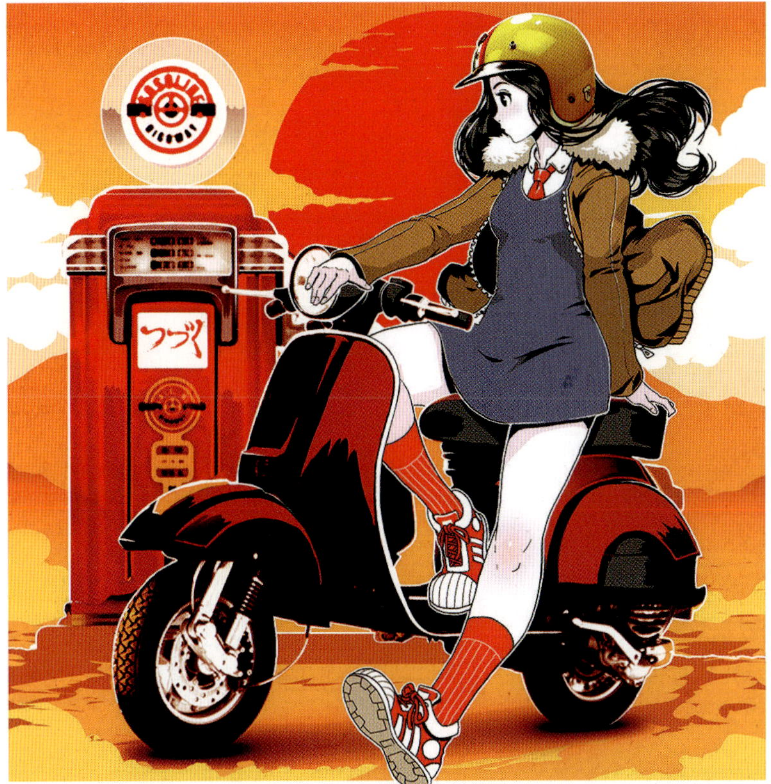

"DeviantArt's viewing public is very different to Tumblr's, Pixiv's, or Instagram's, so you need different content for each," says Gonzalo Ordoñez.

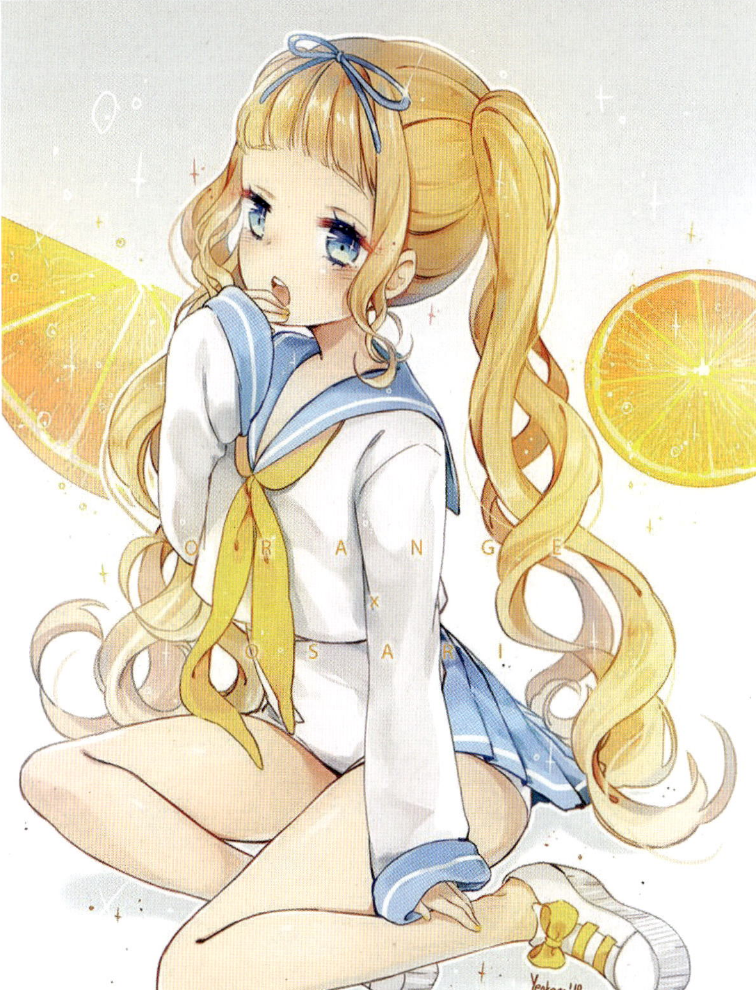

"Setting up my Facebook and Instagram profiles were the main turning point for me," says Aleksandra Spryszynska.

going to experiment with fan art, make sure it's something you have a true passion for. "It's so obvious who's actually into the fandom, and who's just out looking for likes and shares," she cautions.

IMMERSE YOURSELF

The same principle, of course, applies to the discipline itself. Manga isn't just one style, but a deep and rich culture going back decades, and the more you can study and immerse yourself in it, the better your art will become.

"Many people think manga is only Shonen [manga aimed at teenage males] or Moe [childlike characters that aim to elicit a strong emotional response], which is what audiences outside Asia tend to see," says Gonzalo. "But there are many genres, artists, and visions within manga, so I'd encourage young people to learn as much as they can about its origins.

"Explore the work of Osamu Tezuka, Shotaro Ishinomori, and Go Nagai," he says, "as well as other types of Japanese artists, such as Yoshiharu Tsuge or Yoshihiro Tatsumi. This helps you diversify, because if we're all doing similar styles, we'll end up competing with one another. A manga artist doesn't have to be a one-trick pony, but can be as versatile as any other type of creative."

In short, it's about being original and finding your own, distinct path. "When I was starting out, I copied pages from *Dragon Ball*, and recreated the style of artists like Kazushi Hagiwara," says Gonzalo. "But there's a point where you have to try new things, so people don't see you as 'the imitator of,' like the art equivalent of a covers band."

And after that, it's down to persistence, hard work, and just continuing until it starts to happen for you. "Believe in yourself," says Larienne Chan. "Get engaged with the art community. Ask questions, experiment, and practice a lot."

And Aleksandra adds, "Don't give up. It's very hard. People aren't fair, social media isn't fair. But you can be fair to yourself. Do what you love and what defines you. Work hard and it will pay off!"

JOURNEY
"The cover of *The Art of Heikala* describes my works—a magical girl on her way to adventures ahead, accompanied by wildlife and beautiful nature."

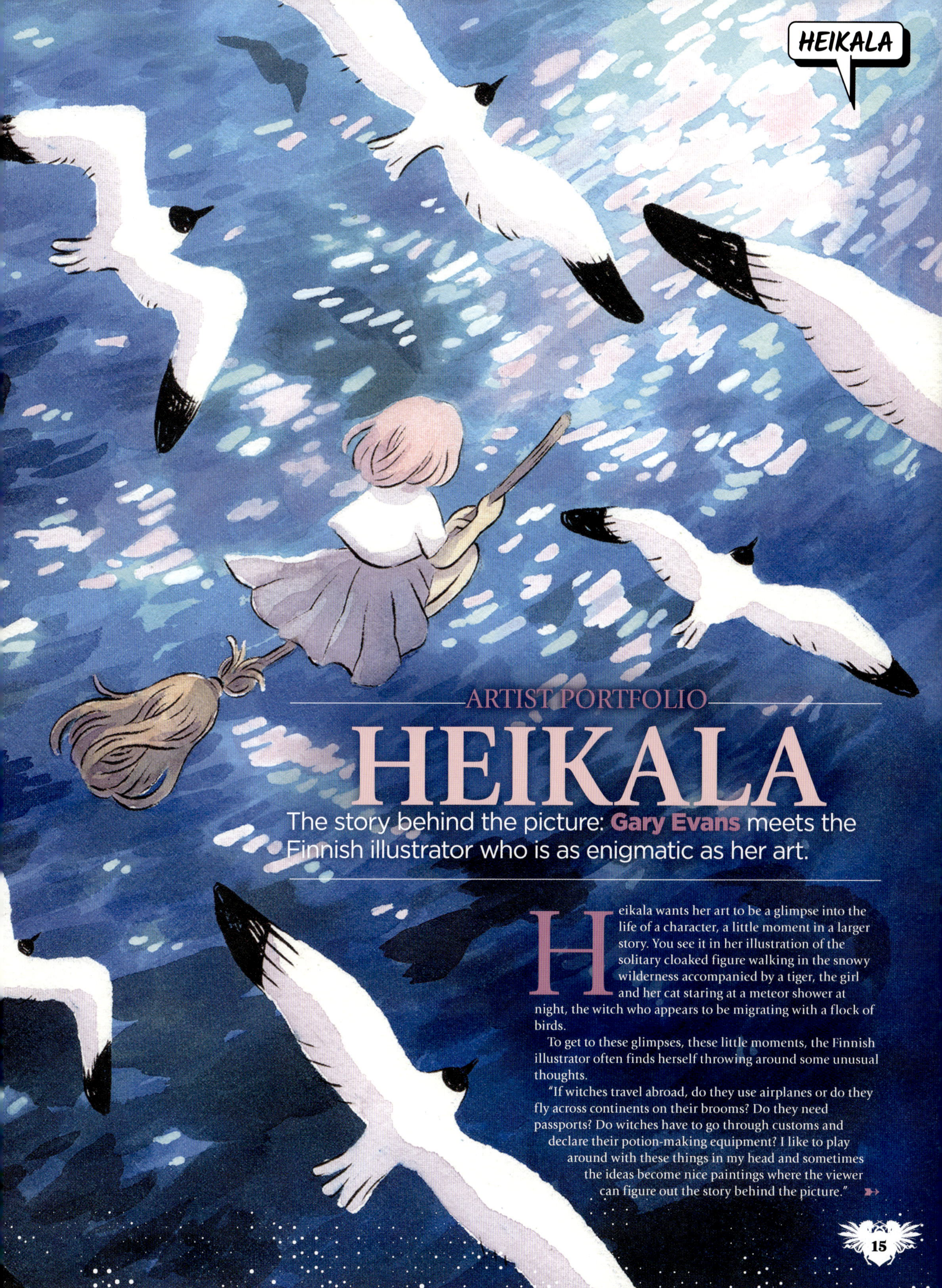

ARTIST PORTFOLIO

HEIKALA

The story behind the picture: **Gary Evans** meets the Finnish illustrator who is as enigmatic as her art.

Heikala wants her art to be a glimpse into the life of a character, a little moment in a larger story. You see it in her illustration of the solitary cloaked figure walking in the snowy wilderness accompanied by a tiger, the girl and her cat staring at a meteor shower at night, the witch who appears to be migrating with a flock of birds.

To get to these glimpses, these little moments, the Finnish illustrator often finds herself throwing around some unusual thoughts.

"If witches travel abroad, do they use airplanes or do they fly across continents on their brooms? Do they need passports? Do witches have to go through customs and declare their potion-making equipment? I like to play around with these things in my head and sometimes the ideas become nice paintings where the viewer can figure out the story behind the picture." ➳

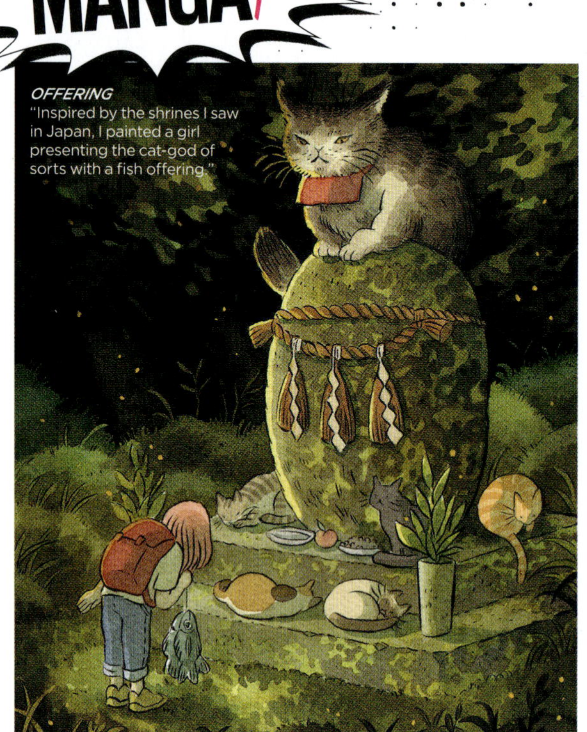

OFFERING
"Inspired by the shrines I saw in Japan, I painted a girl presenting the cat-god of sorts with a fish offering."

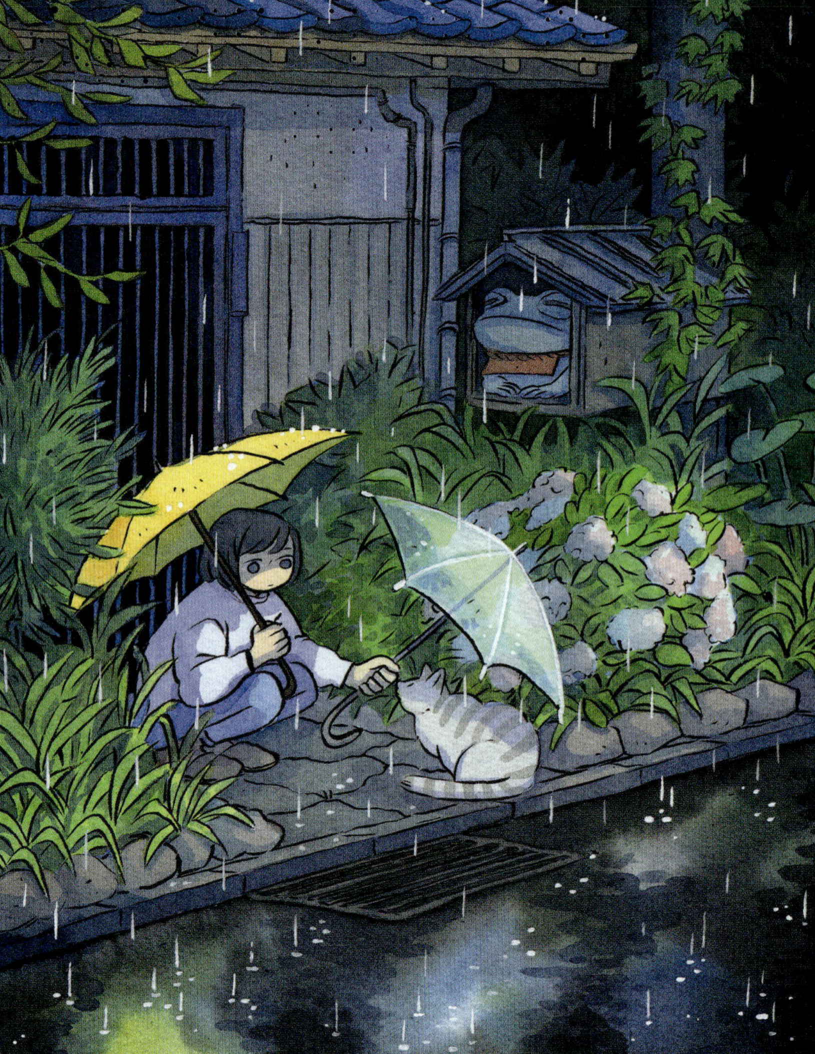

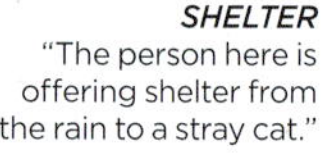

SHELTER
"The person here is offering shelter from the rain to a stray cat."

Heikala lives in a large house in Oulu, Finland. She has a whole room to handle stock and postage for the online shop she started straight out of university, and has since built into a very successful small business. In the corner of her workspace, the house's former living room, she keeps equipment for making and editing the videos that have helped her earn nearly two million followers on social media. Her desk stands in the same room, under the big window that lets in lots of light, and here she keeps the pens, paper, brushes, and colored inks used to give her illustrations that distinctive look—tools she'll soon release as part of her own range of art supplies.

This makes Heikala sound entrepreneurial, influencing, hustling. But she describes Oulu as a good place for an introvert. She doesn't disclose her full name and never posts photos of herself. The story behind this requires a bit more investigation.

> **“I didn't have to worry about getting a job to support myself during the studies.”**
> **—Heikala**

Maybe the answer lies in the bottom of two drawers of the desk under the big window. It's here that Heikala keeps her most prized possessions.

GOING IT ALONE

Heikala was always drawing. It was animals when she was very young, then Pokémon arrived in Finland, and for years her sketchbooks were full of Bulbasaurs and Charmanders. At school, she had an art teacher who encouraged her to experiment with a range of materials and techniques. She sculpted. She got into oils. In the early 2000s, manga appeared on magazine stands in her hometown, Oulu, so Heikala advanced to sketching humans in the style of Japanese comics such as *Ranma ½*.

At 16, she was accepted into a high school specializing in art in Helsinki, a six-hour train ride away, which meant leaving home. Her parents were always very encouraging and so, after high school, she went on to university in Lahti. It was on the five-year graphic design course that she first learned about the importance of branding, product design, and visual storytelling.

These days, Heikala does the odd bit of illustration work for clients, but only if it comes with complete creative control. Still at university, she started going to conventions, to artist alley, where her artwork sold surprisingly well. This meant she was torn between getting a job at a graphic design studio or trying it make a living from her own art. She tried freelance graphic design, but learned pretty quickly it wasn't for her. After graduating, she started building her own business:

Artist PROFILE

Heikala
LOCATION: Finland
FAVORITE ARTISTS: Yoshitaka Amano, Zao Dao, Tove Jansson, Jun Kumaori, and Akane Malbeni.
MEDIA: Ballpoint, brush pen, colored inks, Procreate, and Photoshop.
WEB: *www.heikala.com*

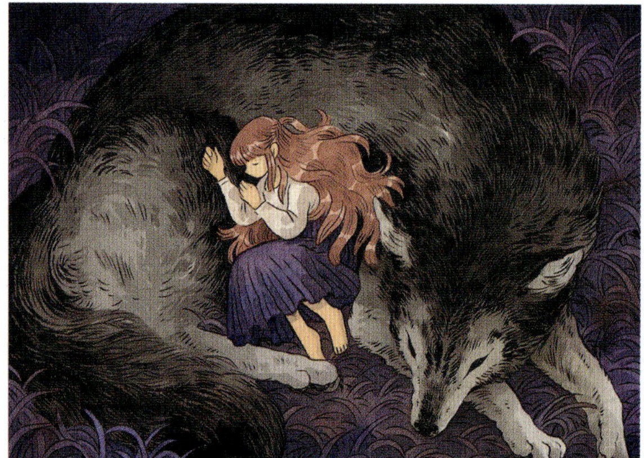

CHILD
"I made this piece earlier this year during the annual Inktober challenge."

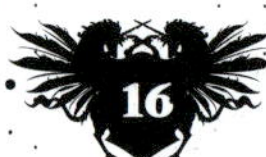

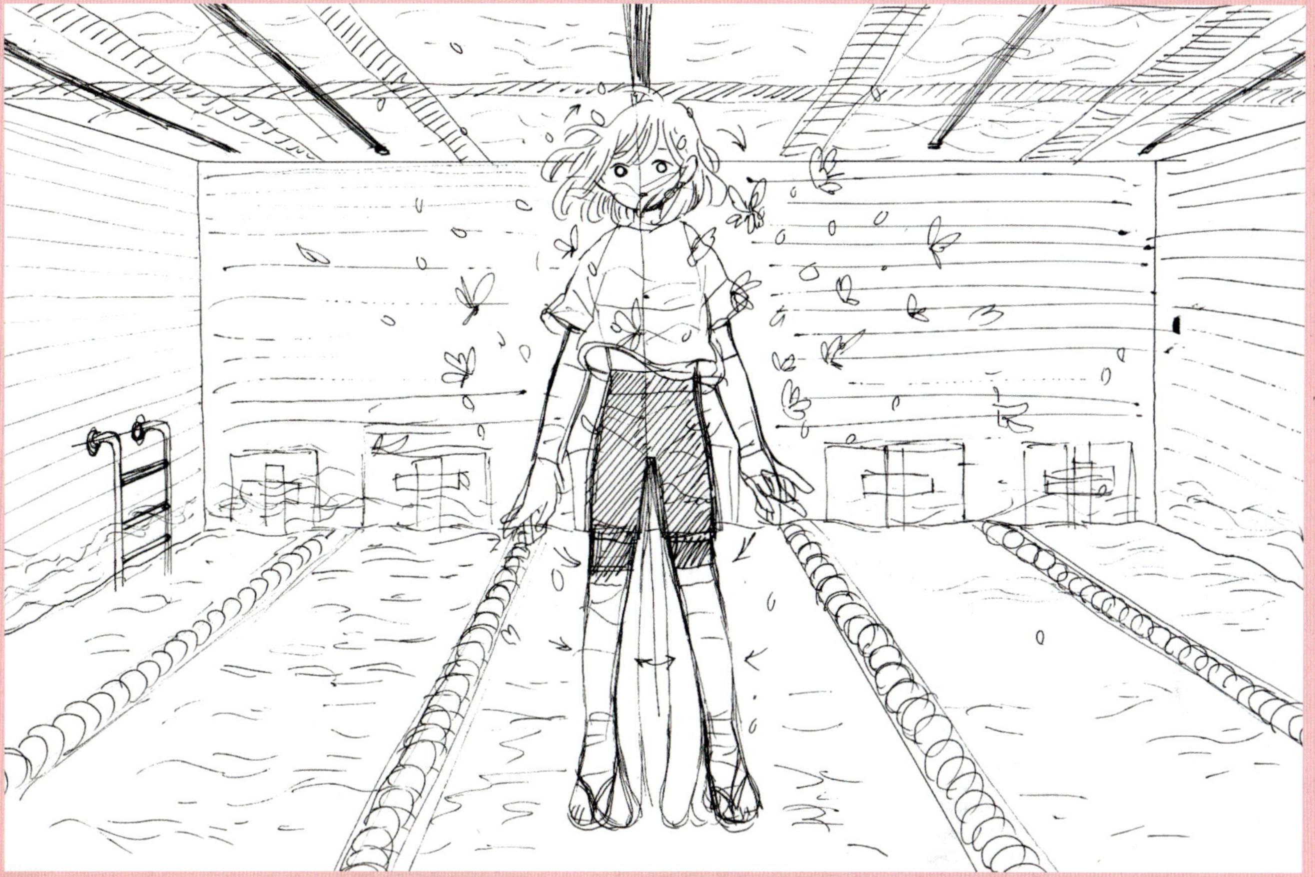

ECHOES
"I struggled with the pose and proportions of the character, and whenever that happens I scan the sketch and make final adjustments digitally by resizing/skewing."

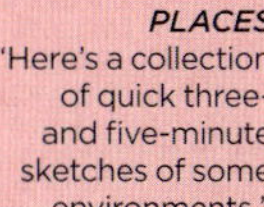

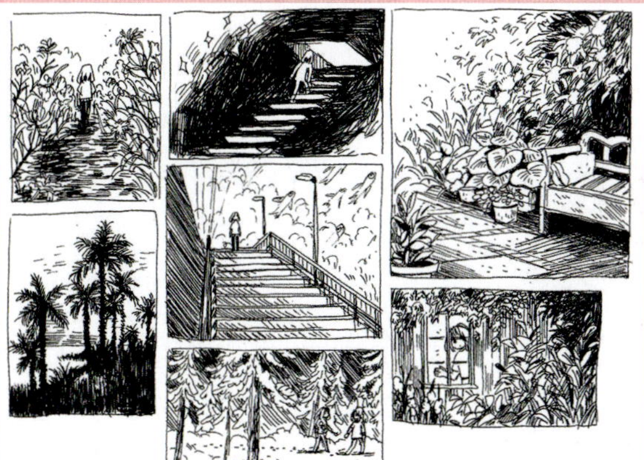

PLACES
"Here's a collection of quick three- and five-minute sketches of some environments."

DON'T GET HUNG UP ON DETAILS

Heikala explains why she sketches fast and small—and never uses an eraser.

"Whenever I sketch, I always use a pen or a ballpoint pen. I made a decision maybe six years ago to not use an eraser at all when sketching. This has streamlined my process and helped me not get hung up on details during the sketching stage, and to work around my mistakes rather than erasing my process.

I start off by drawing in my sketchbook. I use either Deleter or Muji sketchbooks, and I like to sketch on slightly textured paper. For some reason, I prefer sketching on a horizontal page rather than vertical—I don't quite know why that is. I somehow feel restricted when there's too little space horizontally, which is why I mainly use spiral-bound sketchbooks, so I have the freedom to sketch across the page. But I end up flipping my sketchbook upside down on every other page so I don't have to rest my hand on the spiral.

I always sketch really small. My average sketch for a painting idea is usually matchbox-size and it only has the bare essential components for a composition. I scan the tiny sketch and print it out in a bigger size, and then start to work on the smaller details for the sketch. When I'm happy with everything, I trace the sketch onto watercolor paper and start working on the line art, and then start adding colors."

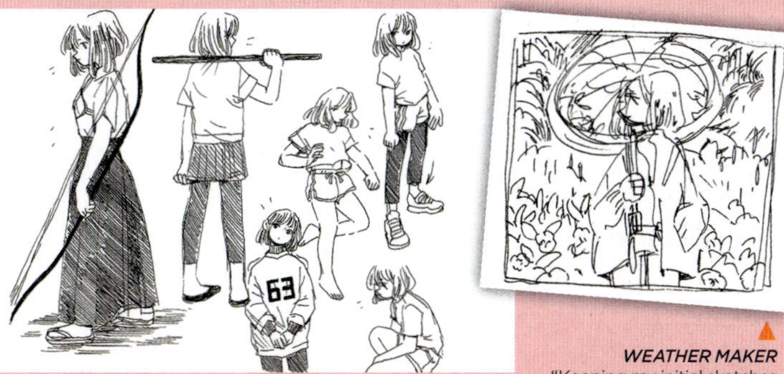

QUICK POSES
Sketches of people and poses from some photo reference."

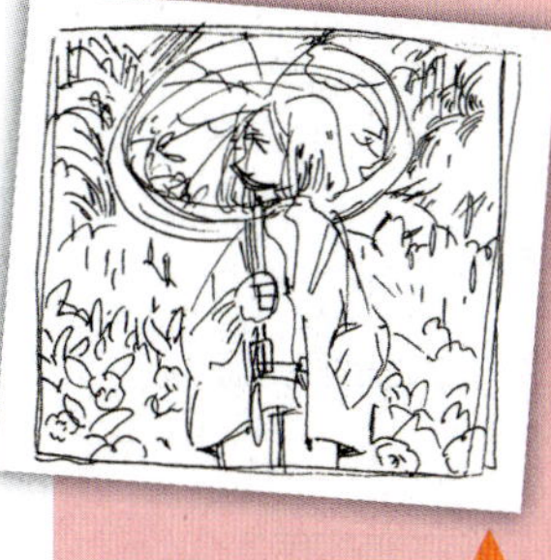

WEATHER MAKER
"Keeping my initial sketches rough helps me flesh out the composition of a piece without getting caught up in details."

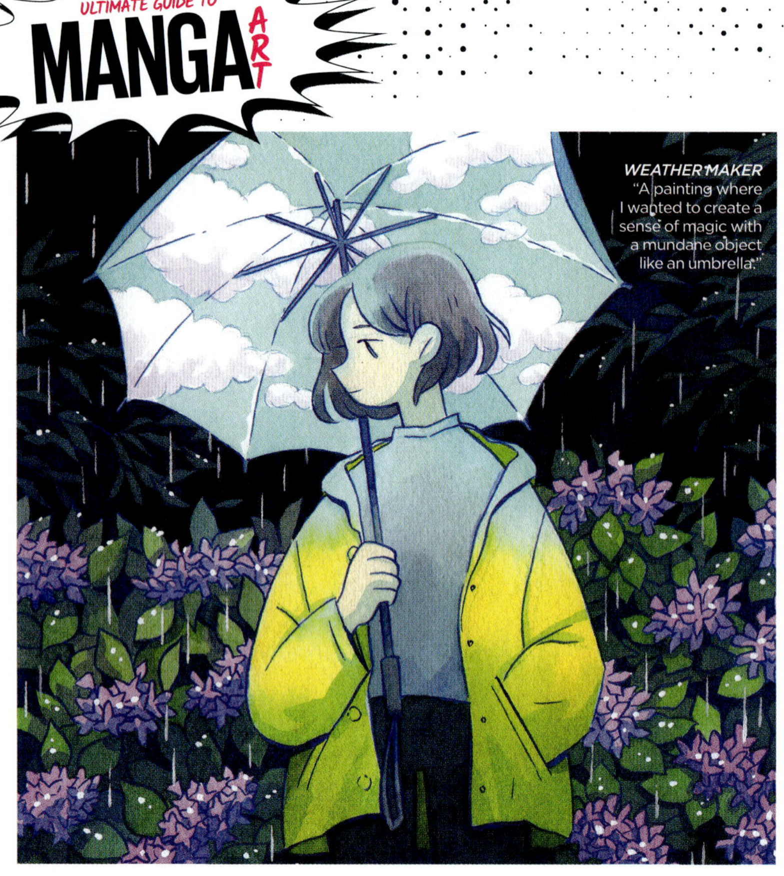

WEATHER MAKER
"A painting where I wanted to create a sense of magic with a mundane object like an umbrella."

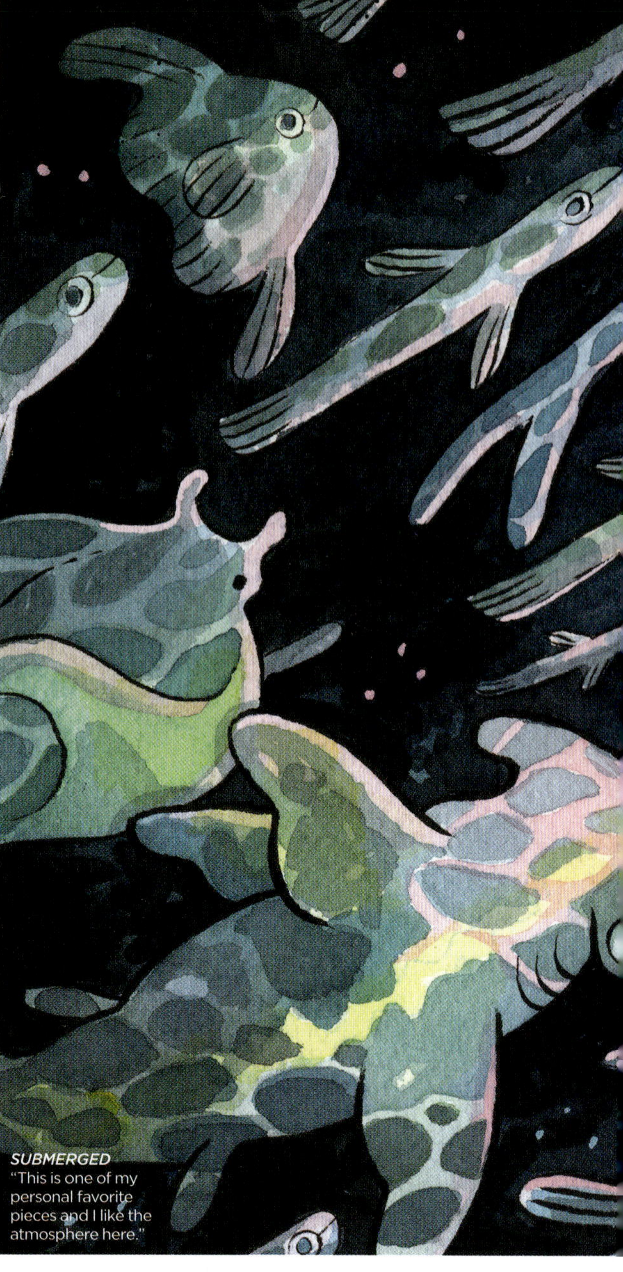

SUBMERGED
"This is one of my personal favorite pieces and I like the atmosphere here."

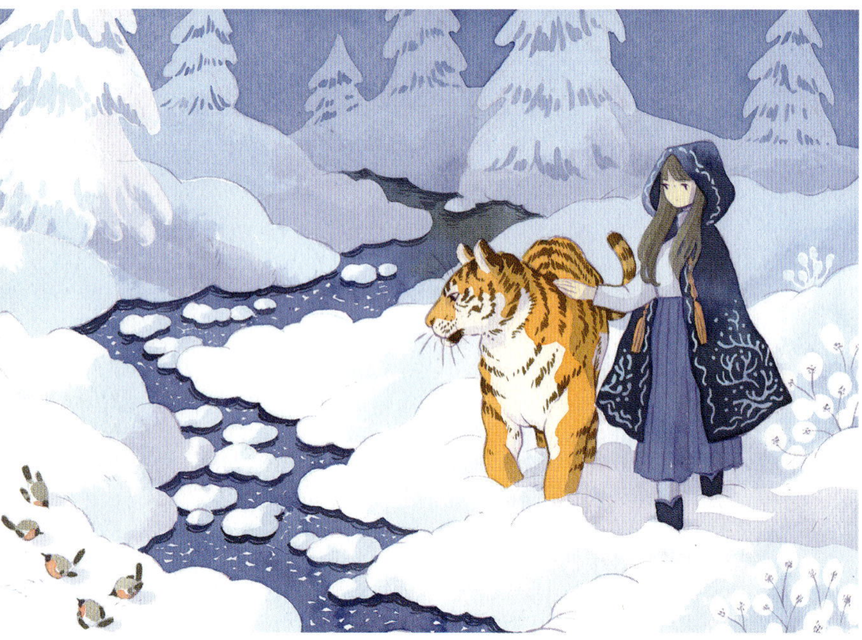

STROLL IN THE SNOW
"I really like how the snow looks in the foreground of this piece, and I'd like to experiment with making snow more in the future."

"Thanks to the free education system in Finland, I didn't have to worry about getting a job to support myself during the studies, nor did I have to take out a loan to study. I'm extremely fortunate that it all worked out."

Working for herself means she has time to experiment on her own large-scale projects, like her book published in 2019, *The Art of Heikala*, and the range of art supplies, mugs, and other merchandise that she has released in the last few years. Most of the supplies she uses herself are only available in Europe and Japan. So she spent a year contacting suppliers and putting together a range to sell worldwide through her online shop. The aim is to encourage more people to make things with their hands.

"Since it's a project that's close to my heart, I didn't want to compromise on any aspect of it, so I decided to make this happen from start to finish by myself, but that also means that I'm taking the financial blow if it doesn't end up working out.

"Making solo projects is of course a big risk financially, but I'm at a point in my life where I want to prioritize projects with full artistic freedom over doing something that I don't have my heart in—even if it ends up being a financial failure."

HUNTING FOR INSPIRATION

Heikala doesn't wait for inspiration to find her. She goes looking for it. Often it's a numbers game: she sits down at her desk and sketches as many as 30 matchbox-size images, but will usually develop only a few. Before that, for an idea to take shape, she has to take in a lot of visual stimulation. She looks through a ton of images on Pinterest and in her own photography.

Japan still plays big part in her art. She's visited the country eight times so far. She's also into magic, fantasy, and mythology. Finland's wealth of natural

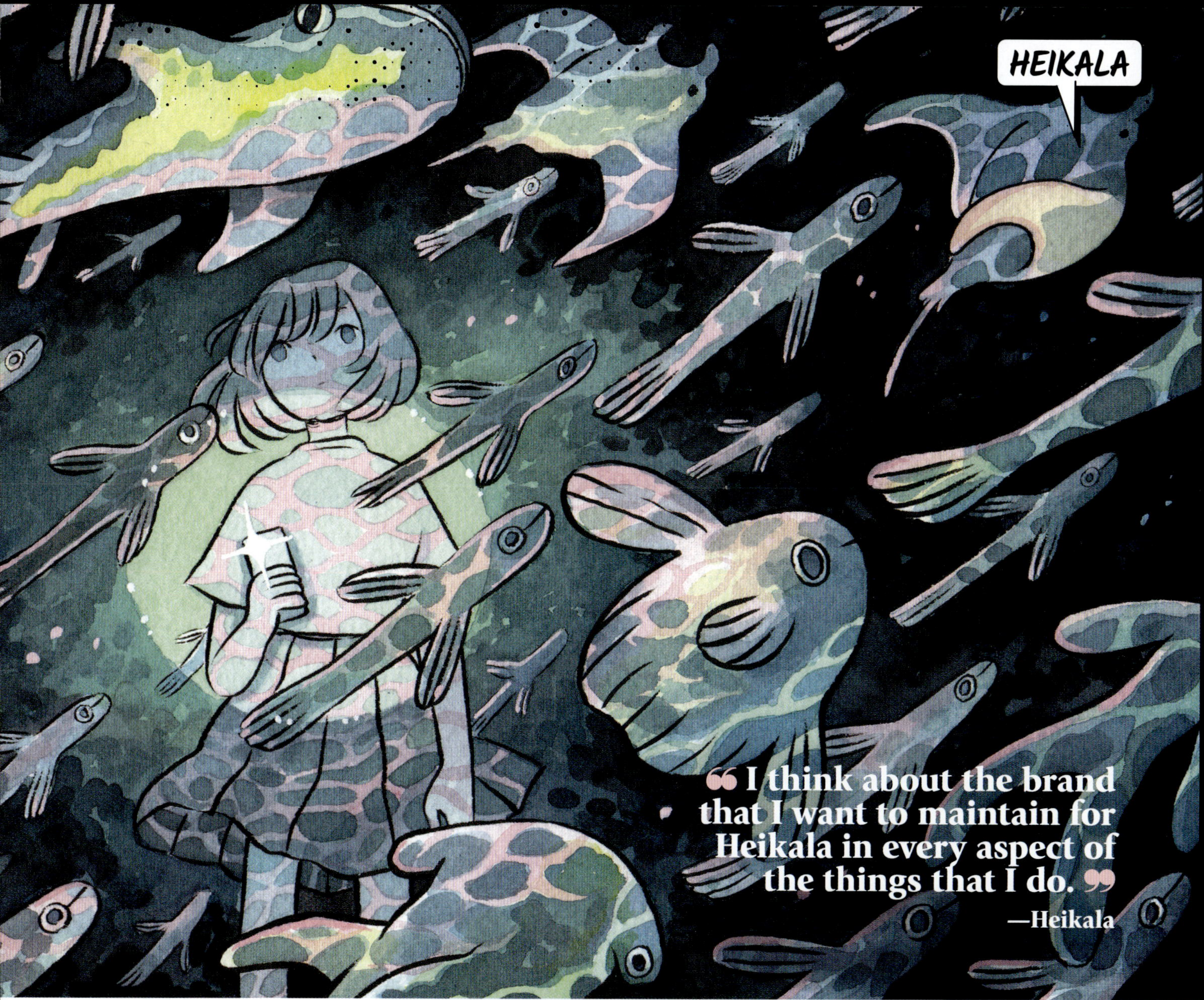

HEIKALA

> “I think about the brand that I want to maintain for Heikala in every aspect of the things that I do.”
>
> —Heikala

beauty increasingly influences her work, as do Finnish children's book illustrators like Rudolf Koivu and Tove Jansson.

She sketches very quickly with a pen or ballpoint pen and never erases anything. Mistakes are worked around. Details aren't important just yet. The small sketch is scanned, printed large, and finished with colored inks.

THE ART OF BRANDING

"In my opinion, as a commercial artist, it's good to have skills in branding and creating a visual identity for yourself. When thinking about brands, it's not only the logo that some company has, but everything that company does.

"I think about the brand that I want to maintain for Heikala in every aspect of the things that I do: how I interact with my followers, what kind of art I want to make, the subjects I want to tackle in my art, what kind of ➳

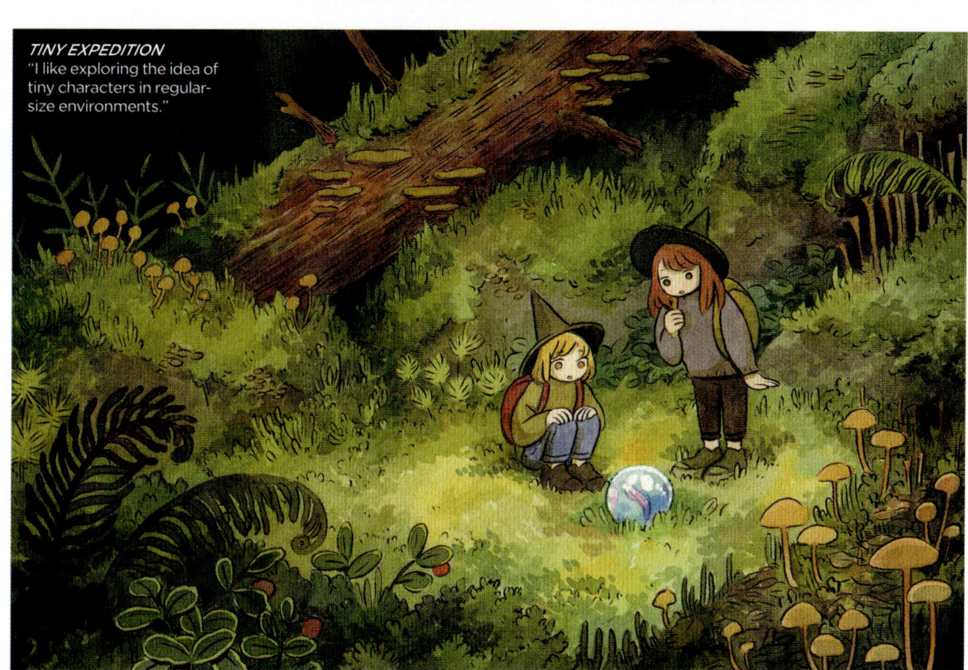

TINY EXPEDITION
"I like exploring the idea of tiny characters in regular-size environments."

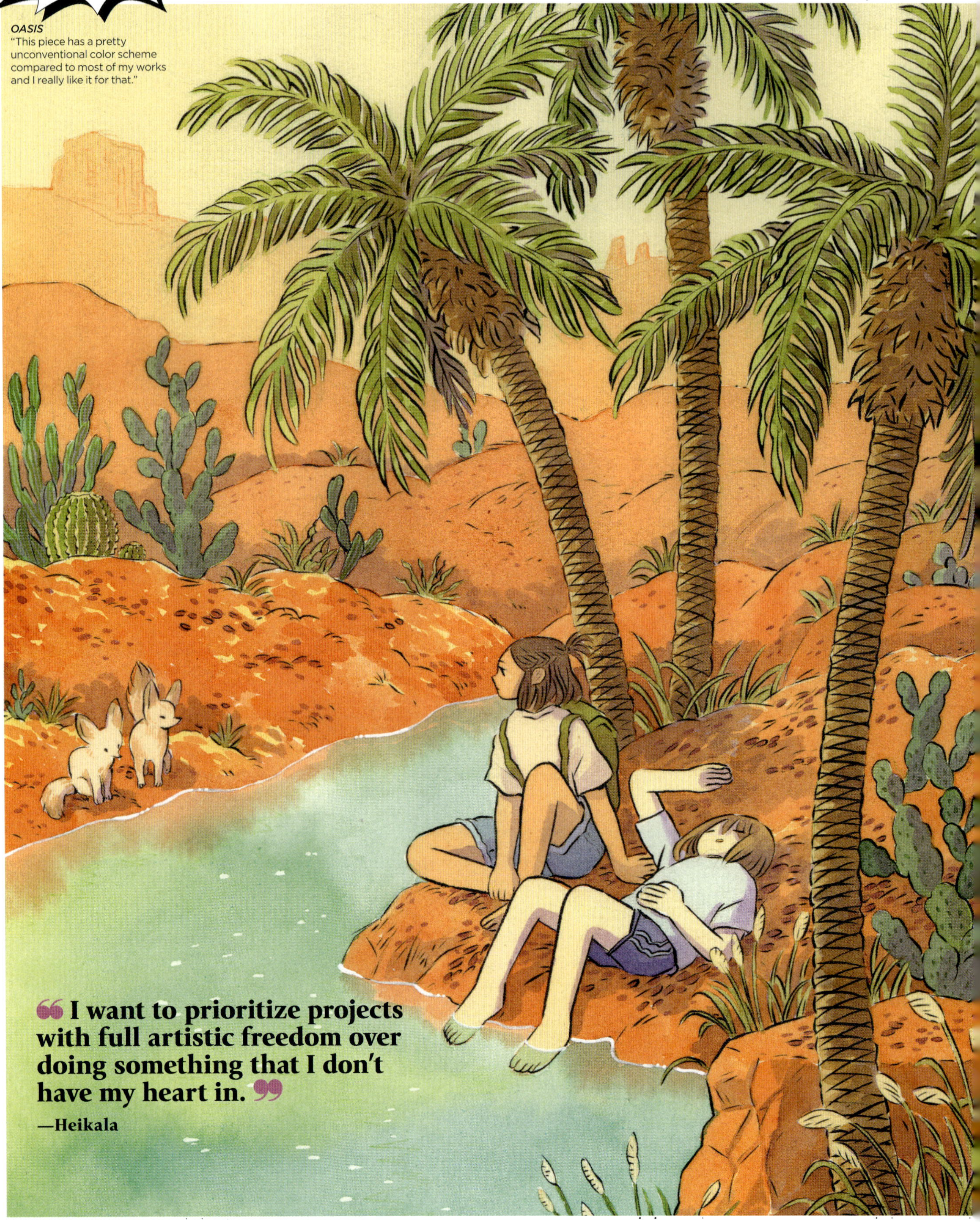

OASIS
"This piece has a pretty unconventional color scheme compared to most of my works and I really like it for that."

"I want to prioritize projects with full artistic freedom over doing something that I don't have my heart in."

—Heikala

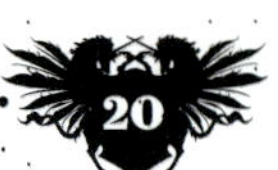

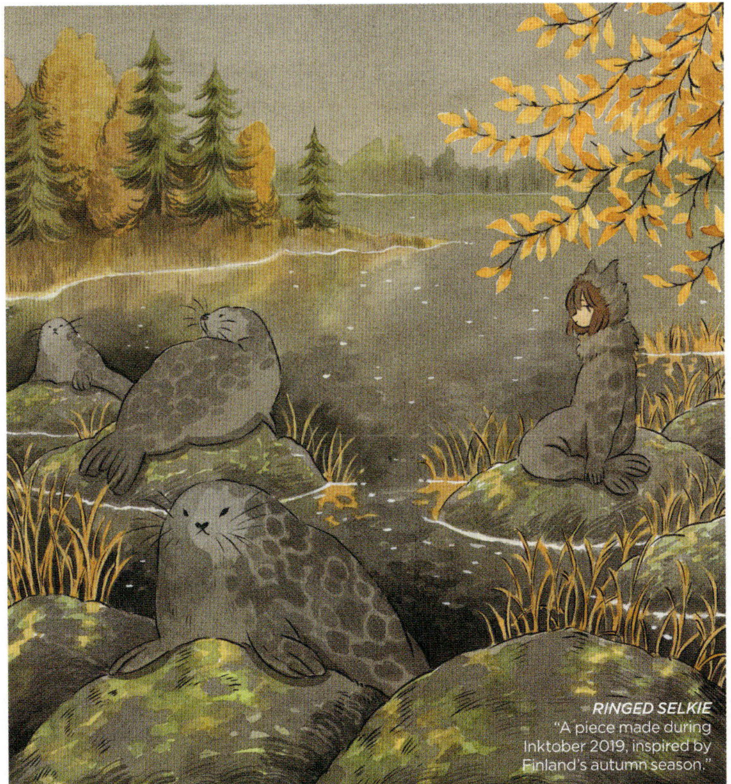

RINGED SELKIE
"A piece made during Inktober 2019, inspired by Finland's autumn season."

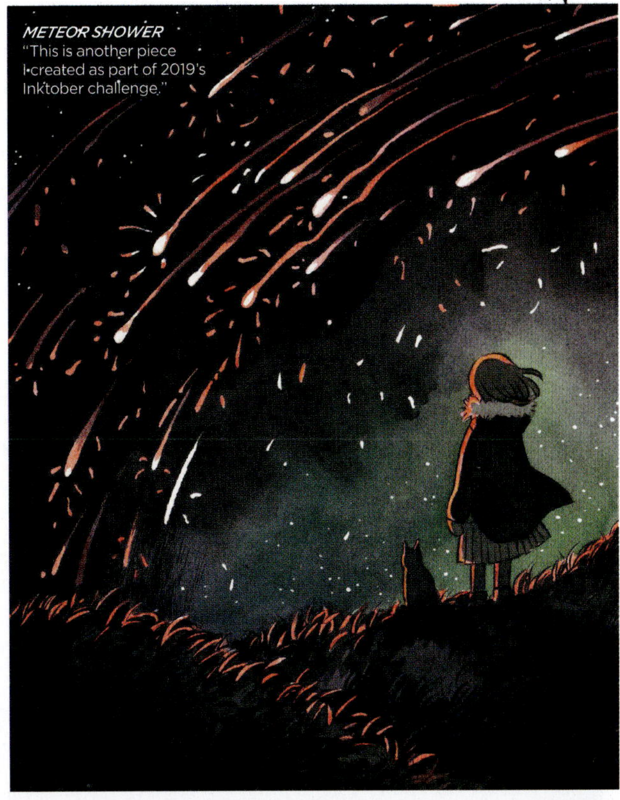

METEOR SHOWER
"This is another piece I created as part of 2019's Inktober challenge."

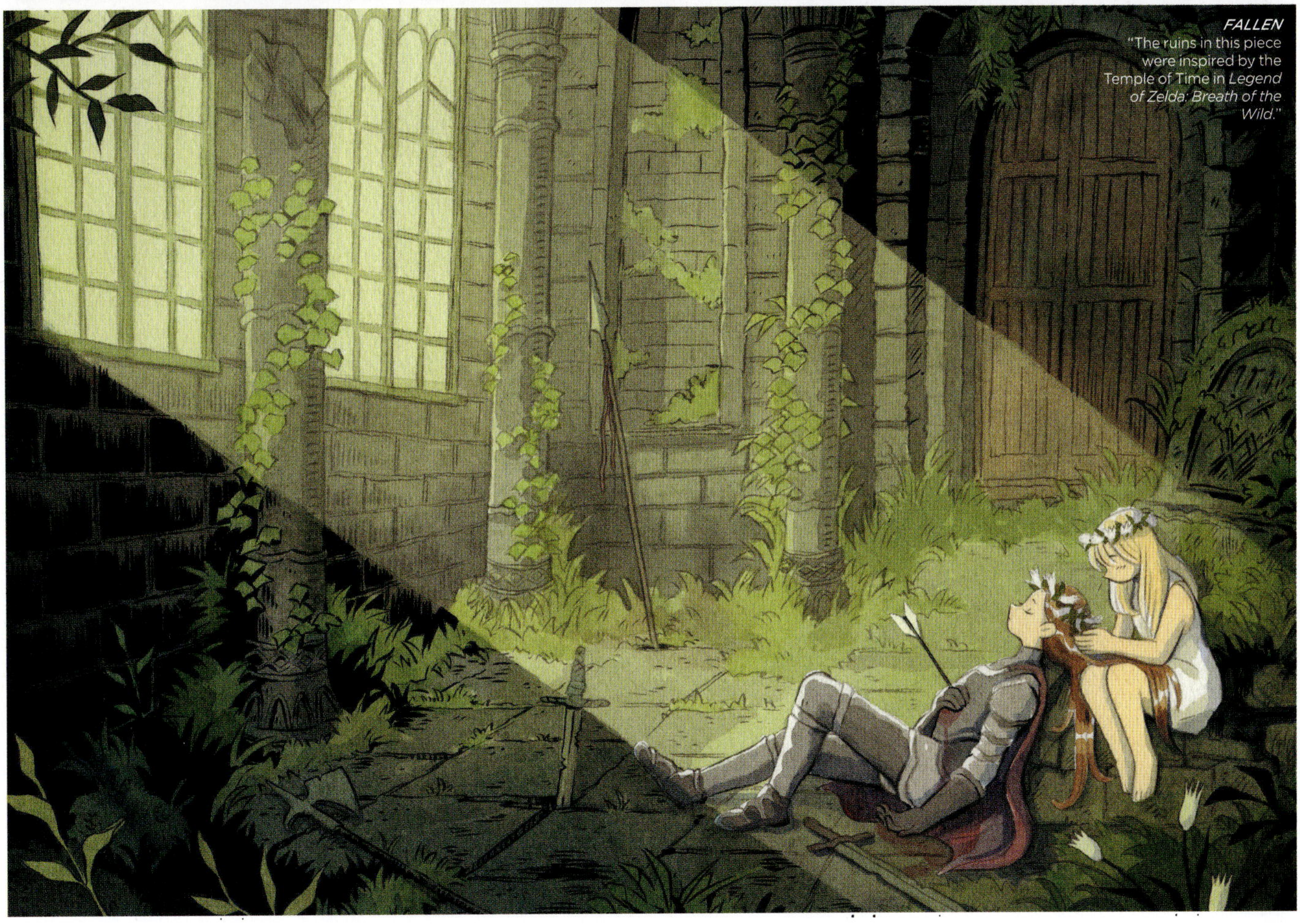

FALLEN
"The ruins in this piece were inspired by the Temple of Time in *Legend of Zelda: Breath of the Wild*."

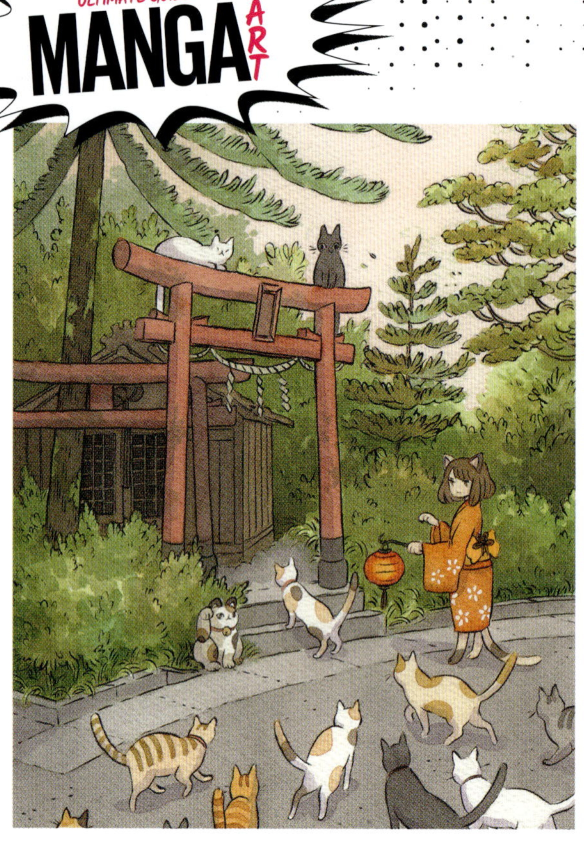

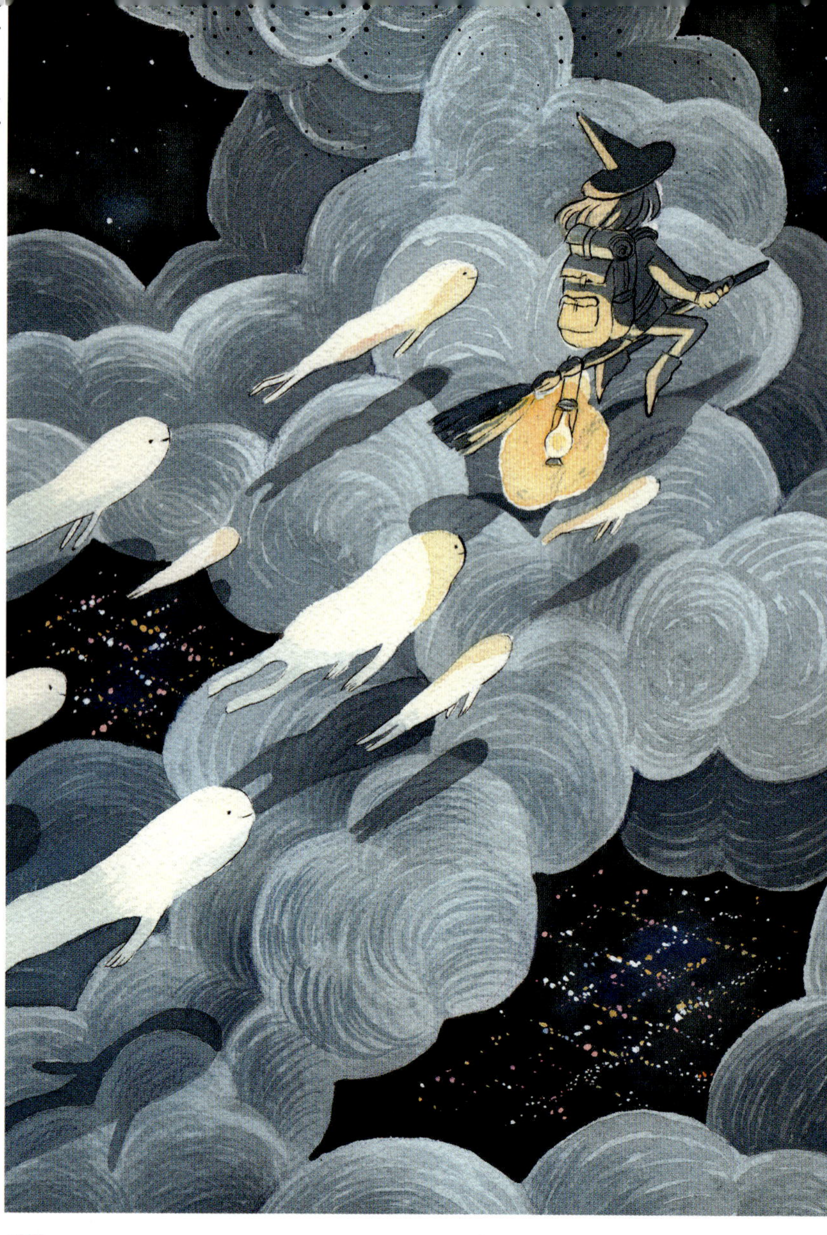

products I want to create, and how I want to utilize my social media. I've made a conscious decision not to do sponsored content on my social media for whichever company, and I carefully choose the people I want to work with and make products with. Most of these things, I guess, basically come down to my own ethics."

In the same way that Heikala wants the viewer to figure out the story behind her art, she seems to want the viewer to figure out the story behind the artist who made it. She gives us glimpses into her life—little moments in her larger story—but the rest she keeps for herself. It's good for business.

▲ *GATHERING*
"A piece made during Inktober 2019, inspired by a photo I took on one of my trips to Japan."

▶ *GHOST MIGRATION*
"This piece shows a witch guiding a herd of ghosts with a lit storm lamp."

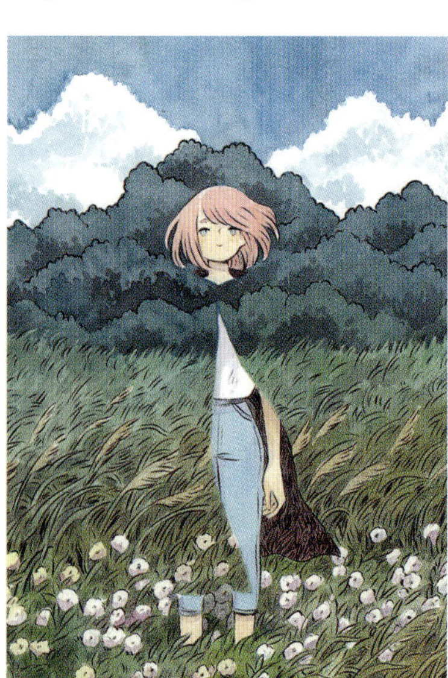

◀ *GRANDMA'S CLOAK*
"I like to add depth to my art by choosing a name that develops the story even further."

"I try to create paintings that are true to who I am. I may not always succeed, but that's something I actively strive to achieve."
—Heikala

It's an excellent bit of branding. But it's much more than that. Heikala has not only solved the age-old problem of making money versus doing the thing you love to do—she's turned the solution into a story, into a work of art. And that means she's free to focus on the one thing that matters most.

PRIZED POSSESSIONS

Whenever Heikala finishes a piece, she puts it in one of the bottom two drawers of the desk under the big window, the place where she keeps her most prized possessions.

"I try to create paintings that are true to who I am. I may not always succeed, but that's something I actively strive to achieve. If those works that are important to me speak also to the audience that views them, then I can feel happy knowing I've reached people who also feel my paintings are true to them. There's so many different kinds of art in the world, and so many different people to experience art, that I find it easy to accept that not everyone will love my art, in the same way that I don't love or understand all art. But I'm so extremely happy to have found the way I love to make art, and to have found my niche and the people who also like to view the art I make.

"Those drawers are used only to store finished originals and whenever I can slide one of those drawers open and place a new work inside, I feel this huge sense of accomplishment."

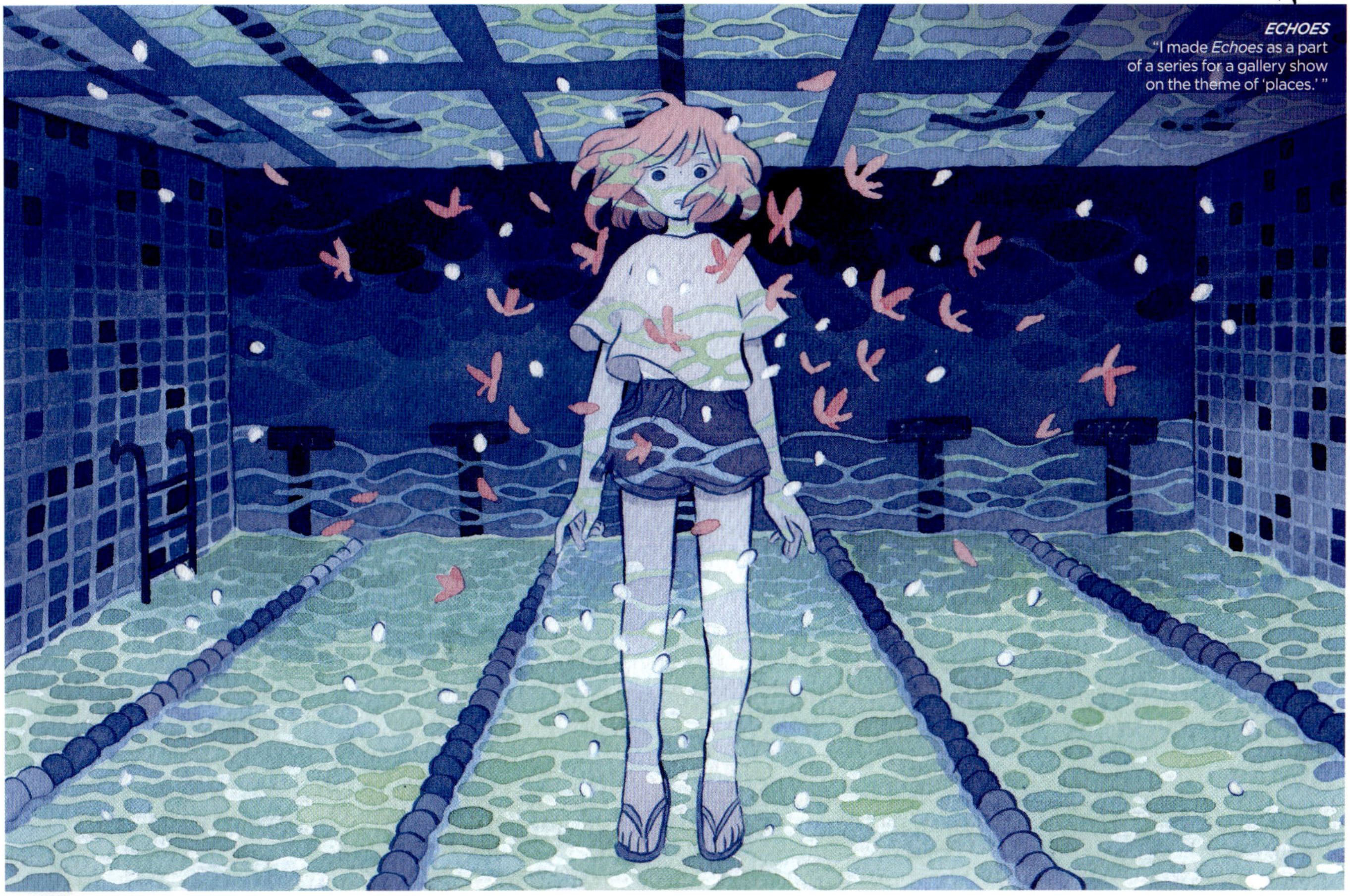

ECHOES
"I made *Echoes* as a part of a series for a gallery show on the theme of 'places.'"

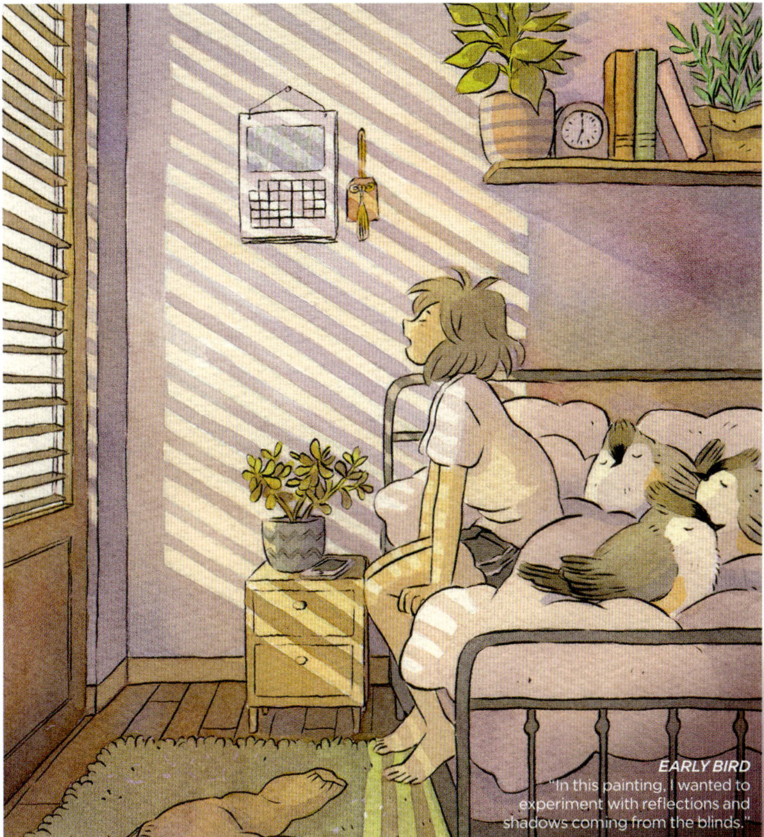

EARLY BIRD
"In this painting, I wanted to experiment with reflections and shadows coming from the blinds."

TRUE COLORS

Heikala fills us in on the techniques behind her distinctive color work.

"I use colored inks in a similar manner to watercolors, but there are some key differences to these mediums. With watercolors, you need to work your way from lighter tones to darker tones and from warm tones to cold tones, otherwise colors will bleed into areas you've painted.

Colored inks are waterproof once they're dry, so it enables me to work in any order, from dark to light, and to lay down bright tones next to one another without them bleeding. It's also easier for me to create shadows. However, working with inks is a bit more difficult. If you make a mistake, you can't lift it up like with watercolor.

I use Rohrer & Klingner colored inks and a Pentel Pocket Brush pen, which is waterproof once dry and a good match with colored ink. I also use a water brush filled with colored inks to make colored outlines. I use a porcelain palette to mix my inks then paint with varying sizes of synthetic watercolor brushes. If you want to try colored inks, get one sheet of good-quality cotton watercolor paper, size two and four synthetic watercolor brushes, and four colored ink bottles: cyan, magenta, yellow (medium chrome), and black. With those four colors, you can create a variety of different tones."

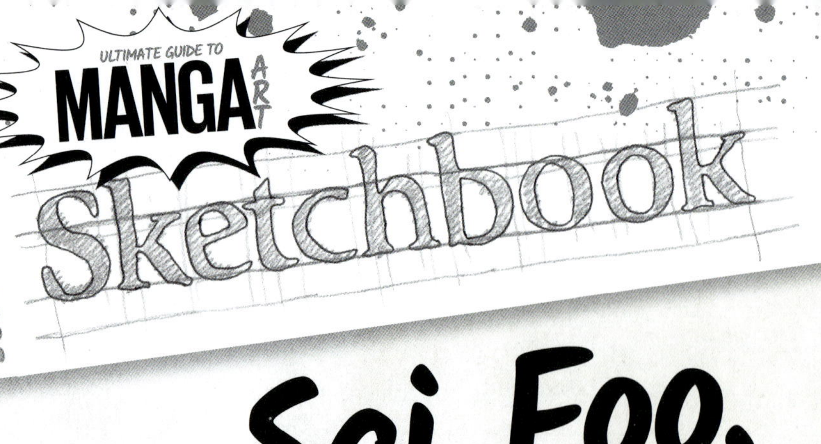

Sai Foo.

Here's an artist who's happy to address his perceived illustrative shortcomings in his sketchbook . . . and it's all the better for it.

Artist PROFILE

Sai Foo

LOCATION: Malaysia

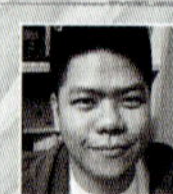

Sai has worked in advertising, animation, and video game industries. He loves creating dynamic line-art poses, sketching in his free time, and trying out various drawing styles and techniques. The artist readily admits that he struggles with some character poses, and says he still has a lot to learn.

www.artstation.com/sai

NAP LADY

"I had this idea to draw a figure lying down. After a brief struggle with the perspective, I managed to come up with something I was satisfied with."

ASTRO REUNION

"I'd been watching lots of space rockets documentary and wanted to draw an astronaut returning from a space mission and greeting his family."

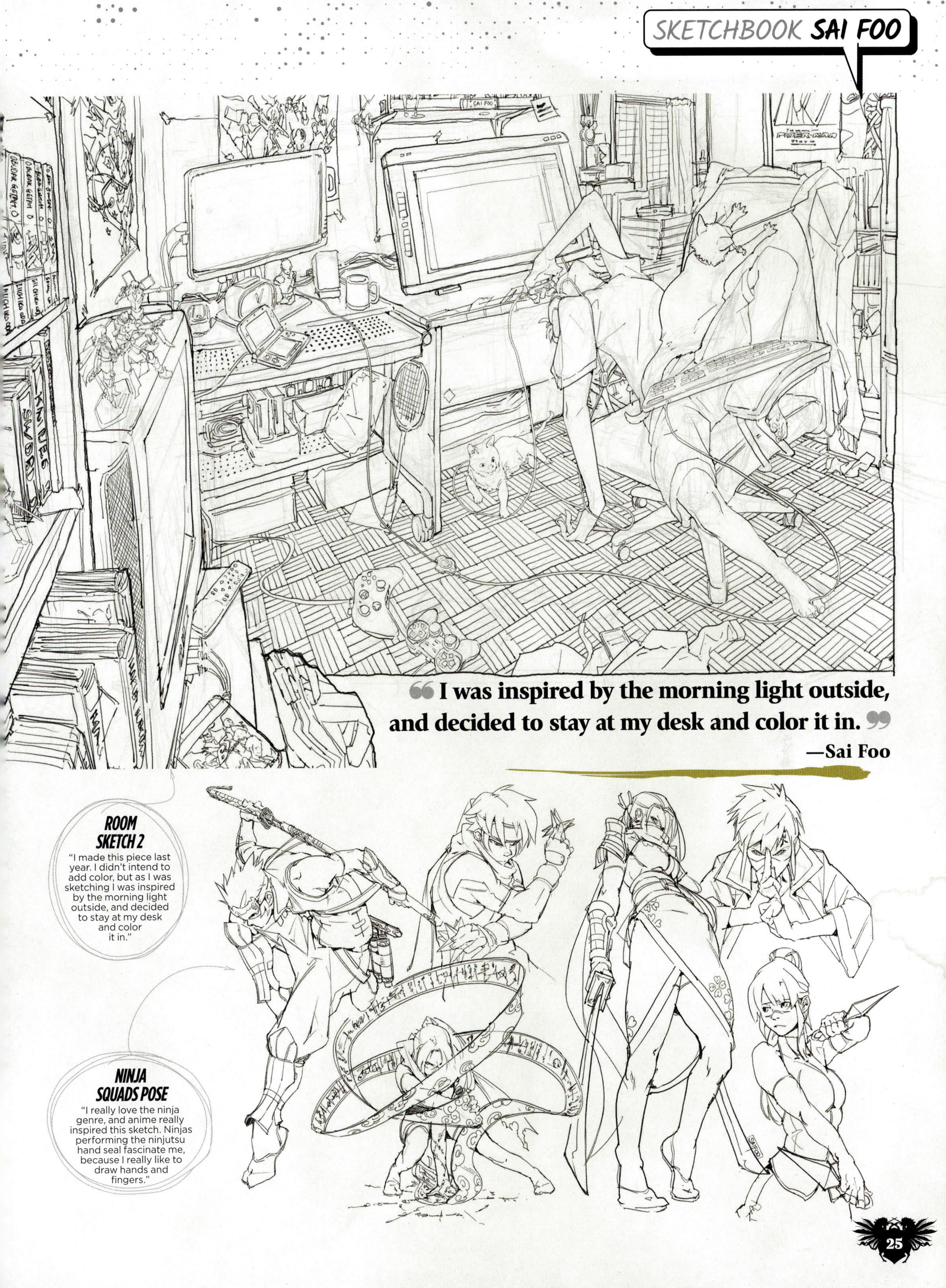

“I was inspired by the morning light outside, and decided to stay at my desk and color it in.”

—Sai Foo

ROOM SKETCH 2
“I made this piece last year. I didn't intend to add color, but as I was sketching I was inspired by the morning light outside, and decided to stay at my desk and color it in.”

NINJA SQUADS POSE
“I really love the ninja genre, and anime really inspired this sketch. Ninjas performing the ninjutsu hand seal fascinate me, because I really like to draw hands and fingers.”

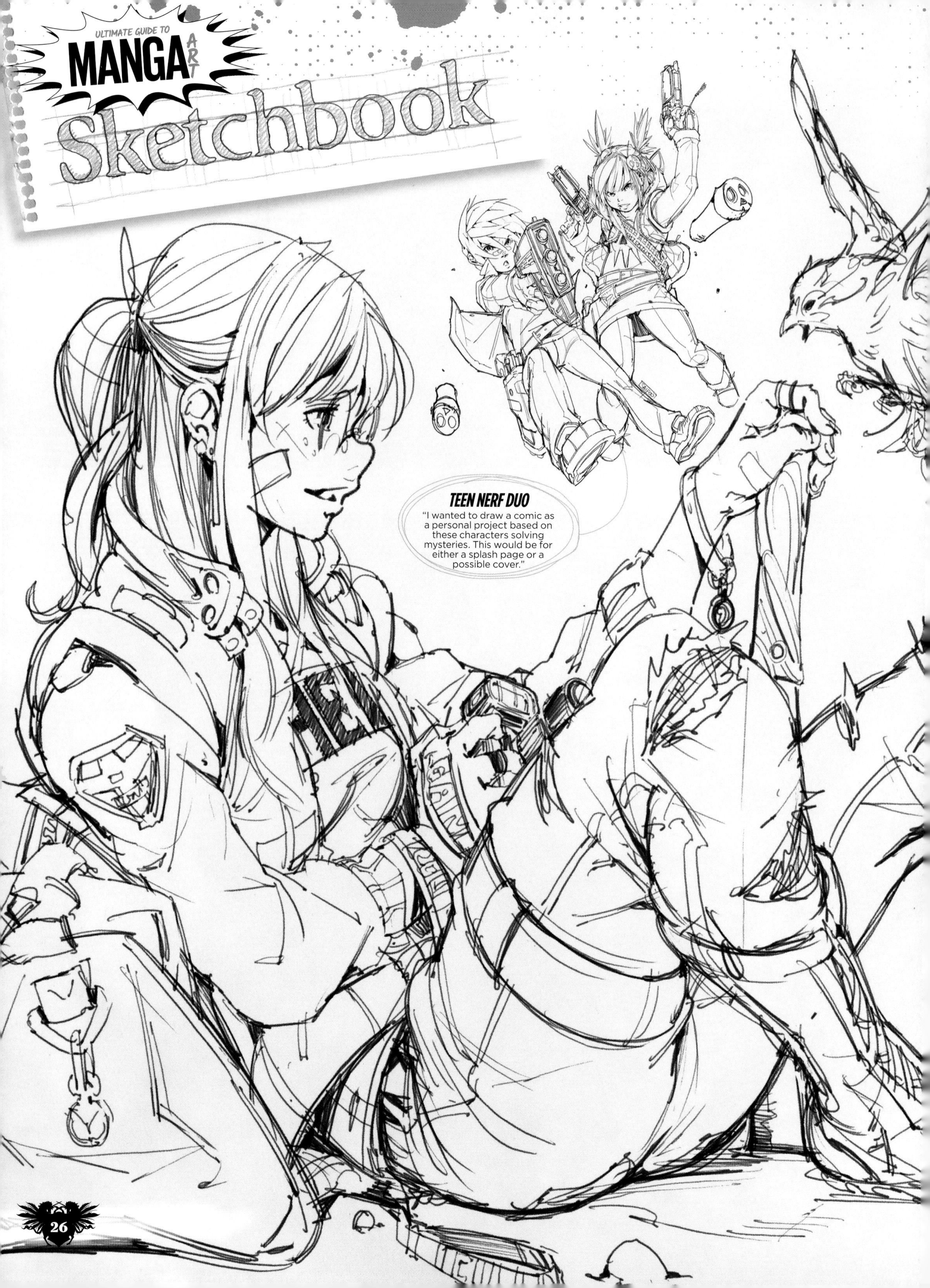

TEEN NERF DUO

"I wanted to draw a comic as a personal project based on these characters solving mysteries. This would be for either a splash page or a possible cover."

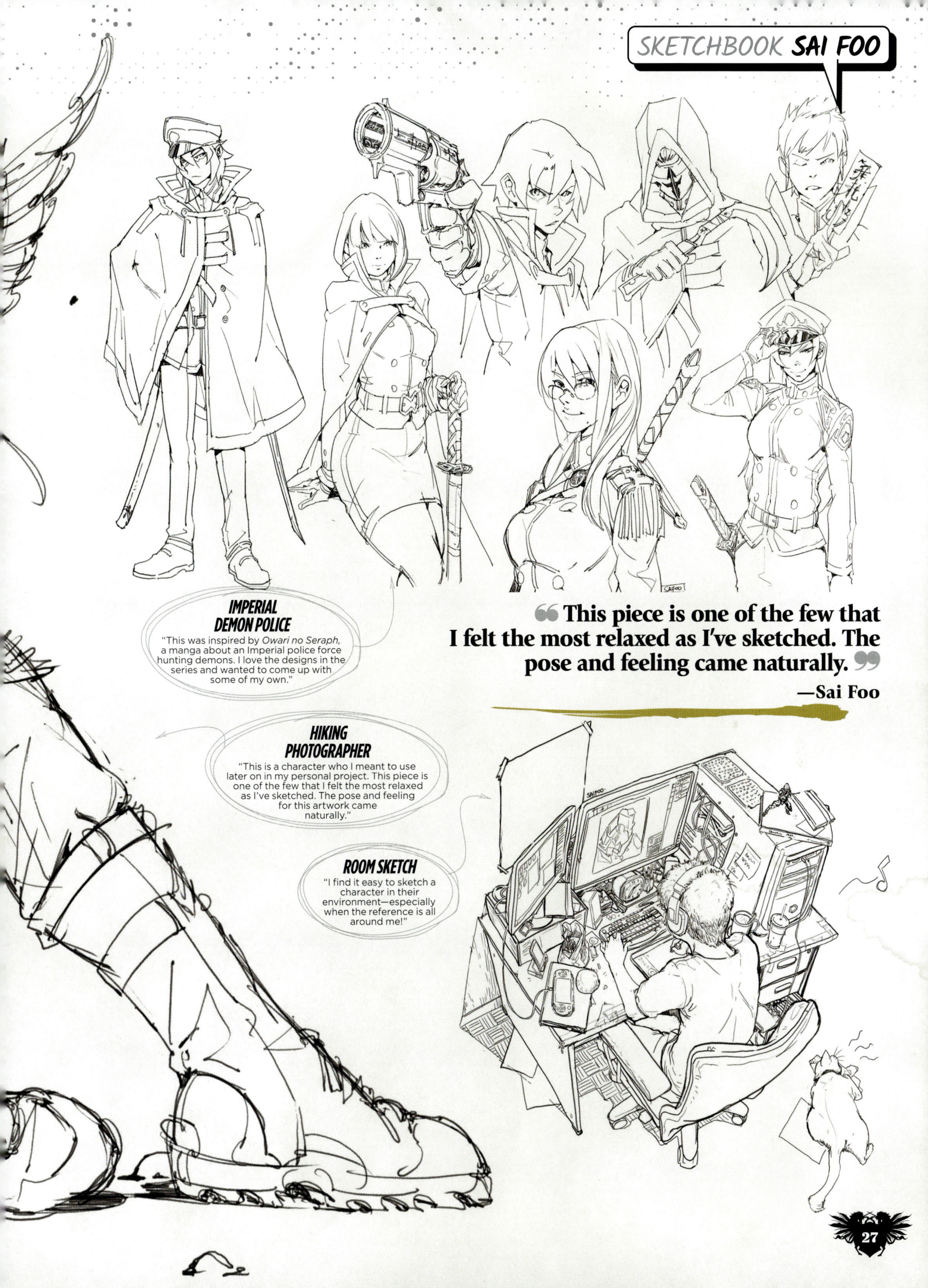

IMPERIAL DEMON POLICE

"This was inspired by *Owari no Seraph*, a manga about an Imperial police force hunting demons. I love the designs in the series and wanted to come up with some of my own."

"This piece is one of the few that I felt the most relaxed as I've sketched. The pose and feeling came naturally."

—Sai Foo

HIKING PHOTOGRAPHER

"This is a character who I meant to use later on in my personal project. This piece is one of the few that I felt the most relaxed as I've sketched. The pose and feeling for this artwork came naturally."

ROOM SKETCH

"I find it easy to sketch a character in their environment—especially when the reference is all around me!"

Sketchbook

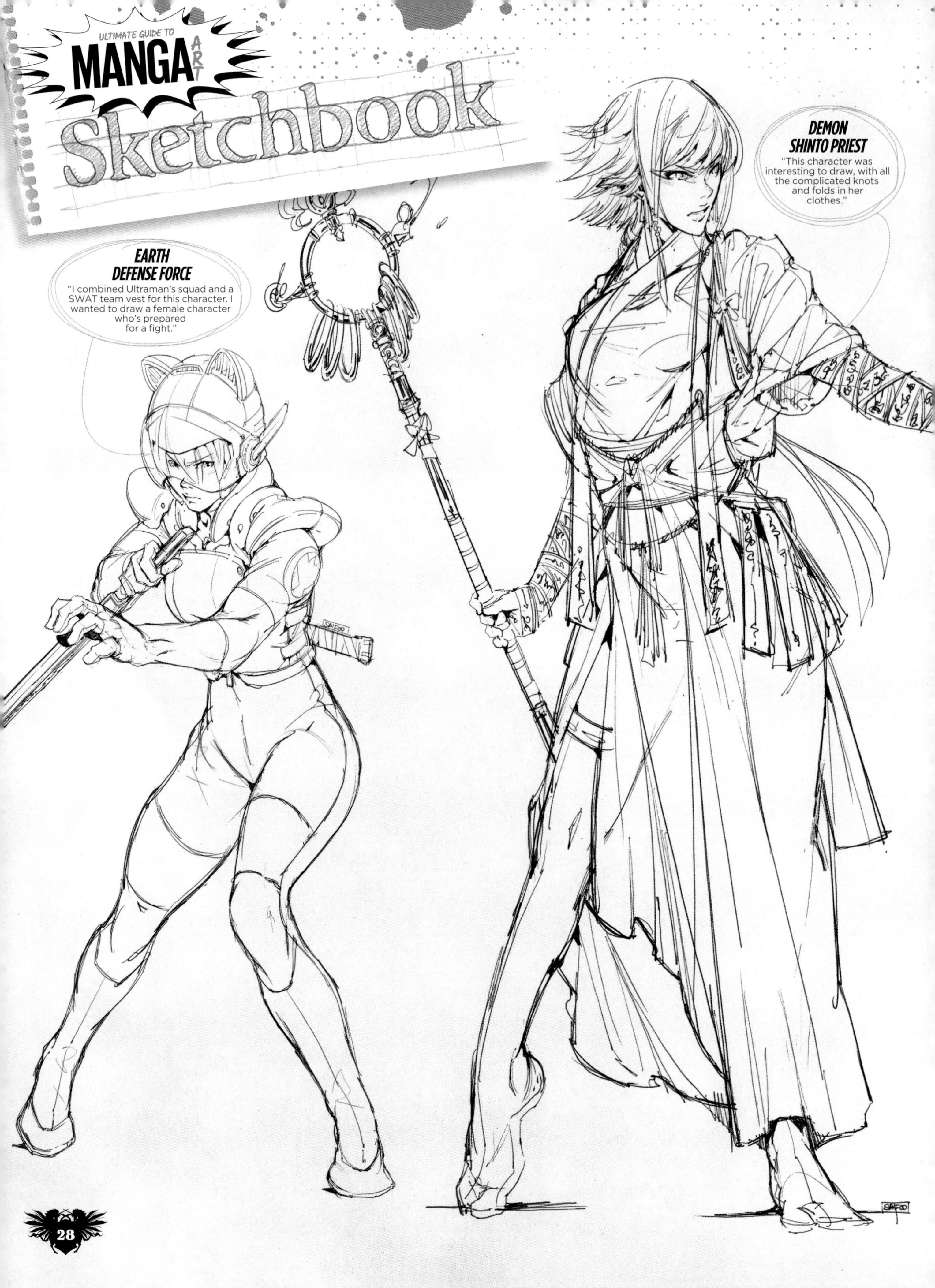

EARTH DEFENSE FORCE

"I combined Ultraman's squad and a SWAT team vest for this character. I wanted to draw a female character who's prepared for a fight."

DEMON SHINTO PRIEST

"This character was interesting to draw, with all the complicated knots and folds in her clothes."

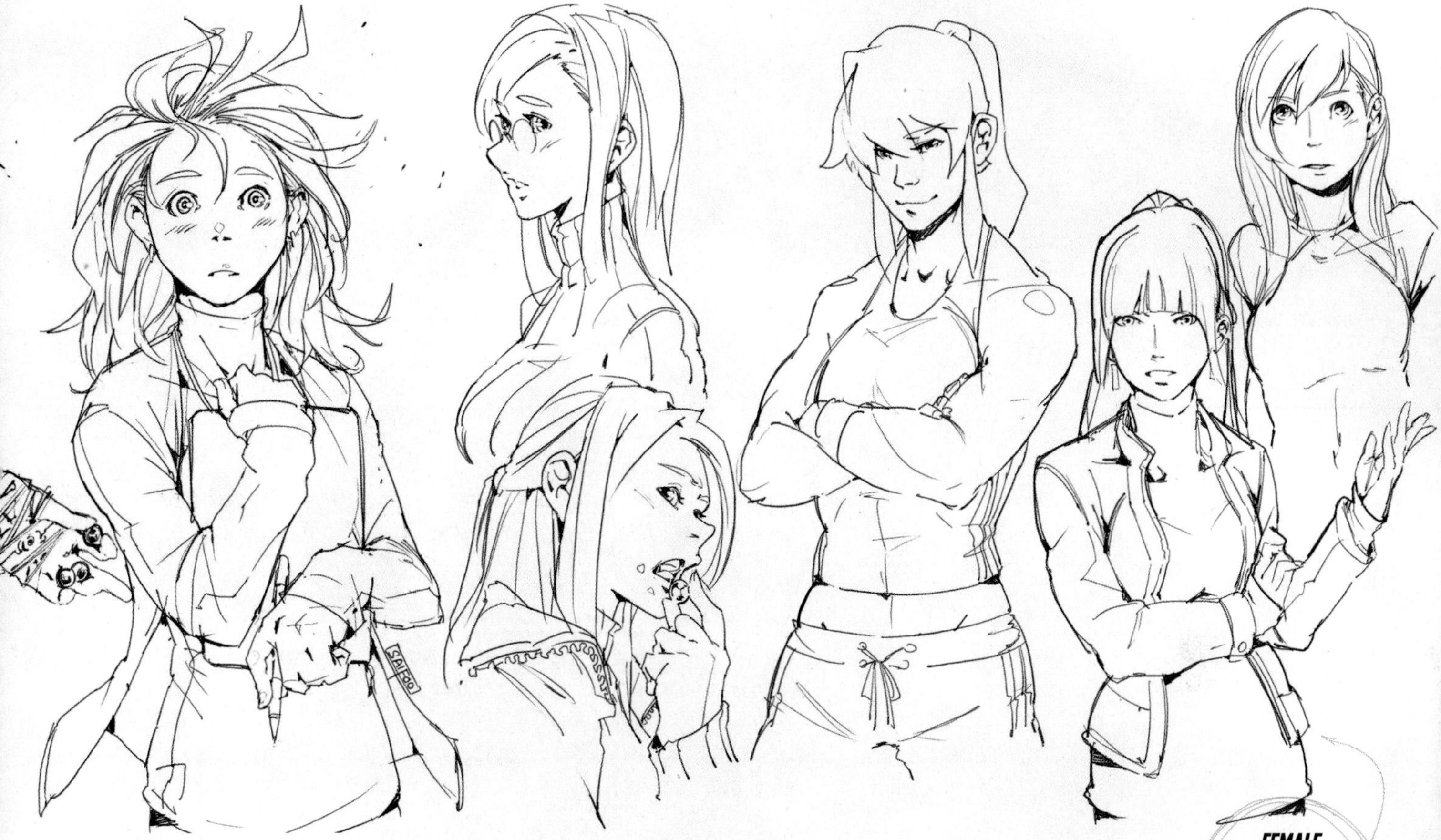

FEMALE TRAINING

"I've been told that I draw female characters like they're men, especially when it comes to their faces. So I've been working on that, although I'm not finding it easy."

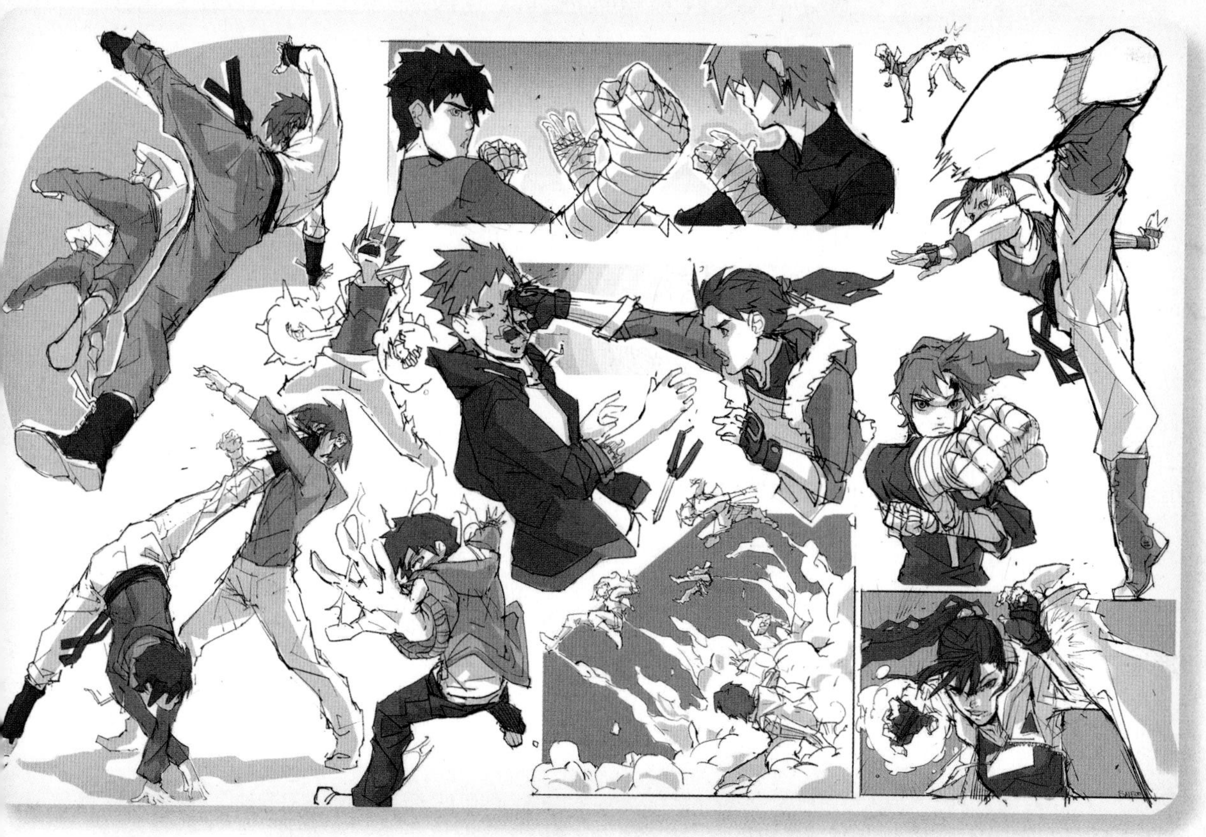

FIGHT POSES

"I sketched this a while back, to practice drawing a believable fight scene. I don't think I've nailed it yet, but I like the feeling I got from these poses."

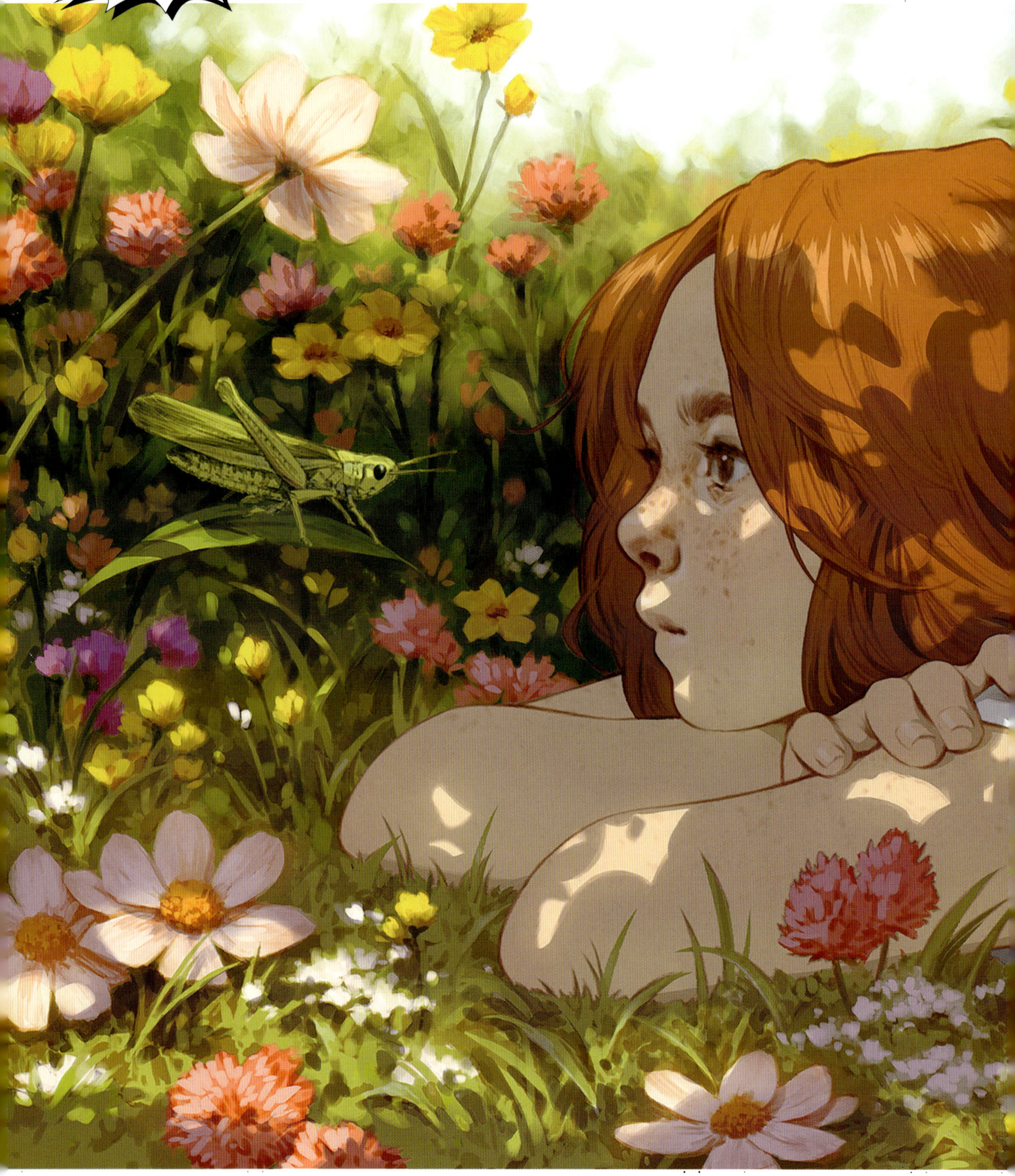

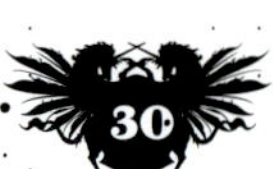

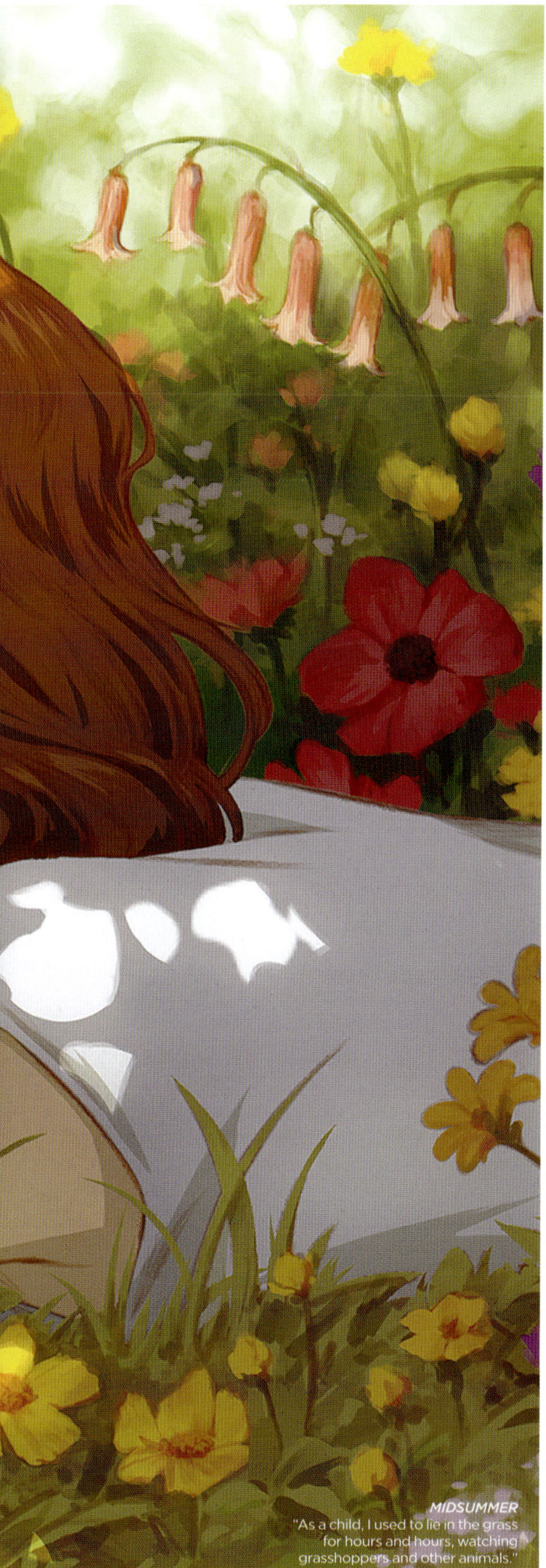

MIDSUMMER
"As a child, I used to lie in the grass for hours and hours, watching grasshoppers and other animals."

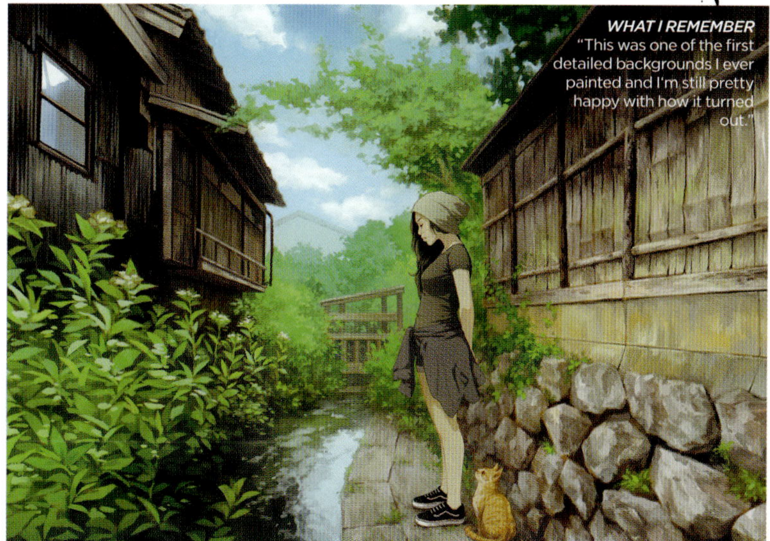

WHAT I REMEMBER
"This was one of the first detailed backgrounds I ever painted and I'm still pretty happy with how it turned out."

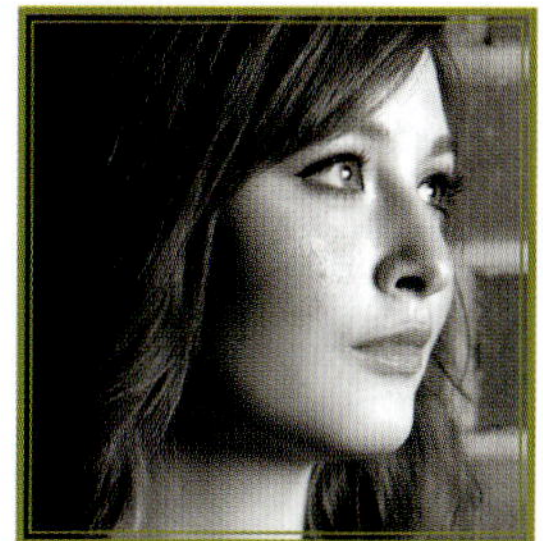

ARTIST PORTFOLIO

DJAMILA KNOPF

The artist tells **Gary Evans** about practicing in secret, losing her artistic voice, and being told to try "real art."

Djamila Knopf's website has a page of FAQs. One of the questions the German illustrator gets frequently asked is this: can you give me career advice?

"If you're an artist wanting to become a professional," she writes in response, "I can give you the following three pieces of advice: 1) Work on your craft, 2) Don't try to force yourself into a style that isn't natural to you, and 3) Share your work on social media."

Good advice. It's solid, precise, and applicable to pretty much any line of work—artistic or otherwise. But these three seemingly simple points come from years of trial and error. It's hard-won advice.

Not that long ago, it looked like Djamila was going to quit working on her own craft. Then, when she did commit to art, she tried to force herself into a style that wasn't natural. Her work became a big success on social media, but only after practicing it in secret because the people she initially shared her work with said it wasn't real art. Behind each piece of Djamila's advice there's a story.

WORK ON YOUR CRAFT

Djamila doesn't speak publicly about her childhood, except to say it was "the kind of upbringing I wouldn't wish on anyone." A couple of things got her through it: one was visiting her grandparents, making fishing poles, bows and arrows, running

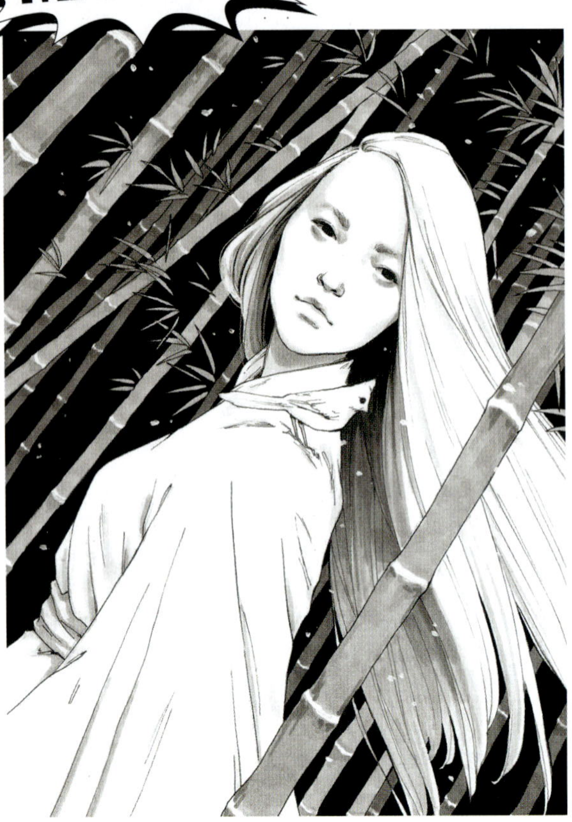

GEIST
"This is my version of Yuki-onna, the snow woman from Japanese folklore. I wanted her face to appear slightly alien and otherworldly."

around their garden, and exploring the surrounding forests, canals, and fields. The other was a group of animated TV shows that looked a little different, and told stories about heroines and magic.

Growing up in the 90s, Djamila never felt connected to her native culture. But she loved anime before she knew it was anime. She was very young when she started watching shows like *Attack No. 1*, about a high school volleyball team. Djamila loved the show's main character and would bounce a volleyball off the wall for hours on end, driving everybody around her crazy.

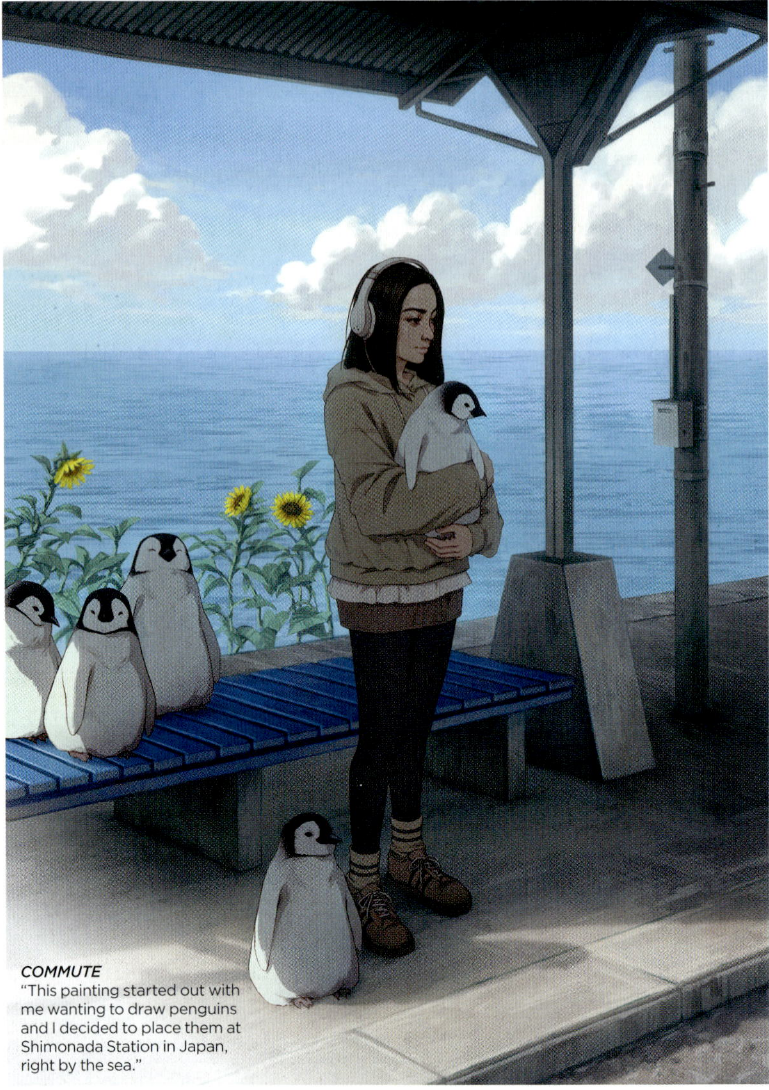

COMMUTE
"This painting started out with me wanting to draw penguins and I decided to place them at Shimonada Station in Japan, right by the sea."

Her favorite anime was *Sailor Moon*. She was five when she first saw it and remembers "being completely mesmerized." For ages, all she drew was *Sailor Moon* fan art.

These days, Djamila is "very schedule-oriented." She's up at 8 a.m., eats breakfast, gets dressed, but there's no great rush. This is one of the perks of working for herself: she gets to start the day slowly. By 10 a.m., or 11 a.m. at the latest, she's sitting at her desk, opening her Todoist app, and checking what's needs doing that day.

"Watching YouTube, I got the art education I was craving."
—Djamila Knopf

The app holds appointments and illustration tasks, but also things like birthdays and when to do laundry. Djamila tracks her time on another app, Toggl Track. This helps her work out how long each task should take and compare it to how long it actually takes.

There's temptation to put all this down to that old German stereotype: efficiency. But there's more to it than that. The first app helps her focus entirely on art, without nagging thoughts about missing her friend's 30th, or not having enough clean socks. The second app helps separate

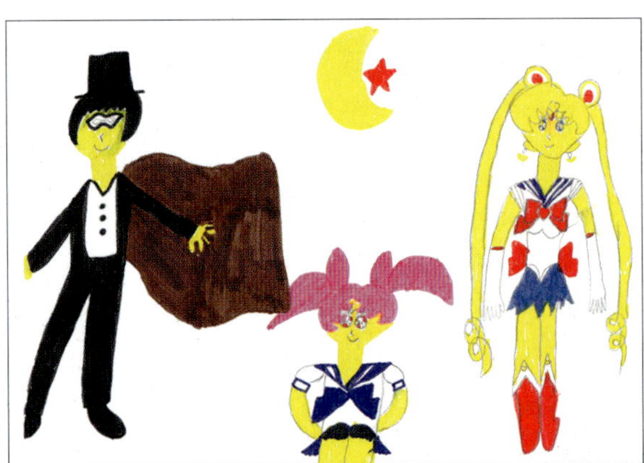

SAILOR MOON FAN ART
"This is one of my earliest drawings. I've kept because it reminds me of how much I loved drawing these characters when I was five."

Artist PROFILE

Djamila Knopf
LOCATION: Germany
FAVORITE ARTISTS: Iain McCaig, Hayao Miyazaki, Tran Nguyen, Kazuo Oga, Amei Zhao
MEDIA: Photoshop, Blender, Alchemy, Copic Markers, Pentel Poc ket Brush Pen, Winsor & Newton black ink, Schmincke Acrylics
WEB: *www.djamilaknopf.com*

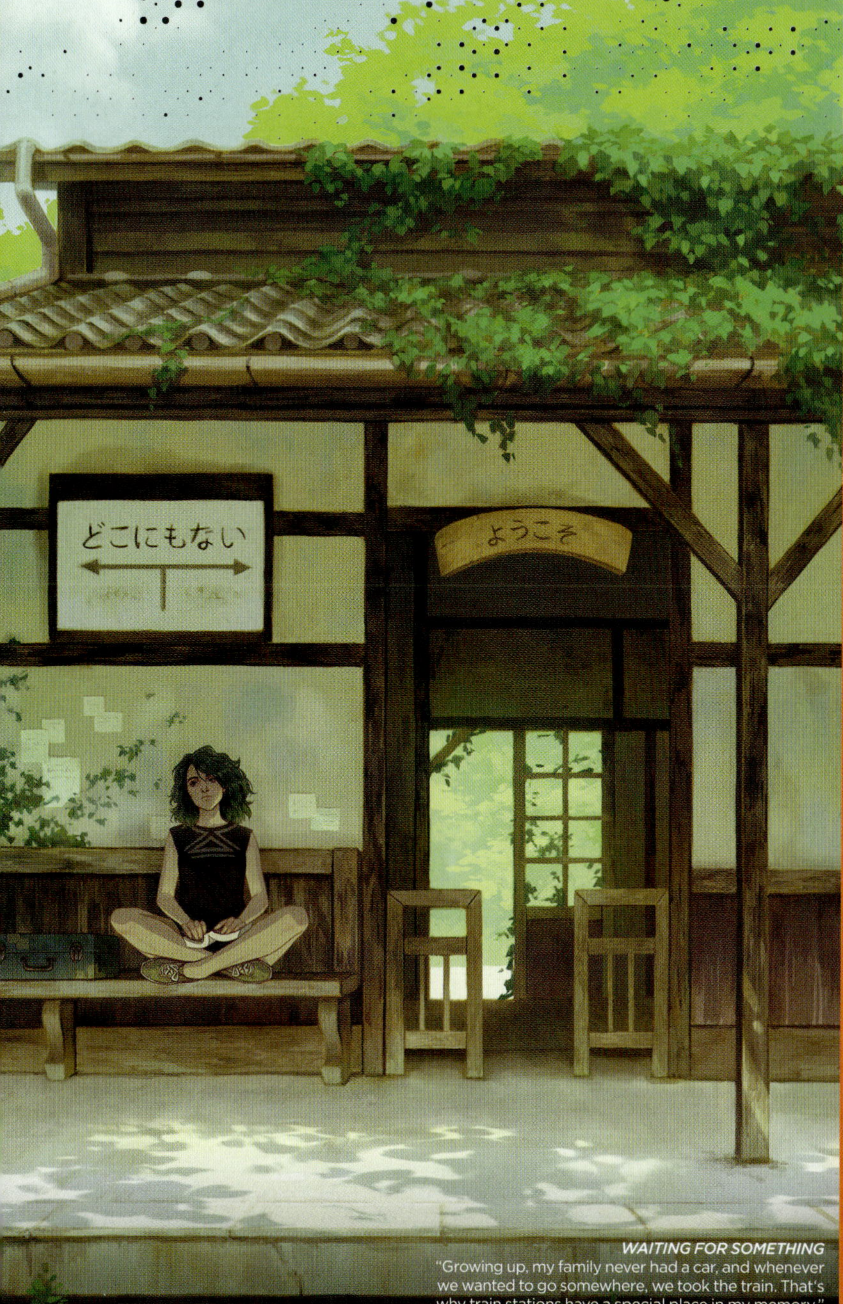

WAITING FOR SOMETHING
"Growing up, my family never had a car, and whenever we wanted to go somewhere, we took the train. That's why train stations have a special place in my memory."

STORY-DRIVEN ILLUSTRATIONS

Djamila shares tips on how to tell better stories through your art.

"Storytelling is something I'm very passionate about. In fact, these days I find it difficult to paint something that doesn't tell a story. There are two artists I admire more than any other: Iain McCaig and Hayao Miyazaki. Incredible storytelling is something they both have in common. I look at their work and it feels as though I've discovered a missing piece of myself.

I want to create something that can move people in the same way characters from TV shows influenced me as a child. There's such a strong emotional component that you can introduce to a piece of art when you include storytelling. It enables people to connect with your art on a deeper level, and to immerse themselves in it, because your personal story can remind them of their own.

I find it a lot easier to start a story when I start out with a location. If I think of a train station, for example, I immediately get a couple of ideas what could be happening there and what characters are populating the scene. That approach is something I can recommend for people who are stuck when trying to come up with stories!

Also, don't try to come up with 'clever' ideas. There probably are countless paintings of train stations out there already, but every person has their own take on it. The design, composition, palette, and mood you choose . . . that's what makes it unique.

Finally, I think the basis for successful storytelling is interaction. That could be a character interacting with another character, with an animal, with a prop, or with their environment. You could keep it simple: a kid looking up into the clouds is them interacting with their environment, and that's your story. Just try to have something happen in the scene that makes the viewer care—something that they can relate to, even if they've never been in the same situation."

work and free time. She draws at her sit-stand desk—two monitors, a Wacom Intuos Pro, Photoshop—in sessions of two hours, then takes a break before getting back at it. In short, these things help ensure she's spending as much time as possible working on her craft. But it wasn't always this way.

DON'T FORCE YOUR STYLE

At school and at university, Djamila's teachers weren't particularly fond of her anime-influenced illustrations. They suggested she make real art ("whatever that means"). This knocked her confidence. The conflict between her own influences and the influences of her teachers meant her art became confused. It had no clear voice.

Unsurprisingly, making a living from art never seemed possible. ➔ She

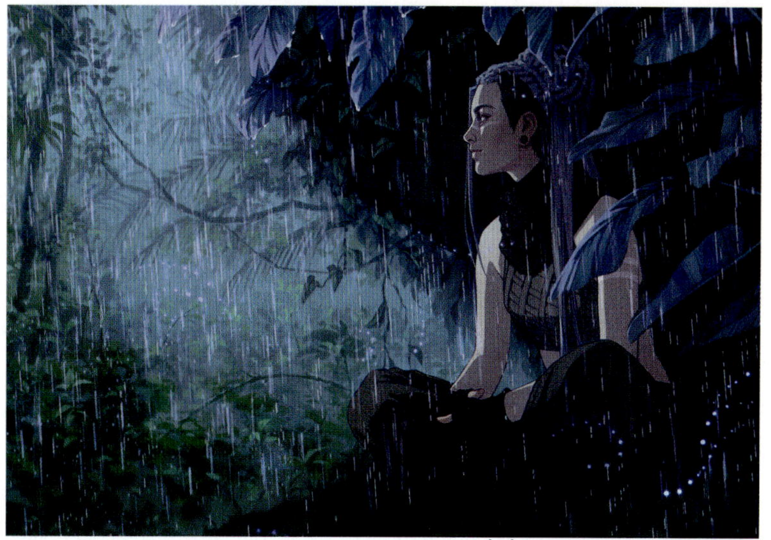

THE SMELL OF RAIN
"This illustration shows my character Leigh. I've had this scene in mind for a very long time, and I actually managed to capture the atmosphere I was going for."

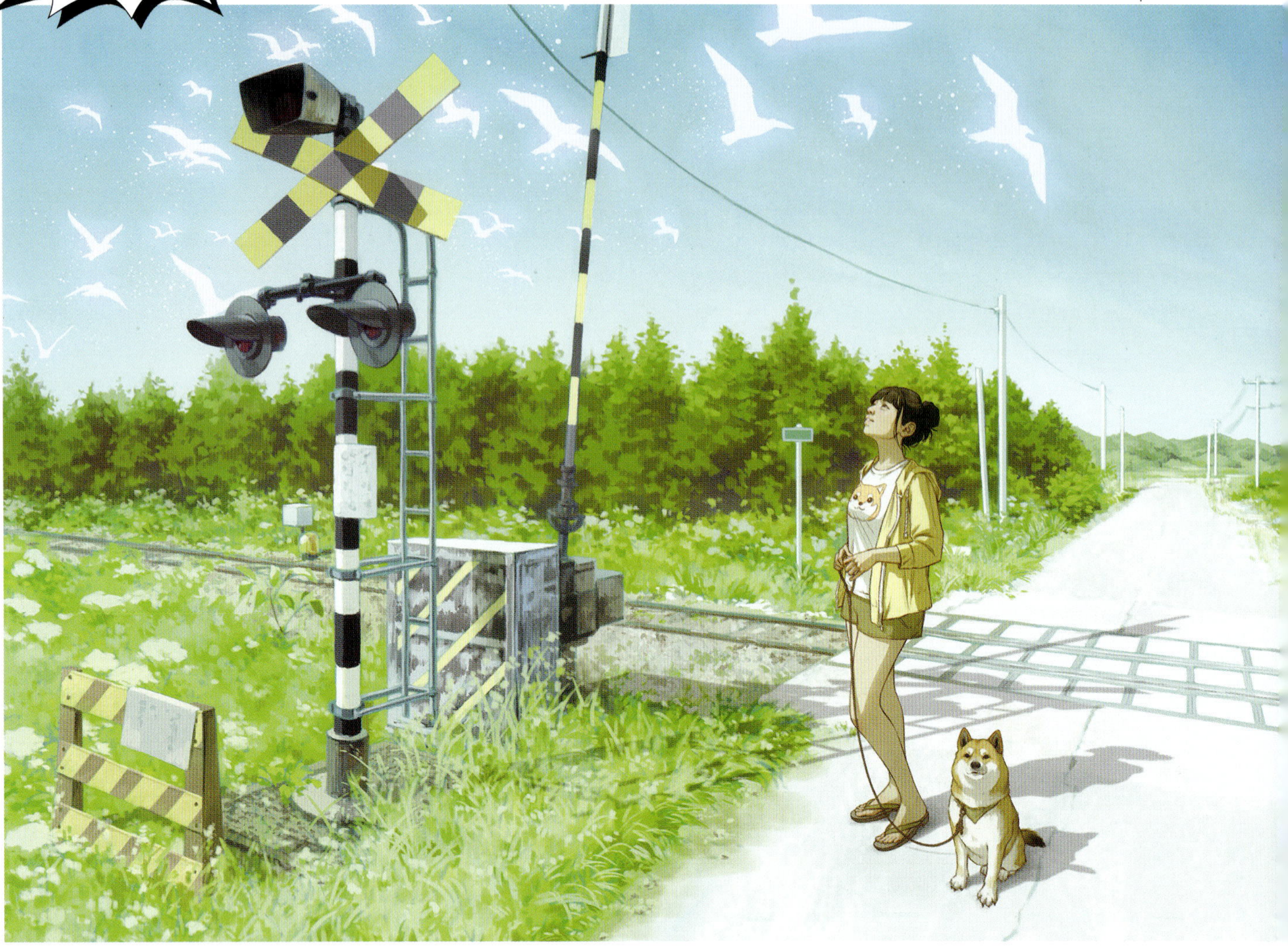

considered art-related alternatives—graphic design, fashion, makeup—but enrolled in Japanese studies at Leipzig University in 2009, then switched the following year to art and English education. She completed her master's degree in 2017, so she's a qualified school teacher. But, halfway through her university program, Djamila secretly decided to pursue a career in illustration.

ONLINE ART EDUCATION

She worked on the art her teachers disapproved of by reading books and watching YouTube tutorials: "I got the art education I was craving and that my school wouldn't provide. And more importantly, I learned that there were people out there on the internet, thriving and making a living doing the kind of work I was always told was inferior and childish."

Still at university, Djamila's DeviantArt page attracted illustration commissions for books by indie authors. It wasn't enough money to live on, but it was a start. After her master's, she went full-time as a freelancer, working for various publishers and game companies. She tried to mimic the style of big-name fantasy artists, big-name outfits like *Magic: the Gathering*, but realistic rendering wasn't really her thing. Plus, if she was being completely honest,

CROSSING
"I wanted to paint a railway crossing, and as I developed the idea, I added the girl walking her dog, as well as the ghost-like birds."

> **"People freak out over the idea of an artist charging for their time and effort."**
>
> **—Djamila Knopf**

Djamila didn't really care about high fantasy. She'd never read *The Lord of the Rings*. She'd never played *Dungeons & Dragons*. She was trying to force herself into a style that wasn't natural.

"Being told that my personal aesthetic wasn't good enough throughout my education probably made me apply the same mindset to my illustration jobs. I was sure clients couldn't possibly be interested in the things I liked, so I adjusted to what I thought they wanted to see from me. But it made me so unhappy that I had to change something."

SHARE YOUR WORK

Djamila was burnt out. She spent months experimenting, questioning herself, looking back through old sketchbooks, and returning to her early influences. She started over, opened a Patreon account, an online store, and started taking prints and merchandise to conventions. She was able to stop taking commercial freelance work and focus entirely on personal projects, artwork that meant something to her.

This new career path wouldn't have been possible without social media. Djamila believes her audience—over 500,000 followers on Instagram alone—helped her get a book deal and teaching work with Schoolism ("my education degree won't

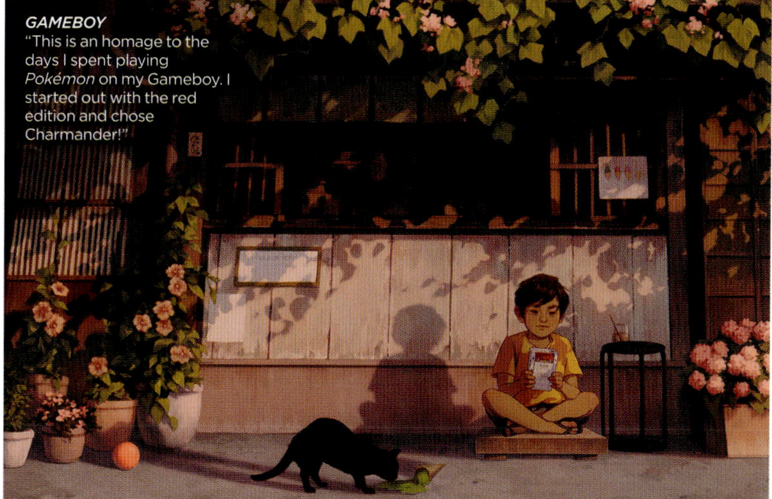

GAMEBOY
"This is an homage to the days I spent playing *Pokémon* on my Gameboy. I started out with the red edition and chose Charmander!"

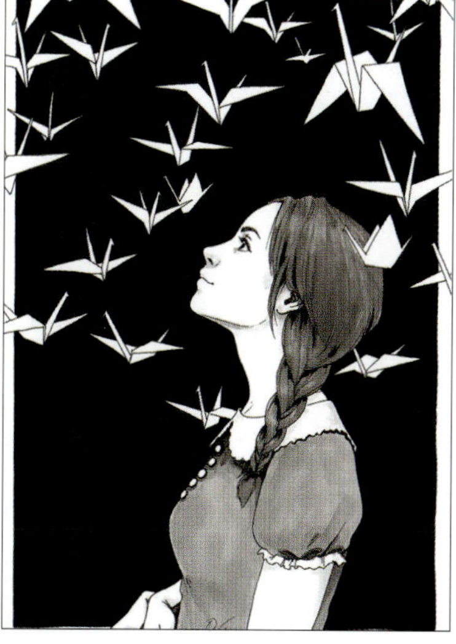

FAR AWAY
"I love the simple elegance of origami animals, so I decided to incorporate them into a drawing, They have something magical about them."

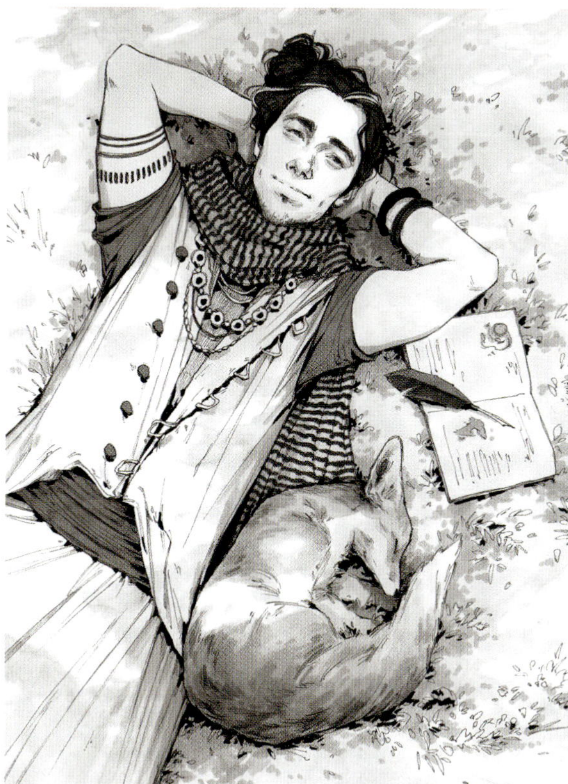

SPRING
"One of my favorite ink drawings. I always enjoy characters chilling out with their animal companions."

completely go to waste!"). The problem with posting online is that her art is constantly reposted without credit, and it'd be a full-time job chasing down everybody who did it. The other thing is self-promotion—still a bit of taboo for artists. Some people get annoyed when Djamila promotes a new project, especially if she's charging money.

"Nobody expects a plumber to fix their sink for free, yet people freak out over the idea of an artist charging for their time and effort. It's something that a lot of artists are deeply uncomfortable with

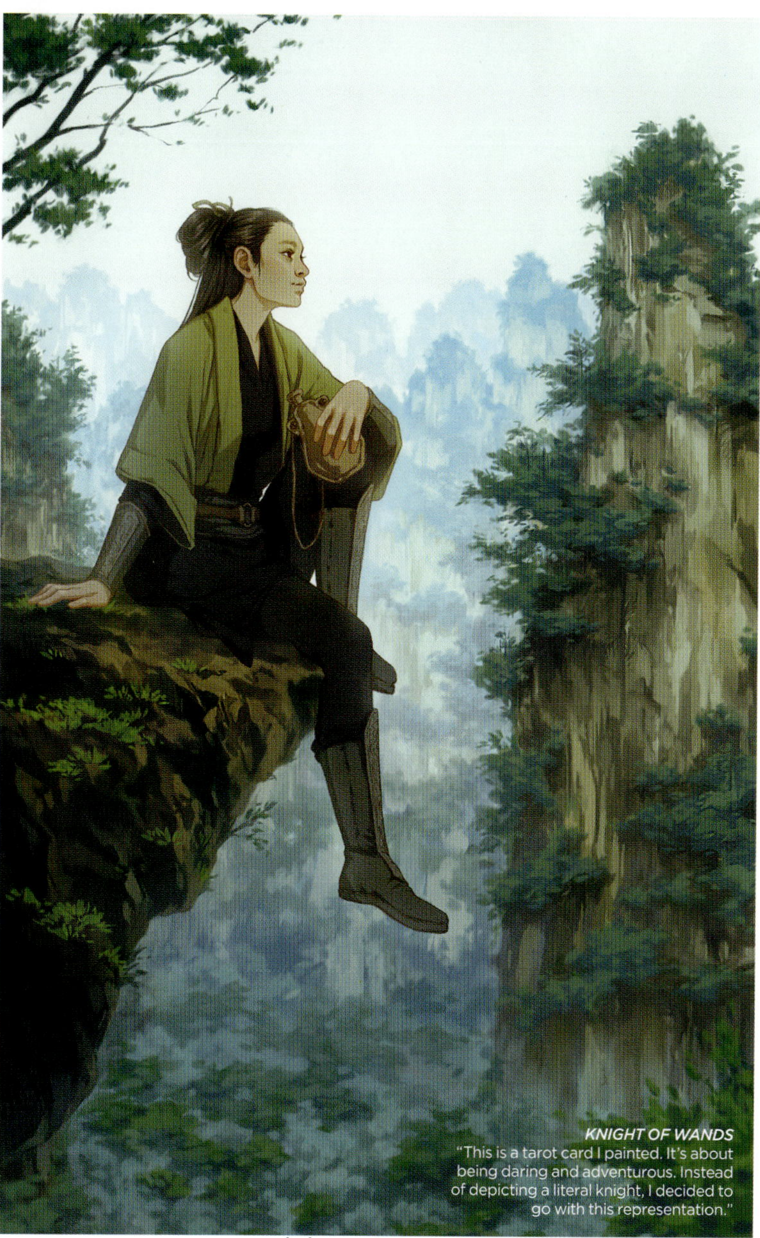

KNIGHT OF WANDS
"This is a tarot card I painted. It's about being daring and adventurous. Instead of depicting a literal knight, I decided to go with this representation."

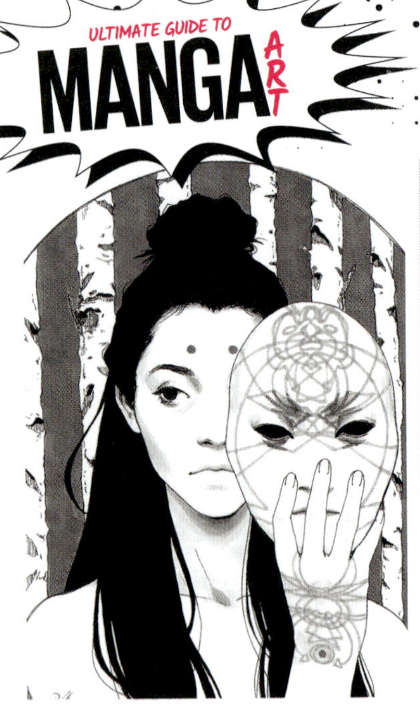

HIDE
"I enjoy masks as a symbol for a facade that you put on—to hide behind or to take on a new identity."

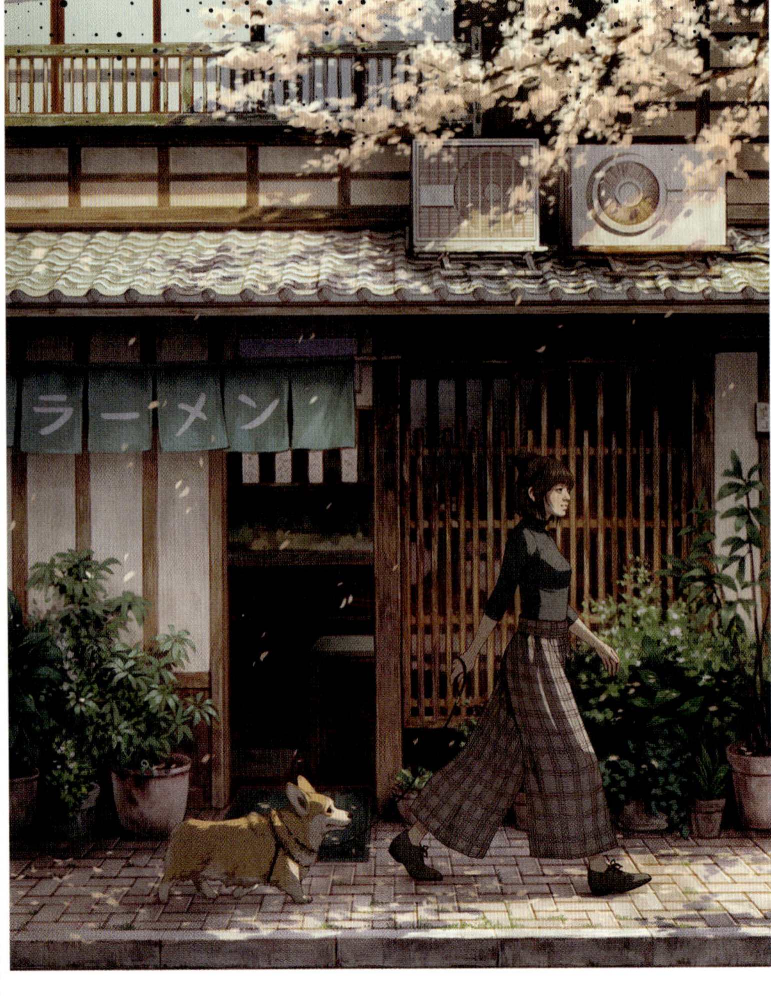

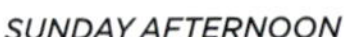

SUNDAY AFTERNOON
"This one started out with me wanting to paint a girl walking her dog, and I decided to set the scene in front of a little ramen shop."

because they don't want to intrude or come across as demanding or greedy.

"I don't worry about that. This is my job and I constantly post artwork without asking for anything. I think, in return, my followers should be able to forgive me for promoting something every once in a while. I still put a lot of effort into making the posts visually pleasing, and I only put the info in the caption. People can easily ignore it if they're not interested and don't need to get offended. The ones that do are the ones I don't want around anyway."

HEARTWARMING FEEDBACK

But Djamila mostly enjoys social media. Talking to followers, getting their feedback, reading that she's

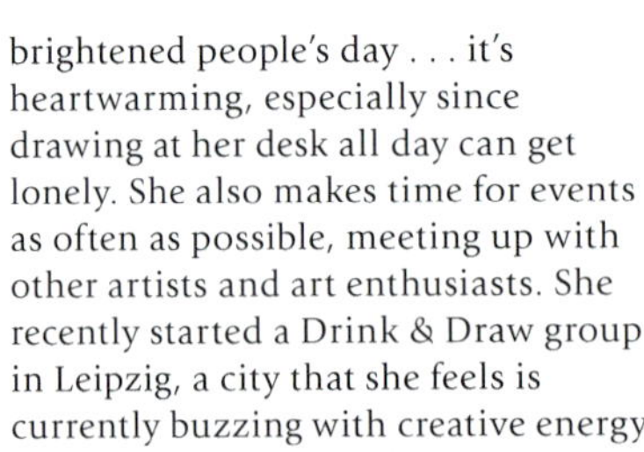

brightened people's day . . . it's heartwarming, especially since drawing at her desk all day can get lonely. She also makes time for events as often as possible, meeting up with other artists and art enthusiasts. She recently started a Drink & Draw group in Leipzig, a city that she feels is currently buzzing with creative energy.

But does Djamila worry she's doing too much, that she's in danger of burning out again?

"It seems like a lot, but the different elements build upon each other and work together seamlessly," she says. But the most important part is making new artwork. That's how I'm able to share content through Patreon and to make prints and merchandise that I can bring to conventions and put up in my online store.

"I'm in the fortunate position where everything I create is personal work. I've have a couple of long-term projects I started and I enjoy jumping around between them. I don't want to force myself to continue working on something that I'm not excited about. This freedom is what I love most about my job, and it is what keeps me motivated."

PUTTING ADVICE INTO PRACTICE

Back to Djamila's advice: "1) Work on your craft, 2) Don't try to force

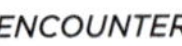

ENCOUNTER
"I painted this scene in winter. I always enjoy using the weather as an inspiration because it has a big effect on my mood."

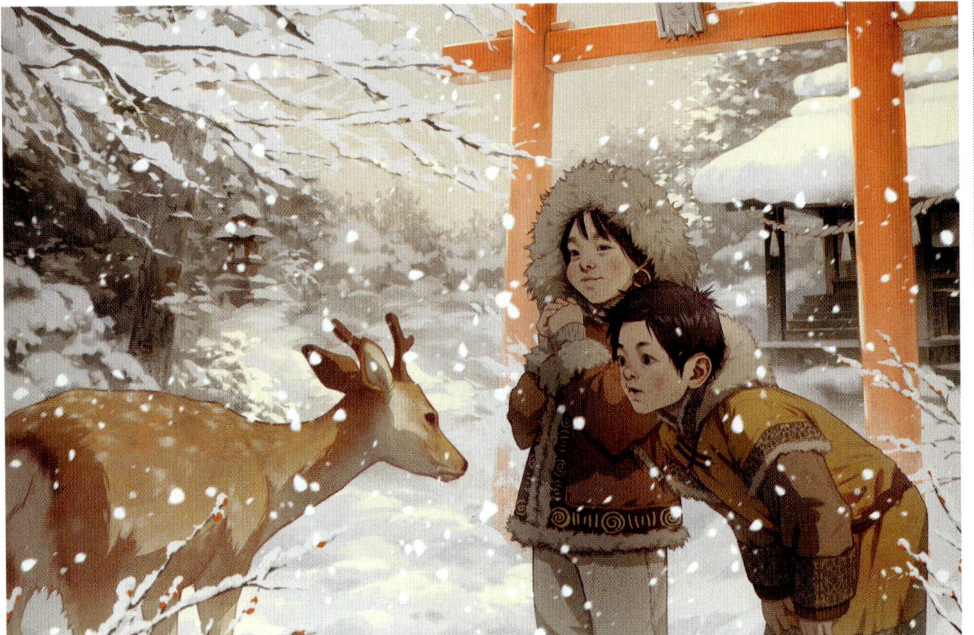

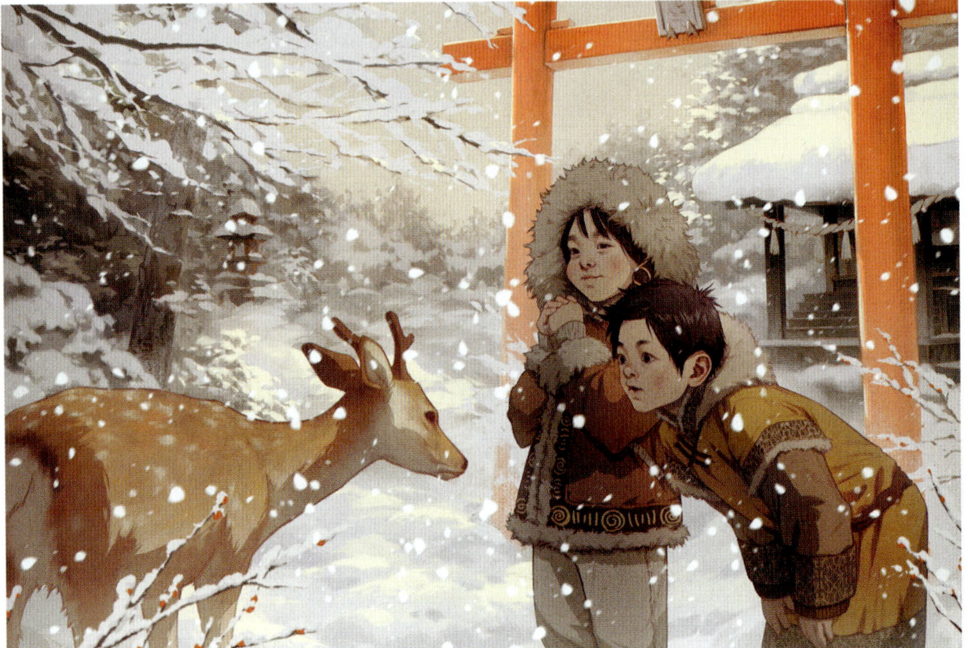

> **"Who am I to deem something worthy or unworthy?"**
>
> **—Djamila Knopf**

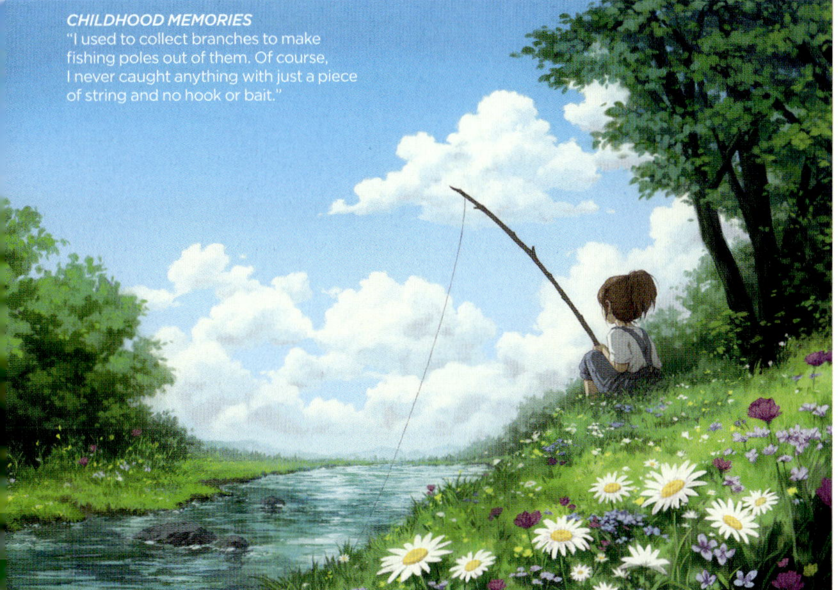

CHILDHOOD MEMORIES
"I used to collect branches to make fishing poles out of them. Of course, I never caught anything with just a piece of string and no hook or bait."

EVOKE A SENSE OF WONDER

Djamila's nostalgic illustrations stem in part from taking a child's viewpoint.

"When it comes to describing my art, the short version is: 'I create illustrations that evoke a sense of wonder and nostalgia,' because these are the themes that are most apparent in my work. I didn't come up with it myself. It's just what people have been telling me over and over again. My goal is to create images that feel as if they're taken from animated films—with a backstory that the viewer can explore.

My illustrations usually start out very vague. I use Pinterest a lot (*www.pinterest.com/djamilaknopf*) and I have a ton of boards with images that inspire me. If something sparks an idea, I develop it further by browsing more related images and by writing down word associations. I have a document on my phone that includes a list of illustration ideas that I eventually want to get to and develop further. Right now, among them are 'ghost children' and 'girl on a train with headphones'—just to give a few examples.

That description is pretty much the extent of it at the moment. The character design, set design, color palette, and composition are all things I'm still figuring out. I use a lot of references for a single illustration because I don't want to stick too closely to a single one. For poses, I usually shoot my own reference, because it's a huge help with anatomy and lighting.

I find myself gravitating to themes such as nature in concrete and magic in the mundane. I enjoy images that are peaceful, contemplative, and bright and colorful, so that's what I want for my own work. The feeling of nostalgia comes from the way I paint the world. I want to show it through a child's eyes: more pure, vibrant, and magical than it actually is."

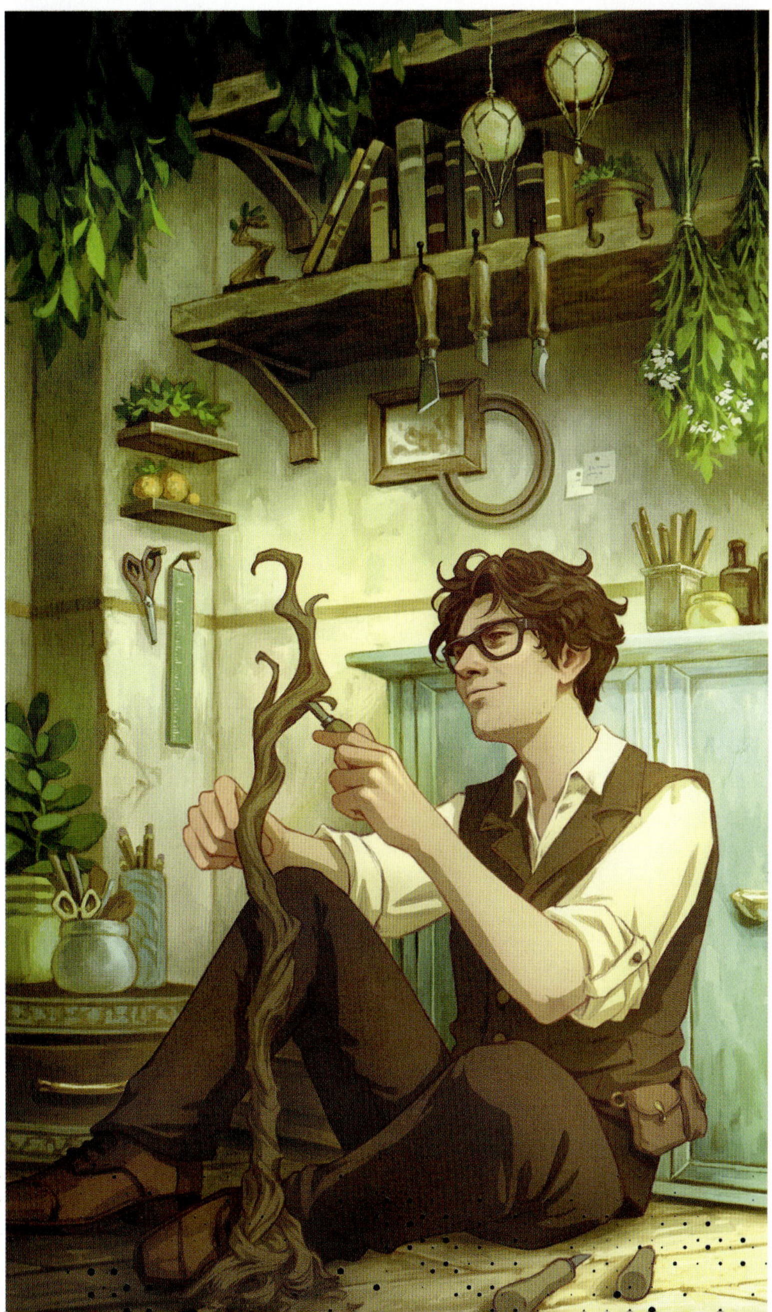

PAGE OF WANDS
"This tarot card stands for creativity, enthusiasm, and confidence, and so I decided to show an artist at work, because that's what I associate with those concepts."

yourself into a style that isn't natural to you, and 3) Share your work on social media." Like all the best advice, it's easy enough to understand, but not so easy to put into practice. So how do you know when you've made it? How do you know when you're making good art, when you're making something that's worthwhile?

"I don't like describing art as good or bad because it's all incredibly subjective. Who am I to deem something worthy or unworthy? So instead of trying to be a 'good' artist, I think it's a healthier mindset to try to simply be honest and open.

"None of us are ever going to reach technical perfection because it simply doesn't exist. And there's always going to be someone 'better.' So instead, just strive to be yourself and to channel your personal experiences and influences through your work. That level of personal connection is what's going to make the art stand out more than anything else."

Photoshop

DRAW AND PAINT FANTASY MANGA

Yueko shares her process for painting a female knight in an anime-inspired art style, paying particular attention to the hair and face.

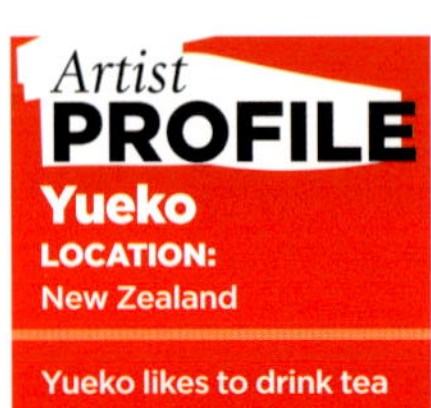

Artist **PROFILE**

Yueko

LOCATION: New Zealand

Yueko likes to drink tea and contemplate how to draw cuter girls.

www.yue-ko.com

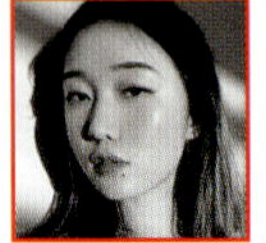

This artwork (page 39) was commissioned by the *ImagineFX* team for their cover! I was given a reference for the pose they wanted, based on a sketch I had previously drawn and some ideas for the character.

The idea of beauty and strength being non-exclusive is something I like a lot, which is why I often turn to the theme of female knights for my original character designs. In the past, I found armor quite difficult to draw, but I've always tried to push myself through challenges instead of avoiding them.

Crystal horns from a past artwork of mine caught the team's eye, so I incorporated them into this design. I added similar embellishments on her sword and armor because I thought the crystal would look a little out of place if it were only on her horns, especially as this character's hair is warm and bright. Because it's a close-up of a character and the team wanted the focus to be on her face, I spent extra time painting the details and softening her features.

How I create...

A STYLIZED MANGA HAIR LOOK

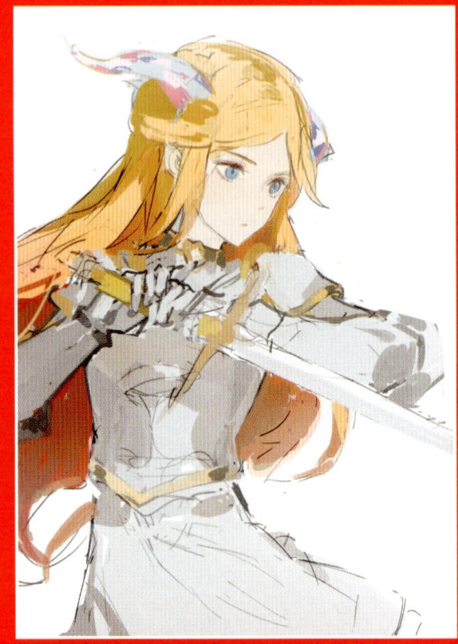

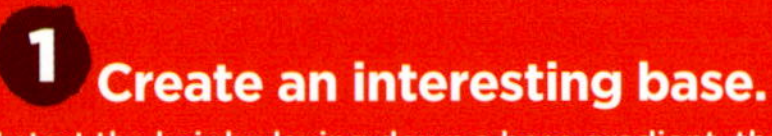

1 Create an interesting base.

I start the hair by laying down a base gradient, then applying some shading using a Linear Burn layer. By locking that layer, airbrushing lighter tones within it, and then adding a soft Overlay layer to brighten it up, the base becomes more interesting.

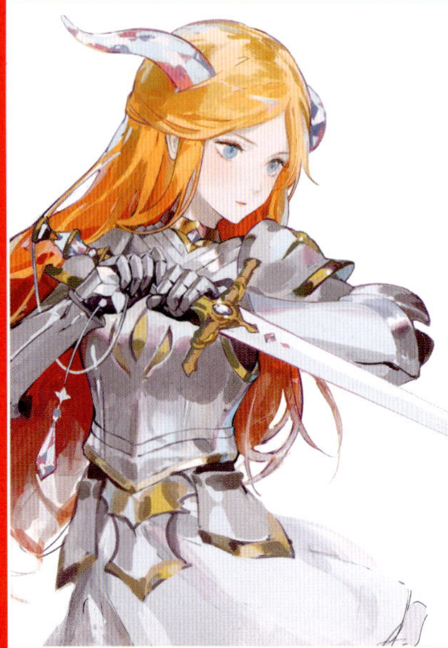

2 Build up texture.

For the next stage, I flesh out the overall shape of the hair and add more strands around the edges to hint at the texture. I blend the shading of the hair down, because hair doesn't often cast harsh shadows onto itself.

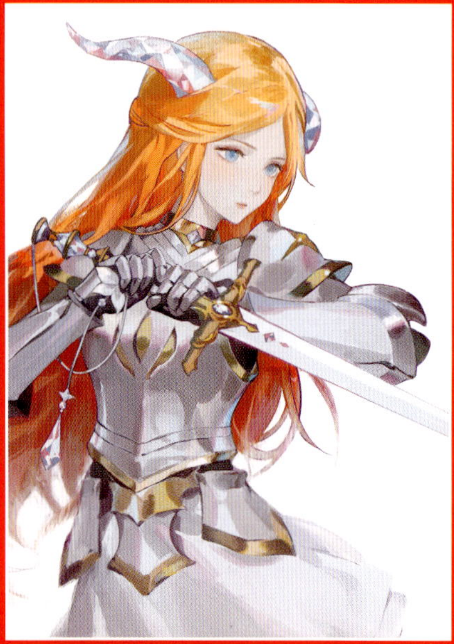

3 Refine the hair's shape.

In the final stage, I focus on cleaning up the smaller details and flesh out the strands around the face. I decided to break apart the large strand in front of the ear to soften the hair and make it appear less thick and solid.

BRING A KNIGHT TO LIFE

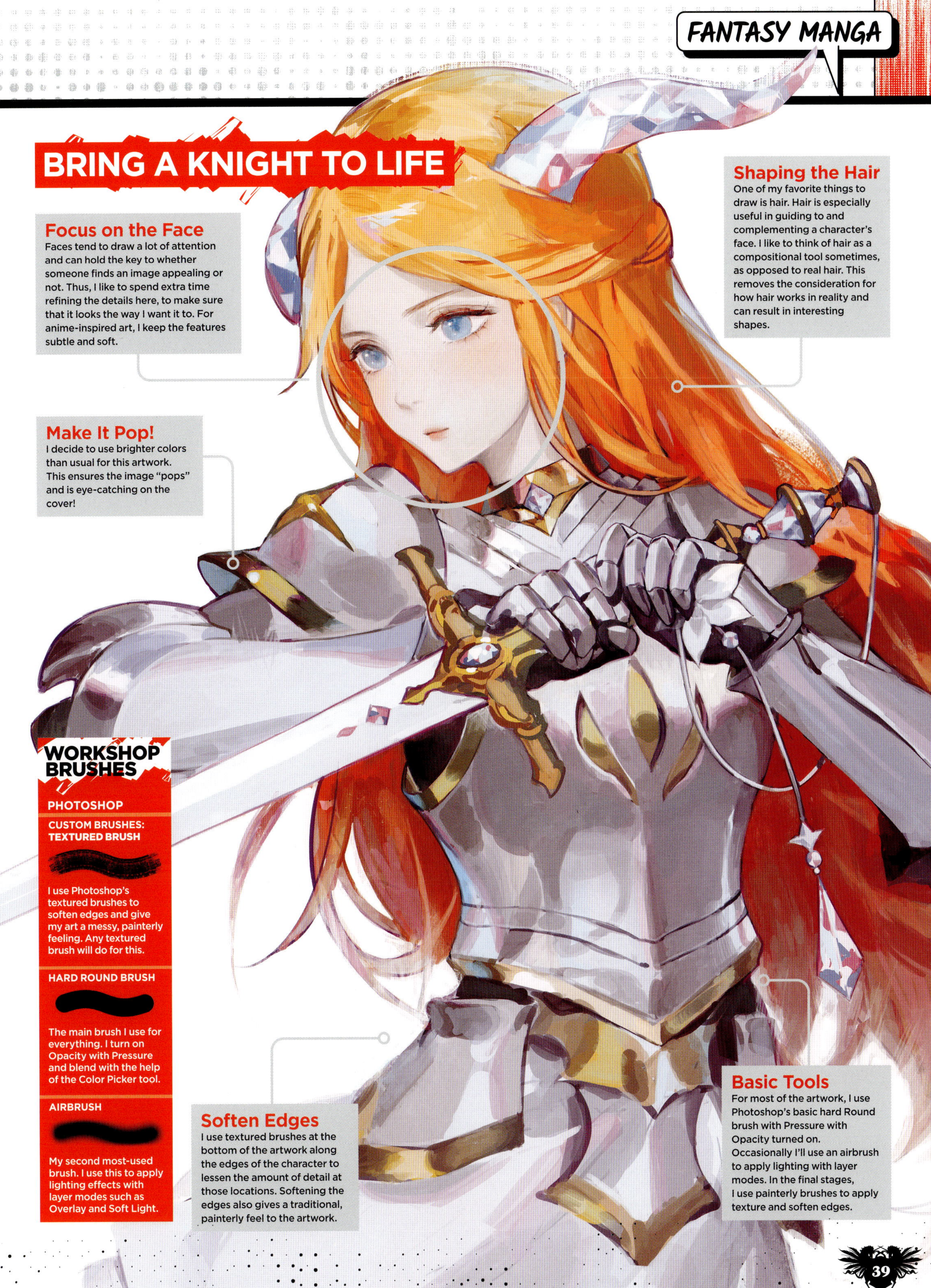

Focus on the Face
Faces tend to draw a lot of attention and can hold the key to whether someone finds an image appealing or not. Thus, I like to spend extra time refining the details here, to make sure that it looks the way I want it to. For anime-inspired art, I keep the features subtle and soft.

Make It Pop!
I decide to use brighter colors than usual for this artwork. This ensures the image "pops" and is eye-catching on the cover!

Shaping the Hair
One of my favorite things to draw is hair. Hair is especially useful in guiding to and complementing a character's face. I like to think of hair as a compositional tool sometimes, as opposed to real hair. This removes the consideration for how hair works in reality and can result in interesting shapes.

WORKSHOP BRUSHES

PHOTOSHOP

CUSTOM BRUSHES: TEXTURED BRUSH

I use Photoshop's textured brushes to soften edges and give my art a messy, painterly feeling. Any textured brush will do for this.

HARD ROUND BRUSH

The main brush I use for everything. I turn on Opacity with Pressure and blend with the help of the Color Picker tool.

AIRBRUSH

My second most-used brush. I use this to apply lighting effects with layer modes such as Overlay and Soft Light.

Soften Edges
I use textured brushes at the bottom of the artwork along the edges of the character to lessen the amount of detail at those locations. Softening the edges also gives a traditional, painterly feel to the artwork.

Basic Tools
For most of the artwork, I use Photoshop's basic hard Round brush with Pressure with Opacity turned on. Occasionally I'll use an airbrush to apply lighting with layer modes. In the final stages, I use painterly brushes to apply texture and soften edges.

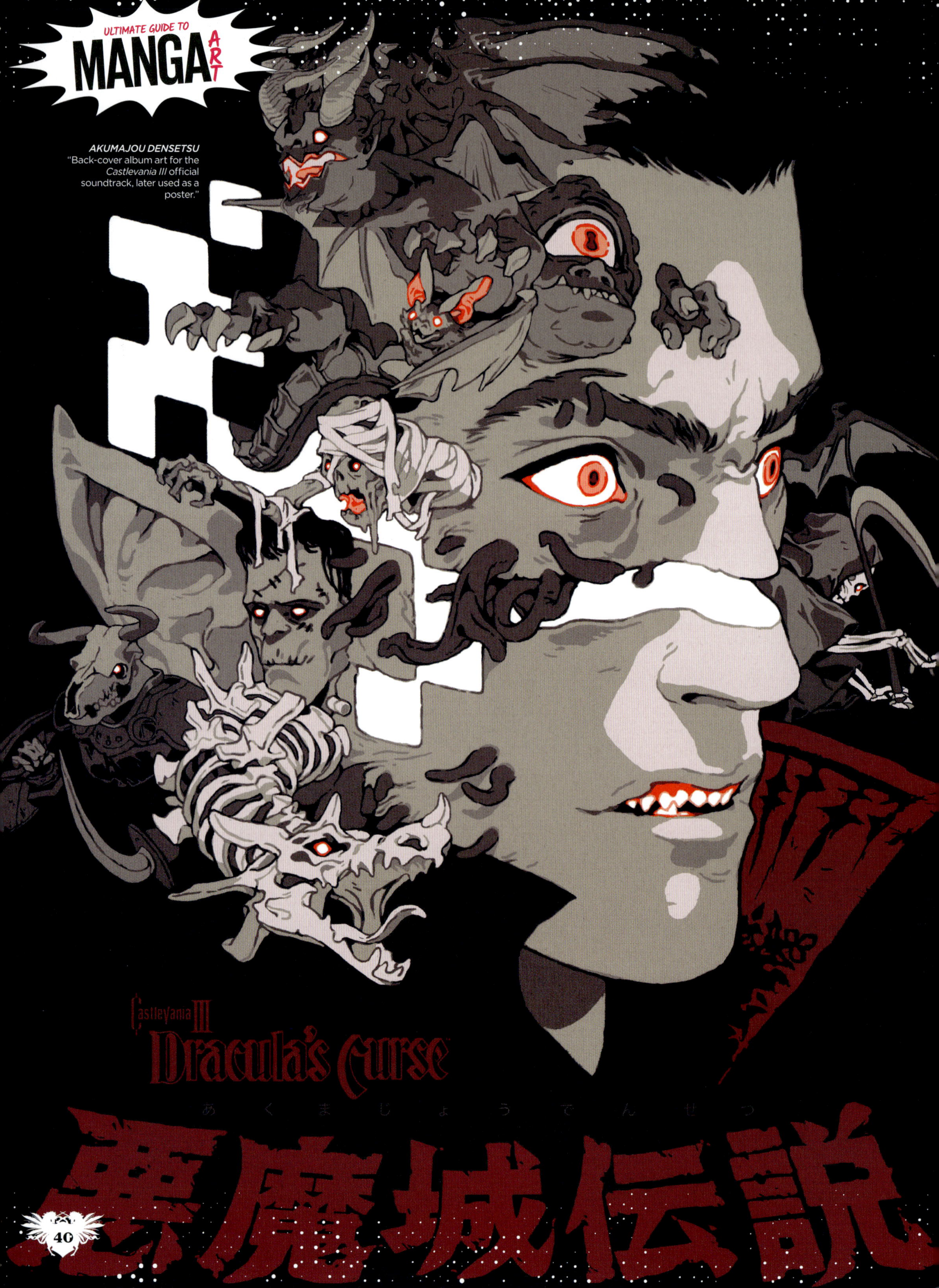

AKUMAJOU DENSETSU
"Back-cover album art for the *Castlevania III* official soundtrack, later used as a poster."

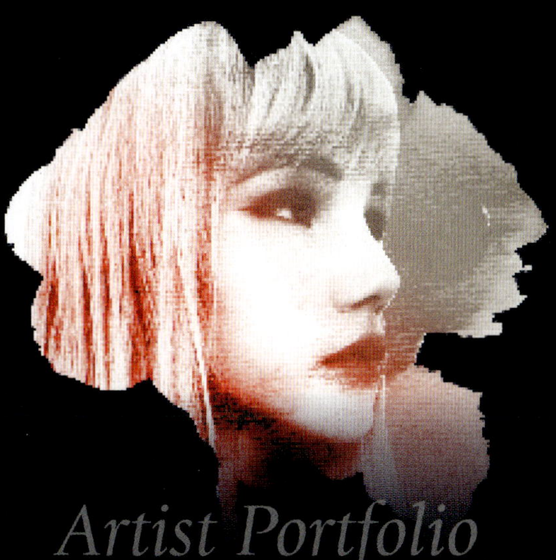

Artist Portfolio

SACHIN TENG

Dropping out of college, roughing it in motels, working up a mountain: the US artist tells **Gary Evans** about the highs and lows of a roller-coaster career.

Sachin Teng hadn't been to bed for six days straight. She was busy preparing for a show—Pratt Institute's notorious end-of-semester exhibition known as Survey. Everybody from the college was going to be there and, more importantly, so were the people from the Society of Illustrators. Sachin was lagging. She decided to have a power nap, another of the hour-long snoozes that kept her going this past week. She finds an empty classroom, makes a bed out of a couple of drawing benches, and closes her eyes.

Before Pratt, Sachin worked mainly in monochrome, pen or pencil drawings, still-life, line art. In 2007, she enrolled in communication design, focusing on illustration, but during her first year she almost failed a couple of classes. The New York college made her realize she wasn't as advanced as some of her peers.

In the past, teachers preached lofty ideas about art: what art was, what art did. They said all the stuff Sachin was into—comics, movies, video games—

> **"No one woke me up. They just stared and thought 'Yeah, same.'"**
>
> **—Sachin Teng**

that wasn't real art.

Pratt believed otherwise. Communication design was a fancy way of saying commercial art—art for money. Here, teachers taught Sachin how to get clients, run a business, market herself. They showed her how to do the one thing every working artist must learn to do: pay the rent. They set tight deadlines because tight deadlines are the reality of art for money. The Survey event was Sachin's chance to put this into practice.

The artist woke up from her hour-long power nap and saw the classroom was now full. A group of sophomores were in the middle of critique session. The students left Sachin to sleep because they were all in the same position: busy preparing for Pratt's end-of-semester exhibition.

"No one woke me up," the US

Artist PROFILE

Sachin Teng
LOCATION: US
FAVORITE ARTISTS: James Jean, Shintaro Kago, Josh Keyes, Katsuhiro Otomo, and Kehinde Wiley
SOFTWARE USED: Photoshop, Illustrator
WEB: *www.sachinteng.com*

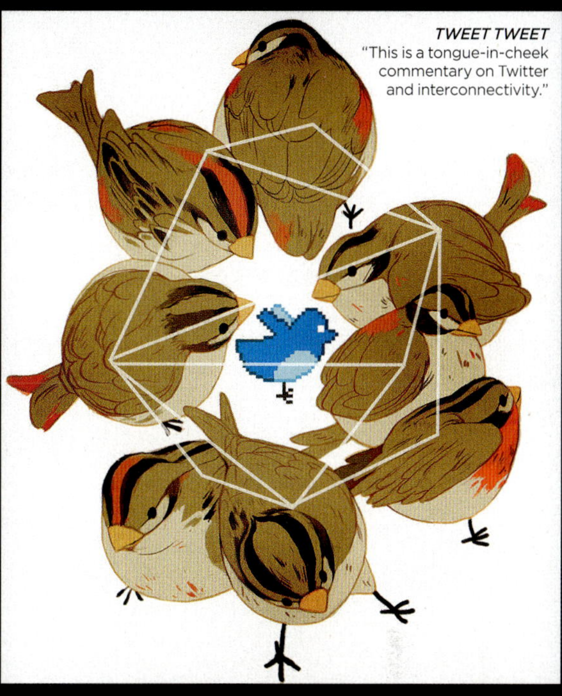

TWEET TWEET
"This is a tongue-in-cheek commentary on Twitter and interconnectivity."

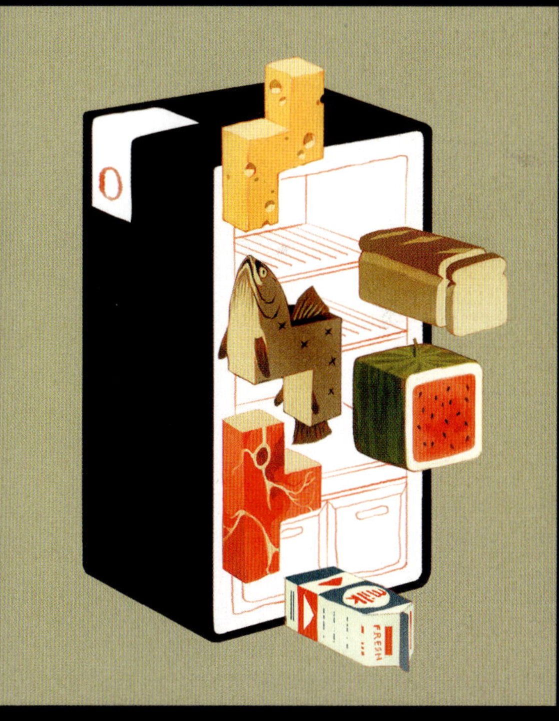

FRIDGE TETRIS
"Millennials always say that we have to 'Tetris' our stuff—fitting luggage into a tight space or food in a full fridge. So I made a literal reference to it."

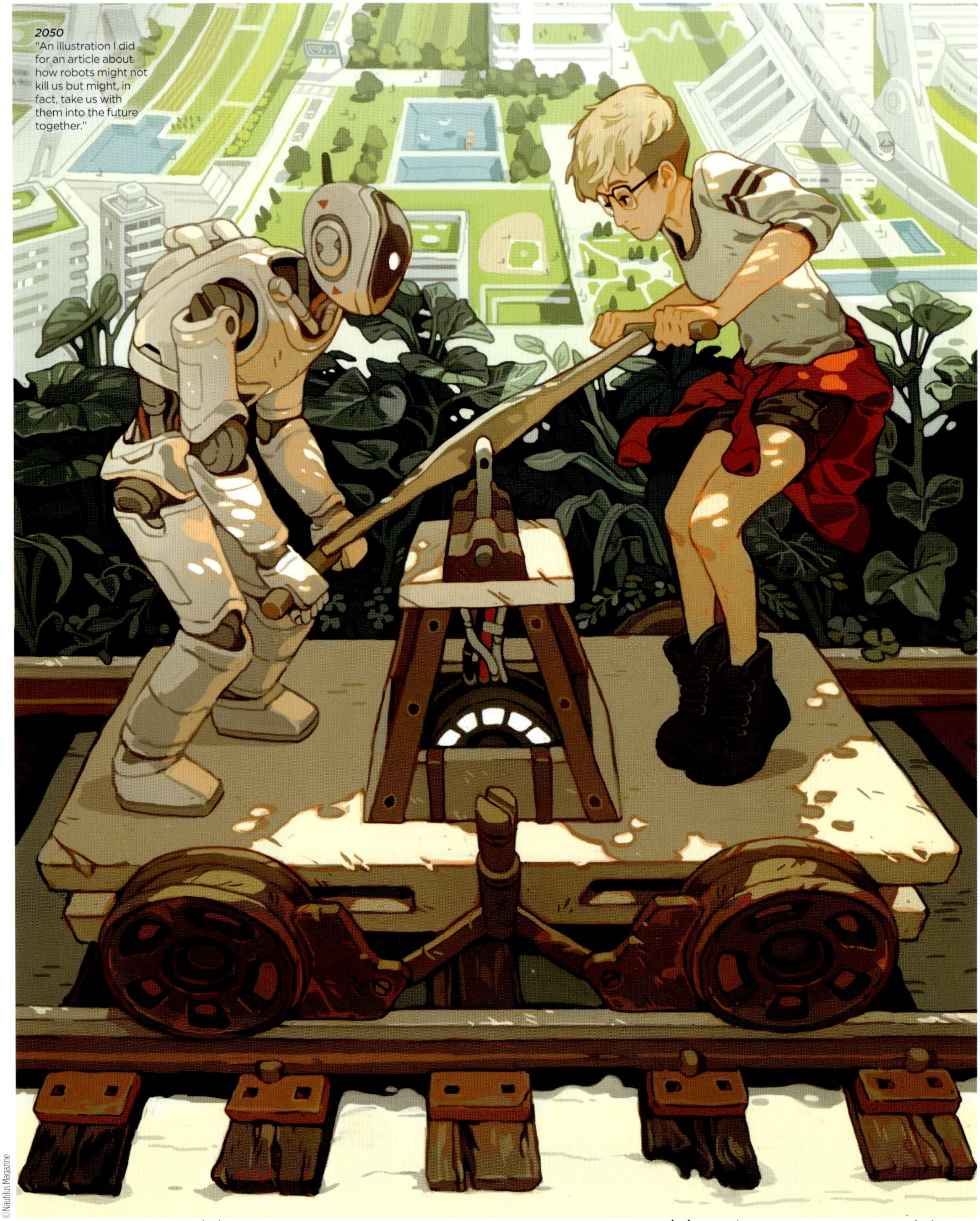

2050
"An illustration I did for an article about how robots might not kill us but might, in fact, take us with them into the future together."

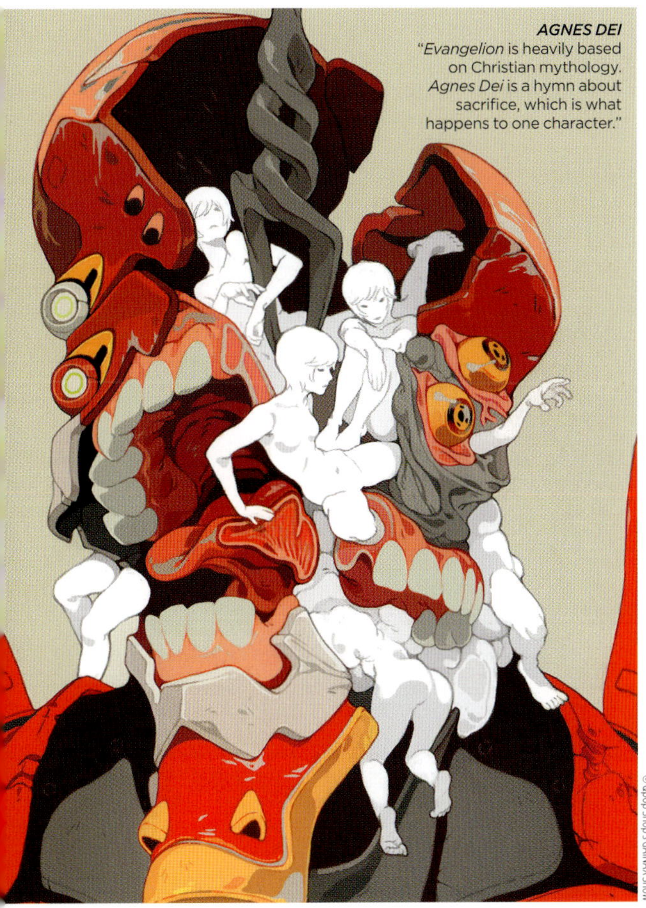

AGNES DEI
"Evangelion is heavily based on Christian mythology. *Agnes Dei* is a hymn about sacrifice, which is what happens to one character."

illustrator says. "They just stared and thought, 'Yeah, same.' Survey was hell. We all had horror stories. I used to pull all-nighters end on end. But it got me a couple of spots in the Society of Illustrators, and even one award. When it was over, all I remembered was the exhaustion."

What Sachin did next seemed like a gamble. She quit. Maybe Pratt taught her too well, because she decided to use the final year's tuition fee to set herself up as a working artist for real. Her mother agreed—on one condition. If it didn't work out, she had to go back to college. Her mother also gave tight deadlines: two years.

THE FREELANCER'S FIX

Sachin went on vacation with her family. They went on a tour of the mountains. Everybody else took in the scenery, enjoying the experience of the open road. However, Sachin set up office in the back of the car, working on her laptop with a SIM card in a USB stick for Wi-Fi. She had a deadline. She needed to finish an illustration, send it off to the art director for approval, and she had an hour left to do it. Then her battery died.

The tour stopped at a store in the middle of nowhere. The rain lashed down on a small building made of corrugated iron. Sachin ran inside to ask if they had an outlet to charge her laptop. They did. With the clock ticking, she breathed enough life into the battery to turn it on, catch a Wi-Fi signal, and send off her work.

"This, supposedly, was a vacation," Sachin says. "It's funny to me now, but at the time I was so stressed out. Work-life balance is hard as a freelancer."

This is the freelancer's fix. Starting out, you're going to be broke—possibly for years. Sachin was. After college, she left New York, her hometown, and moved to Los Angeles. Slowly, steadily, work came in. She overcompensated. She said yes to everything, anything. She worked weekends, worked holidays. "If you turn down work," Sachin says,

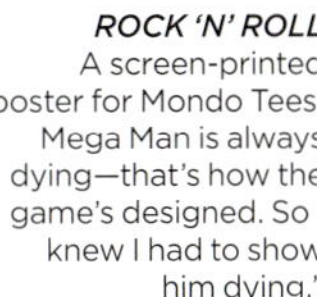

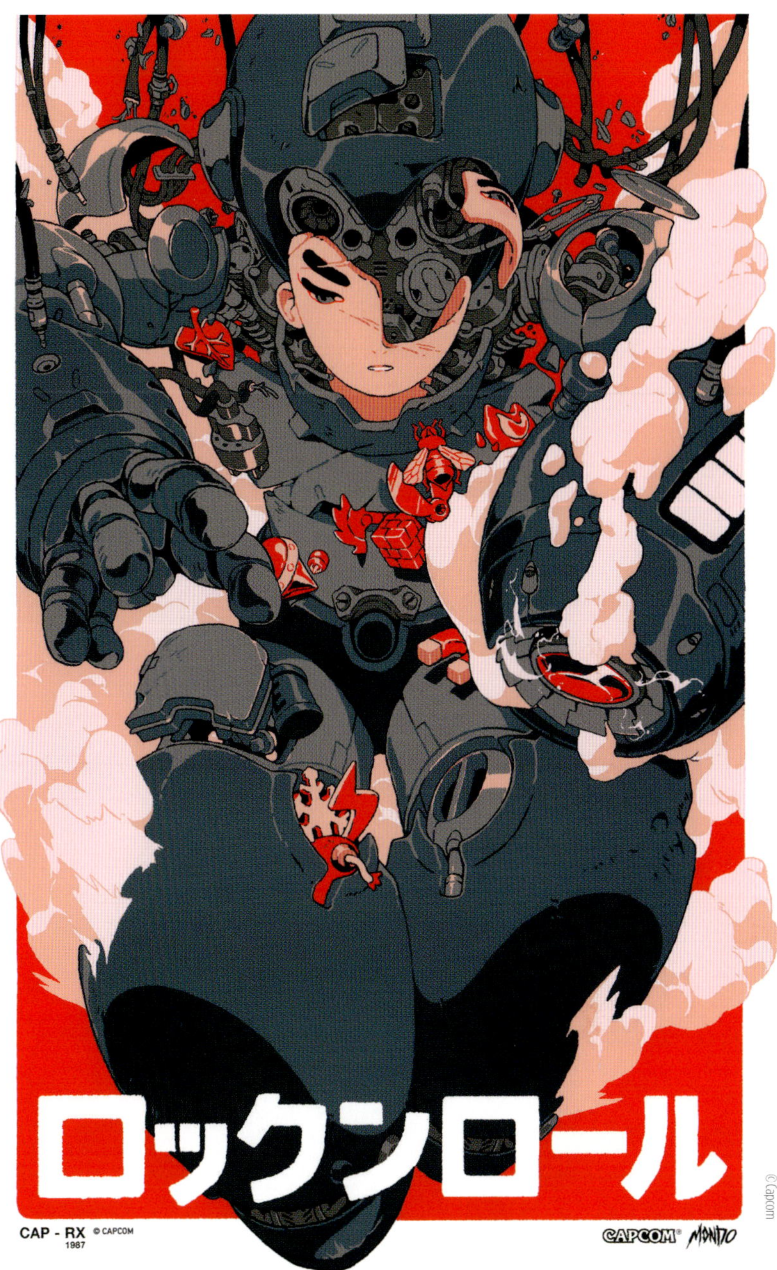

ROCK 'N' ROLL
A screen-printed poster for Mondo Tees. Mega Man is always dying—that's how the game's designed. So I knew I had to show him dying."

> **"If you turn down work you feel like you're turning down money, which is scary as a freelancer . . ."**
>
> **—Sachin Teng**

CREATING ART BY DESIGN

Sachin reveals how she thinks like a designer while illustrating this poster for an animated film.

1. CREATE AN INITIAL SKETCH.

This is a poster based on the animated film *Ponyo*. I wanted it to feel like two worlds colliding. In the film, the entire world is briefly flooded, so I wanted to make the canvas to feel that way. Sosuke is being forced into this small space. It's almost claustrophobic. The other thing was the conversation between the two characters. The canvas is split in half and two objects mirror each other on either side. The colors in the initial sketch are quite unrelated to the colors I actually ended up using. When you're trying to sell an idea, you have to make it read in the simplest terms. I was color-coding objects more than designing a color composition.

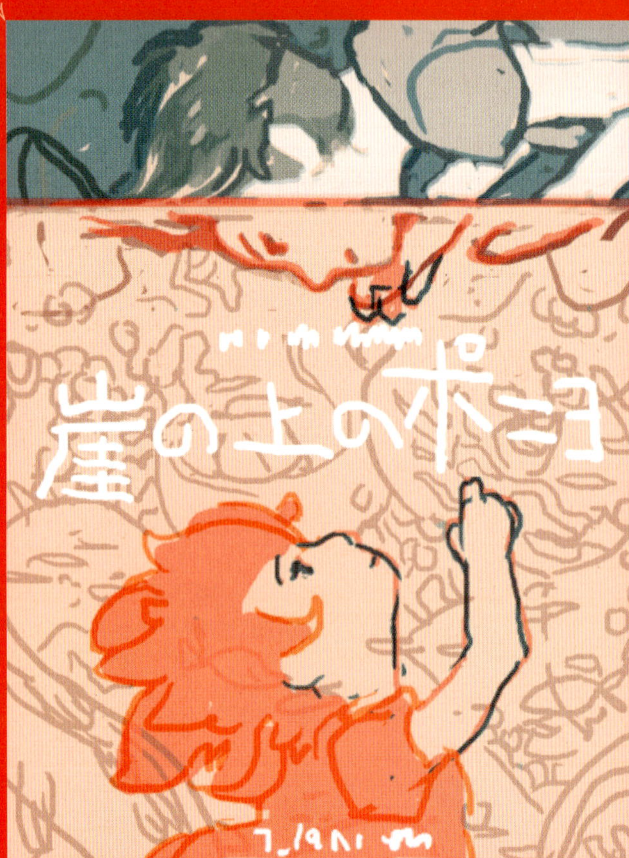

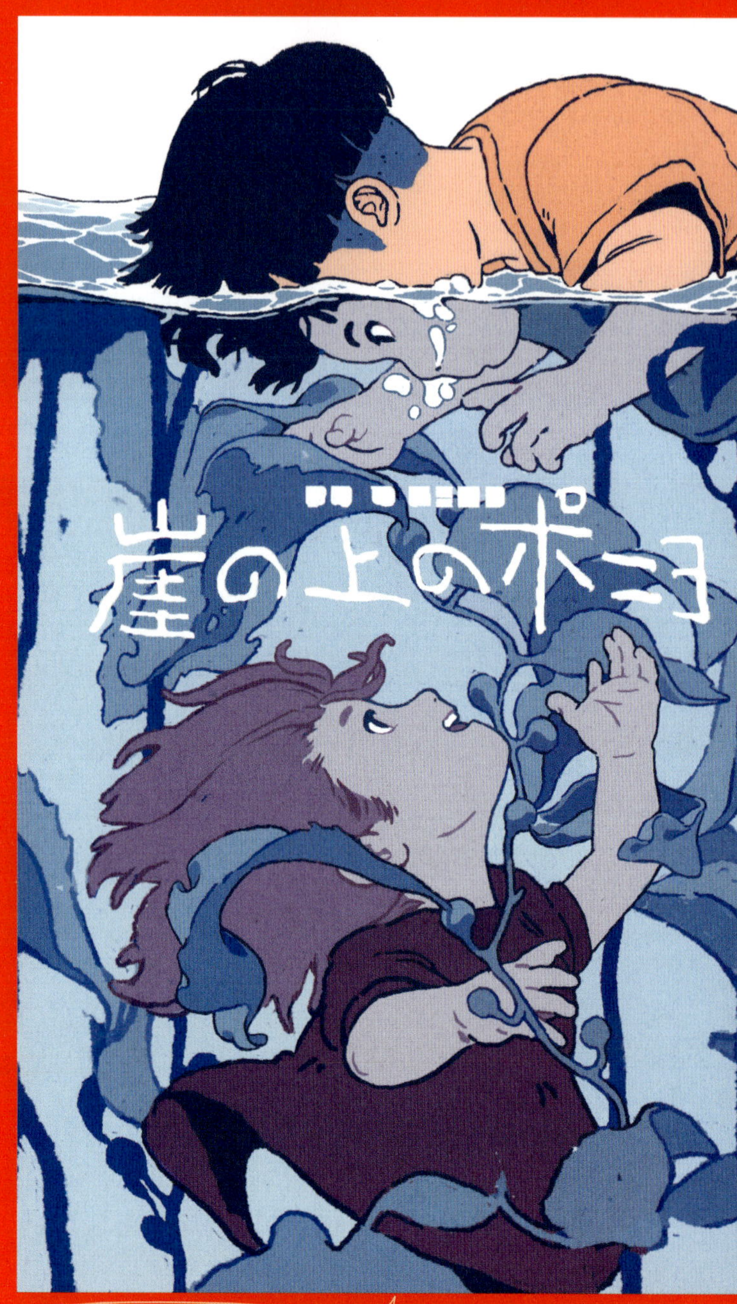

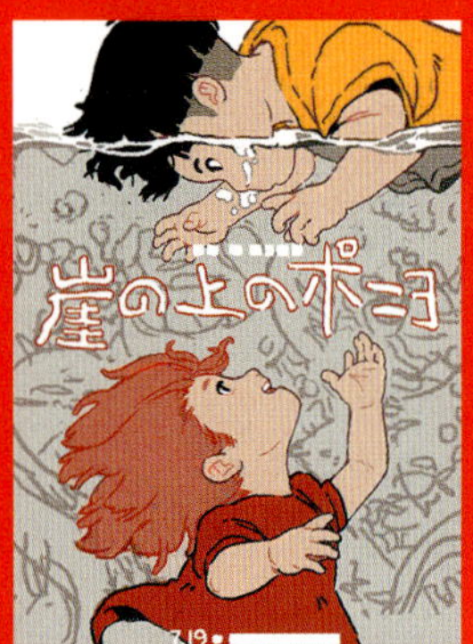

2. ANCHOR THE COMPOSITION.

Here I'm starting to render the main focal points of the illustration. They're the anchors of the composition, so they take priority. And I also want to establish the water refraction on Sosuke early on. This one of those uneasy moments: if you're not paying attention you don't see it right away, but you eventually see that the above doesn't line up with the below.

3. SET THE STAGE.

Once the actors are in place, I set the stage by creating the environment of kelp in which they'll rest, so it's grounded. I knew I was going to have dozens of fish and marine life, and without grounding everything it was going to be messy and impossible to know where to place them in space. At this point, you'll notice the large swath of blue I laid over the entire piece. I wanted to being unifying the color palette so the colors would be cohesive and feel like they belonged to the same world.

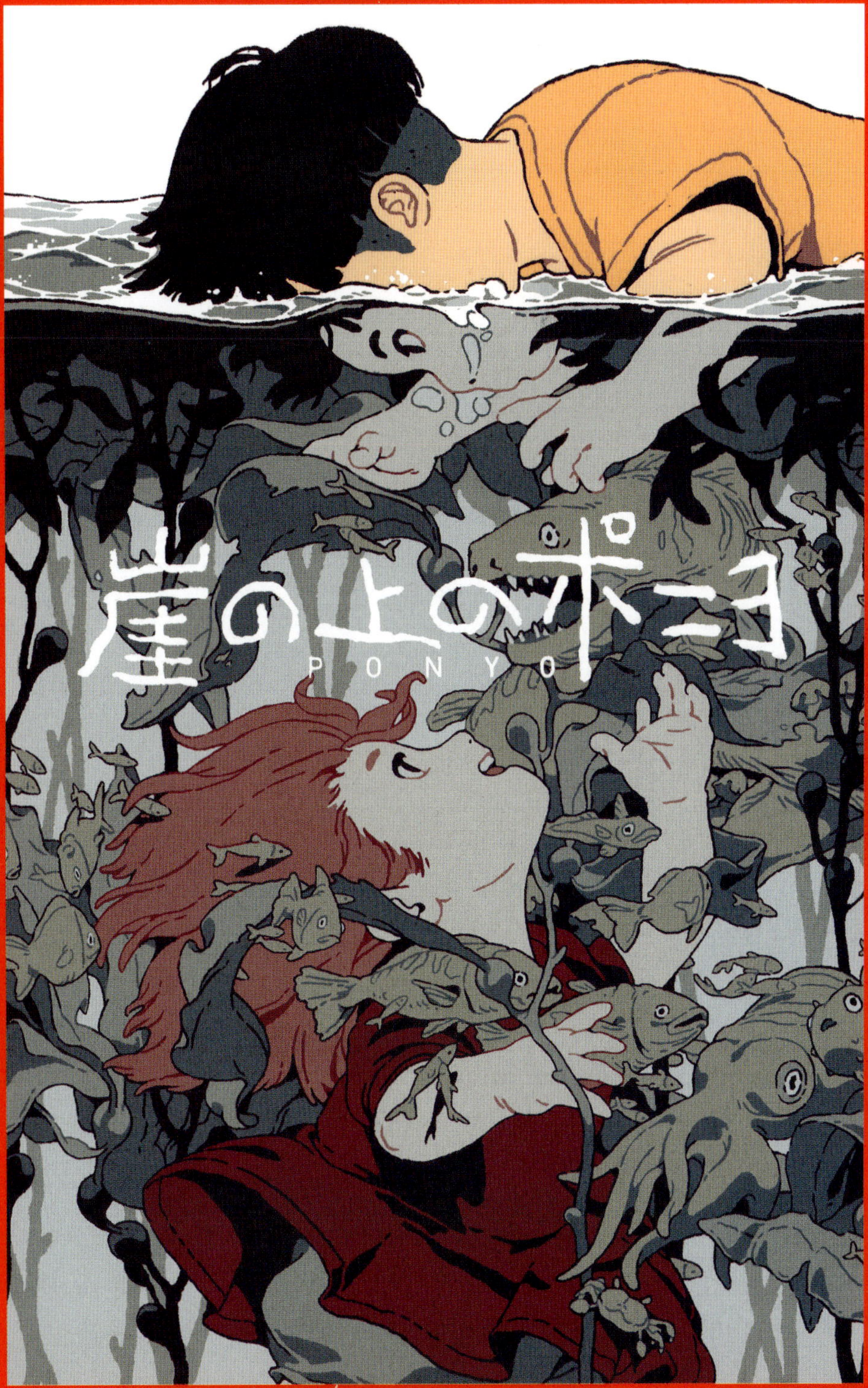

4. FILL IN DETAILS.

More kelp gives depth and pushes the space inwards. To ensure it's not busy or hard to read, the marine life forms a spiral around Ponyo and I don't let too much background light through the fish. Going from big fish to little fish creates a healthy variety of scale. Limit the numbers of the largest objects, and have lots of the smallest objects. I changed the colors of some lines, because too much black in the line art tends to flatten the image out. Details are always last, big shapes and colors first. You don't start hanging ornaments before you have a tree.

"you feel like you're turning down money. Which is scary as a freelancer, because they might never contact you ever again. But you have to learn to be okay with that."

Sachin's best art comes when the client enables her to do her own thing. But commercial work is often about compromise. The client is entitled to give detailed instruction. They're paying for it, after all.

"The confusing and weird clients are the ones that want you to do art in someone else's style, which is theft, plain and simple. And it makes about as much sense as calling an electrician to fix your plumbing. You just have to take it on the chin and try not to take it personally. Enjoy your art as much and as often as possible.

> **"Details are always last . . . You don't start hanging ornaments before you have a tree."**
>
> **—Sachin Teng**

"Not every piece can be your magnum opus, which means if you have to mail it in to meet a deadline, you'll have to submit work you don't think is finished. I don't know anyone who hasn't submitted work they wish they could add just one more detail to."

Sachin has worked for a wide range of clients in a diverse range of fields: advertising (Coca-Cola, Disney), editorial (*The Atlantic, The New Yorker*), and publishing (Dark Horse Comics, Penguin Random House). A professor at Pratt, Rudy Gutiérrez, taught Sachin how to market herself in this way. The economy's up and down, client's come and go, but you've got to make sure things are always moving. Finish a job and you're on to the next. If you're not making money in editorial, switch to advertising. You're not stuck in any one field. This is the best thing about being a freelancer.

LANDING THE THING

Sachin starts every new piece with research—reading the book, watching the film, listening to the album—getting to know whatever it is she's illustrating. Research is especially important for

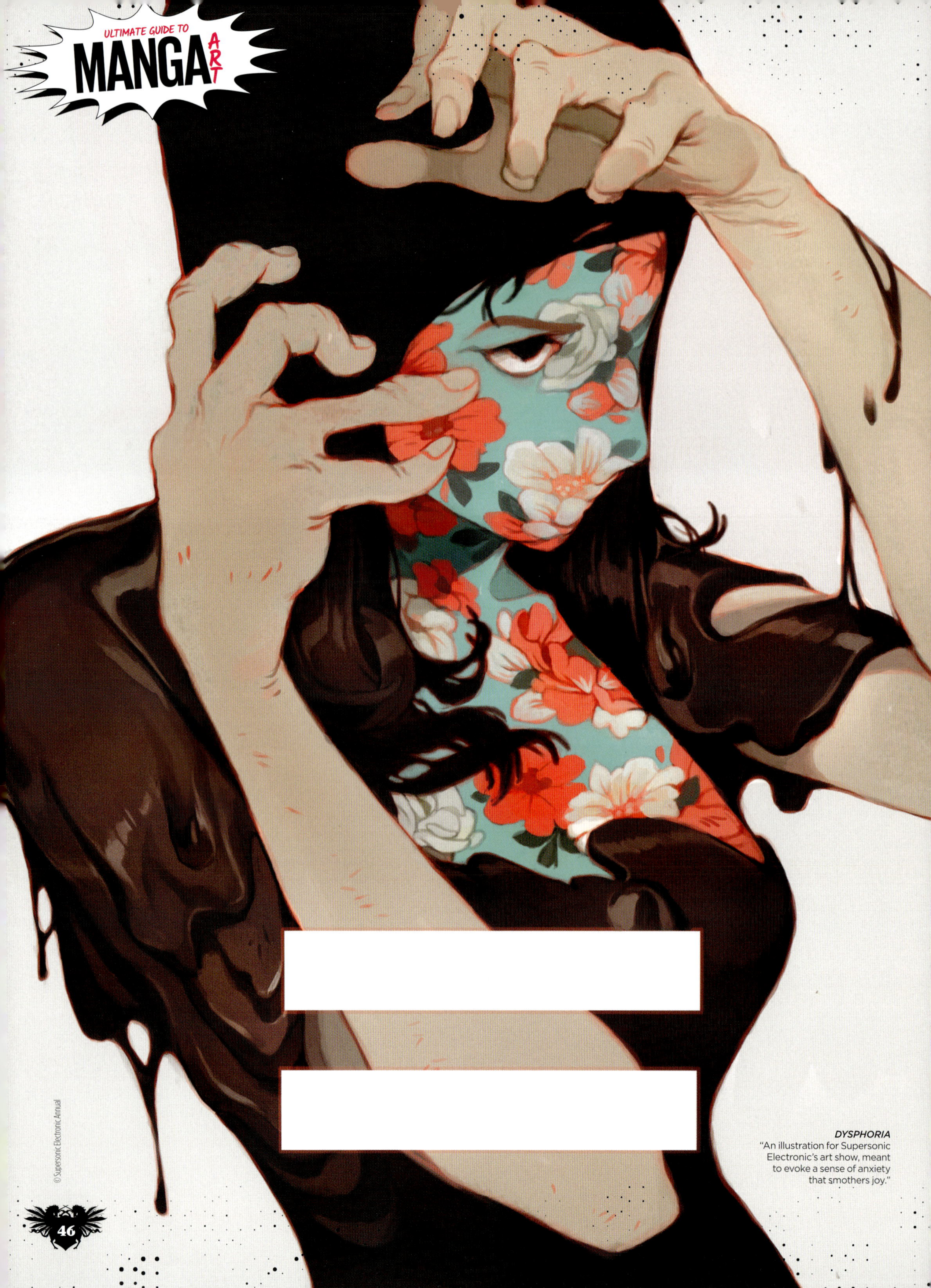

DYSPHORIA
"An illustration for Supersonic Electronic's art show, meant to evoke a sense of anxiety that smothers joy."

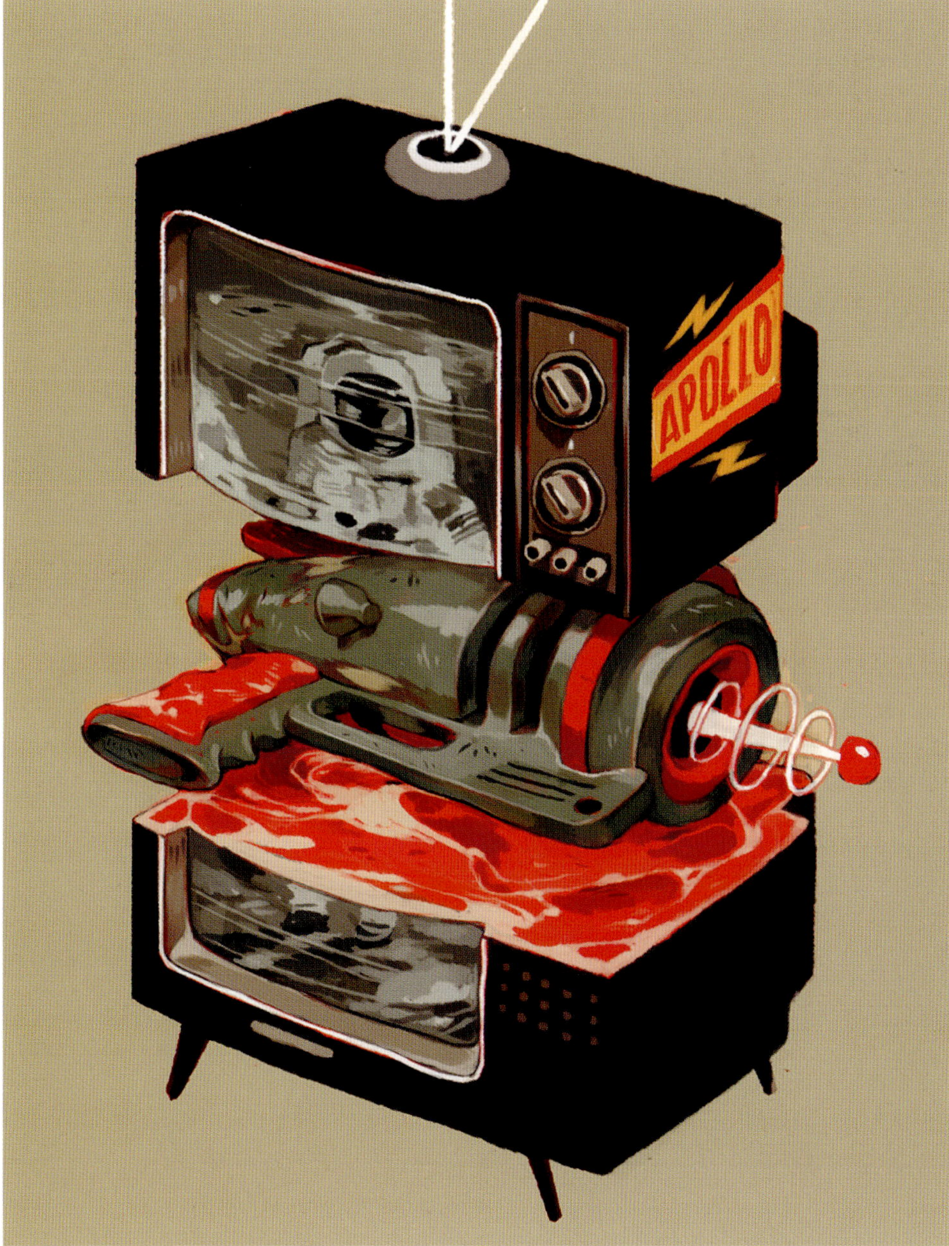

DAYS OF FUTURE PAST
"Done for an art show about retro futurism. It shows the wonder and imagination of what we thought of the future would be, juxtaposed with the moon landing - which is the real-world counterpart."

editorial work on social or political issues. Sachin makes a comprehensive mood board of relevant images, then sketches and brainstorms, mostly in Photoshop or Illustrator. Occasionally an idea jumps out, but usually she has to work at it. She never forces this stage: "Making a good illustration is about problem-solving. The conceit is to finesse it into an elegant solution."

From here it's about "logistics." The thing's flying. All Sachin has to do is land it smoothly. But that's easier said than done, and it's frustrating when the illustration on the page doesn't match the idea in her head.

"You have to see what it is about the choices you've made that steered it off course, which can take time you may not have. A lot of the time, a successful illustration comes down to whether or not I can figure it out in time."

"I'm a little illustrator, a little designer, a little fine artist. It's more fun that way."

—Sachin Teng

ESCAPE FROM THE BED ZONE

Sachin works from home, always near a window, and struggles with the "biblical temptation" of her bed being a few feet from her desk. Not a morning person, shes wake up and turns on music or the TV as loud as possible to force herself out of bed. She walks to Starbucks for coffee or, if she's really struggling, the corner store for Red Bull. A lot of the day is spent answering emails, or printing, assembling, and posting merchandise. When she gets to work, it's on a Wacom tablet connected to an iMac.

Her work features lots of pop culture icons—the Nintendo Game Boy, the Sony Walkman, the Nike Dunks. This is because her art is a self-portrait. New York City kids like her grew up with these things. Artists who are starting out always worry about finding their styles, their voice. Sachin says you've always got it—you just don't realize. "Your style is just you," she says. "It's ironic because to be original means to do something no one has ever done before. I'm a little illustrator, a little designer, a little fine artist. It's more fun that way."

MOTHER'S DEADLINE

Sachin moved to Los Angeles to financially support her partner, who'd been offered a job there. They lived in a motel for a couple of weeks, then took the first apartment that would take them in the Van Nuys area, where they slept on an air mattress for another three months. Pretty

HOW TO BEAT ARTIST'S BLOCK

Sachin explains why drawing like a child can help when you're stuck.

I was working on my junior thesis for illustration at Pratt. No matter how hard I tried, I just couldn't catch a break in this class. Nothing that had carried me before mattered to this professor. And I couldn't understand what he meant by "confounding"—his favorite descriptor for conceptual work.

It was about to be the end of the semester and I still hadn't made a breakthrough. My initial sketches for the thesis were shot down. So I had to start over. I was certain I was just going to fail. Painting alone wasn't getting me anywhere, so I decided to just read a lot. There had to be books or articles, essays, something that would give me some insight I wasn't seeing. I eventually landed on a book called *Visual Thinking*, which contained a description about how children draw compared to adults, the way people think and perceive, and it made something click.

I got to work and I ended up with this image, one of a five-painting series. No rendering. No drawing. And the airplane blueprint is just collaged on top. I had never collaged anything in my life. I don't make work like this anymore, but the mindset that helped me make it sticks with me to this day.

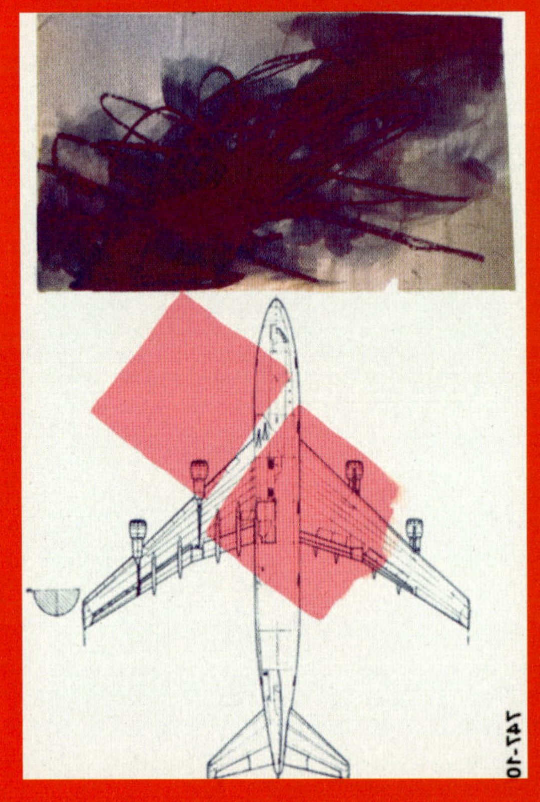

Sachin channeled her inner child when she was struggling with course work at Pratt, and came up with this artwork.

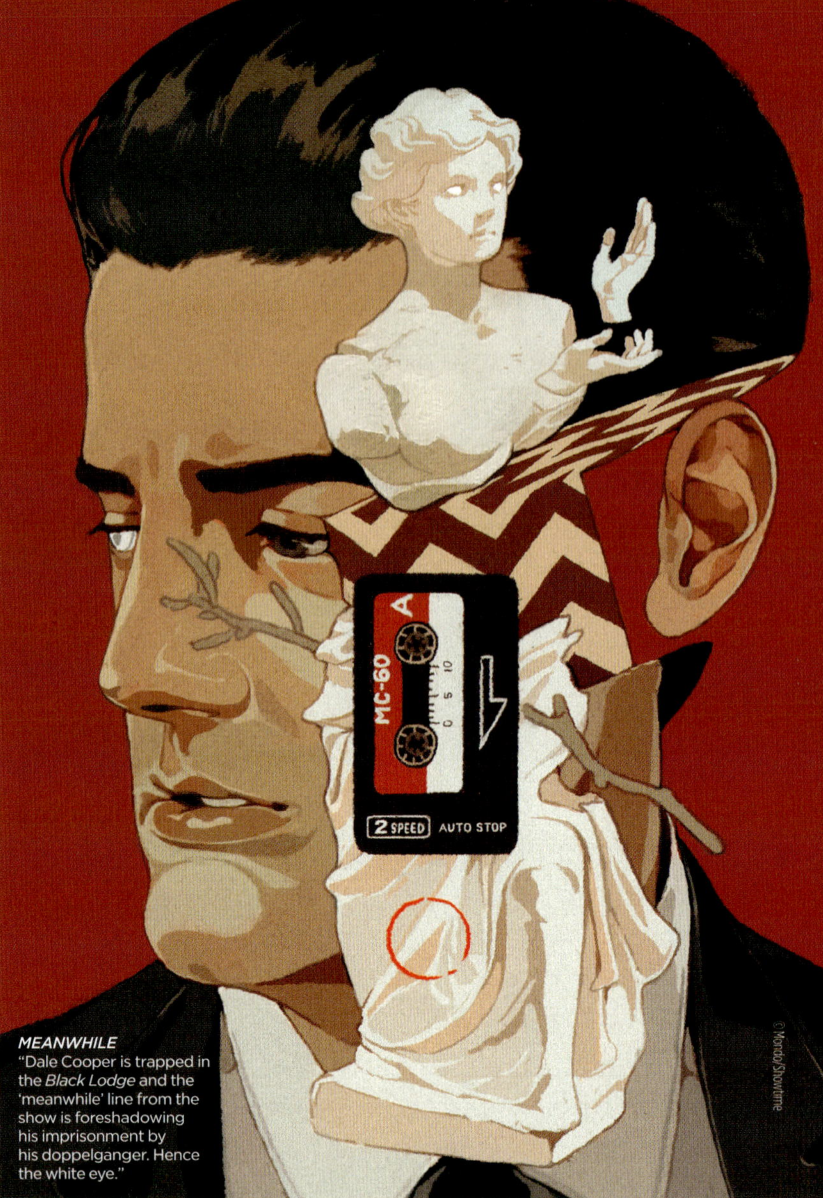

MEANWHILE
"Dale Cooper is trapped in the *Black Lodge* and the 'meanwhile' line from the show is foreshadowing his imprisonment by his doppelganger. Hence the white eye."

> **"The only thing that will set you apart and move you forward is to be the most faithful version of yourself you can manage . . ."**
>
> **—Sachin Teng**

soon, Sachin had used all her savings. She considered getting a "real job." But by then, her partner was making money and able to support the both of them. Sachin hated not paying her own way. Plus, her mother's two-year deadline was almost up.

"This was the one time I truly, deeply felt leaving school had been a mistake. But my mom saw me busting my ass and, even though I wasn't quite there, she could see it. So she lifted the two-year deadline and let it play out to see where it went. My mom's a saint."

LEAVING LA

Sachin left Los Angeles after a decade and moved home to New York. Pratt showed Sachin how to do the one thing every working artist must do: pay the rent. These days, that's not so much of a struggle. But the life of an artist will always come down to the conflict between doing good work and making good money. Sachin's still working on that one.

"My own art still lacks fearlessness, because at the end of the day I need to make a living. I always regret the work I make when I'm being a coward, and I never regret the work I make when I'm confident.

"The only thing that will set you apart and move you forward is to be the most faithful version of yourself you can manage, and stop stressing yourself out and beating yourself up trying to live up to what you think you need to be. A lot of artists can be way too hard on themselves."

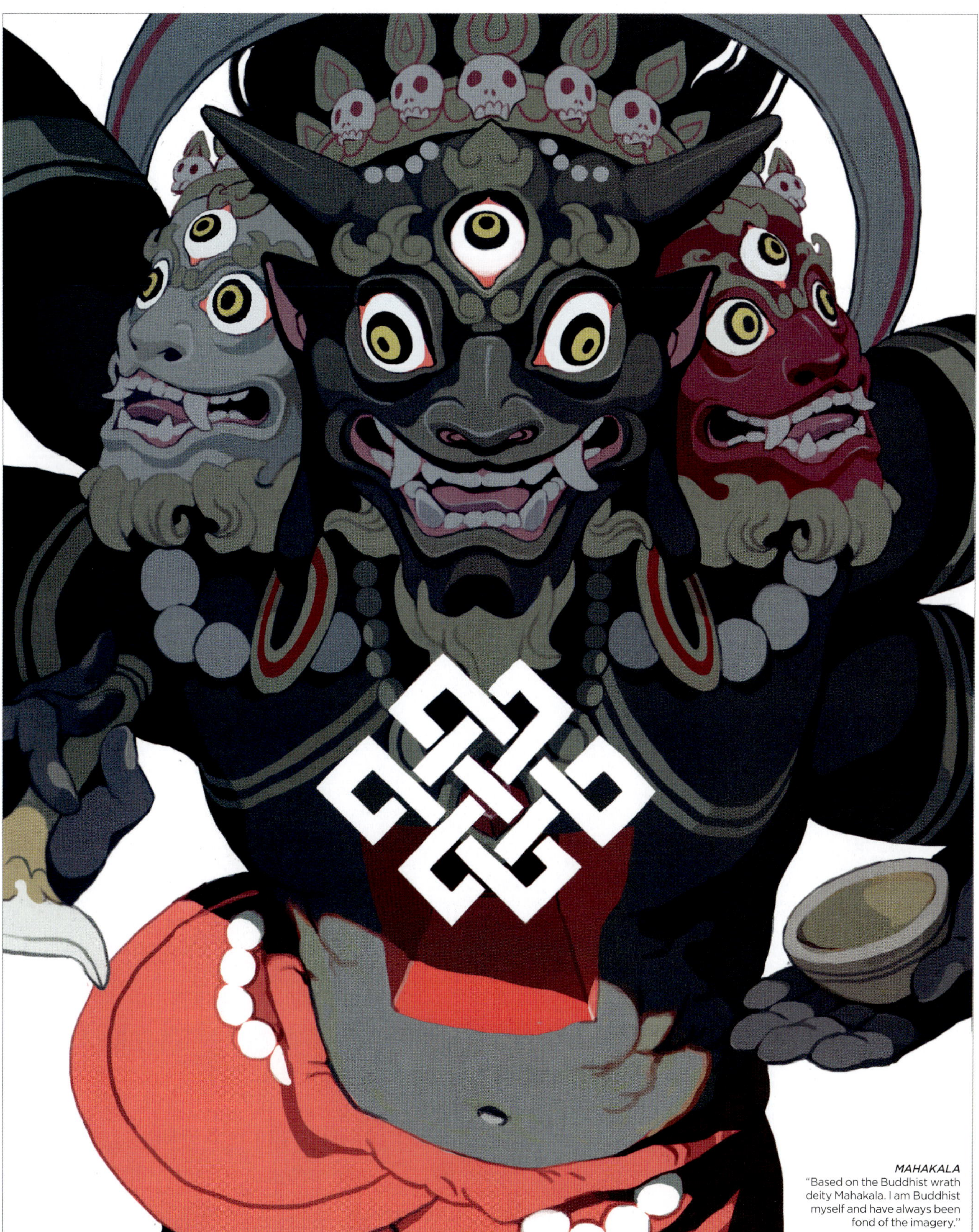

MAHAKALA
"Based on the Buddhist wrath deity Mahakala. I am Buddhist myself and have always been fond of the imagery."

Clip Studio Paint

COLOR MANGA IN CLIP STUDIO PAINT

Asia Ladowska reveals her process for creating a manga portrait, while passing on essential advice on sketching, shadows, and lighting.

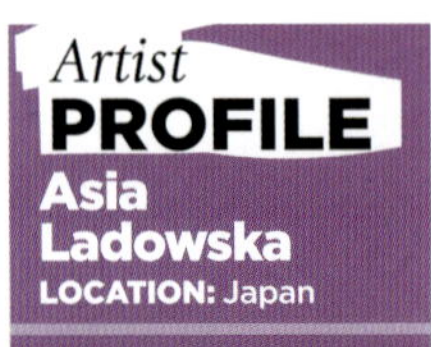
Artist
PROFILE
Asia Ladowska
LOCATION: Japan

The Polish artist, who is currently residing in Japan, is the author of the best-selling book *Sketch with Asia*.
www.ladowska.com

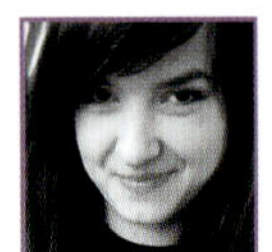

Painting digitally isn't an easy thing to do, especially when you're staring at a blank canvas and the possibilities are endless. I always feel excited about creating a new illustration, but with this joy comes many fears and a lot of self-doubt.

Apart from being unsure where to start, I used to ask myself questions. Is my illustration looking good? What else can I add? Did I add too much? What if I change this? I'm sure many of you feel the same at the beginning of your art journey, so to help you out I've prepared some tips that you can refer to "find yourself" if you ever feel lost when painting.

For this workshop, I created a character: Mai. This simple name comes from the name of the month I painted her in. I started this illustration in May 2020 and didn't open the file until May 2021 when I finally finished it.

Art is a journey, not a destination. If you check the number of my Instagram posts, it's above 1,100. If you take away 10% to be on the safe side, that's at least 990 portraits, and I keep making new ones! Sometimes instead of asking yourself too many questions about your own drawing, all you need to do is finish it and then start another. Painting is incredibly enjoyable, so as a final word, I want to say keep creating, have fun, and don't give up.

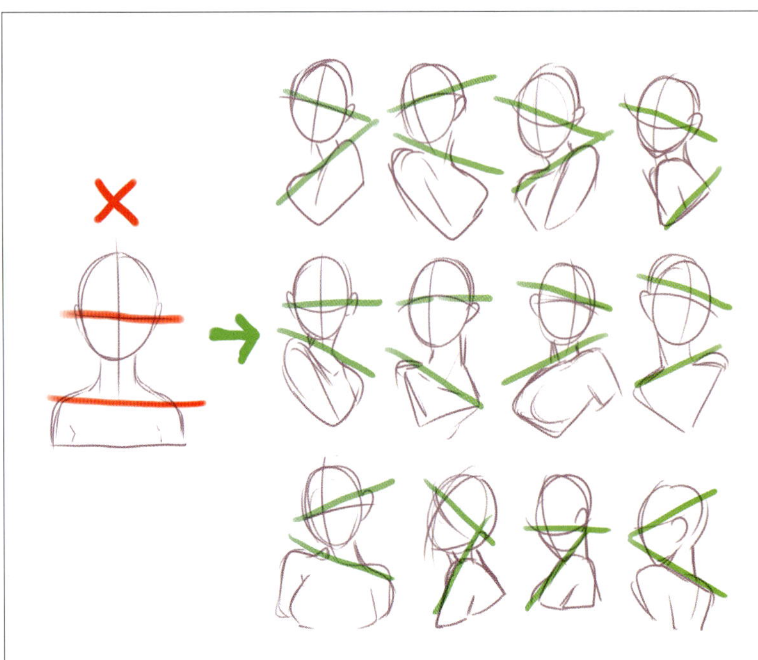

1 Choose an interesting angle.

The most difficult angle to work with when drawing a portrait is the frontal view. It needs careful symmetry, balance, and well-measured proportions, and when you put all of this together it looks a little . . . boring. I always struggle to make frontal poses look interesting, and end up trying to second-guess myself. Even if I push through the process, the result doesn't look very attractive. However, if you choose a slightly more dynamic angle, then you'll be off to a good start!

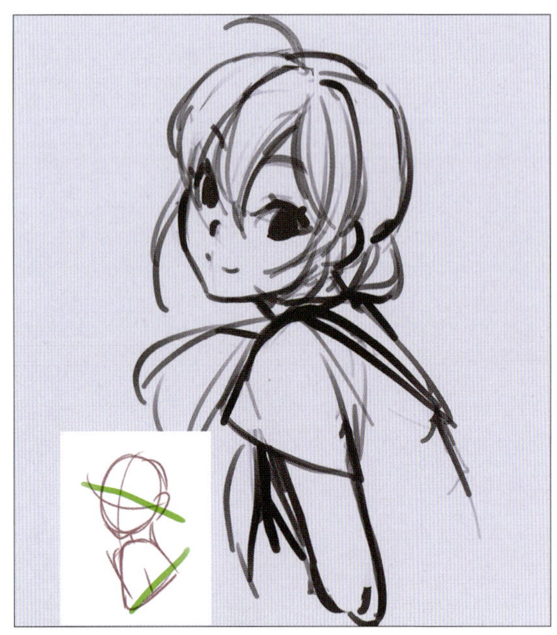

2 Sketch quickly.

I always try to draft a sketch in under 15 minutes. Let's face it—it's just a sketch. I need to visualize my idea before I forget it! My favorite tool to use in Clip Studio Paint is the Darker Pencil. It's good for sketches, line art, and even shading. I mainly use the software's default brushes, but adjust their settings slightly. For the Darker Pencil I always untick the Adjust by Speed option and change Stabilization to around 15.

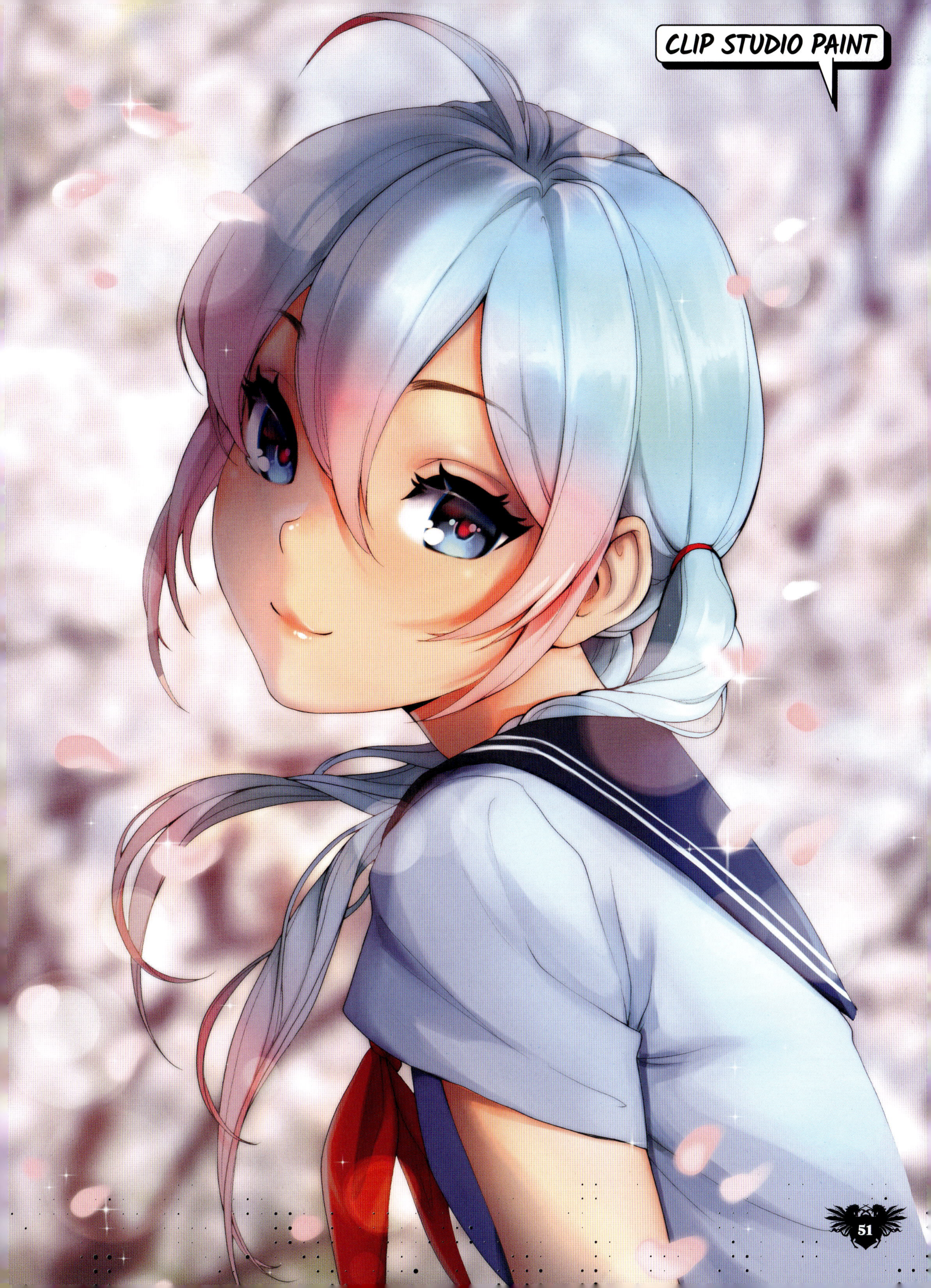
CLIP STUDIO PAINT

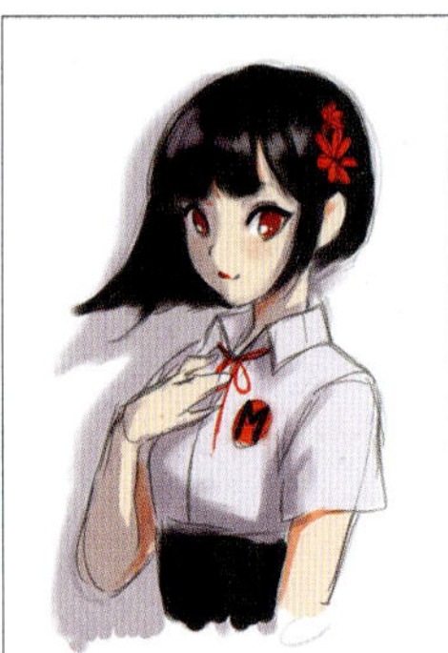
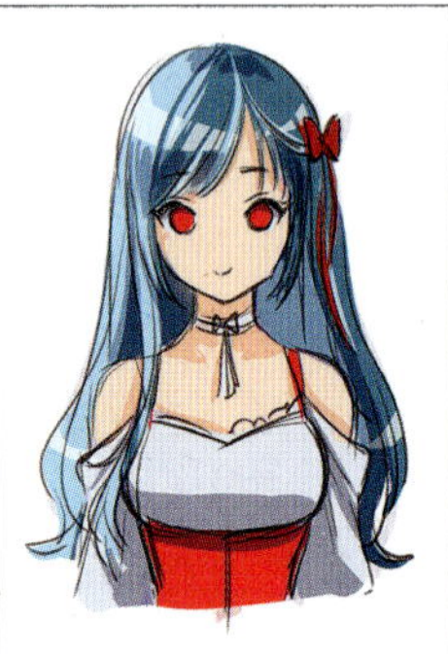
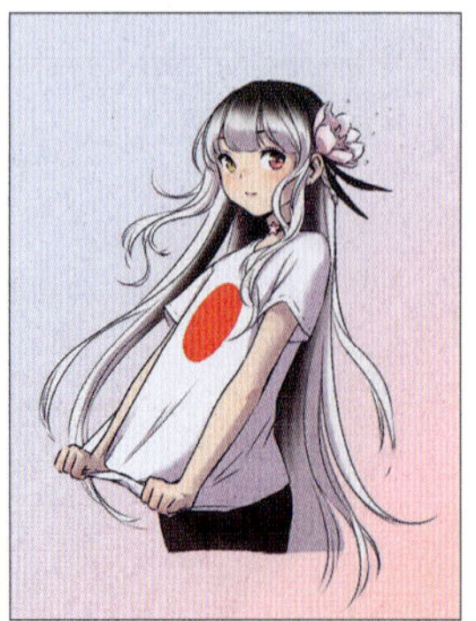
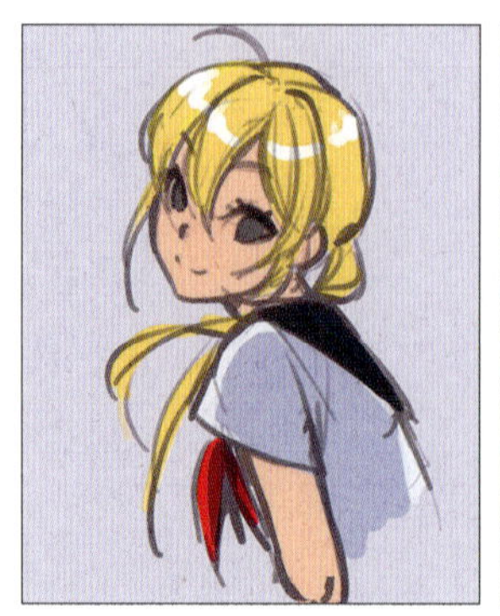
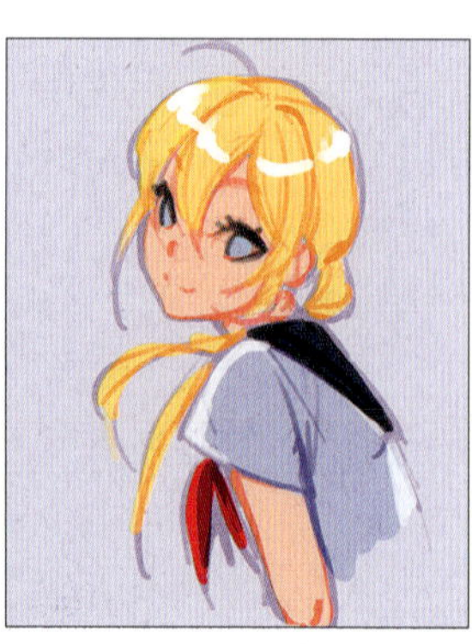

3 Color your sketches to bring out the character.

I usually add a splash of color to my sketches at this stage. Some mistakes can't be spotted when there are just lines in place (and on top of that, many messy lines!). It helps to see the illustration as a shape, and colors help shape sketches. When you squint, you can already see the character. For the lines of this sketch, I used a dark navy color rather than black, and when I changed the layer mode to Color Burn, it resulted in beautiful hues that I can use later for shading my character.

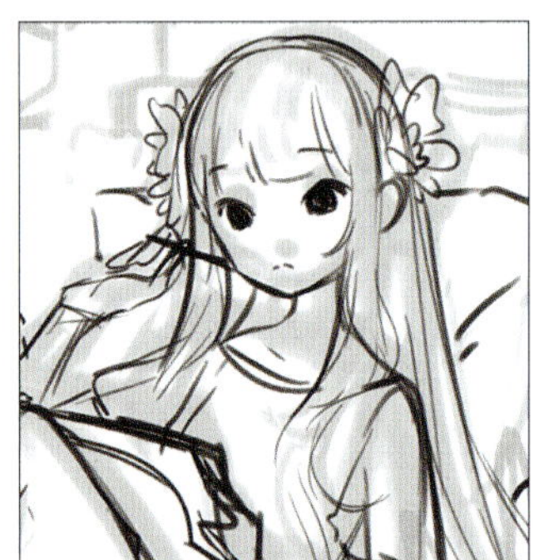
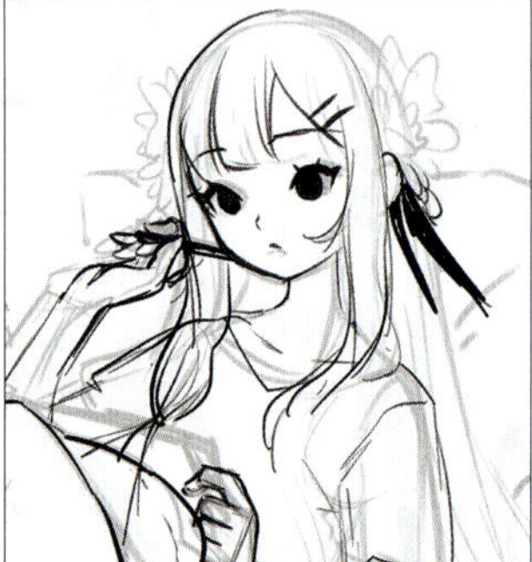
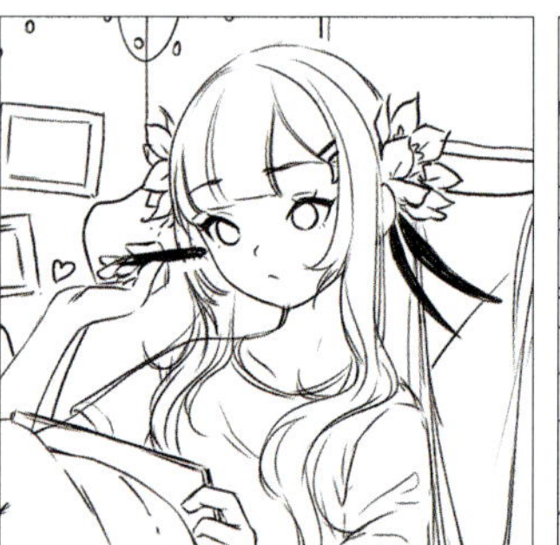
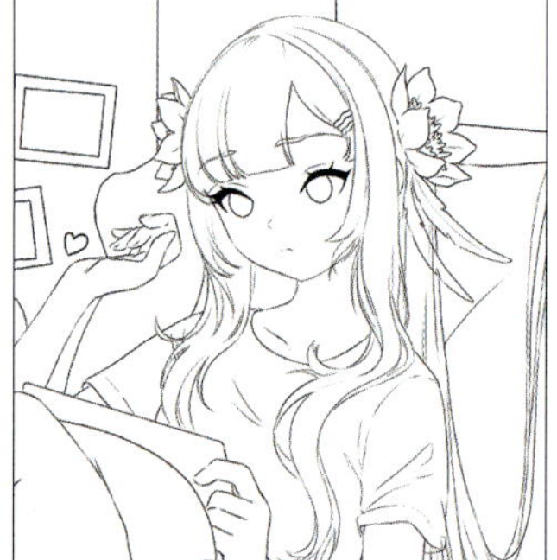

4 Don't rush the line art.

I can break down my process into sketch, line art, colors, and post-processing. Yet each of these steps can become complicated. By saying "don't rush the line art," I don't mean draw slowly, but rather refine the sketch as many times as it takes for the line art to become easier to draw.

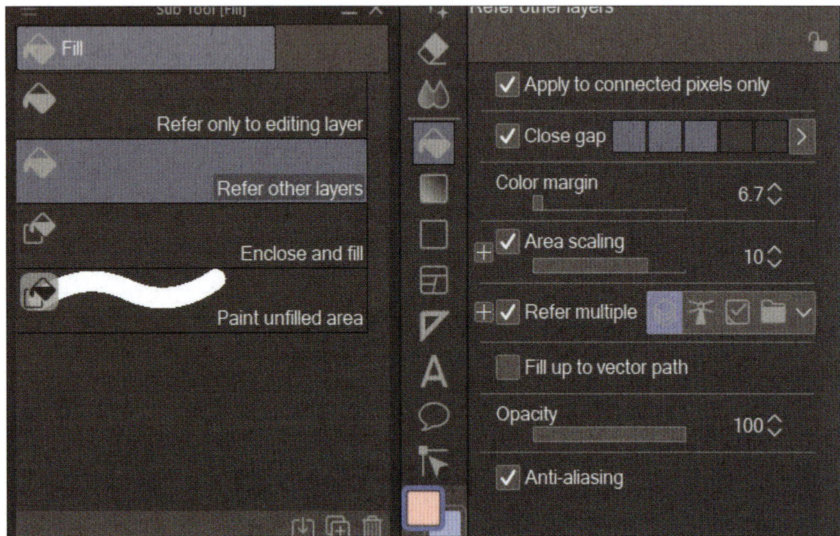

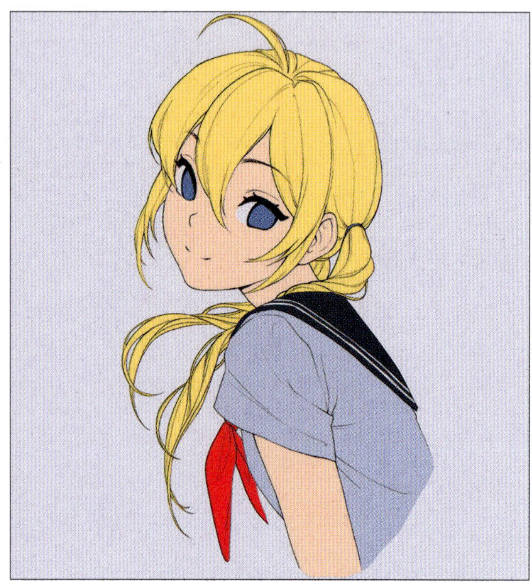

5 Save time using Clip Studio Paint's Smart Bucket tool.

Before I knew Clip Studio Paint, I used to waste countless hours drawing flat layers manually. Luckily, you don't have to make that mistake! The software's Smart Bucket tool is very good at recognizing line art, and with one click I can fill in most of the areas. If you play with its settings it can identify lines that have gaps in them, or even textured lines. To make sure all the pixels in my character are selected, I color the background first on a separate layer. Then I switch off the line art and color the reverse on another layer.

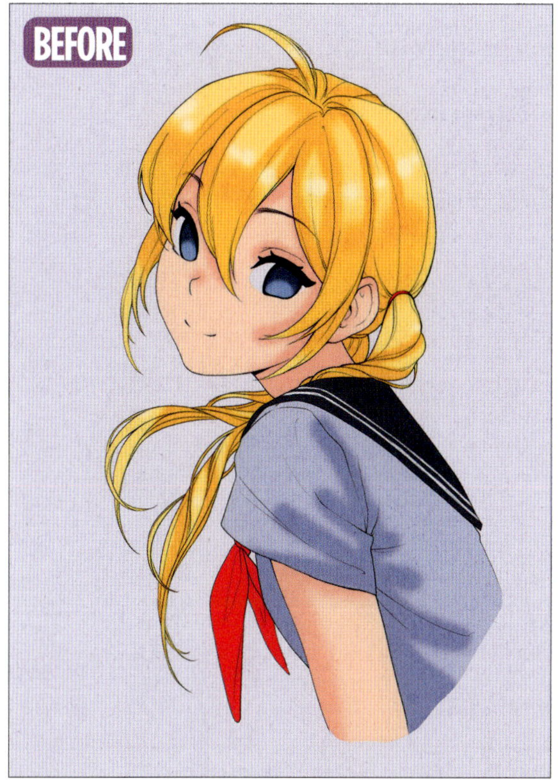

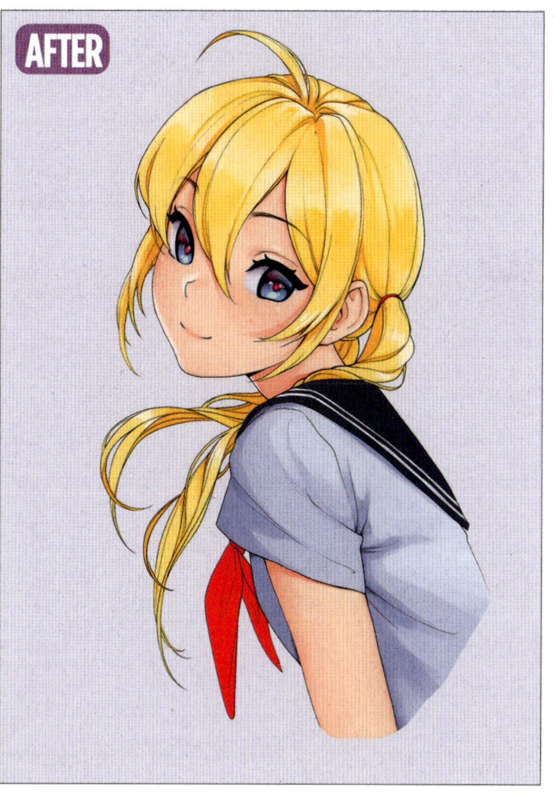

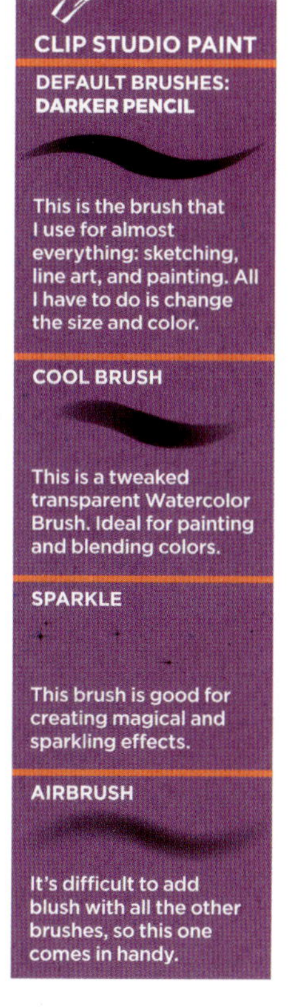

WORKSHOP BRUSHES

CLIP STUDIO PAINT

DEFAULT BRUSHES: DARKER PENCIL

This is the brush that I use for almost everything: sketching, line art, and painting. All I have to do is change the size and color.

COOL BRUSH

This is a tweaked transparent Watercolor Brush. Ideal for painting and blending colors.

SPARKLE

This brush is good for creating magical and sparkling effects.

AIRBRUSH

It's difficult to add blush with all the other brushes, so this one comes in handy.

6 Use a hard brush rather than a soft airbrush.

Good drawings have both soft and hard shadows in place, but if you're not sure what and where they should go, choose the hard edge. Drawings look much better with flat cell shading rather than mellow soft airbrush shading for everything. I always use a hard brush first and then blend selected edges into soft ones if necessary.

In this step, I've added some shading to all the color layers. Much like artists who use ambient occlusion, this shading doesn't define any light source. Rather, it adds some depth to the character and makes her look more interesting. Let me show you how I do it in the next step.

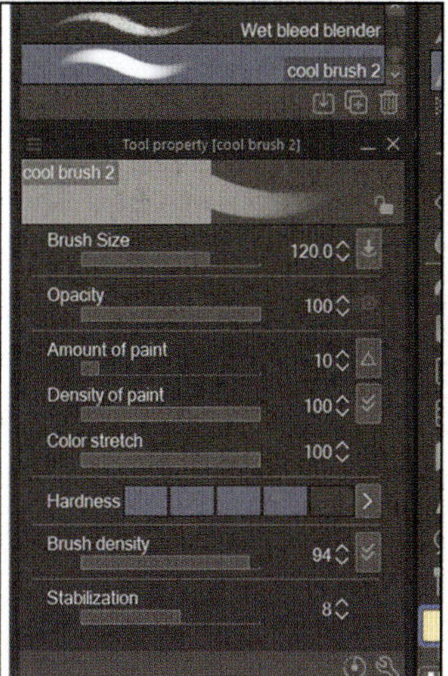

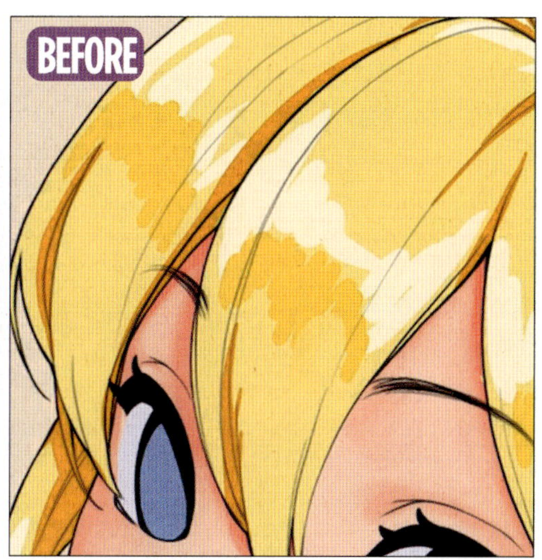

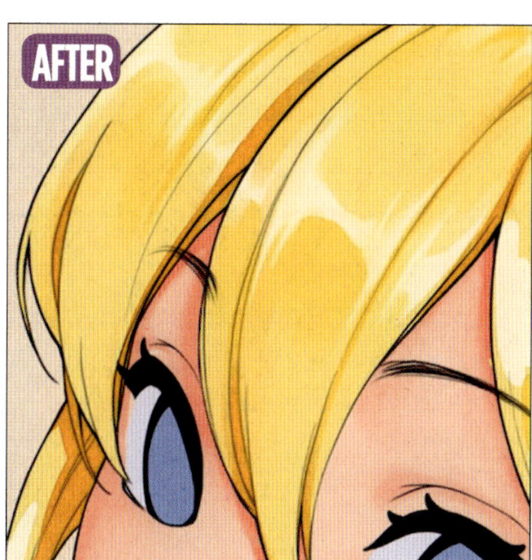

7 You can use the Transparent Watercolor brush as a blender.

For me, a much more powerful tool than the Blending brush or any other paintbrush is the Transparent Watercolor default brush in Clip Studio Paint. You can see the settings I use in the screenshot, but I change them as I paint. If you set Amount of Paint to a low value, it blends the colors together, depending on the direction of your strokes and the pressure you put on your pen, and it doesn't matter what color you've chosen for your brush. If you set that value to a high number, it'll blend the color of your brush with the existing colors. This tool has so much versatility, and surprisingly the results doesn't even look like watercolors. ➽

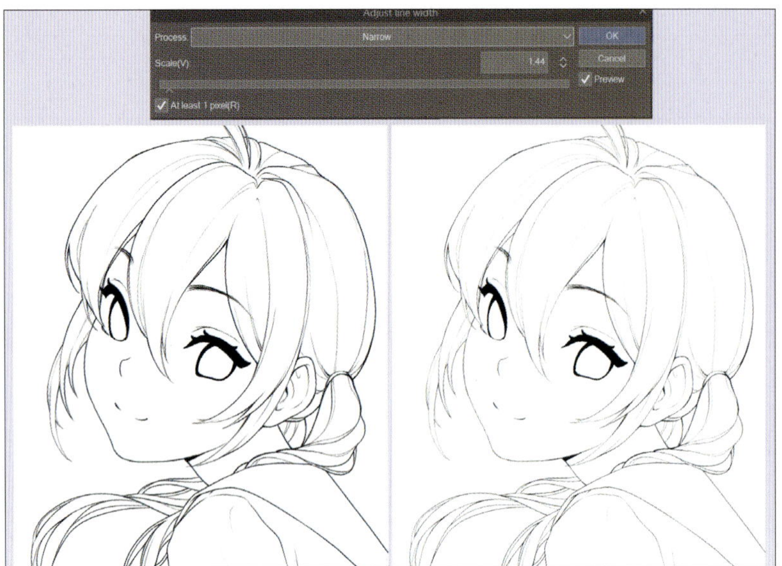

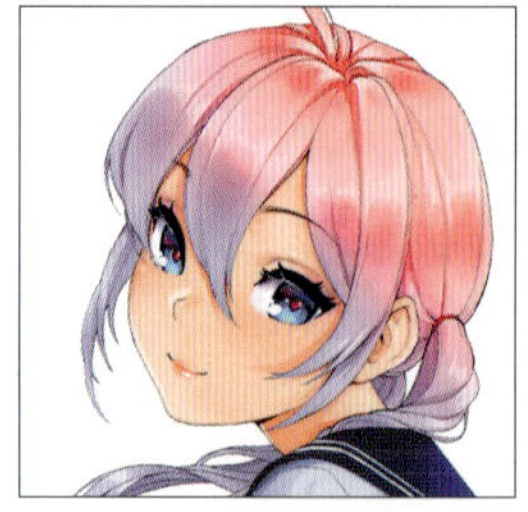
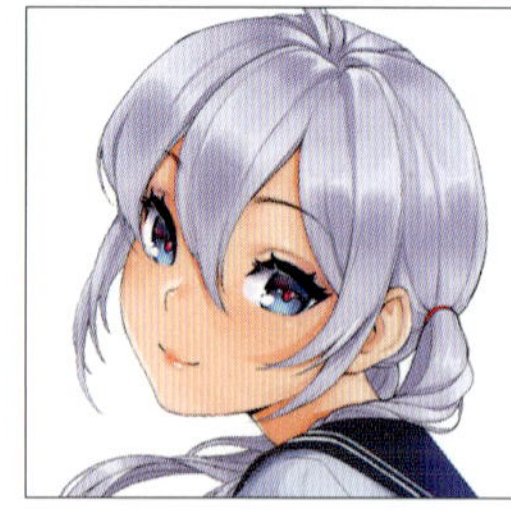
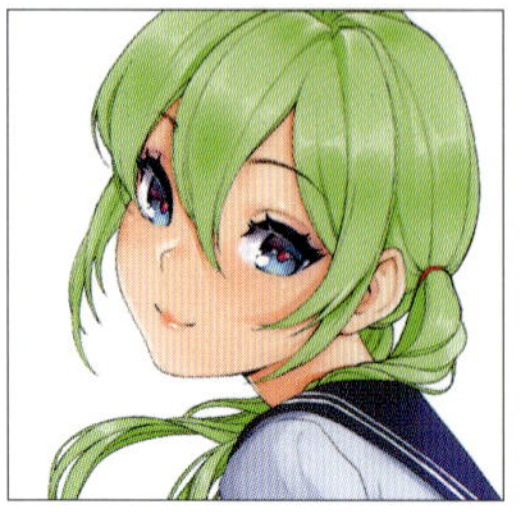
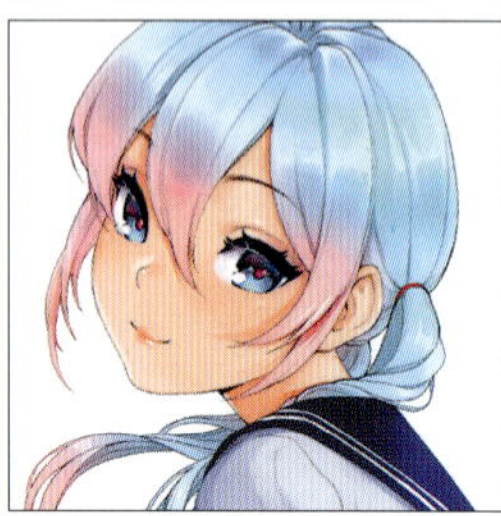

8 Did you know you can adjust your line widths?

Clip Studio Paint is made for painters, illustrators, animators, and manga artists, and is packed with functions to help us work faster and more effectively. One of those functions that I can't live without is being able to adjust line width. You can access it under Filters>Correct line>Adjust line width, and it enables you to thicken or narrow the line art. On the left, you can see the lines I drew originally, and on the right are my corrected lines. Thanks to this function, my illustration became even more delicate. However, if your art now looks rough and pixellated, I'd recommend duplicating the layer of edited line art, blurring it a little with Filter>Blur>Gaussian Blur and setting the layer mode to Multiply.

9 Experiment with colors.

I can never decide what colors to use! I love playing with colors and changing them to see "what if?" There are multiple ways you can do it yourself. You can either select the colored area in question (or apply it to a whole layer) and use Edit>Tonal Correction>Hue/Saturation/Brightness filter and adjust the sliders, or clip a layer to the one you're editing, and set it to Color mode, then add color with the Bucket tool. You can also add new colors using functions such as Multiply, Color Dodge, Divide . . . you name it! You can also mix colors and use gradients, too.

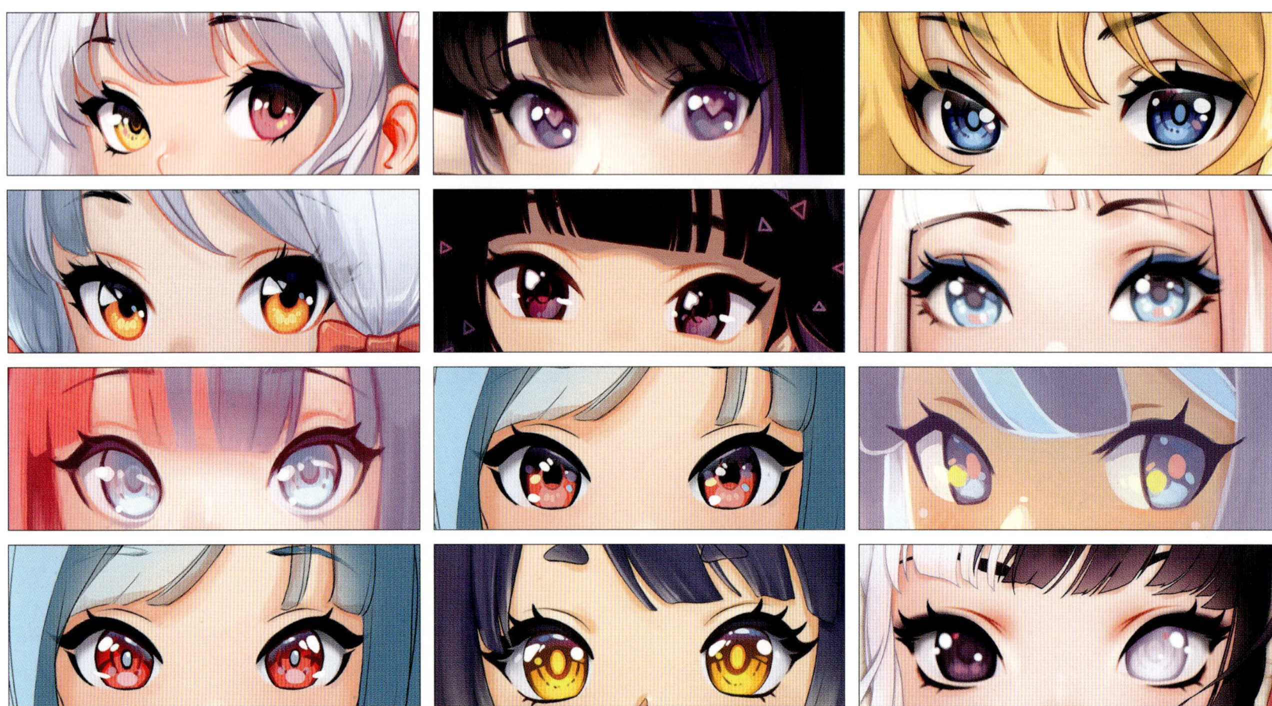

10 Put a whole world into the eyes.

I do believe that eyes are the window to the soul, and I paint them with this in mind. I love painting eyes! It might actually be the eyes that made me fall in love with manga-style art. I endlessly experiment with how I paint them, using a variety of styles, shapes, and colors. I often take inspiration from other artists as well, and mix their styles with mine. I wonder if you can see my inspirations in my drawings.

11 DEFINE THE LIGHT SOURCE AND ADD SHADOWS

Learn how to quickly paint shadows to enhance your manga characters.

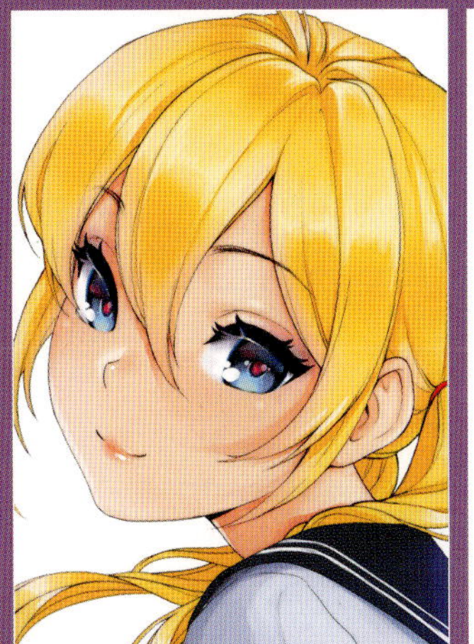

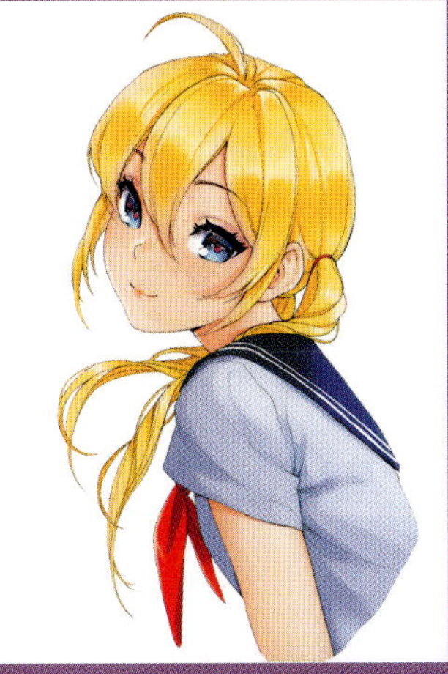

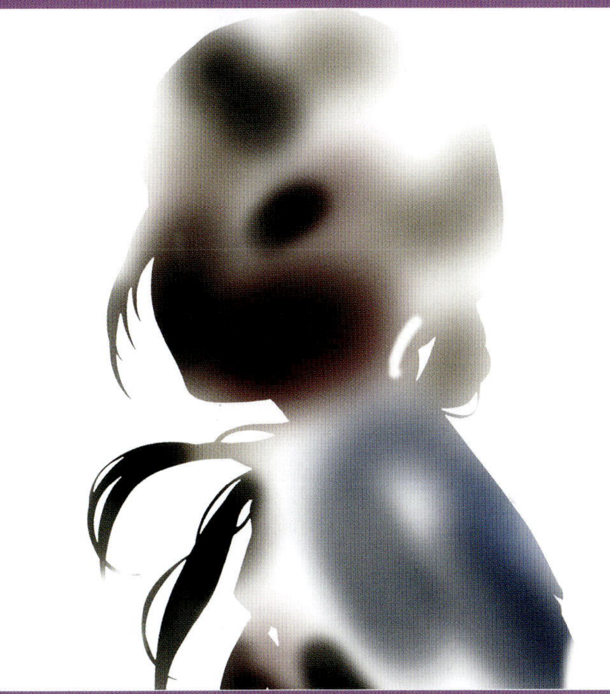

A Create a base for your shadows.
I start by adding basic and delicate shading to my character, without defining any light source. This stage adds depth to flat colors and creates a strong base for the actual shadow.

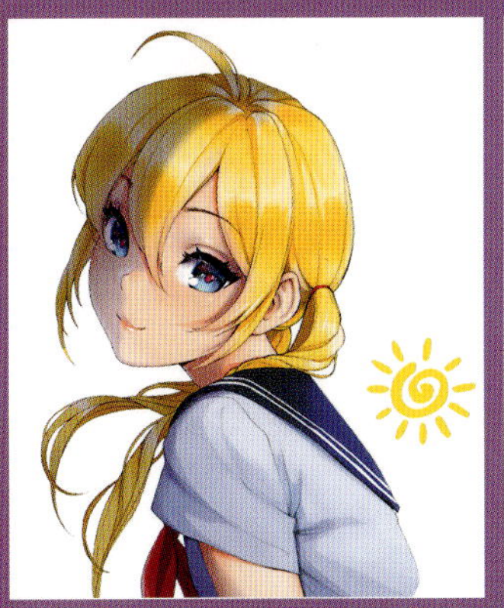

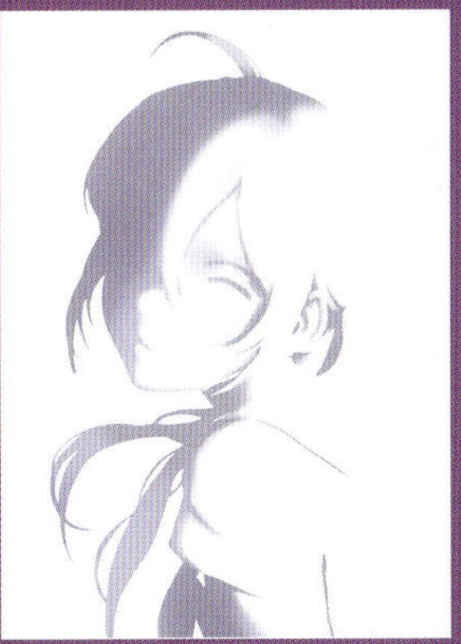

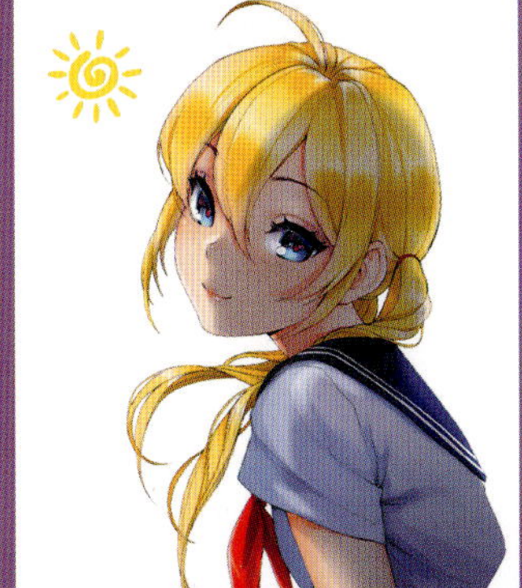

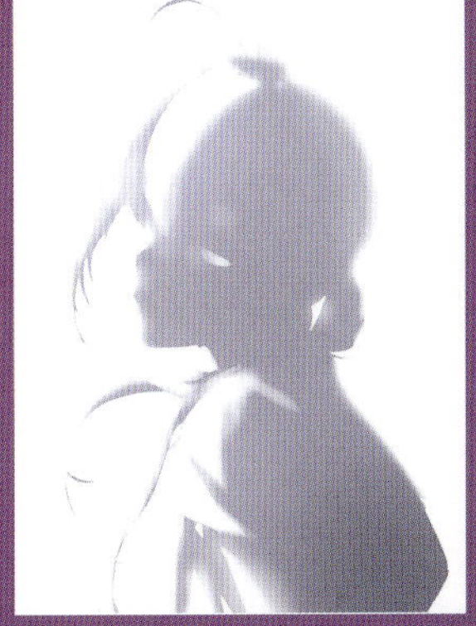

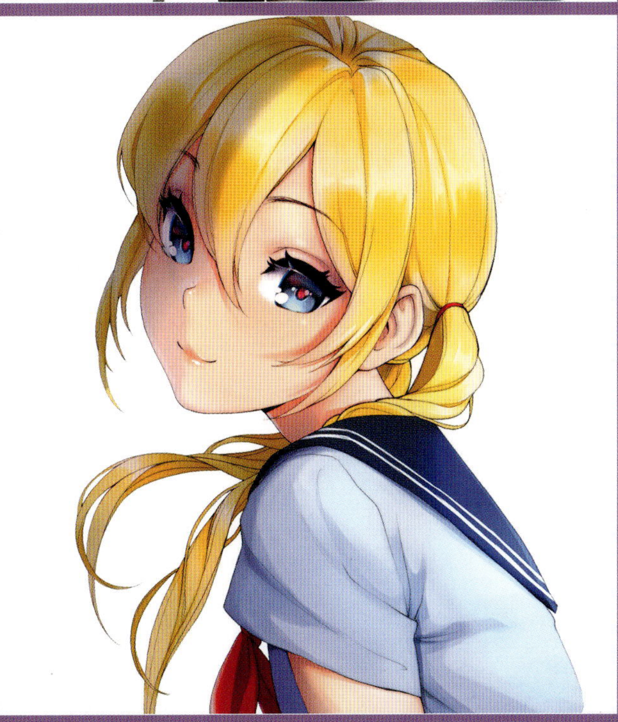

B Paint flat shadows.
I imagine my light source, then add a layer set to Multiply above the Color layers. Next, I paint a shadow with just one color on this new layer. It's usually grayish purple, but depending on what effect you want to achieve, you can use any color.

C Make your shadows glow.
To breathe some life into the flat shadow, I add another layer above my earlier Multiply one and set it to Color Dodge. Now, with a soft brush I paint the areas that I want to glow, using a color that's low on value and high on saturation.

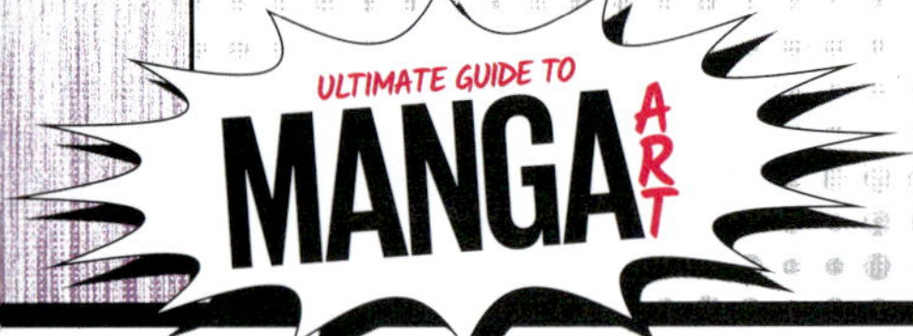

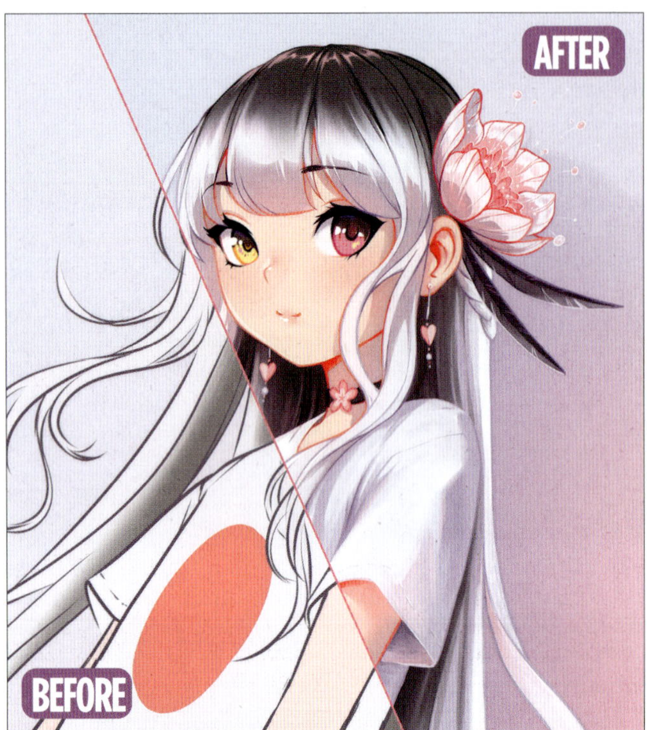

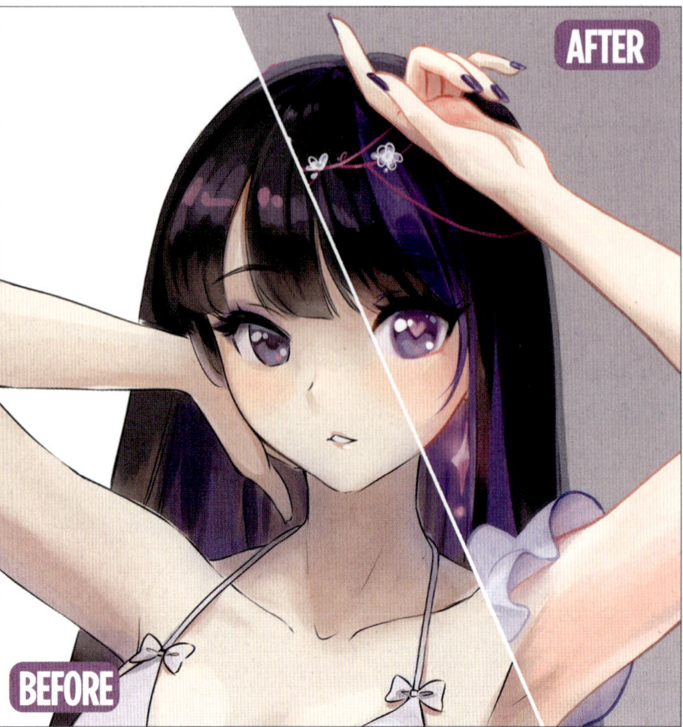

12 Ignore the rules and just paint!

Everything you've just read? Sometimes I don't want to do any of it! To be honest, it's a lot to remember and think about when painting. When I just want to relax while creating art, I get my illustrations as far as I can with a colored sketch, and then add a layer on top of it (or sometimes not even that) and just paint. My favorite tools here are the Darker Pencil and the multifunctional Transparent Watercolor Brush.

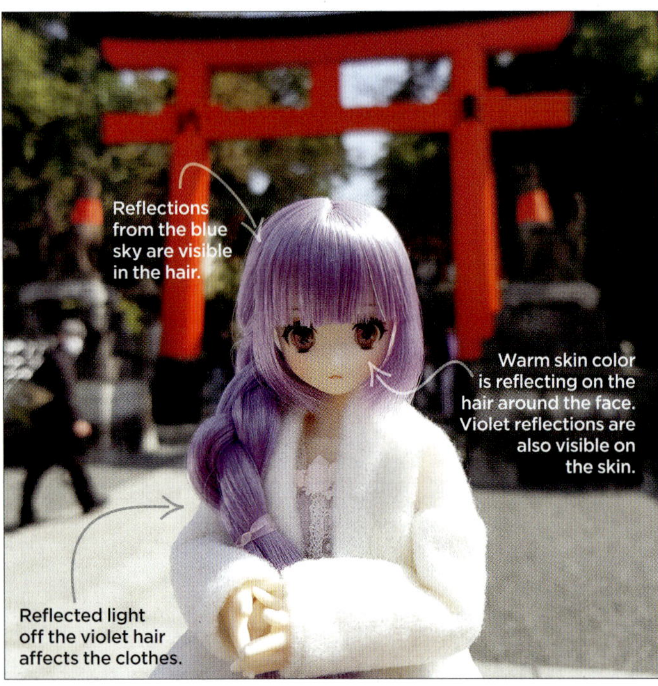

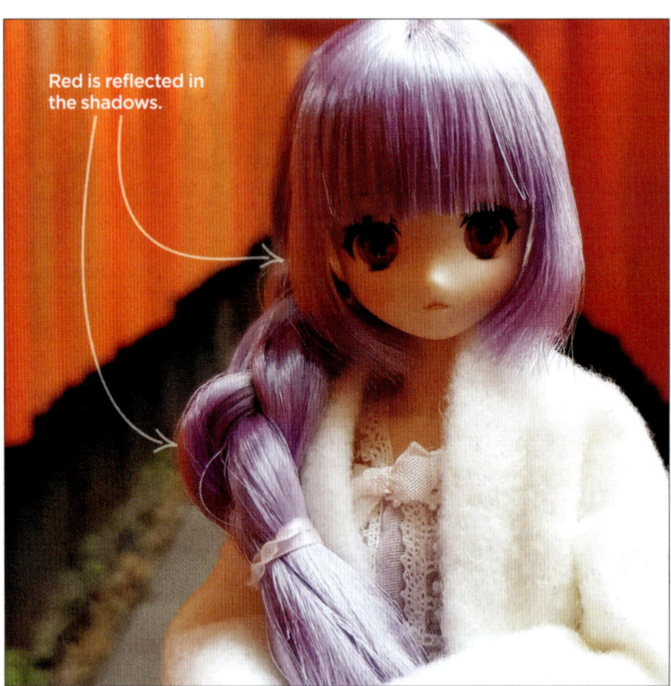

13 Use colored reflections in your art.

Here's a cool technique to bring your illustrations to life: add reflected colors in the shadow areas or on the edges where different colors meet. Colors often reflect each other in nature. If the character is placed in an environment with strong red elements for example, red is likely to reflect in some darker colors. The same goes for the blue of the sky or green from the grass. In illustration it can be exaggerated; manga artists often use skin hue around the face on clothes and hair to make the character's skin look soft, almost appearing to glow.

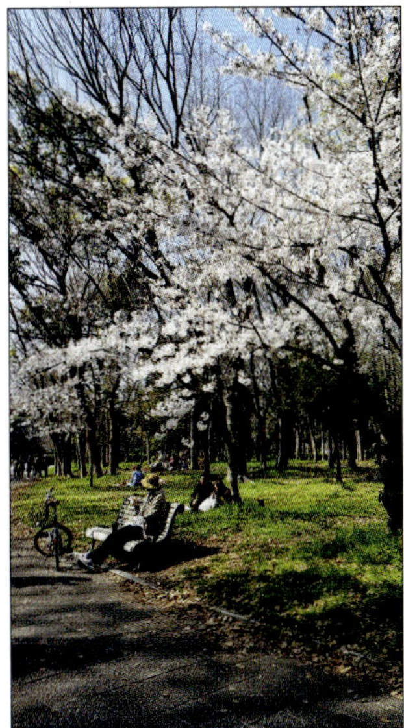
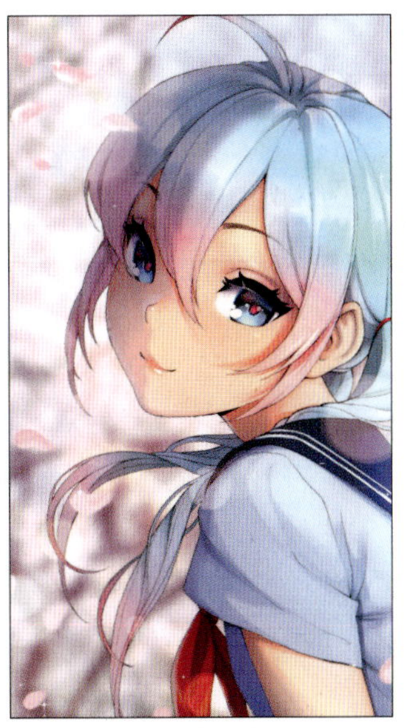
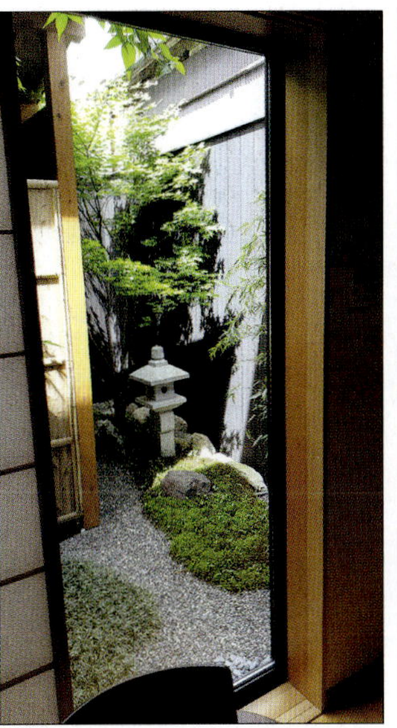
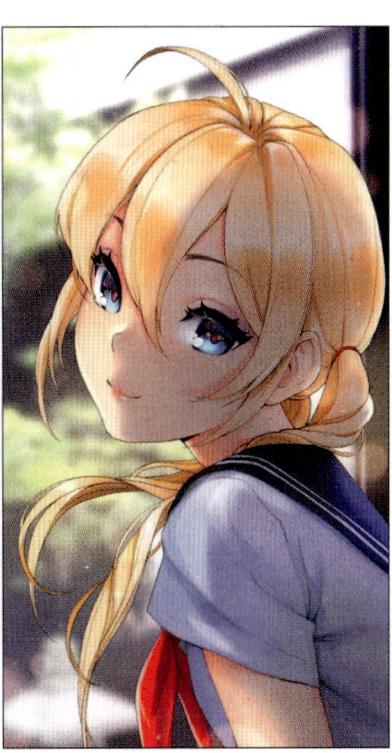

14 Create illustrations with backgrounds.

I'm really bad at drawing backgrounds. I know that I'll get good at this when I start practicing, but I haven't found the drive to do so just yet. That doesn't mean I can't create illustrations with backgrounds. I just need to be a little more creative about the fact that I can't paint them! For this illustration, I'm using photos I took myself and adjusting them using my photo-editing skills. I crop them, blur, brighten, overpaint, and add effects to the point where it's not easy to tell that these are photos in the background.

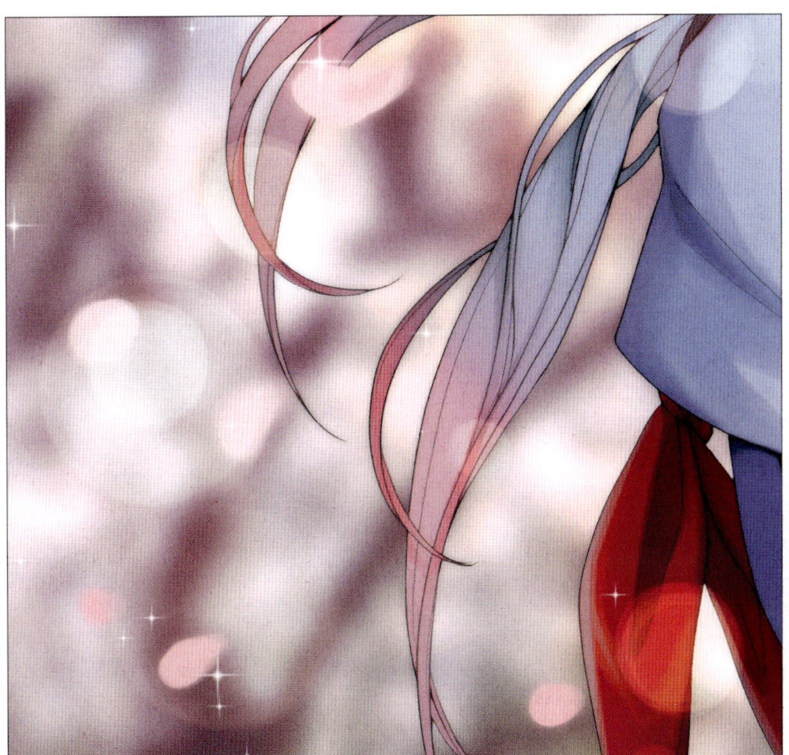
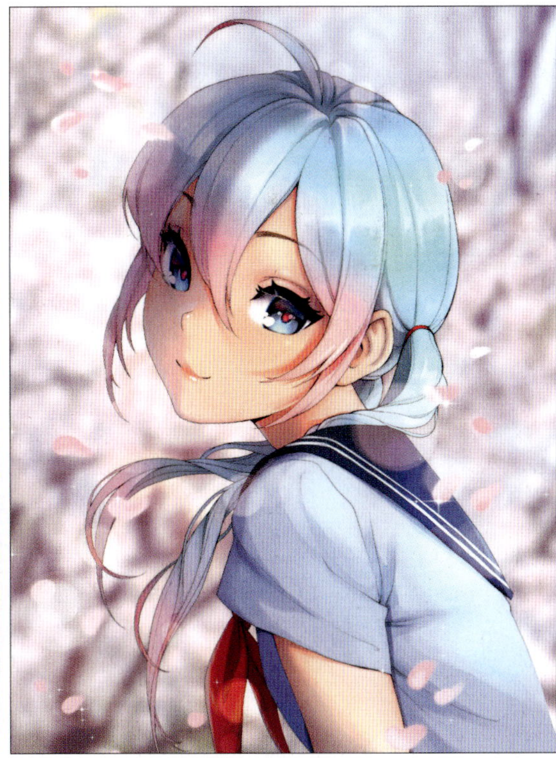

15 Know when to walk away from the drawing.

Often I'll blast through the entire illustration process, then sit in front of the canvas adding and deleting layers for hours, only to end up exactly where I started. Am I finished? Should I add more? Does it look good? Can it look better?

What helps me walk away from the drawing (when I'm unable to grasp that I don't need to create a masterpiece every time I draw) is my list of things I can do to help close the chapter. These steps are: adding a little more Color or Glow Dodge (like the bokeh lights you can see in the picture), adding a Color Balance Layer, and adding a signature. And unless I upload the drawing online, it's likely that I'll come back to it and waste more time. Posting online gives me closure. My social media platforms are a journal of my artistic journey. A trip full of learning, discovering, creating, and of course, mistakes as well.

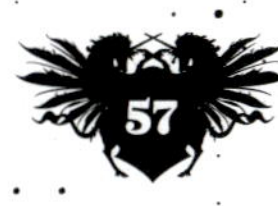

Photoshop

COMPOSE AN ANIME STREET SCENE

Tan Hui Tian uses coloring, lighting, and perspective techniques to paint an urban setting that's full of details.

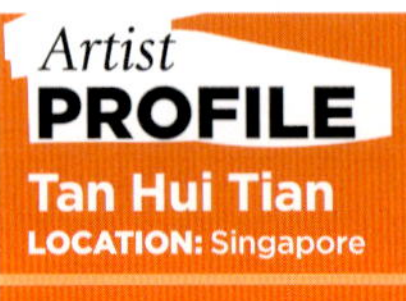

Tan Hui Tian

LOCATION: Singapore

Tan is a senior illustrator at Collateral Damage Studios. She's created the key visuals for conventions such as Anime Fest @ New York Comic Con and STGCC's 10th year anniversary.

https://ifxm.ag/t-h-tian

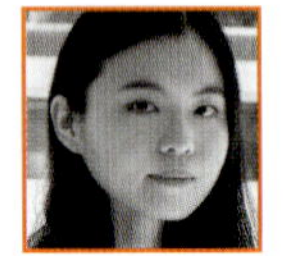

Traditional anime backgrounds are painted with poster paints, but increasingly studios are switching to digital tools. Backgrounds are designed to suit the cel-shaded animation in the foreground, and differ from matte-painted backgrounds created for films in that there are more hand-painted elements, and the colors are more saturated.

For this workshop, I'll be describing my process for creating an anime-style background. It would be good if you had an awareness of basic perspective concepts, such as how to set up a simple two-point perspective grid.

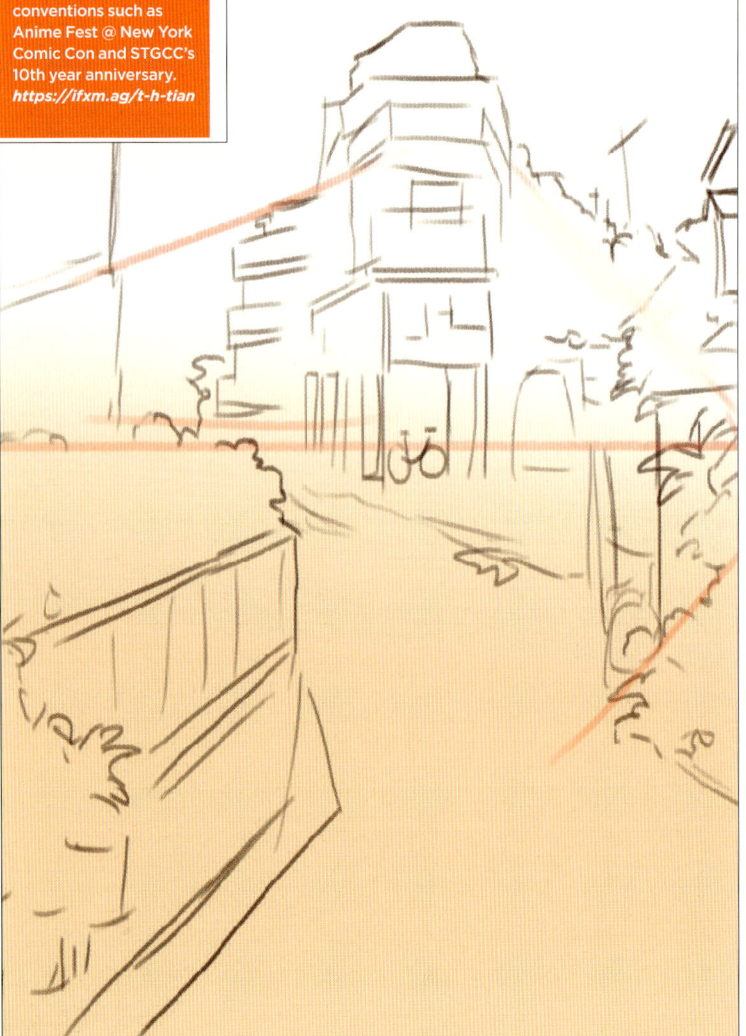

1 Make a compositional sketch.

I start off by searching for inspiration on Pinterest, searching online, and going through my reference folders. I decide to do a common scene in anime: a quiet street in daylight. I have a rough composition in mind, and sketch it out with a simple brush. At this stage, I have a two-point perspective in mind, but choose not to use a perspective grid yet, so that the sketch can be more dynamic.

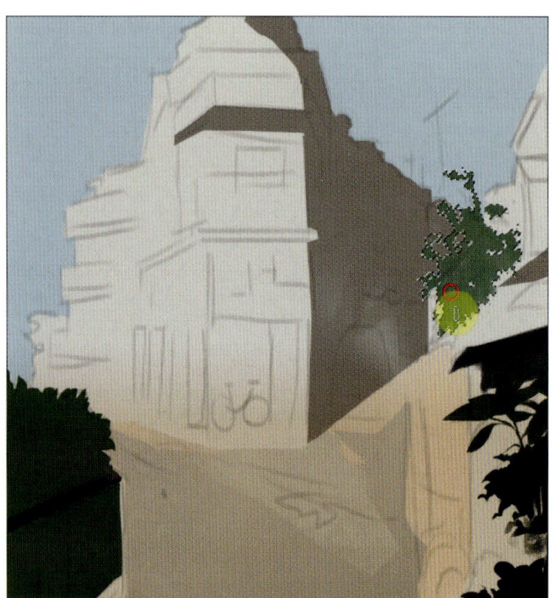

2 Move on to color flats.

I then lay down color flats in different layers. I often merge components that aren't touching into a single layer, to reduce the layer count. I use the Lasso and Paint Bucket tools to create the shapes. At this stage, there's no need for all the shapes to be precise. It's more important to create tonal contrasts and interesting shapes.

STREET SCENE

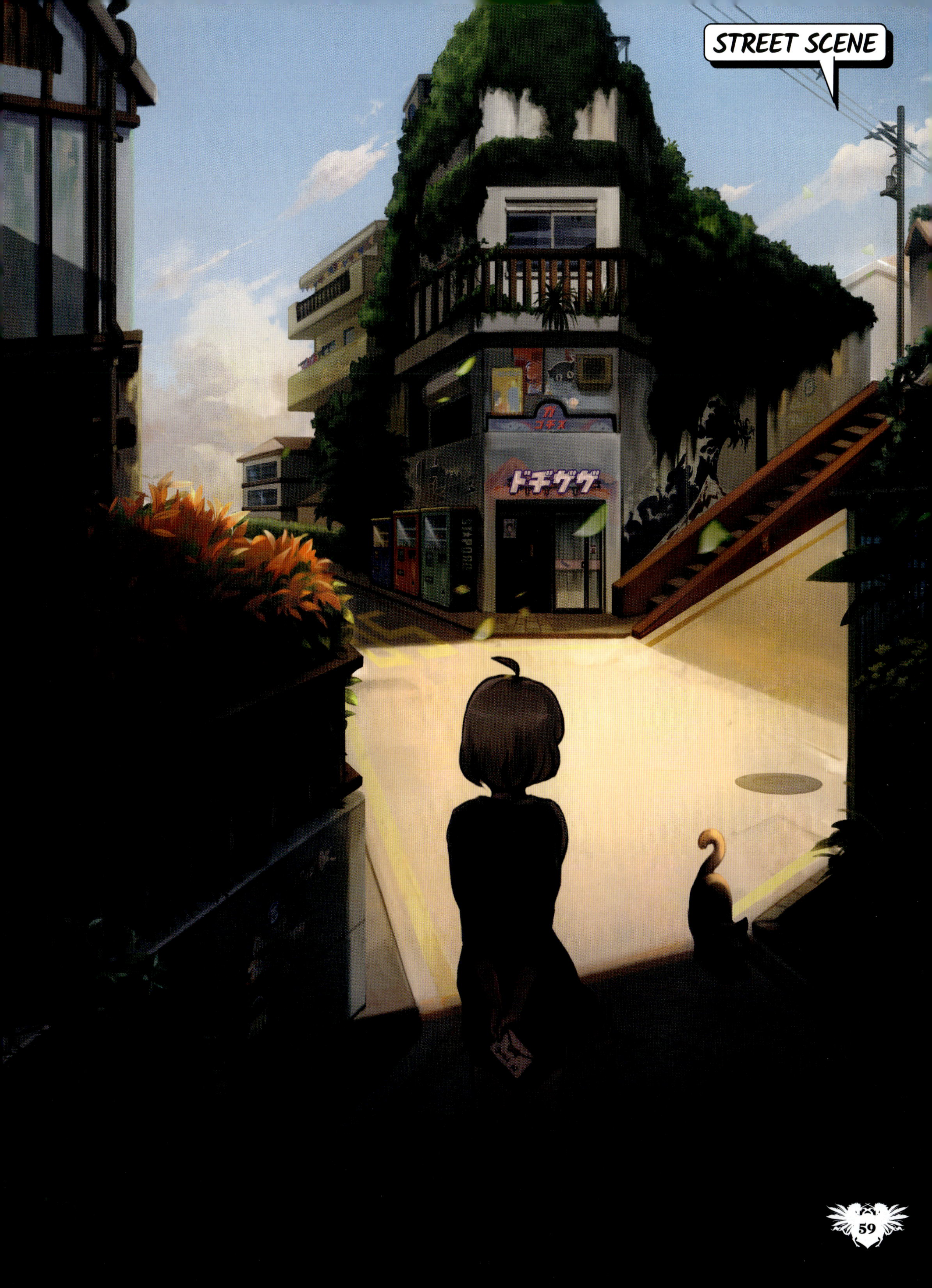

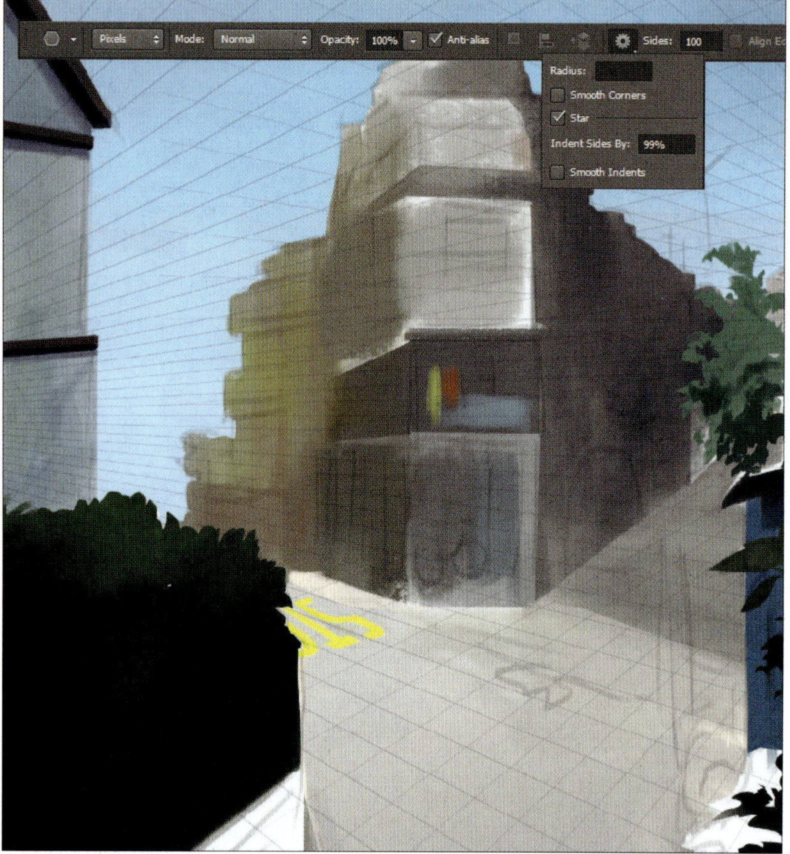

3 Work to the correct perspective.

Once I have the shapes more or less pinned down, I then correct them according to the perspective grid. You can create a perspective grid with the Filter>Vanishing Point tool in Photoshop. For this, I use the Polygon Tool on the Star setting with 100 sides and 99% indented sides.

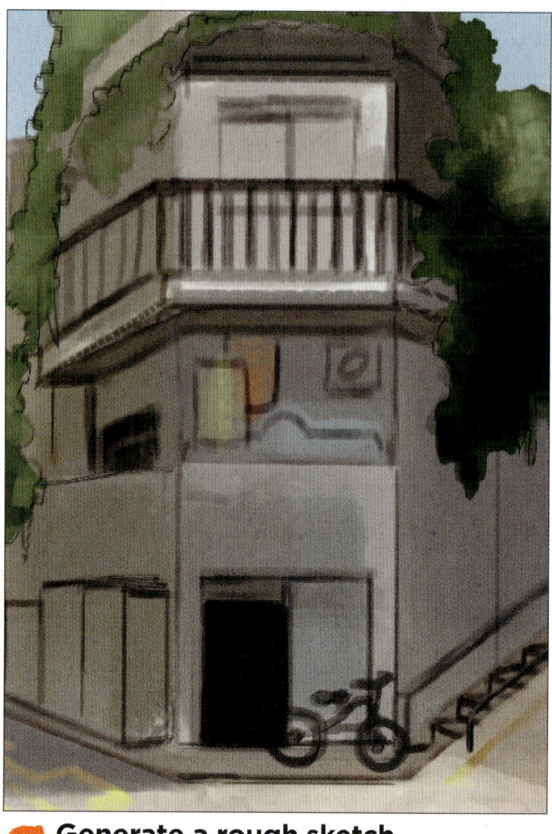

4 Generate a rough sketch.

In the areas that are unresolved, I draw a rough guideline of the shapes that I want on another layer. I find it easier to refine the shapes afterward, rather than drawing precise lines. If the art direction is more line based, then I spend more time refining the undersketch before moving on to the inking stage.

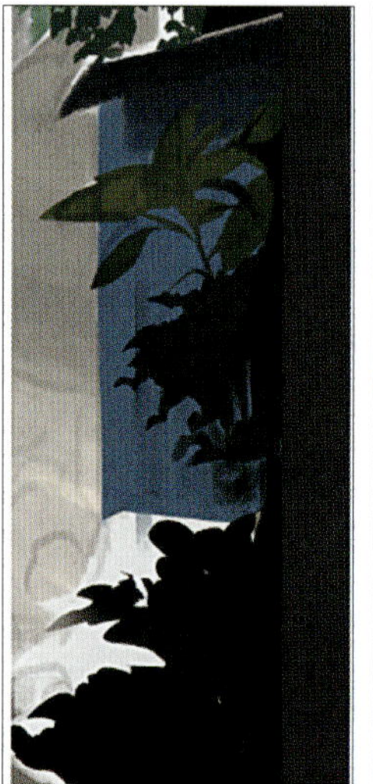

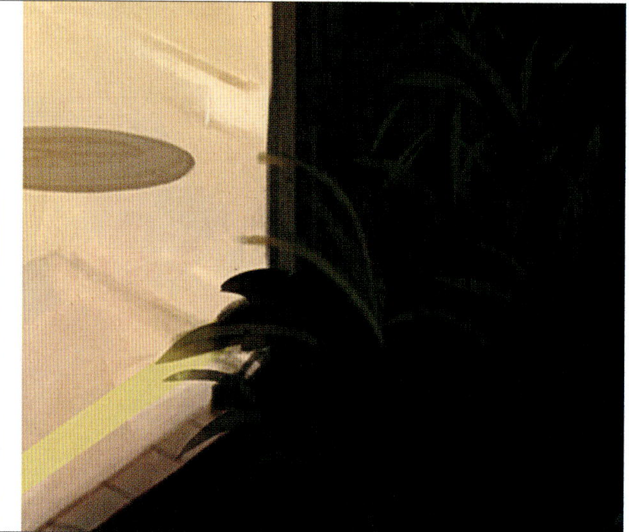

5 Refine shapes without over-rendering.

When rendering, I find references of the real-world objects and simplify that in my artwork. I try to work on the detail without zooming in too much, and finish the overall shading first. For the greenery, a lot of it is suggested so there's no need to over-render it. I skip around from component to component a lot during this stage, so that I'm not tempted to spend too much time on one particular element.

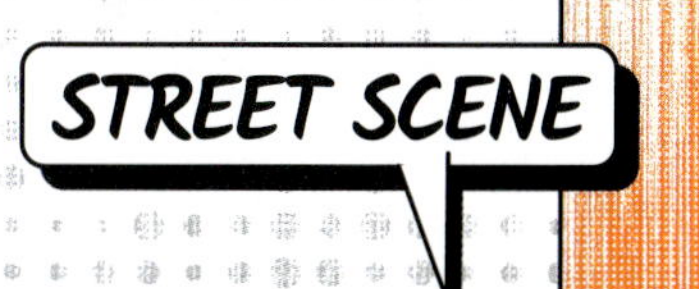

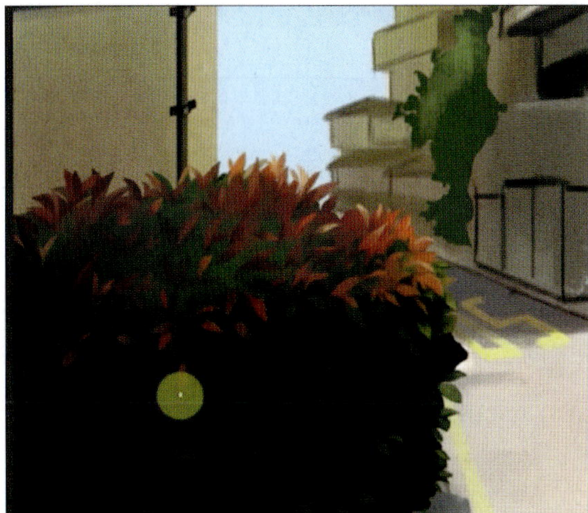

6 Overlay lighting.

A good trick for creating visual interest through lighting is to play around with the tonal contrasts. James Gurney's explanation of the Windmill Principle (*https://ifxm.ag/jg-windmill*) helped me a lot. I decide to have the cast shadow cut across the hedge in foreground left. I use brushes on Dodge and Overlay modes to quickly create the backlit effect on the hedge.

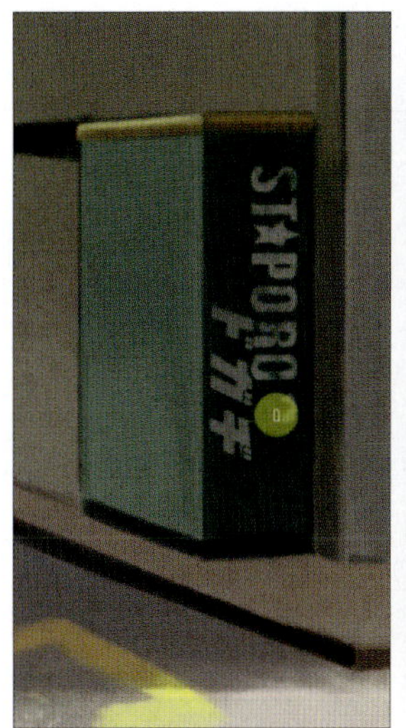

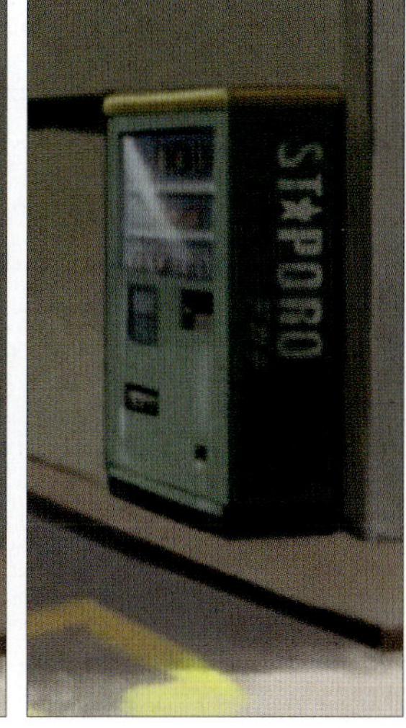

7 Blend details.

I add decals quickly by using the Type or Shapes tool, rasterizing the result and then blending it into the artwork. Make sure that the decal is of the correct tonal value and saturation. If necessary, I color-correct using the Hue & Saturation or Curves tools. I then add a weathering effect by using a textured eraser.

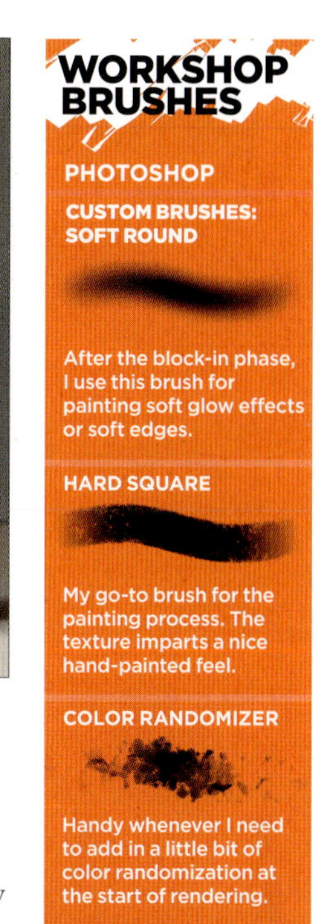

WORKSHOP BRUSHES

PHOTOSHOP

CUSTOM BRUSHES: SOFT ROUND

After the block-in phase, I use this brush for painting soft glow effects or soft edges.

HARD SQUARE

My go-to brush for the painting process. The texture imparts a nice hand-painted feel.

COLOR RANDOMIZER

Handy whenever I need to add in a little bit of color randomization at the start of rendering.

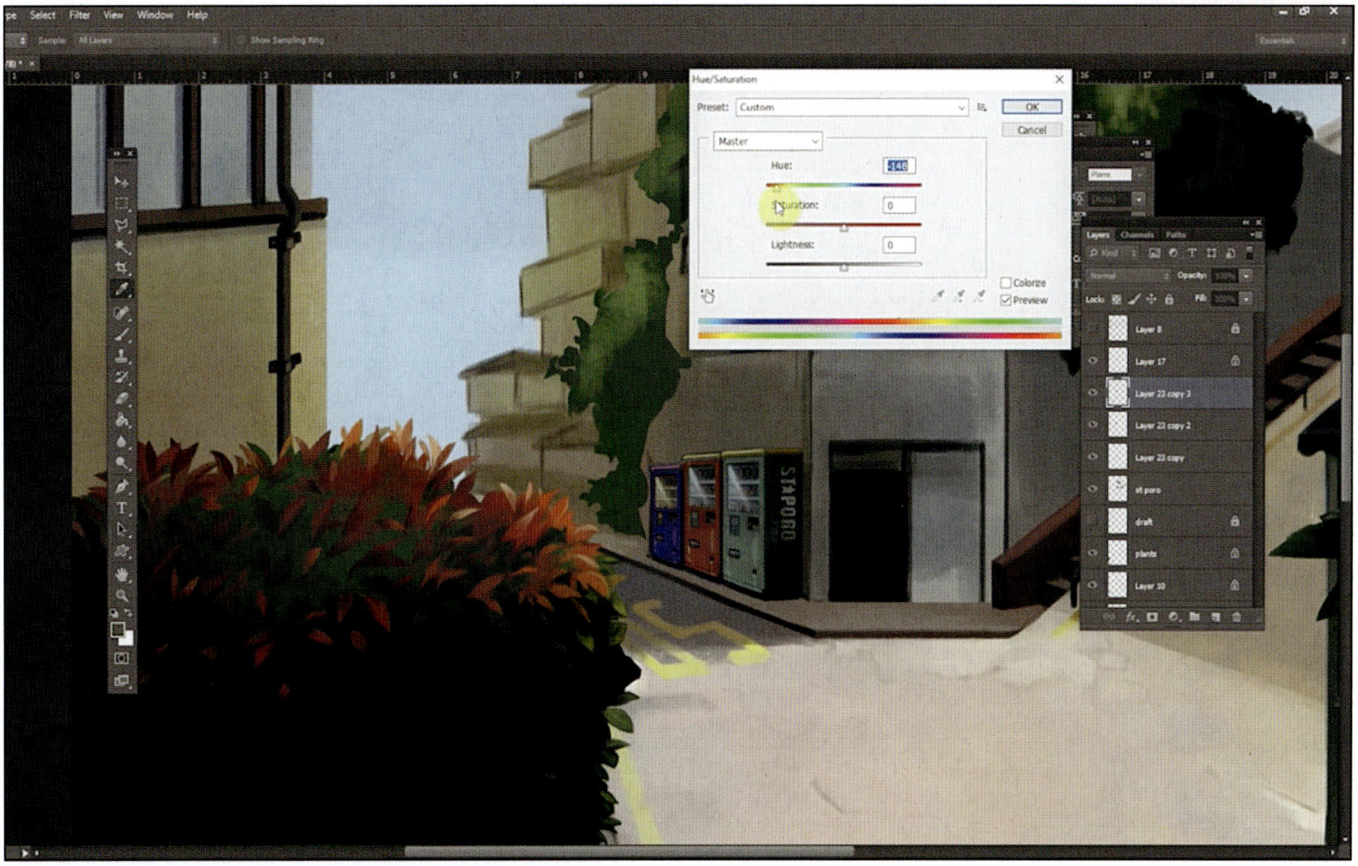

8 Replicate details in the environment.

It makes sense to save time by duplicating items that are repeated around the scene. If the item isn't meant to be a perfect clone, I might change it to a different hue or edit certain details. I use the same trick to create the hand-painted brick tiles.

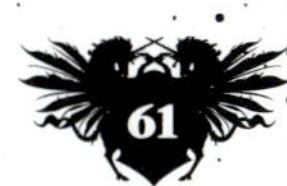

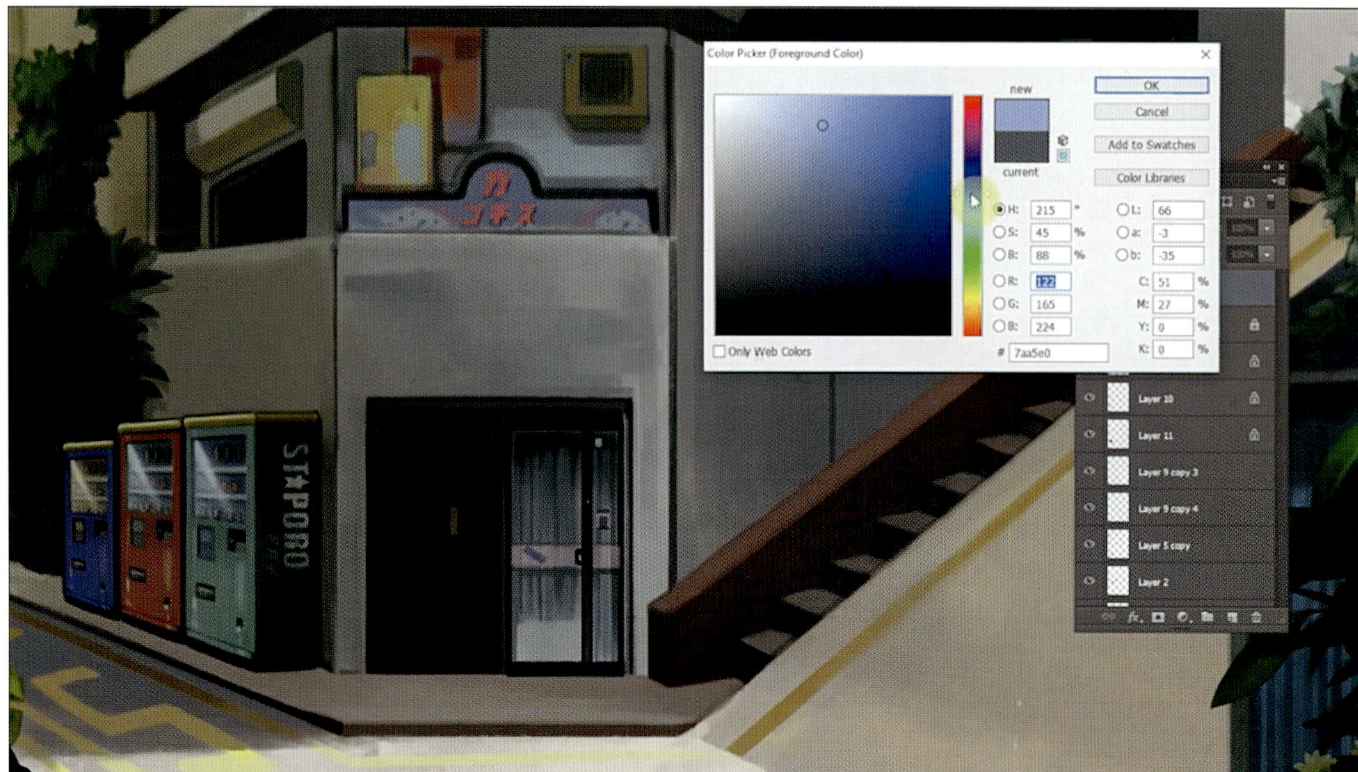

9 Color pick to create cohesiveness.

I didn't have a color palette in mind when I began this piece, but I want to create a cheery atmosphere. To create cohesiveness between the different colors, I use the Color Picker to select colors from other parts of the image, and have spots of colors distributed throughout.

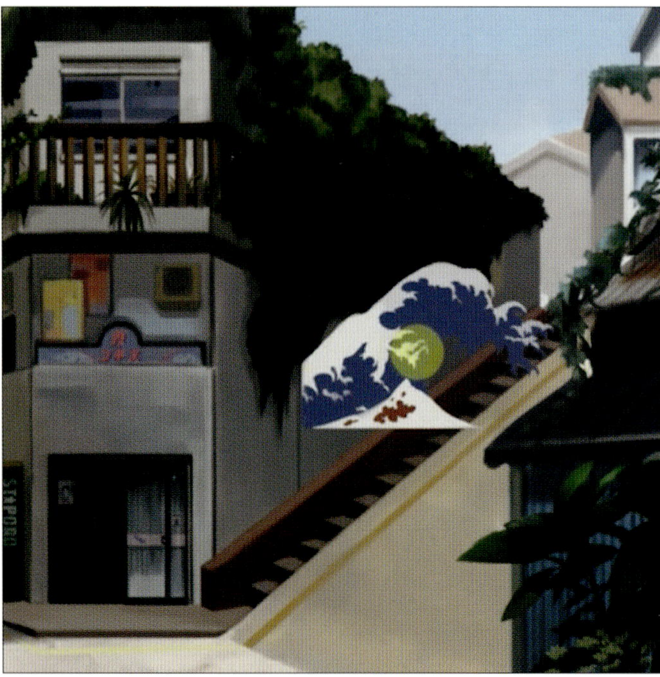

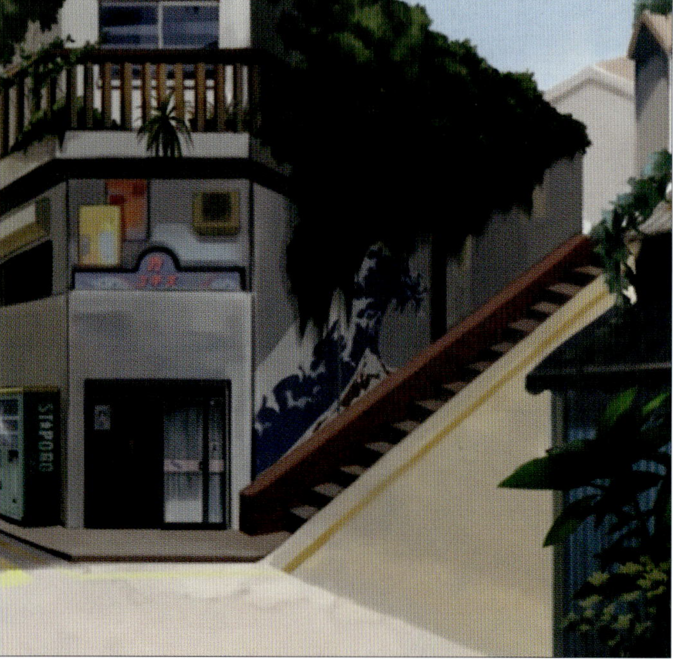

10 Put the wall mural into perspective.

I use the Perspective Warp tool to warp the mural design onto the wall. I like to keep my Move Tool on auto-select, with the transform controls visible. This means that there's one fewer step involved in transforming any layer object. I can also switch between layers easily, and quite often don't have to worry about naming my layers. To transform a layer object manually, go to Edit>Free Transform.

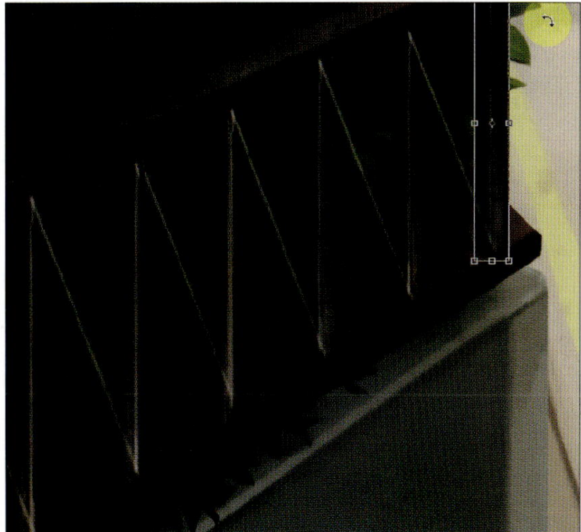

11 Find objects in perspective.

I don't really use the perspective grid because I find that I play by the rules too much when it's visible. However, it's often necessary to refer to it for equally spaced objects. You can use this trick when you need to find out the distance between equally spaced objects in perspective. The zig-zag lines will always be parallel to their corresponding lines (zig to zig, zag to zag).

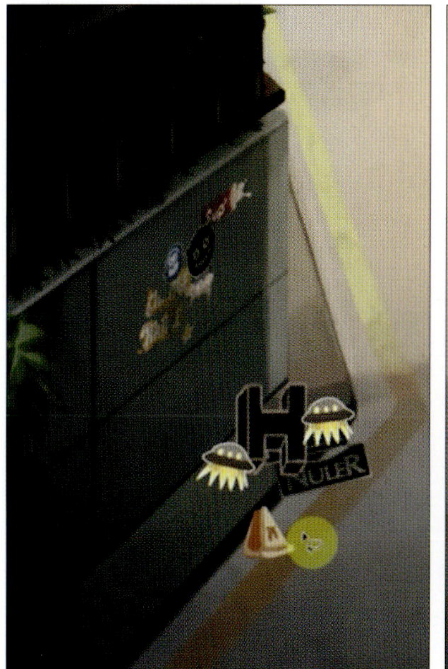

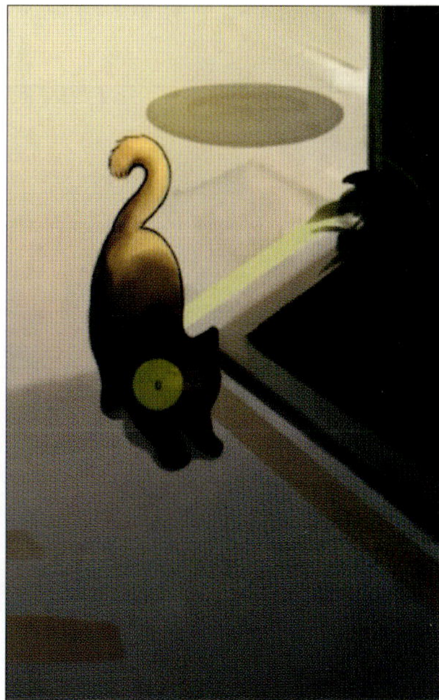

12 Add visual interest.

This is the fun part for me. I add little quirky details into the environment such as graffiti, animals, signs, and posters. I often add my Space Penguin mascot into the artwork somewhere, and other little inside jokes.

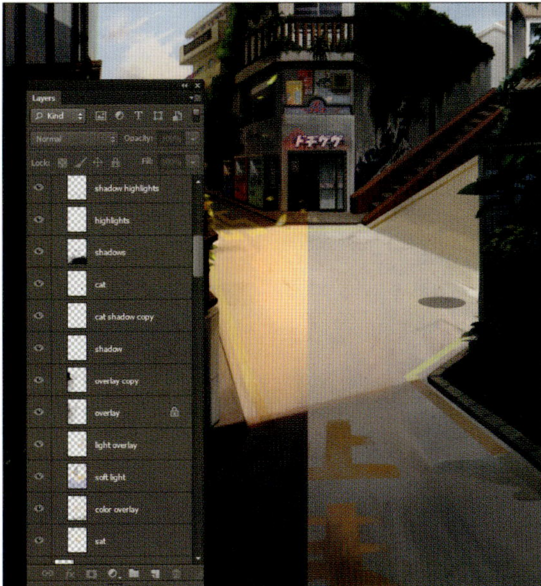

13 Bring the color together.

Color-adjustment layers tie the disparate colors together. I'm using a lot of layers on different blending modes, but the most important ones are the textured brush shape on Multiply mode (for the cast shadow), and the layers with soft Airbrush blobs on Soft light and Color mode that enhances the sunlight and blue shadows. I also make other adjustments, such as adding atmospheric fog or increasing the saturation on the shadow of the clouds. To make sure the layer adjustments don't muddy the colors beneath, I set the layers to Normal, 100% Opacity, and refine the shapes as needed.

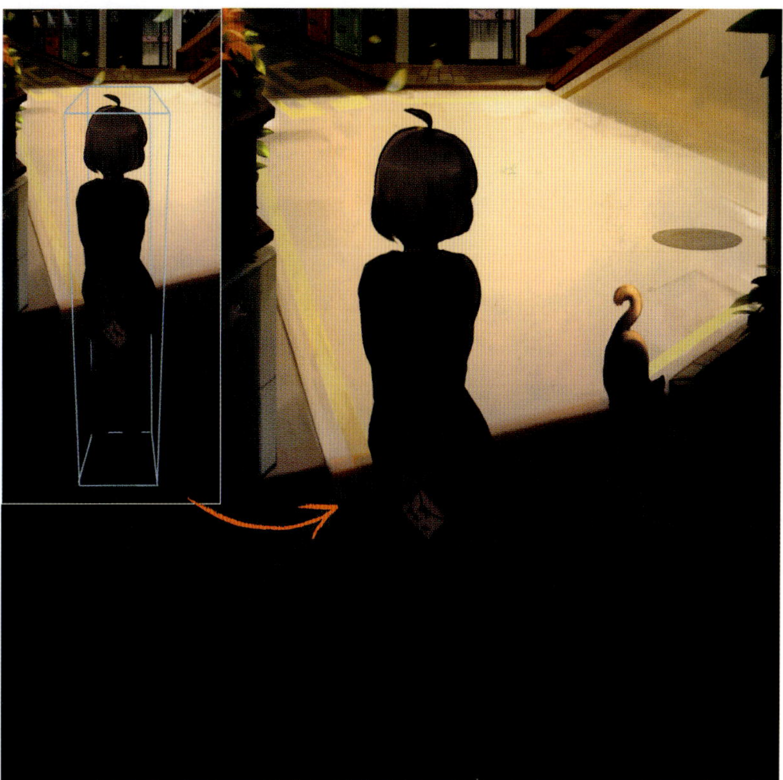

14 Add a character.

When adding in figures into a finished environment, I consider the perspective before blocking them in. Here, I render the young woman in neutral lighting, and then adjust the colors with the Curves tool. I place the character layer under some of the color adjustments layer, ensuring that the colors appear more cohesive.

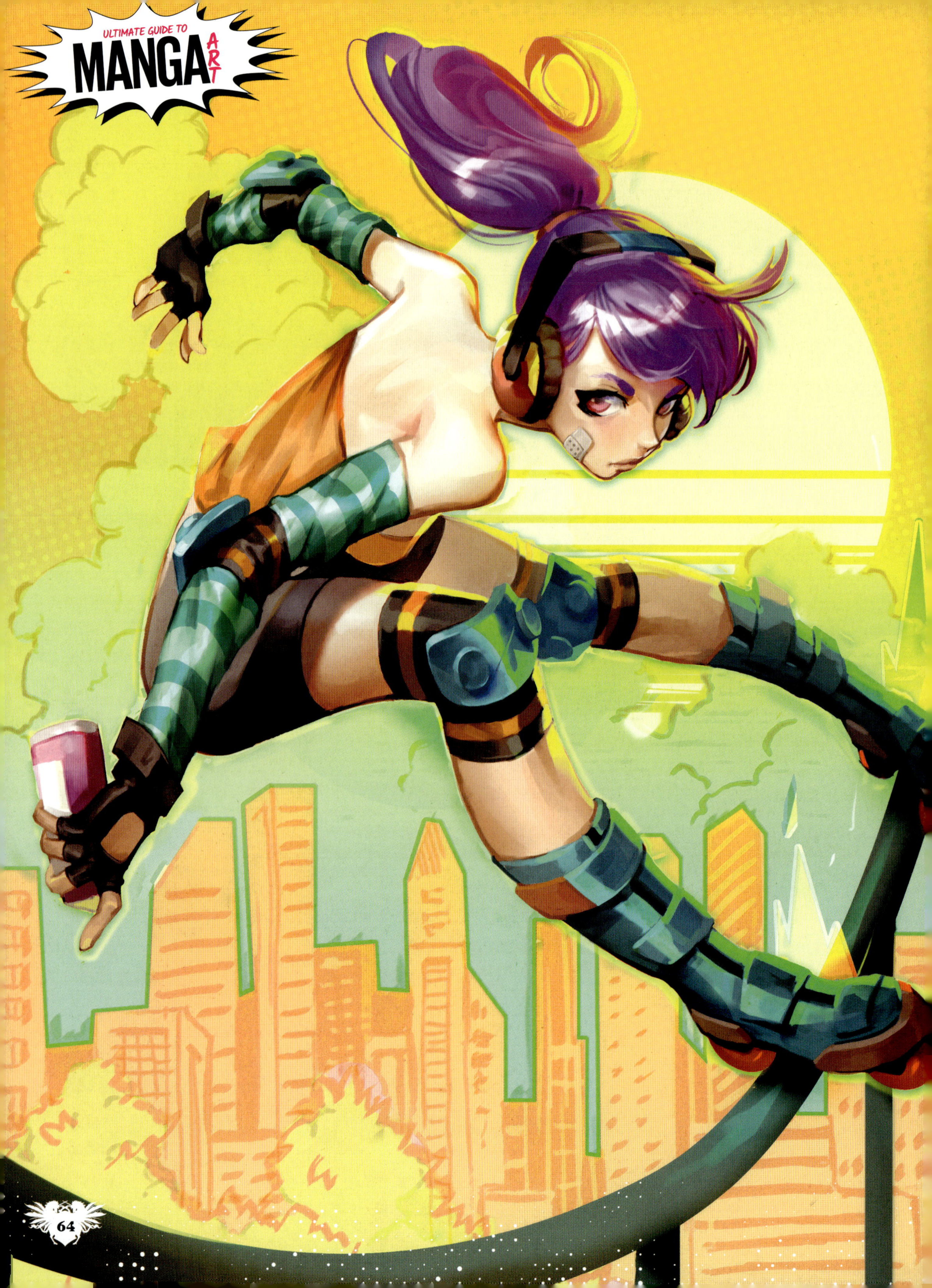

Photoshop

LEARN NEW MANGA COLORING SKILLS

James Ghio breaks down his rendering techniques for creating colorful and appealing manga art without having to render every element.

Artist **PROFILE**

James Ghio
LOCATION: Canada

Cover and concept artist James has worked for companies such as Udon, Capcom, Marvel, Bandai, and Microsoft Studios. He's currently taking a break from the industry and is busy developing a self-published project.
http://ifxm.ag/j-ghio

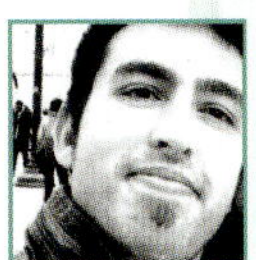

In this workshop, I'll explain the basic rendering techniques that artists can use to effectively manage their illustration process.

There's a primary directional light in my painting that helps show off forms with a strong degree of clarity. I'll be explaining the significance of this lighting scheme and how to render out the lights and darks within a set tonal range. Note that I'll be keeping all the tones within this tonal range until I'm satisfied with their overall forms. After establishing a strong black-and-white base, I'll apply color through the use of Color adjustment layers.

As you decide on your tonal range, think of it as 0 being white and 100 being black. When working in black and white, it's best to keep the tonal range close and maintain the values within 30 units of each other. This means that when rendering, your lightest tone should be only 30 units brighter than your darkest tone.

Once you've finished this tonally controlled rendering, you can add tones outside of this range to enhance your core shadows, drop shadows and occlusions in the dark areas, as well as any highlights or speculars in the light areas.

I'll also discuss color choices and how these decisions reduce the time taken to finish the image. Finally, cover and box art require some design flair in placing elements to strengthen the composition, and so I'll reveal how you can achieve this.

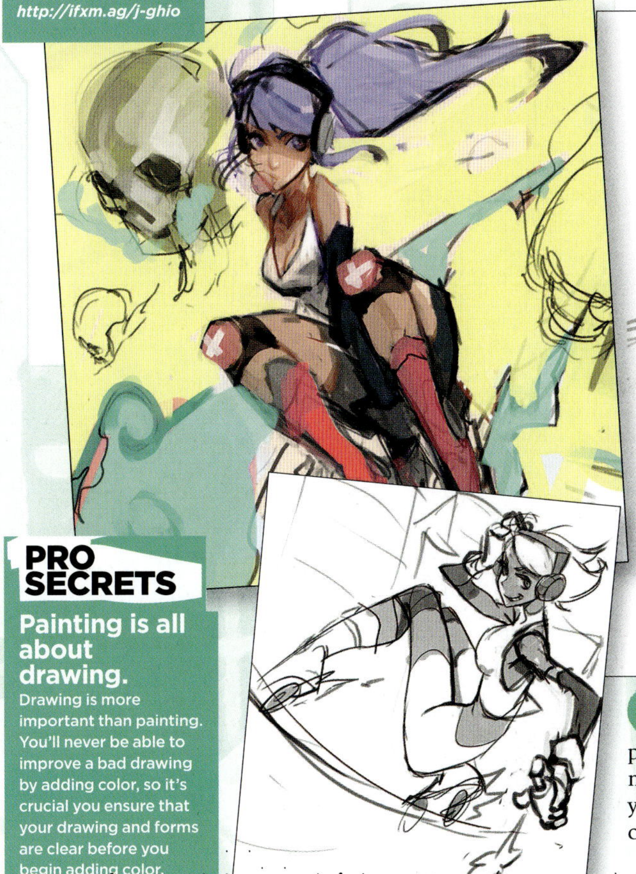

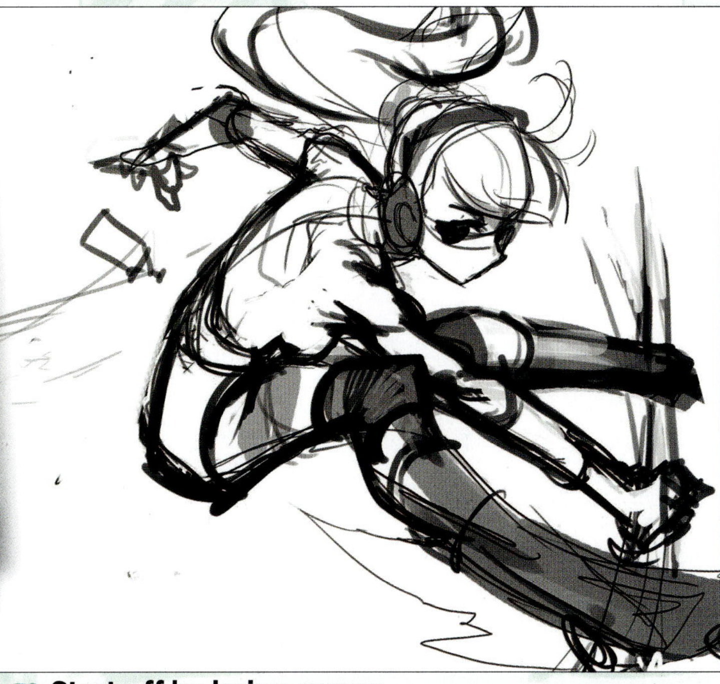

PRO SECRETS

Painting is all about drawing.
Drawing is more important than painting. You'll never be able to improve a bad drawing by adding color, so it's crucial you ensure that your drawing and forms are clear before you begin adding color.

1 Start off by being messy.

Here's the preliminary gesture for the final image. This is the stage in the process in which you can be as gestural as you want to be. Go ahead and be messy, use construction lines and energetic lines until you find the pose that you're looking for. Sometimes you'll find new and interesting ways of constructing a scene through these unplanned lines.

PRO SECRETS

Work smarter in grayscale.
Keep your grayscale forms simple. Some forms aren't shown through tones—they're simply indicated through shifts in color. Hue transitions can trick the eye into seeing forms that aren't grayscale. Depending on the material, you may need to use several layer styles to achieve the color and contrast you want. For example, use an Overlay layer to increase contrast, or a Color layer style to preserve existing contrast in the scene.

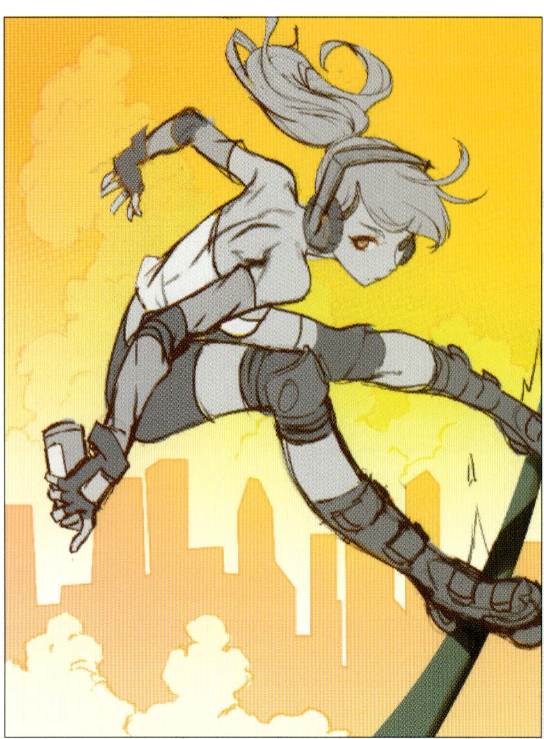

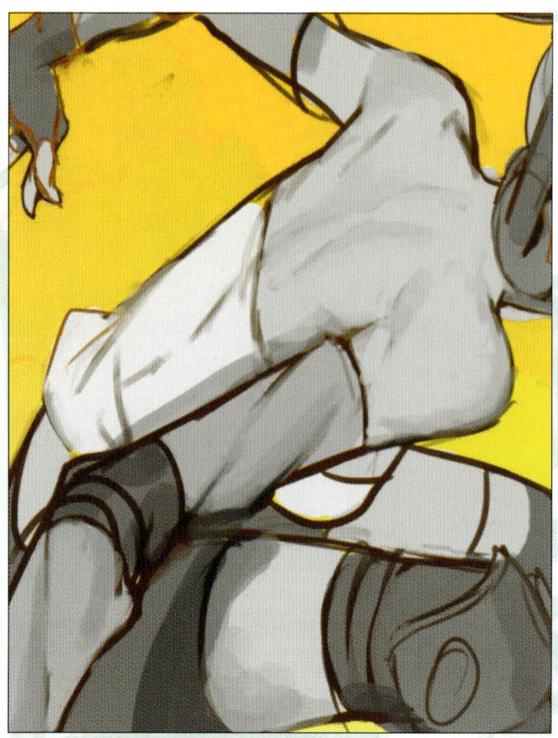

2 Ask around for help.

Manga styles do not come easily to me. I usually have to render the image out to achieve the details I'm after. But there is a shortcut that I've found to be useful—ask another artist friend for help! In this case, my wife helps me draw out the hair and eyes, which comes naturally for her because she's a manga artist by trade.

3 Smooth out the structures.

I always draw plenty of anatomy details during the initial sketch stage. Even though they'll probably fade away during the rendering stages, such subtle details will still leave an impression. As you can see in the character's back, most of the lines are now rendered out. Accurate, low-key anatomy will set your art apart from the crowd.

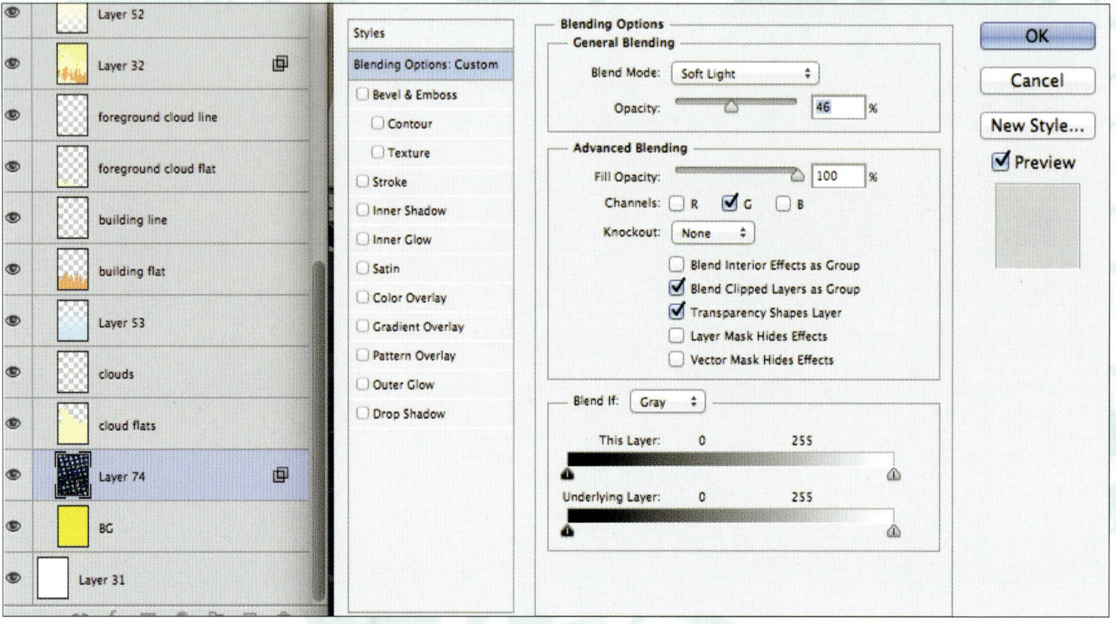

4 Summon the Photoshop gods!

I want the background to pop and feel real, even though it'll eventually have a two-dimensional, stylized look. So I begin messing with Photoshop's blending options, filters, and inverted controls. While doing this, I never know where it's going to end up, but eventually something magical happens as I keep applying layer effects.

WORKSHOP BRUSHES

PHOTOSHOP

CUSTOM BRUSHES: SQUARE

The square bush is for solid forms, and I use it for sharpening edges.

RENDER

This brush helps me draw and render without having to switch brushes.

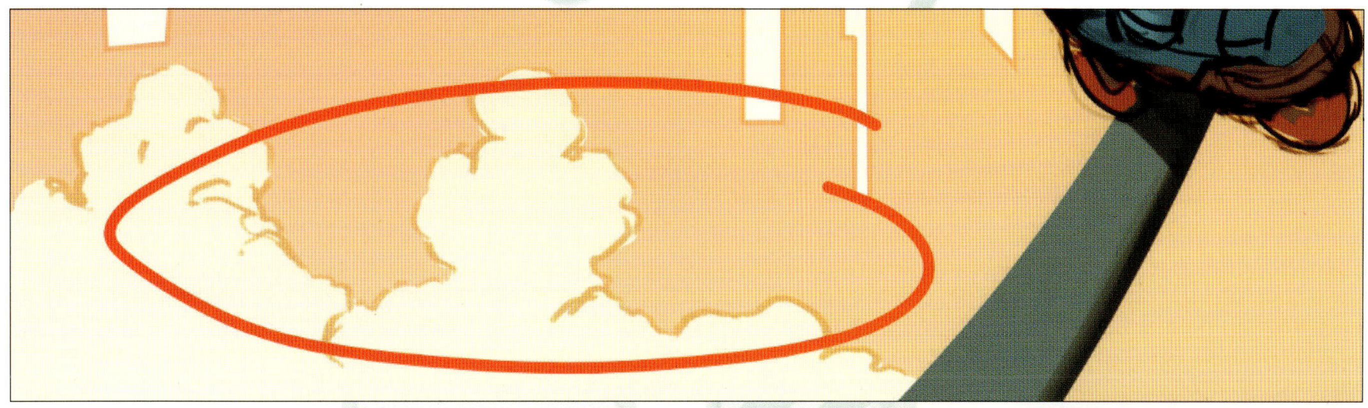

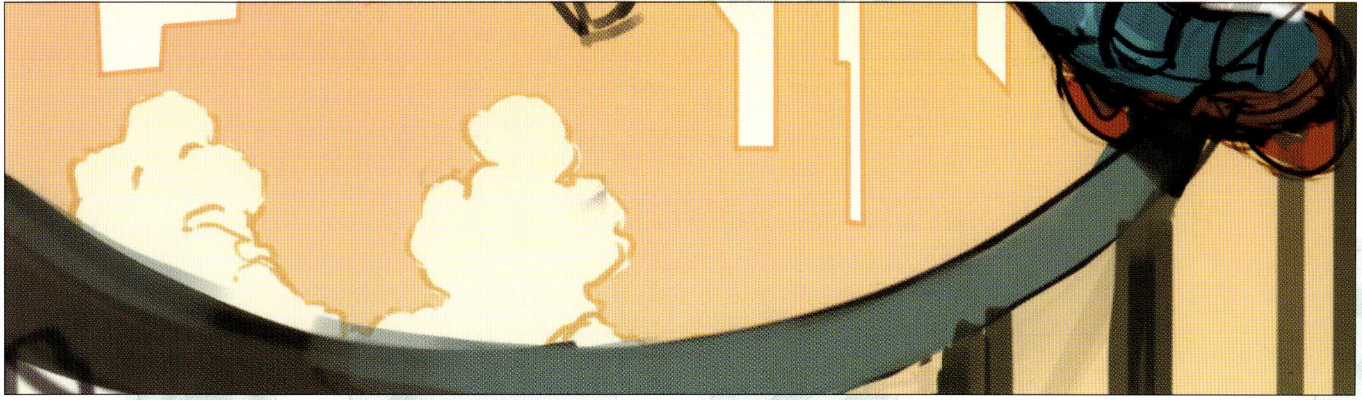

5 Consider the fore-, mid-, and background.

I become aware that something is lacking in the composition. I had initially used the clouds as a filler in the lower left-hand side of the painting. One of the requests from the *ImagineFX* team was to ensure that there was no drastic foreshortening coming from the character's pose. So, bearing this in mind, I need to find another element to work as a foreground component. Moving the rail into view is a good solution.

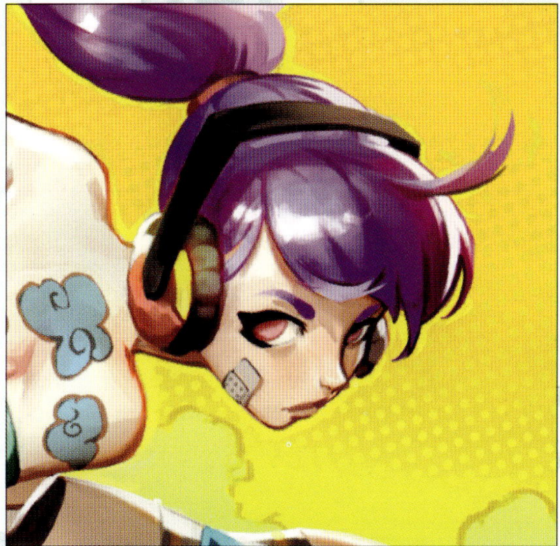

6 Make video game style influences.

All the colors are laid out, which gives me a great opportunity to start transforming features and details. Another request from *ImagineFX* was to have a Jet Set Radio–like underlying theme. So I render out the face with similarities from the game's unique style while trying to maintain a manga likeness at the same time.

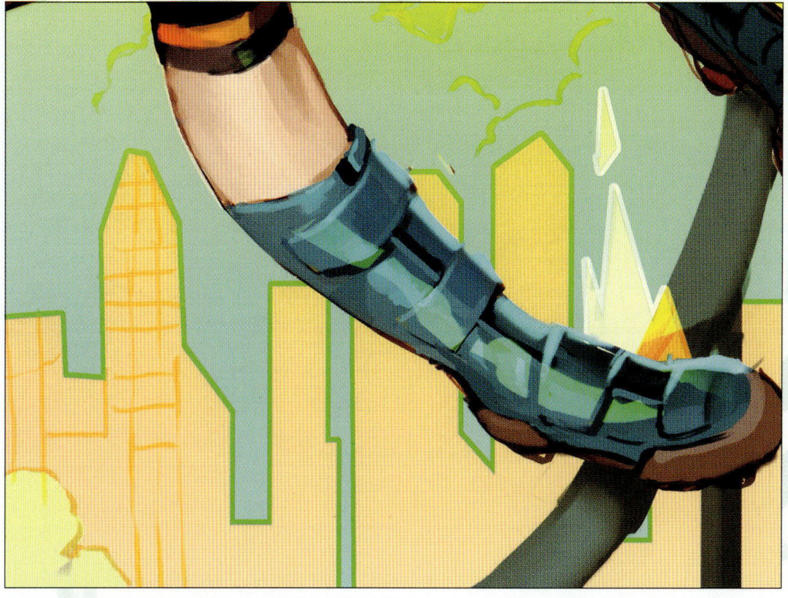

7 Make elements shine.

For my final highlights pass, I use a separate Overlay or Color Dodge layer and draw out a thick highlight with Transparency turned on. Then I use an eraser to create the highlight shape. It's similar to masking, but a little more intuitive, and because it's on a separate layer you can adjust the color with the Hue slider.

PRO SECRETS

Create precise brush strokes. During any stage in the painting process, keep your brush opaque to avoid pushing paint. A soft brush will force you to render endlessly. Using an opaque brush will establish clearer and precise marks. It'll also help prevent muddy color transitions and overly rendered forms.

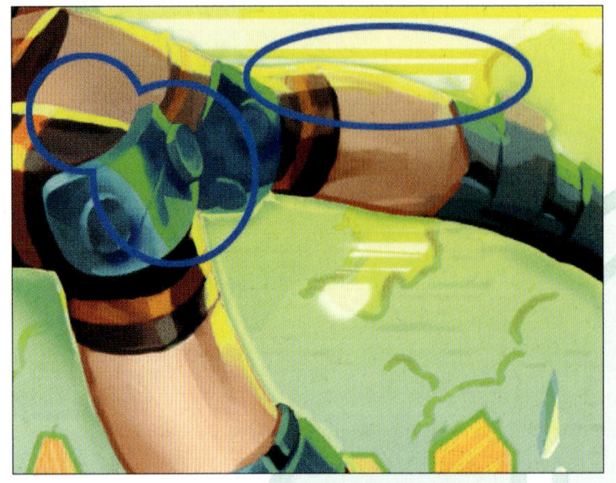

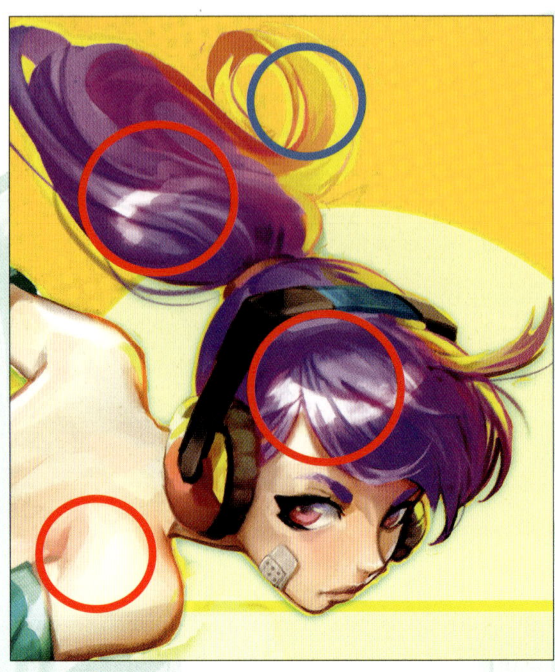

8 Add color to those highlights.

It's important to separate lights by color. Here, the red circles are the primary warm highlights. Notice how the highlights are almost purely white. The blue circles are areas that take on the yellow light from the background. This helps the viewer easily distinguish between the different lights being used. Essentially, it's directional light versus rim light. I use a Darken layer for this process.

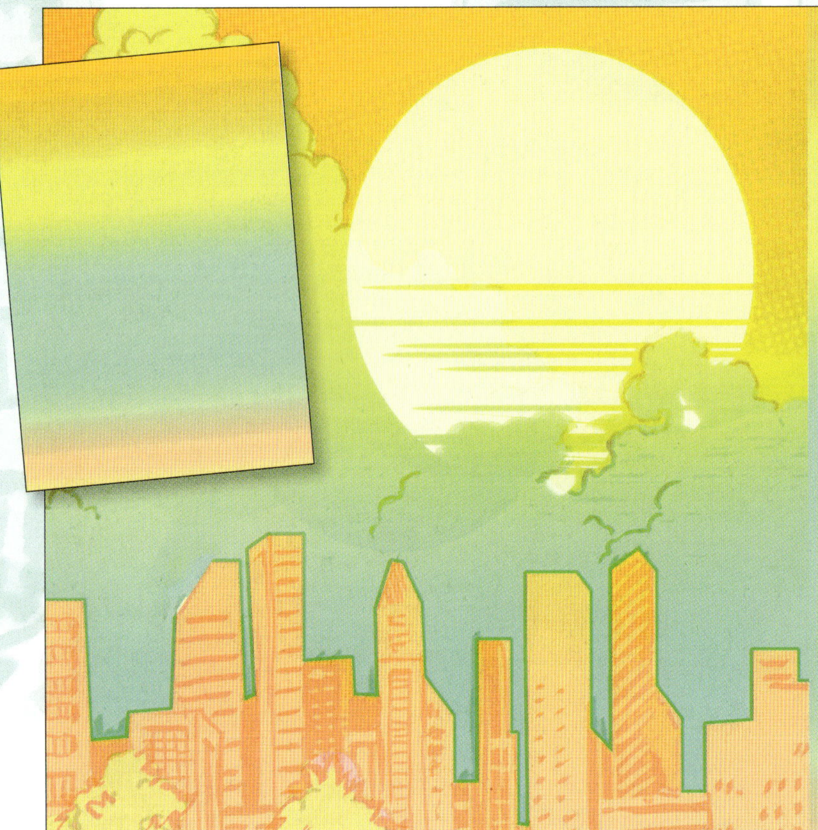

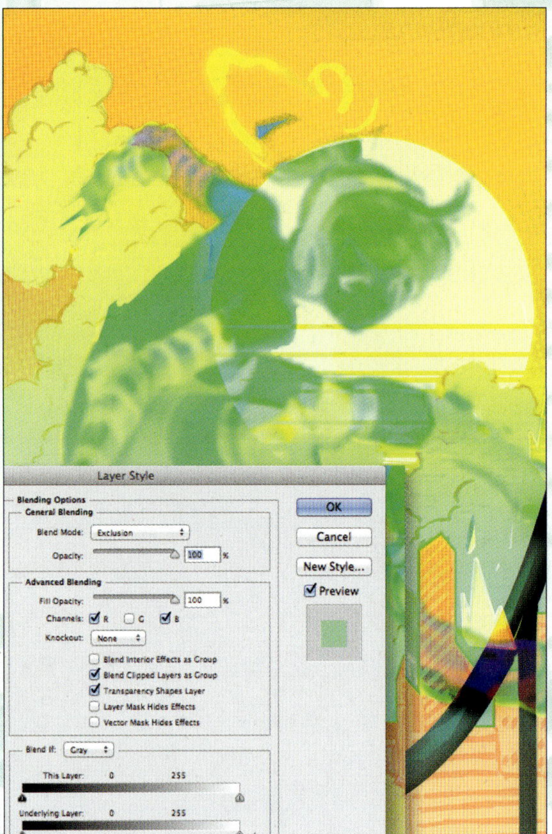

9 Build up a scene around a hue gradient.

Here, I've broken down the background into a color gradient so you can see how there's a smooth transition of color despite having contrasting elements, such as the buildings against the clouds. In everything you paint, you should be looking for ways to implement color gradients. Think of the whole image as one big abstraction of color, and then find ways to bring certain areas of color together.

10 Make it glow.

Of course, with every splash of color you need an element of glow. Using an Exclusion layer, I remove the green channel so that I can have a green knockout glow effect behind the character. It helps lift the main character off the background, as well as pop her off the page.

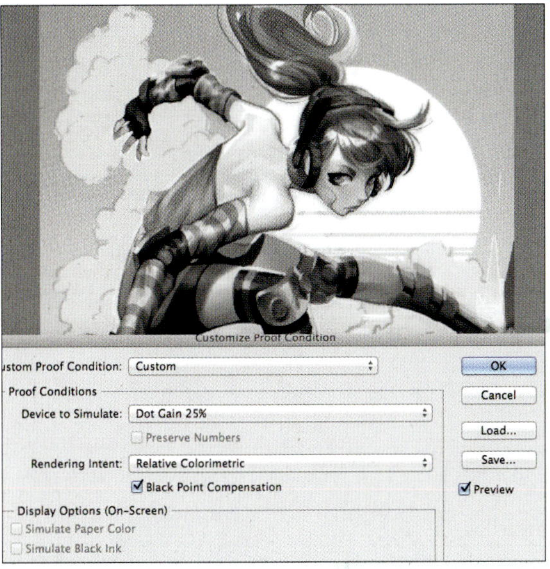

11 Check your tones.

At this point, I need to check the tones within the composition to make sure that I haven't pushed the contrast too far. I strongly believe you should be constantly toggling between color and grayscale views throughout the entire painting process. To do this, select View>Proof Setup>Custom, and apply the settings that are shown above. Now every time you press Y you can see your work-in-progress as a grayscale image.

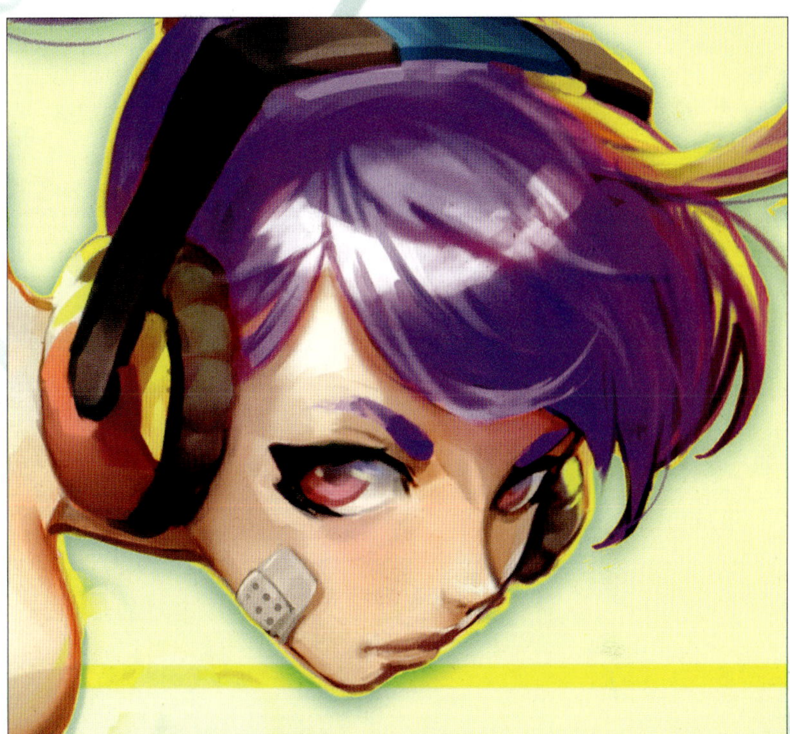

12 Be detailed.

Although I'm keeping this illustration pretty simple, it never hurts to carry on detailing (at least, up to a point). I prefer to detail using highlights.

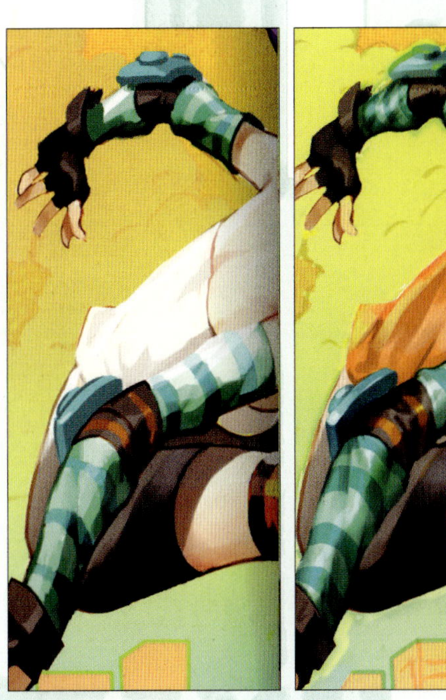

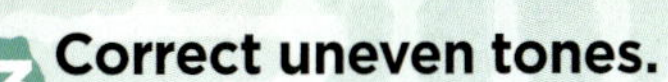

13 Correct uneven tones.

To connect the character to the background's overall palette, I change her shirt to a deep orange. Even though it's tonally correct, her shirt was blending with the background clouds too much. It's never too late to make these kinds of adjustments. Don't settle for what you've painted until your eyes agree with the overall image!

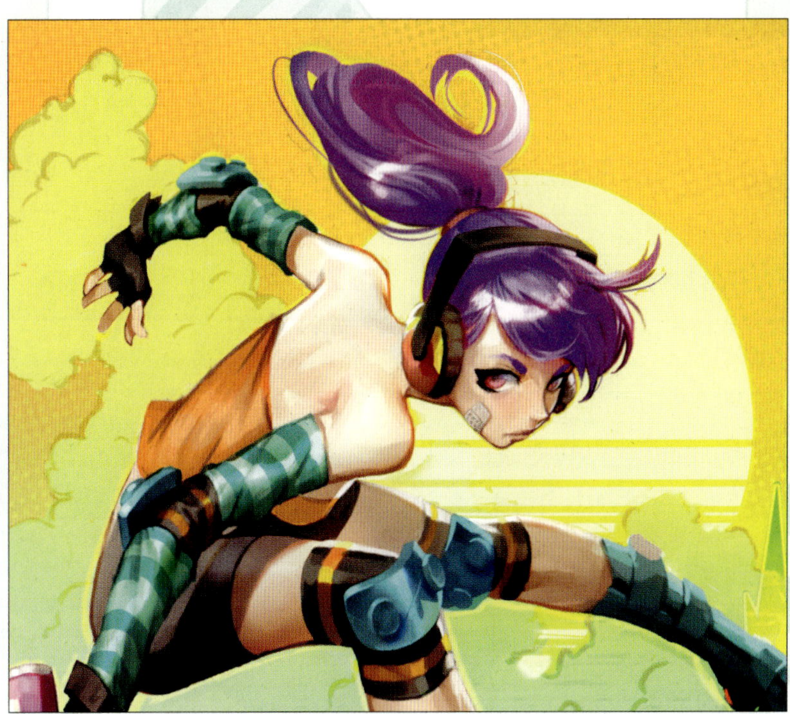

14 Show your reasoning.

I realize I need to justify why there's rim light on the character. Art doesn't always need to make sense, but in this case the colorful environment means I definitely need to show the cause behind the effect. What better way to do this than by painting, a giant stylized sun to match the rest of the background?

Photoshop

BE INSPIRED BY A MANGA CLASSIC

Toni Infante taps into the influence of *Akira*, and uses color, contrast, and composition to create a striking image.

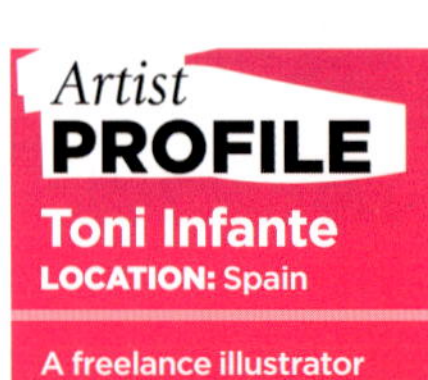

Artist **PROFILE**

Toni Infante
LOCATION: Spain

A freelance illustrator and comic artist from Barcelona, Toni works with clients such as Image Comics, Boom!, and DC. He also teaches.
www.toniinfante.com

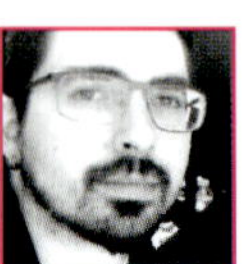

I've been a huge manga fan since childhood, and it's impossible to hide the influence that passion has on my art. In my quest to learn how to paint powerful and dynamic images, I've learned a lot from my favorite manga artists through observation, and trial and error.

Yet, as illustrators we can also make use of a range of visual techniques—composition, color, lighting, perspective—to help us achieve such goals. People rarely spend more than a few seconds looking at something before moving on. So in the case of art that also serves a commercial purpose—such as a magazine cover—it's even more important to ensure those techniques are all working to create an eye-catching composition. It may feel overwhelming at times, but the trick is to divide up the workflow, focus on one step at a time, and solve any problems as they arise.

Because it's a static medium, I always try to create dynamism by playing with and exaggerating these techniques. Use of complementary colors, diagonal shapes, and forced perspectives are some of the elements I repeatedly use in my work, and I'll talk about these and more in this workshop. From the initial rough sketches, creating more detailed line art, adding color, and final touches, I'll dive into this neon world to explain my choices during the process and pass on some tips or observations that hopefully will help you in your own work.

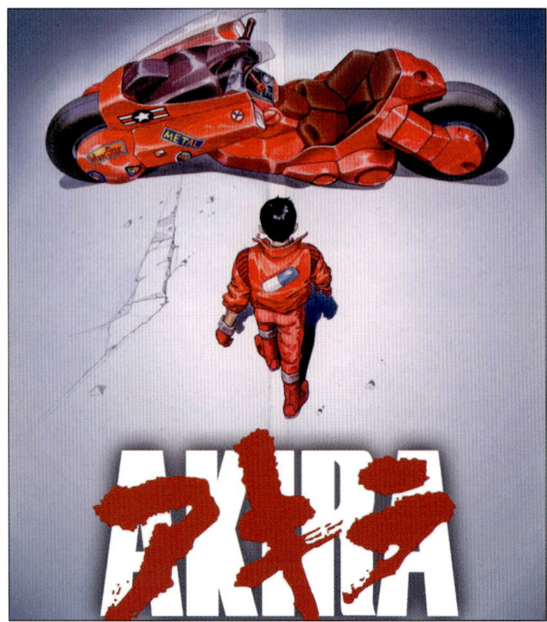

1 Look for inspiration.
Before I begin sketching, I always look around for some reference material. Films, photographs, or any other media can help me generate a raft of original ideas. I'm always trying to make something fresh and different in my art. Having said that, this piece is meant to be a tribute to the manga classic *Akira*, but I'll also include references to some of my other favorite manga series.

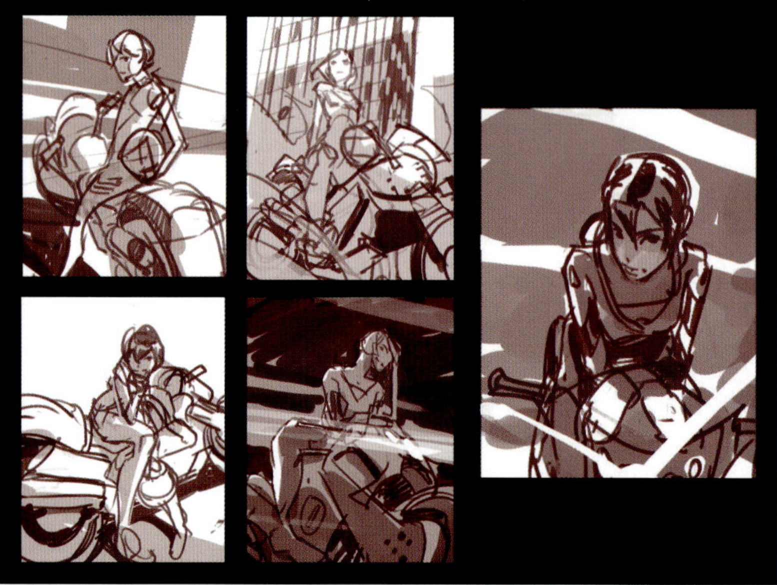

2 Produce quick thumbnails.
While the premise is simple—woman on a motorcycle—there's plenty of potential for introducing different points of view. Those sketches work as a brainstorming session, and as well as arranging elements differently, I try to work with different emotions on each one, too. Black, white, and a mid-tone are all the colors I need at this point, which make things simple yet readable. Those sketches are like the skeleton of the image, and the composition must work even at this early stage. I place my lighting and cast shadows with the narrative in mind, and if I'm lucky I'll start having some ideas for how to color the scene later on.

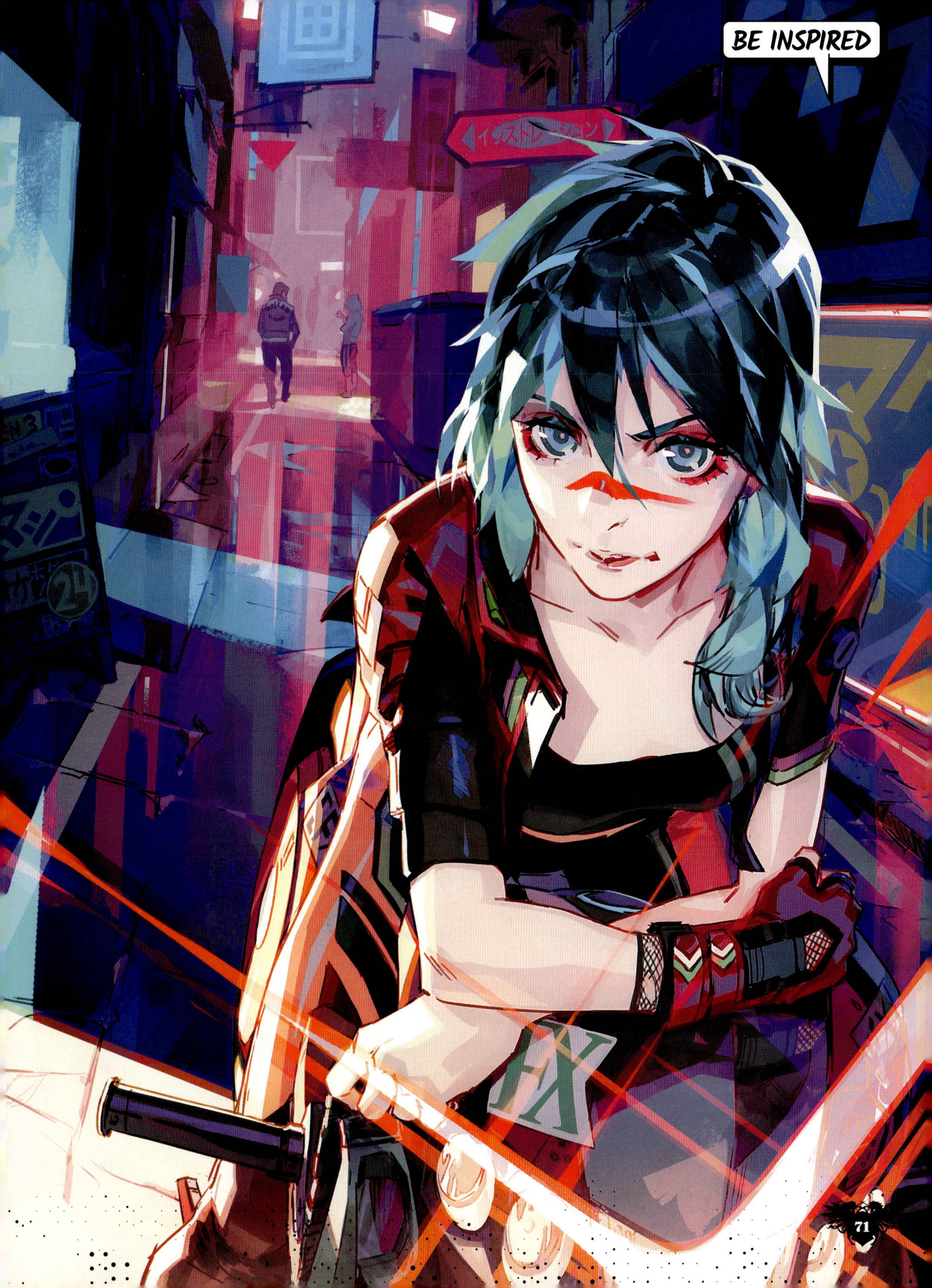
24

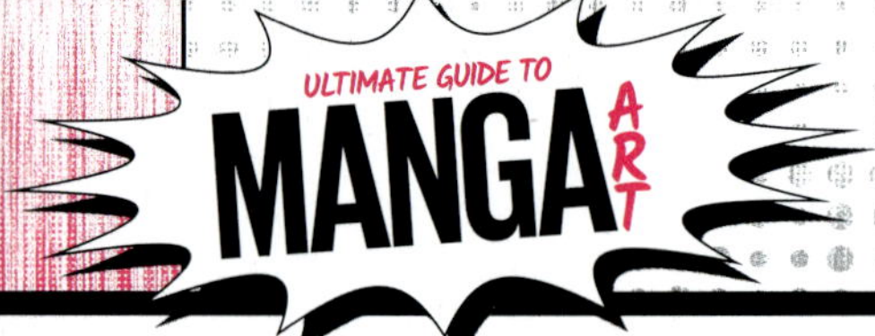

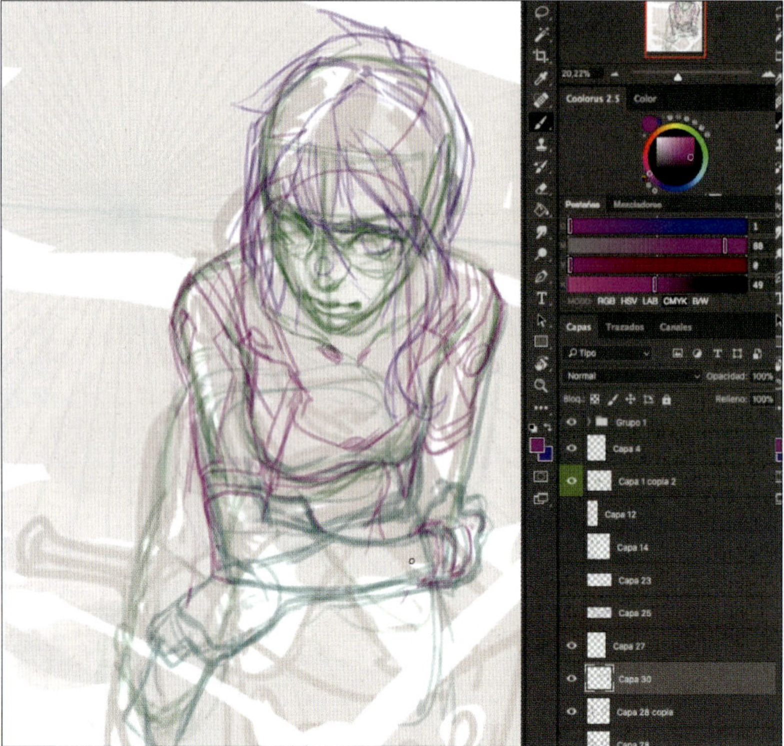

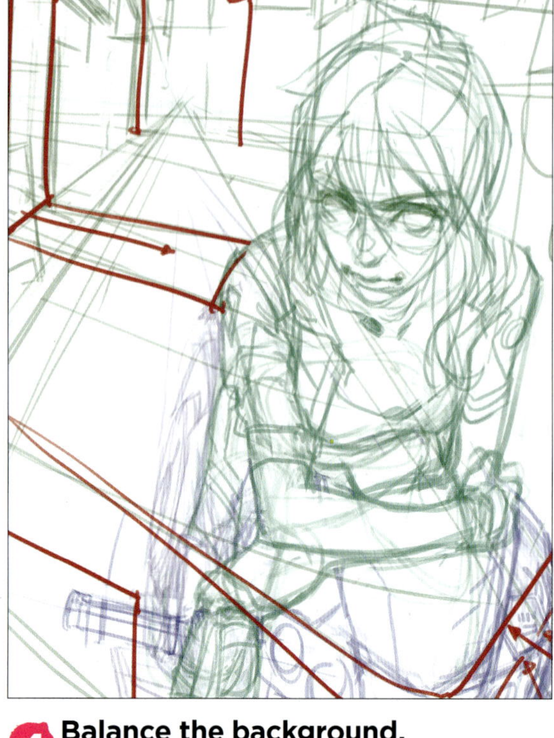

3 Refine the sketch.

It's time to draw over the sketch and place details, just as if I were using a lightbox. I focus on anatomy and perspective, using a one-point perspective grid that I rotate slightly to add some dynamism to the scene. Then I define muscles and the main lines of the character. I draw her clothes, hair, and other details in a different color, so as not to lose sight of the character's anatomy.

4 Balance the background.

Placing the character on the right can make the image look unbalanced. To fix this, I place details in the street behind using some night Japanese street images as reference. I place a huge light source on the store at the left, which creates a key diagonal line going towards the character. The vertical street lines and the motorcycle headlight help balance out the overall composition.

WORKSHOP BRUSHES

PHOTOSHOP

CUSTOM BRUSHES: PENCIL BRUSH

I set this to 100% Opacity for line art, 20-30% for sketches.

TEXTURED BRUSH

Square-shape brush for backgrounds. Ideal for geometric objects.

GENERAL BRUSH

Used on 100% Opacity. Good for flat colors and rendering.

COLOR GENERATOR

Adds random color brush strokes on an Overlay layer.

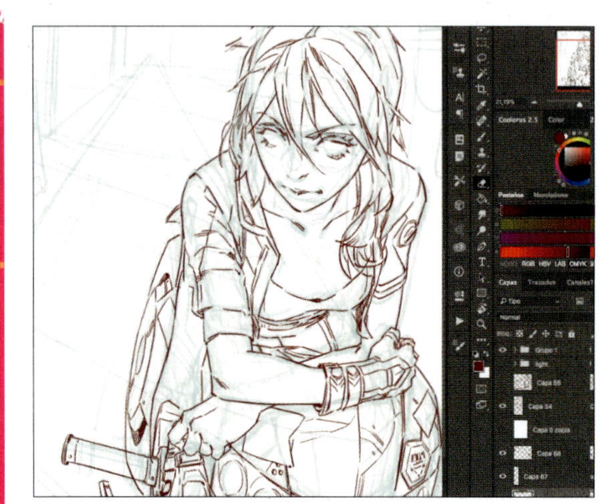

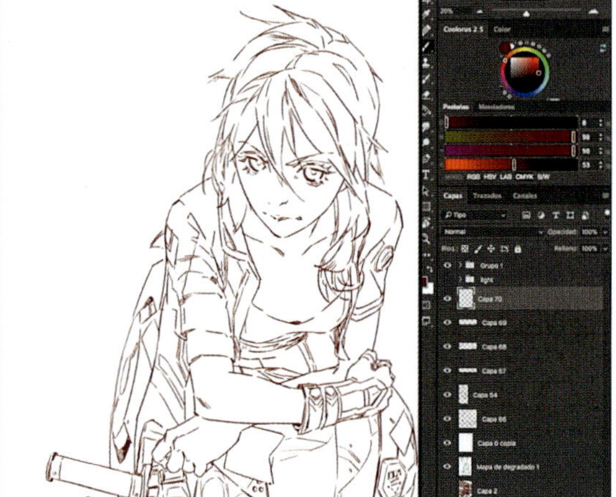

5 Create the final line art.

When everything's set in place, I draw over the rough sketch's lines from before and detail the character and other elements. The background will be detailed using only color, but line art will remain visible on the character and foreground, so I keep them clean on different layers. This line art will play a huge role in depicting the classic manga look.

6 Don't overwork, simplify.

Sometimes it's tempting to start detailing early on in the process. The results are often messy. Instead, try to be straightforward and simplify. Here, the basic structure and anatomy are in place, but it doesn't mean they need to be visible on the line art. The structure lines have done their job, and now it's time to build on them. I simplify objects like her nose and hands into just a few lines.

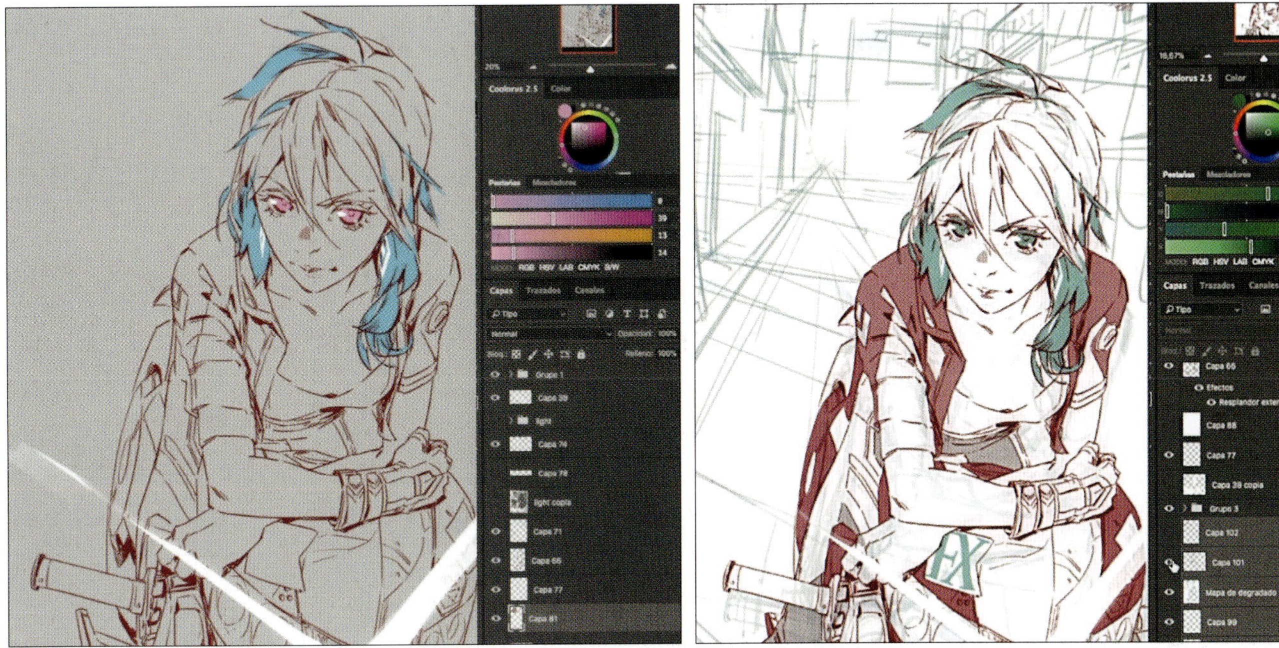

7 Think about character design.

On a portrait piece like this, it's important to define the character. The clothing design, color scheme, and eyes all help add depth to our young biker. I decide to portray her wearing a leather jacket and pants with plenty of triangle motifs and diagonals. You can also see these shapes in her hair. Red-colored elements on her clothes and face convey the impression of strength, despite her friendly expression.

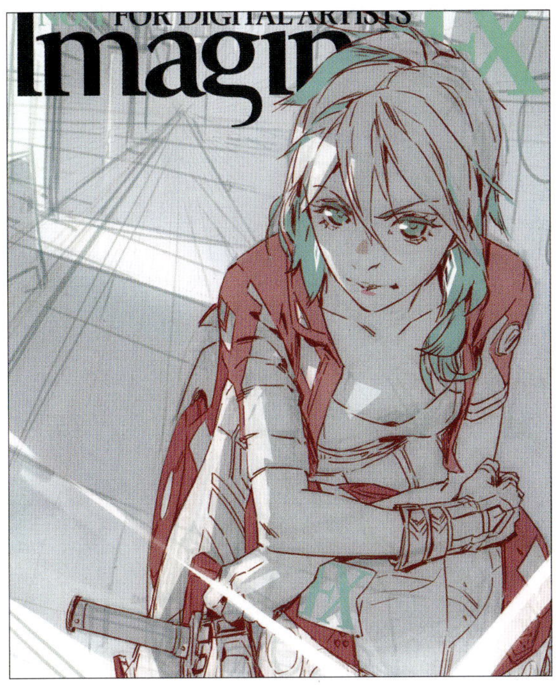

8 Think about lighting.

The idea of setting the scene on a neon-lit street at night was decided early on, but now it's necessary to detail the concept and place highlights and shadows more precisely. I pay attention to the position of the *ImagineFX* logo, too—it's important to keep it readable. I decide to leave that area in dark tones and free from neon lights, enabling the logo to pop out in white.

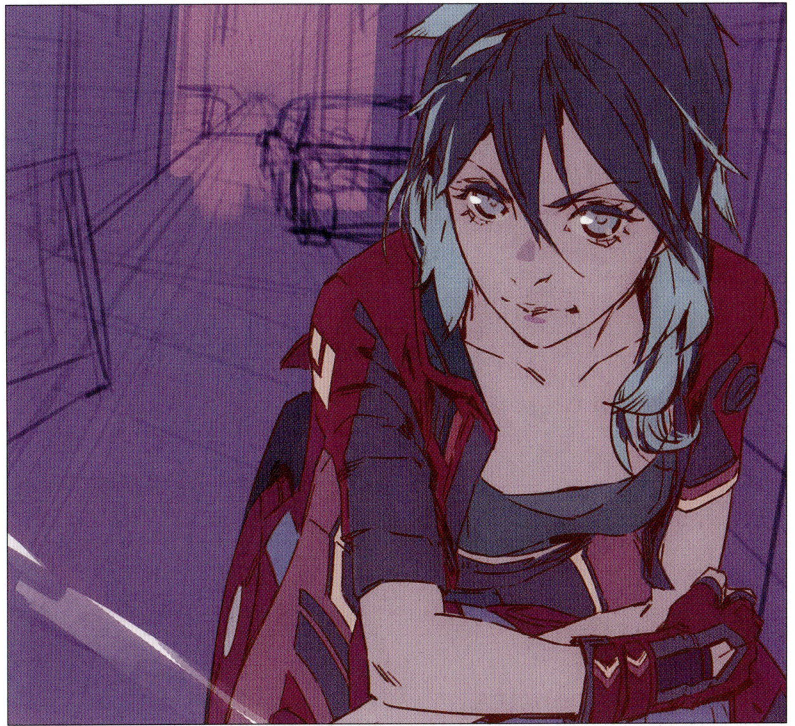

9 Establish general color schemes.

I now make my first color decisions. Depending on the complexity of the illustration, I usually create a full-color key in a smaller duplicate of the file. However, because there's just one big character and I've got a clear idea of the image, I don't need more than my previous light and tone study. Filters like Image> Adjustment>Color balance help me to keep all the tones as a purple hue.

10 Bring life to the world.

To add realism and life, I bring plenty of details into the background: store signs, damp pavements, people, etc. I imagine myself in the scene, and try to express on the canvas what I would feel as I walk through that environment. Exaggerated lighting or a sense of weather are always good tools to employ when creating visual interest.

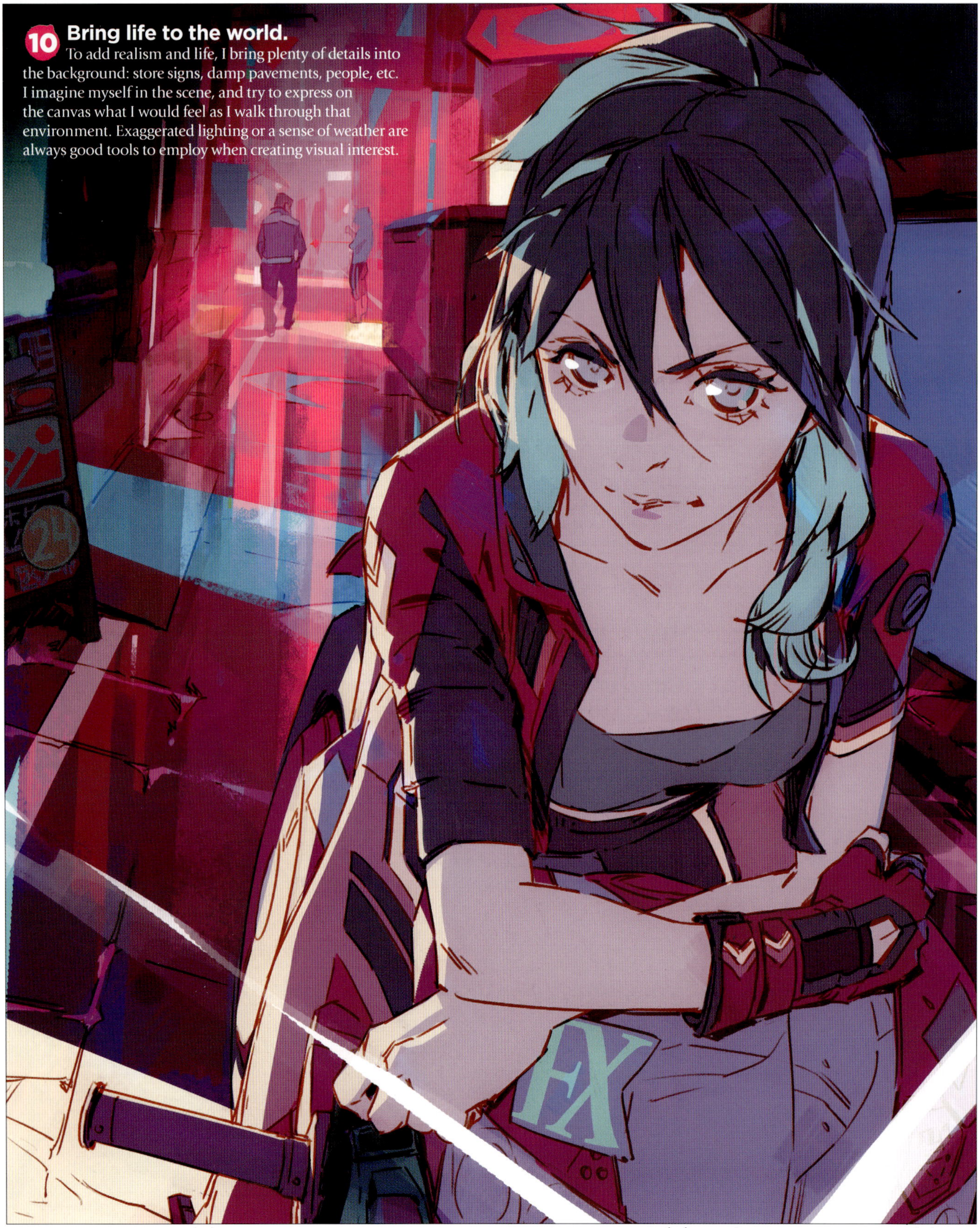

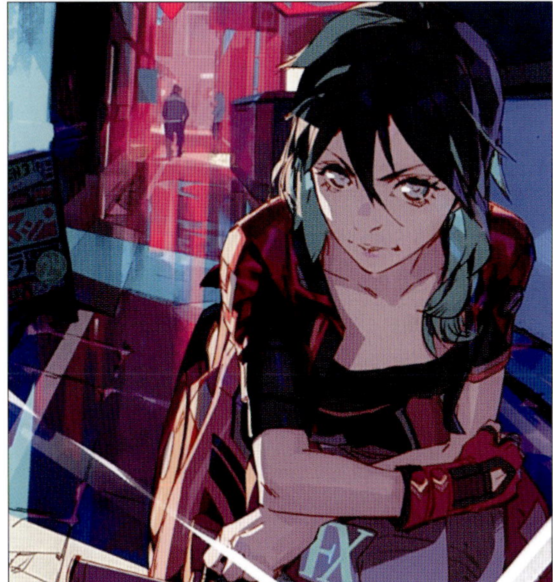

11 Add volume and render.

Using my custom Color Generator brush in Overlay mode, I add some randomness to my colors. This helps enrich the entire image. Then I start on the character. First I put highlight over on the left that will make her stand out, and then I dive into the details. My shading is full of hard edges and flat colors, because I want the image to echo the anime or manga style.

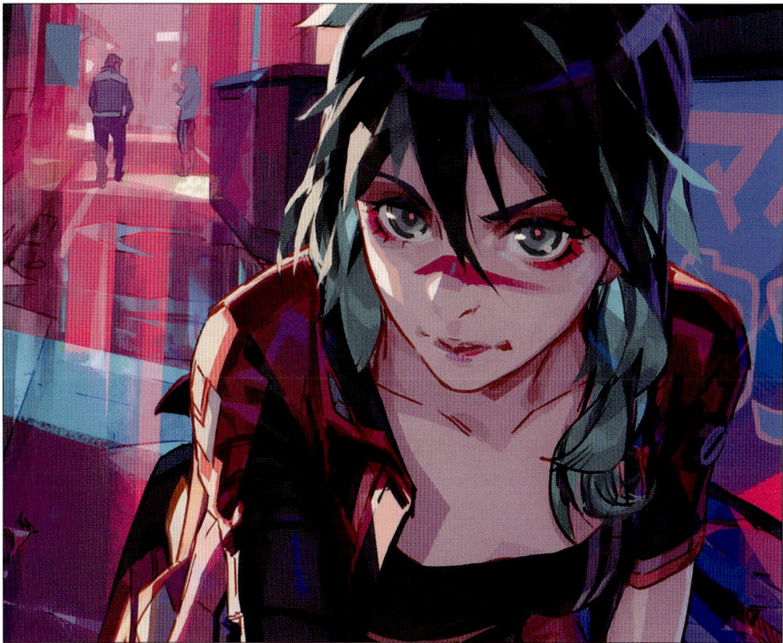

12 Shade the leather and metal.

My colors are already established, so I select the Eyedropper tool (Alt+click) and keep working on shades and volumes, bearing in mind that lighting works differently across a range of surfaces. The darkest zones and contrast are reserved for leather and metal, while skin is worked with a low contrast. I try to merge layers while painting, keeping the background and lights separate from the character.

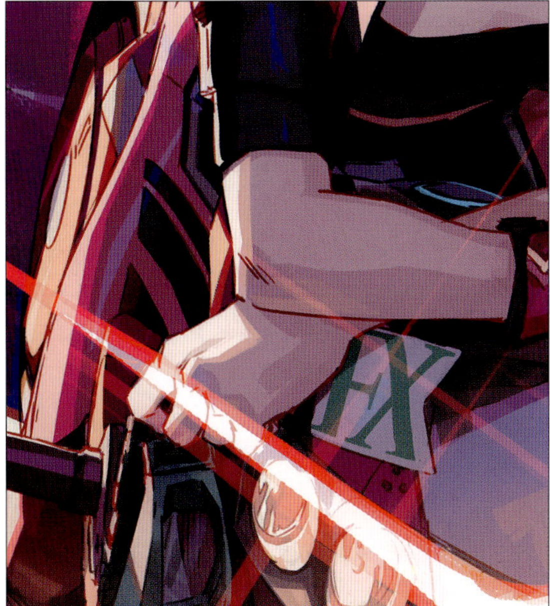

13 Bring in anime-style effects.

I'm almost there now, so I enhance the overall look and apply my final touches. Inspired by anime, I spend a bit of time working up the motorcycle headlights, making them big and strong. These geometric forms also help me fill the composition to the lower-right area of the scene. They're painted with white with some reddish tones on the edges on an Overlay layer mode.

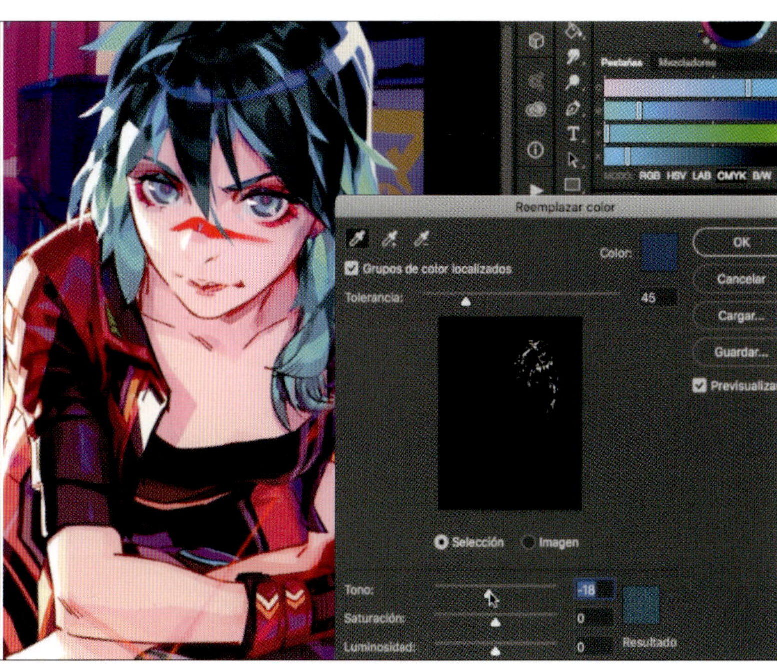

14 Make tweaks from the team.

At the request of the *ImagineFX* team, I change the hair color and light focus to make the character stand out against the logo. I also do some polishing work and get rid of some details on the background to make the cover text more readable. At any point, it's important to stay focused on the important stuff and not fill everything with unnecessary details that might distract the viewer. To finish off, I apply Filter>Focus>Focus mask to emphasize certain shapes in the scene.

Procreate & Photoshop

CREATE AMAZING MANGA FIGURE ART

Manga and anime character artist **Ilya Kuvshinov** brings to life a girl and her toy Totoro, using a range of Photoshop blending layer modes.

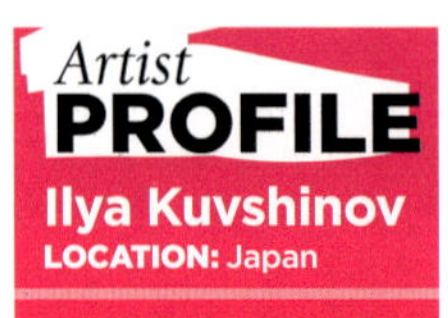

Artist **PROFILE**

Ilya Kuvshinov

LOCATION: Japan

Ilya developed character designs, concept art, and animations for *The Wonderland*, and characters for *Ghost in the Shell: SAC_2045*.

http://ifxm.ag/kuily

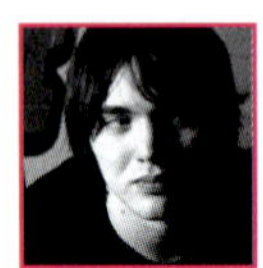

A decade spent in art education, followed by another 10 years immersed in digital painting techniques have enabled me to identify the different ways of approaching commercial work, and helped me to uncover new ways of expressing my ideas in my personal art.

I usually work in Procreate on an iPad, and Photoshop on an iMac Pro, switching between both applications. For this workshop, I created the sketches on an iPad and finished the piece in Photoshop, taking advantage of the bigger screen size and the program's larger range of tools. You'll see how even basic effects such as Lighten, Darken, and Color Burn layer blend modes, Gaussian Blur, and Liquify can help you create those pro-level finishing touches.

Digital art tools either attempt to imitate the effects of traditional media, or take a painting approach that, for the most part, is far removed from real-world processes. My work doesn't resemble a "real" painting at all, apart from during the early sketch and line art stages, and when developing shadows and background. Instead, I rely on Photoshop to enhance parts of the image as I go: first by developing the mood of the artwork, and then adding details throughout the scene. It's a totally different approach to working in traditional media. Here, I've used vivid colors, light blooms and gentle rendering to express my love for the films of Studio Ghibli.

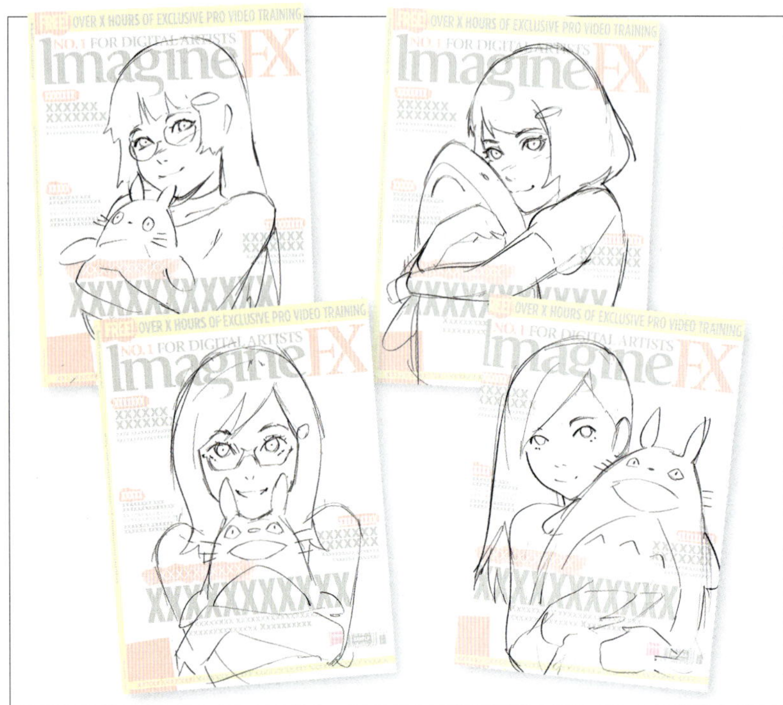

1 Generate rough sketches.
The *ImagineFX* team's idea is "a girl hugging a plush toy, maybe a Totoro one," so I start by creating four sketches in Procreate: three with Totoro, and one with a shark plush toy. I'm mindful of the cover layout, so the face of the girl and her soft toy should roughly be in the middle of the composition.

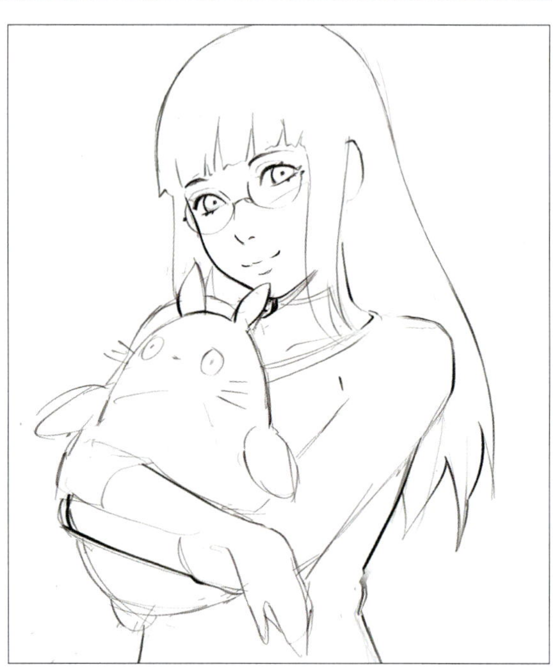

2 Alter the character's age.
It's decided that I should proceed with sketch number one. However, I need to make the girl look much older—between 12 and 18 years old. This means I need to change the size and proportions of her head and facial features, making her head and eyes smaller, the cheeks less chubby, and increase the length of her arms.

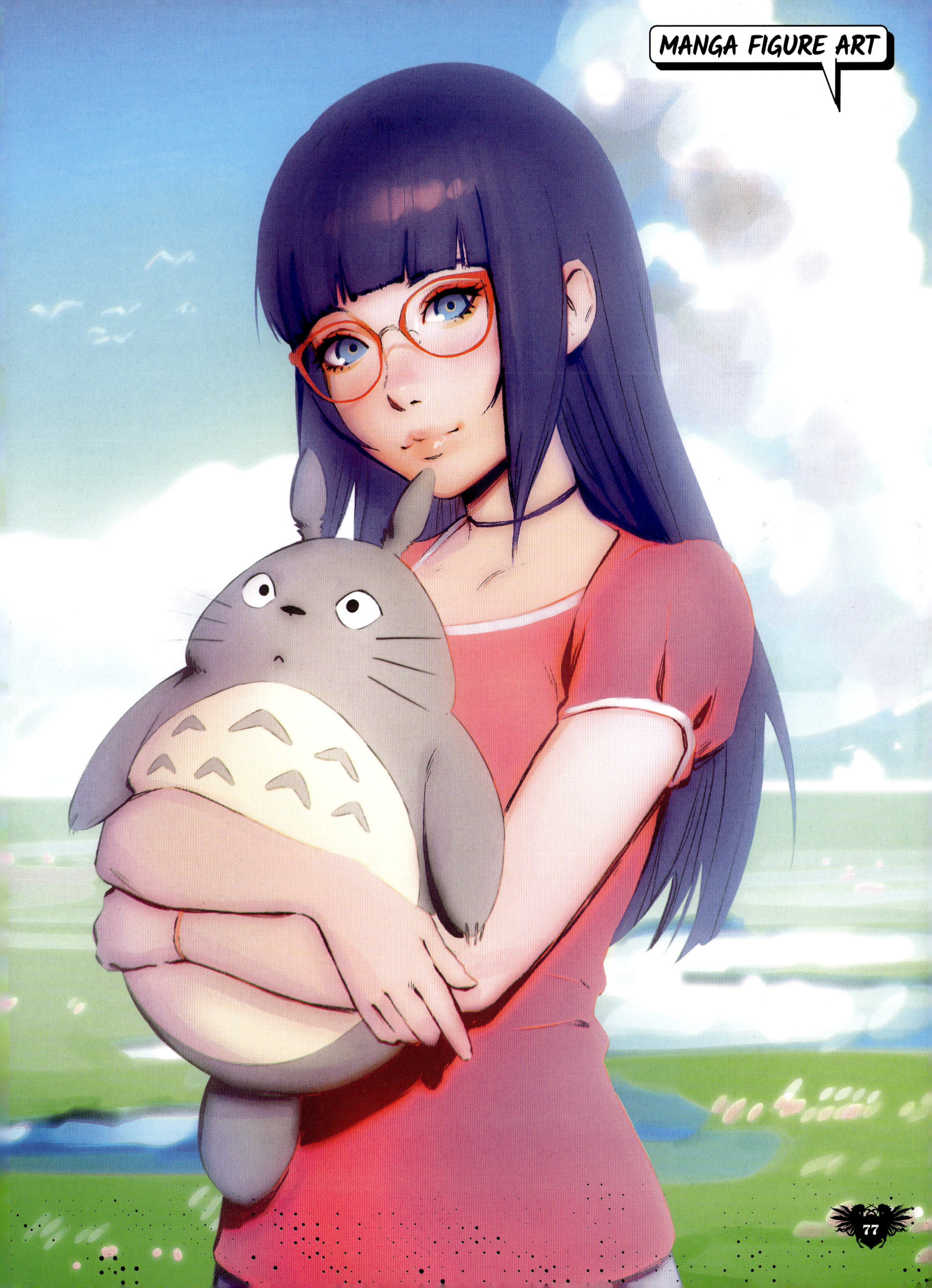

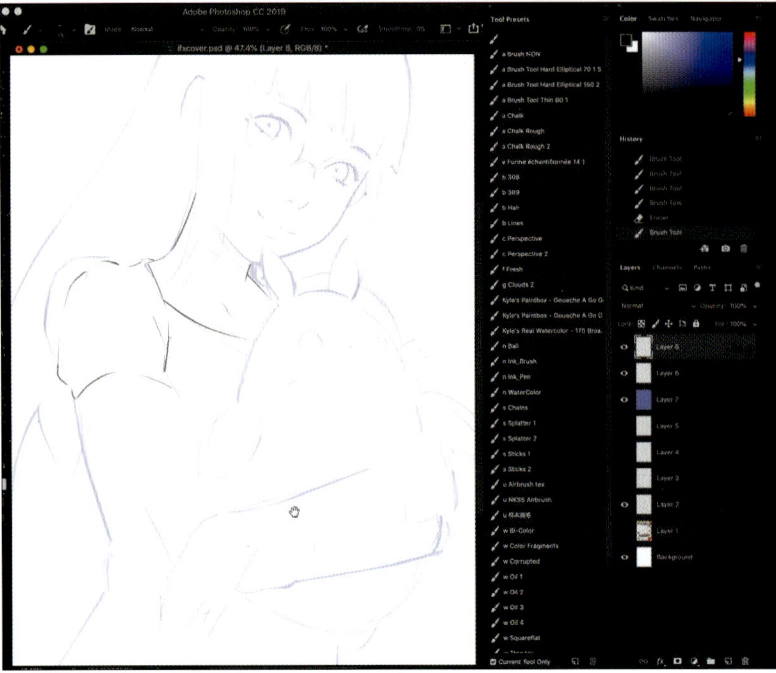

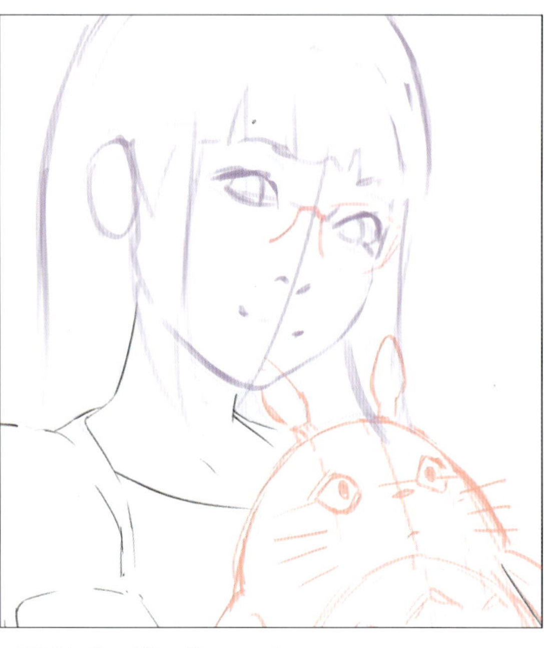

3 Create a line-art layer.

I take the sketch into Photoshop and roughly double the image size, just in case we need to crop the image to make the cover more effective. Before starting to ink, I create a new Lighten blend layer filled with just blue (press Alt+Del to fill the layer) to differentiate the rough sketch from the line art.

4 Make the line art.

I start inking on top of the sketch, fixing any mistakes on the fly. Technically, working digitally means I can correct errors even at a late stage in the painting, so I don't worry about making mistakes as I draw the line art. However, for guidance I add structural sketches for the girl's head and draw Totoro with violet and red lines.

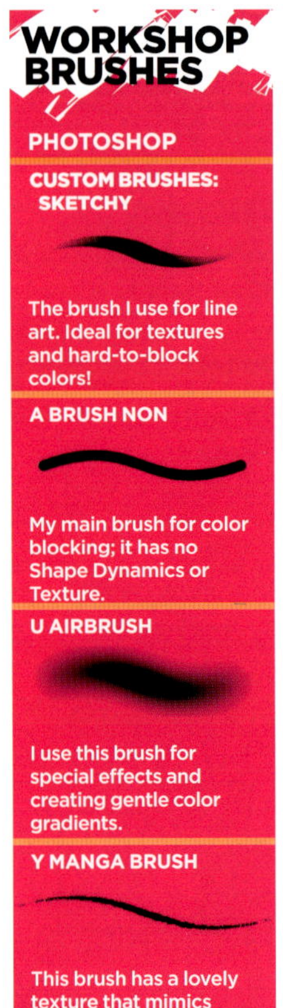

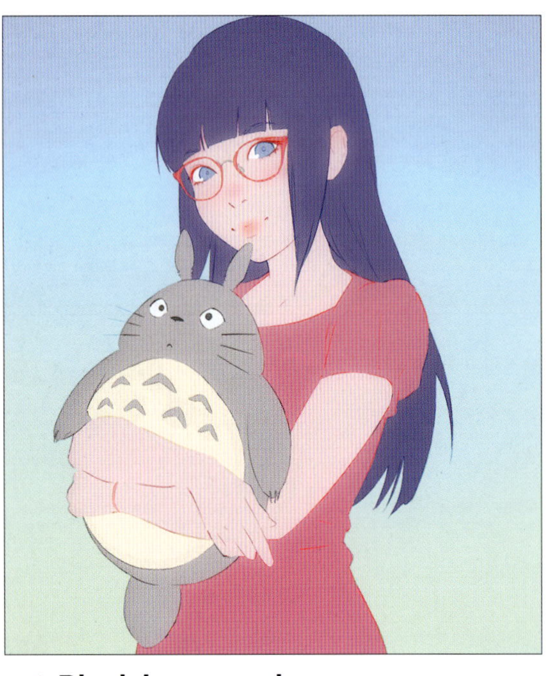

5 Block in your colors.

I regularly flip the image horizontally, finding and fixing more mistakes as I go along. I finish the line art in about an hour, and after another hour, my colors have been blocked in. The brush I'm using for the line art makes it difficult to block the colors with the Magic Wand tool, so I have to do this stage by hand.

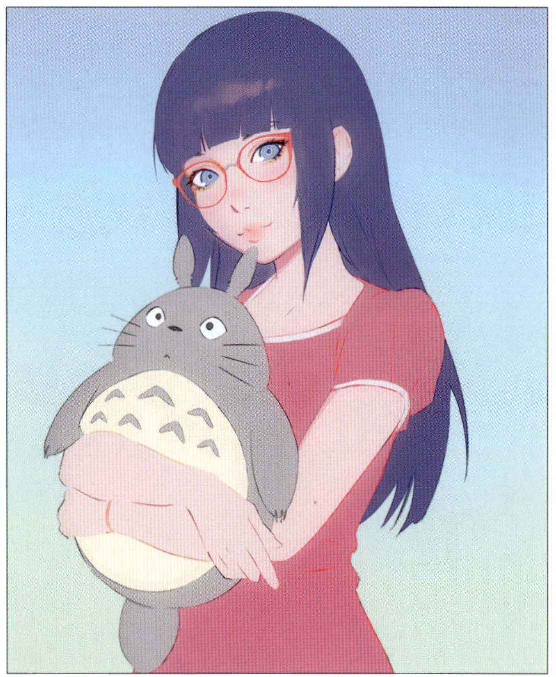

6 Amend the face.

I now decide to make some changes to the face, making full use of the Liquify tool, and cutting out the eyes and moving them around. I also fix the shape of the head and width of the arms and waist. I'll be back to fix the face later on in the painting process, though.

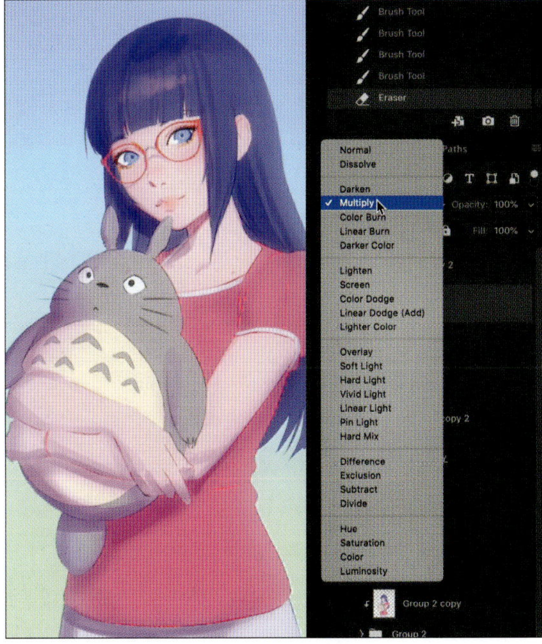

7 Shadow layer techniques.

Using a bright violet color, I roughly add shadows on top of the character using a Multiply layer. I also copy the same layer and blur it with Gaussian Blur on top. This softens the shadows and changes the opacity of both layers, creating an even softer shadow effect.

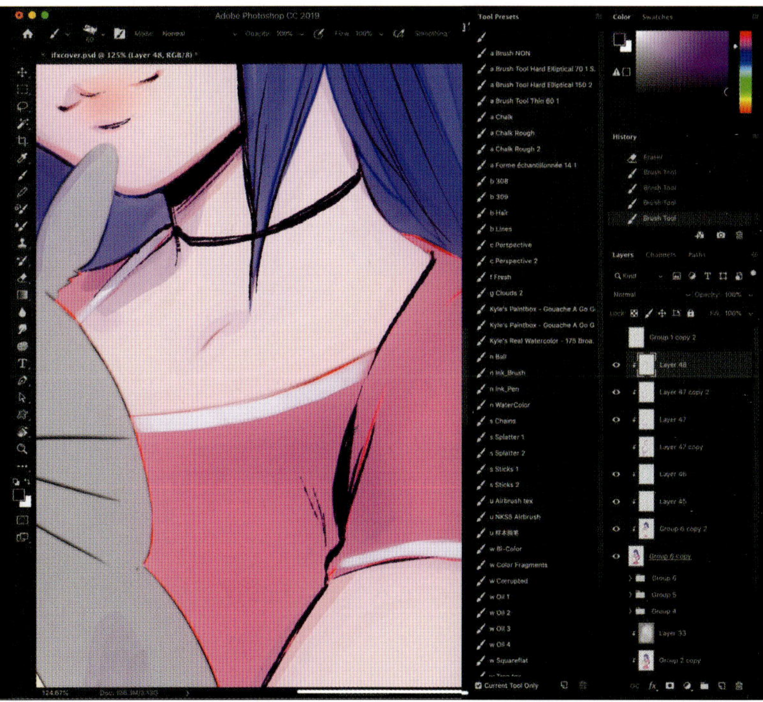

8 Develop a cel-shade look.

I use dark violet with my Y Manga Brush to add contrast shadows and one more line layer to the figure, which gives the image an aged-ink cel-shading appearance. This step wasn't planned, but it suits the theme of the piece.

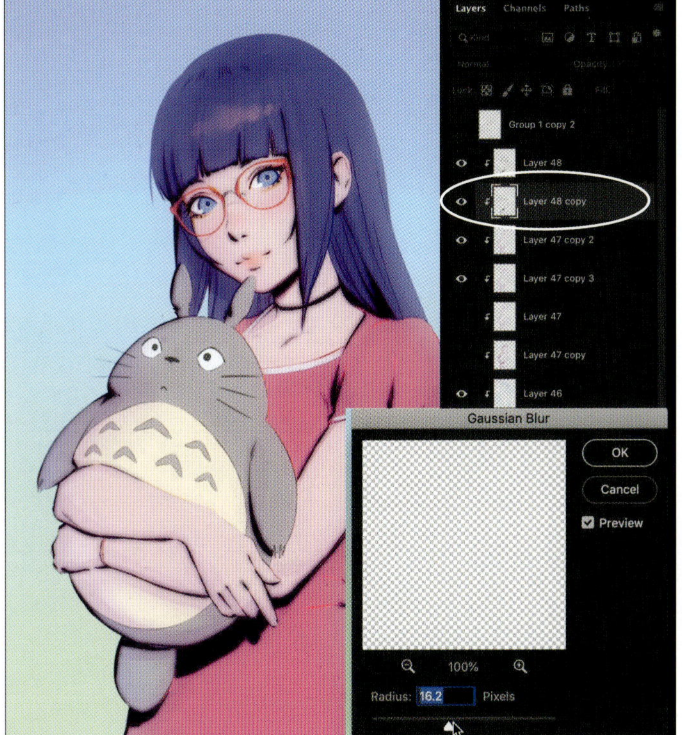

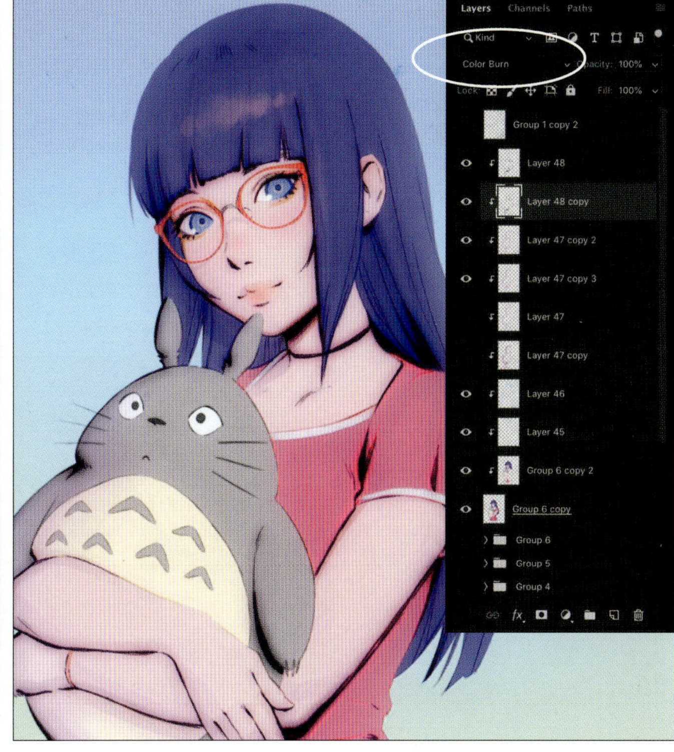

9 Generate a stronger sense of shadow bloom.

I copy my new shadow layer, apply Gaussian Blur to it and change the layer blending mode to Color Burn. This generates more shadow bloom in the piece. I did the same with the initial line-art layers earlier, but the effects weren't as noticeable as they are here.

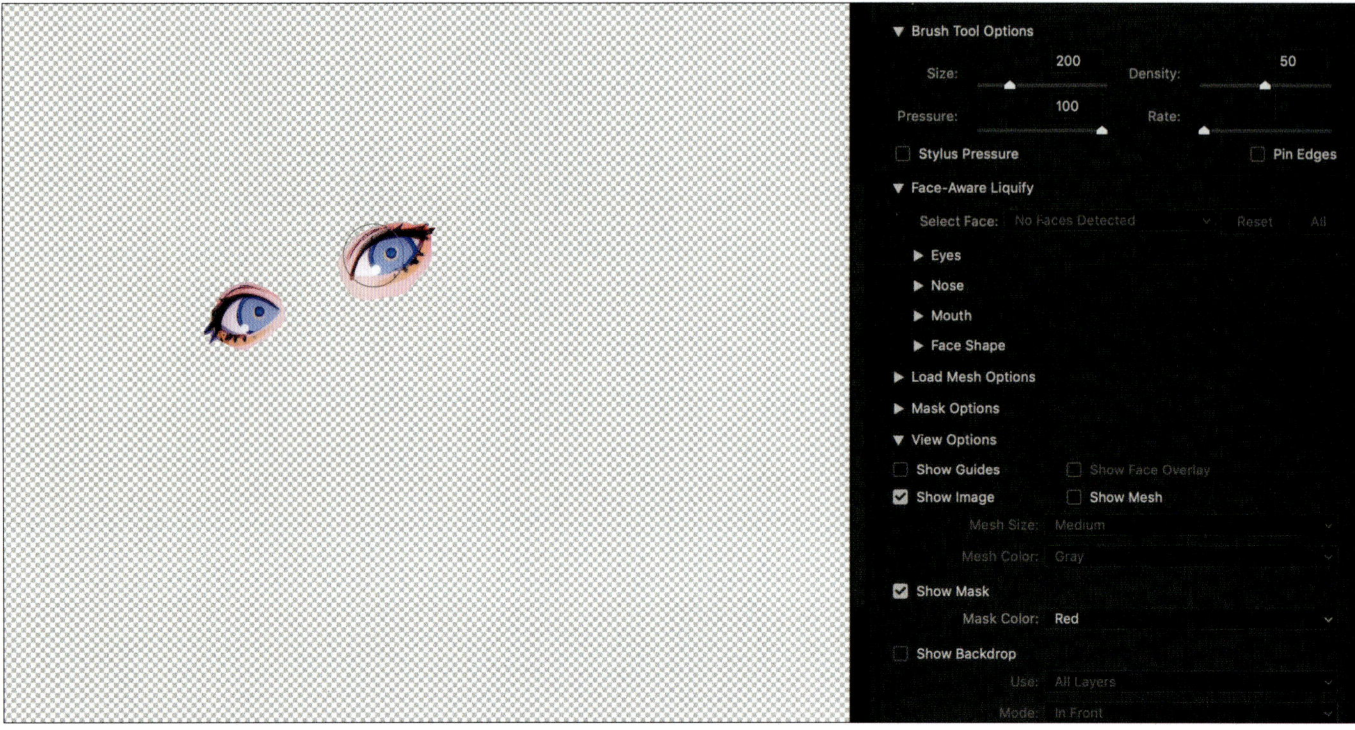

10 Use the Liquify tool to achieve the right eye shape.

I use the Lasso tool to quickly select the eyes again, before cutting and pasting them onto a new layer. Then I use the Liquify tool to edit their shape until I'm happy with their appearance. I usually spend a lot of time fine-tuning the face on every portrait piece I paint.

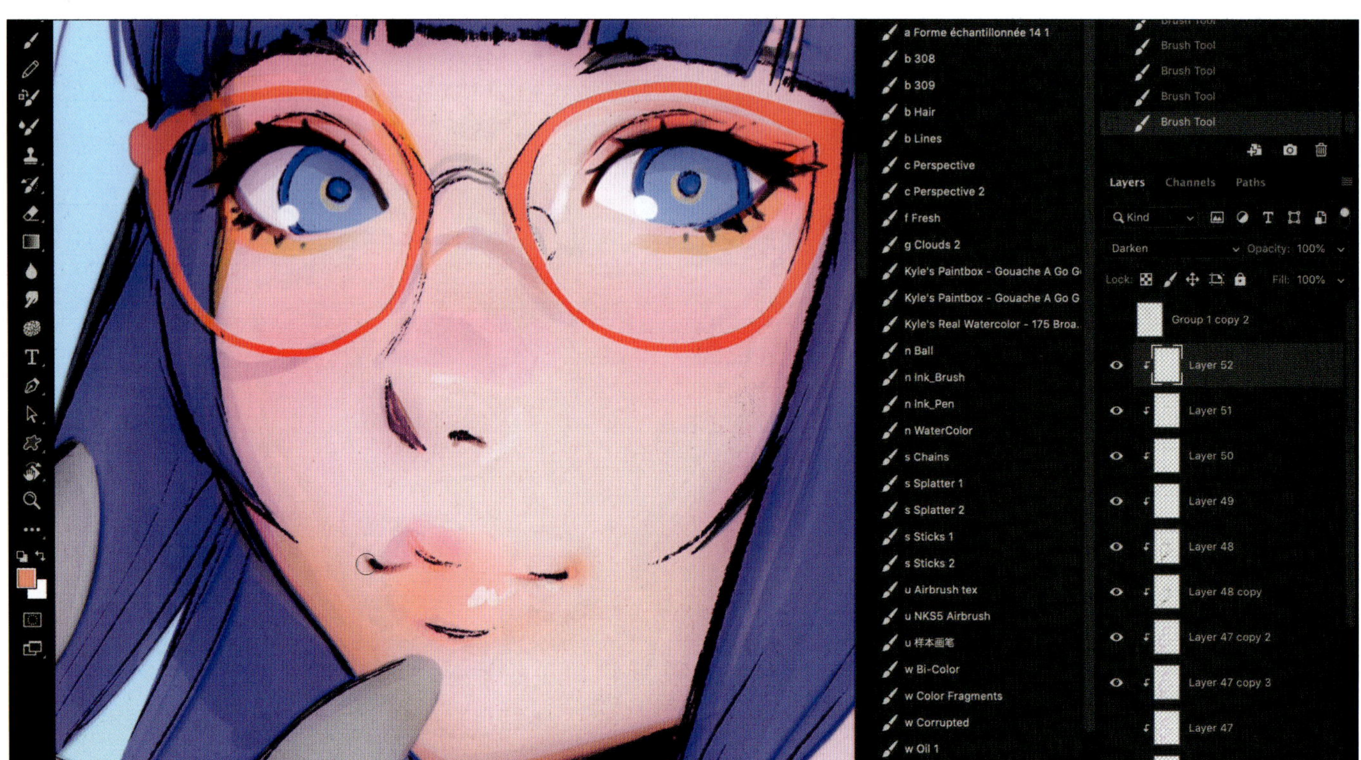

11 Bring in more details using Lighten and Darken layers.

During this stage, I add details (mostly to the face) using a lot of Darken blending layers, rather than painting over the dark part of the piece. I also do the same with Lighten layers as well, which enables you to partially see the layers underneath. For me, this is the fun part of the process!

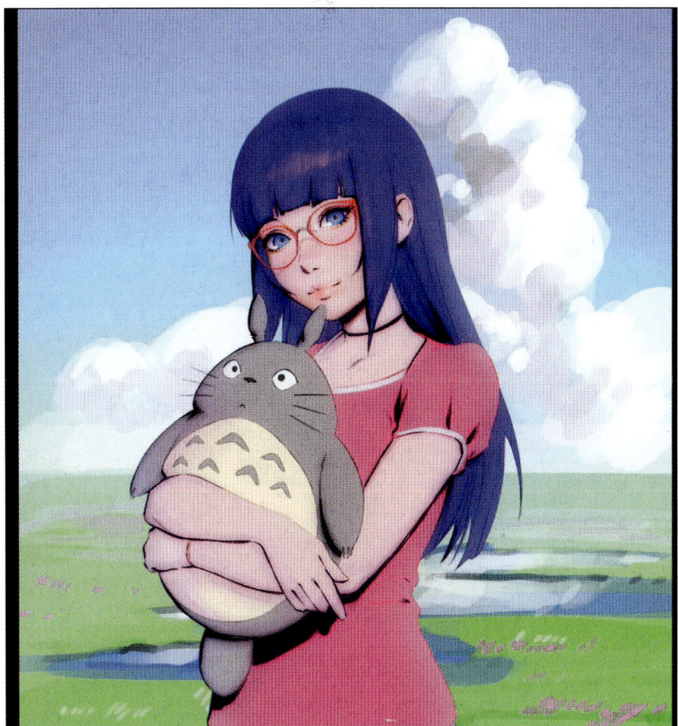

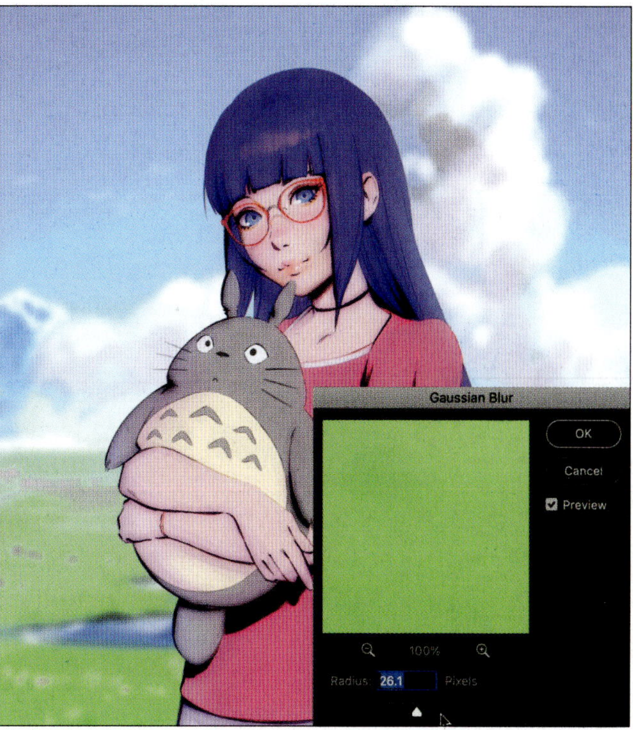

12 **Paint and enhance the background.**
I roughly paint in the background. I then copy it, blur it, and change the blending mode of the blurred layer to Lighten, which generates a depth of field effect while keeping the details visible. I then create a Color Dodge layer and generate some hazy bloom effects with the Air Brush.

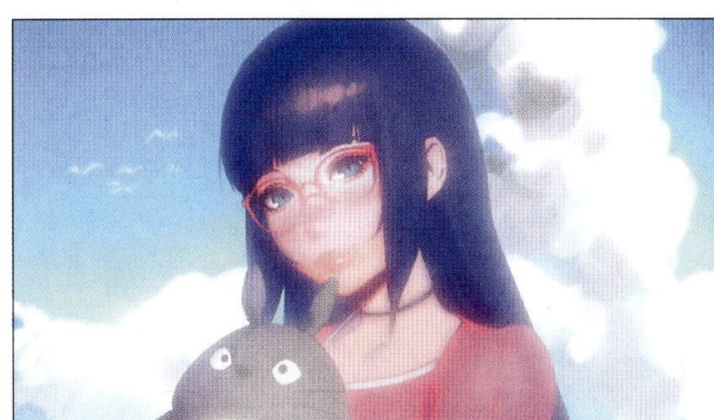

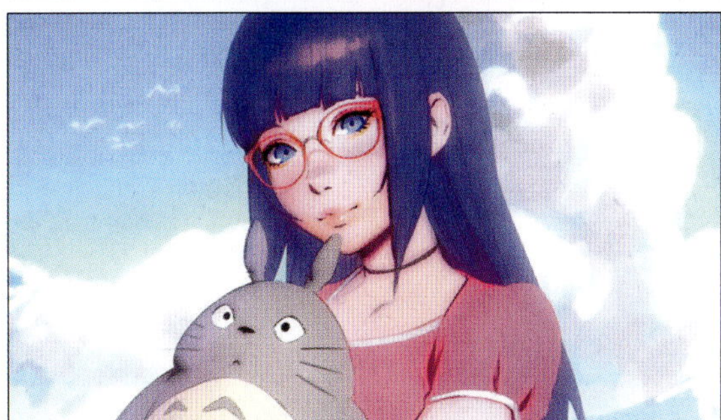

13 **Push the bloom effect.**
To reduce the contrast of the ink shadows, I add more red with a Lighten layer. I now copy the whole character layer (clipping it to the main layer), blur it, Lighten it, and erase the parts where I want the details to be still visible. Some color corrections with the Curves and Selective Color tools and I'm finished . . .. or am I?

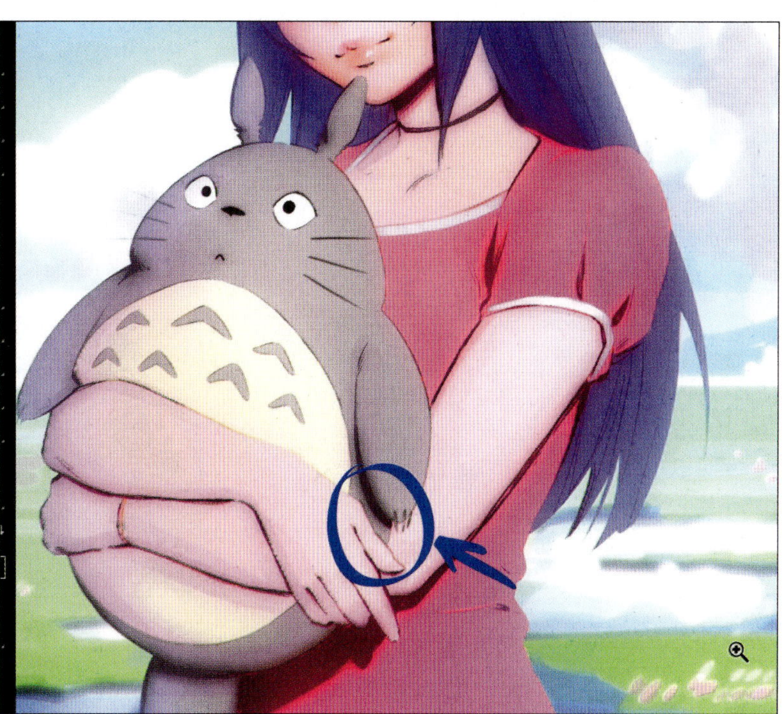

14 **Spot and fix last-minute errors.**
Soon after I start to write this workshop, I notice one more mistake. The left part of Totoro's body is on top of the girl's left hand, which would be physically impossible. I need to fix this ASAP because I've already sent the *ImagineFX* team the final high-res file. Phew, that was too close for comfort!

Photoshop

PAINT A FANTASY MANGA PORTRAIT

Asia Ladowska puts aside her ink pens and markers, and embraces the digital painting process of a soft and colorful manga character.

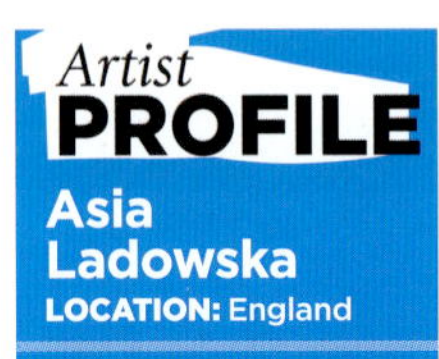

Asia Ladowska
LOCATION: England

The Polish artist and Instagram art ambassador is also the author of the book *Sketch with Asia*. *www.ladowska.com*

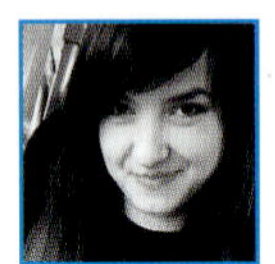

For this workshop, I'm painting a beautiful manga character. My go-to tools are usually traditional media. I'm most comfortable working with ink pens, pencils, and markers, so I'm learning a lot when I'm painting with digital tools.

I have no idea what the end result will look like, so I'll make sure to share in this workshop every important step and my thinking process, as well as why I make certain decisions that affect the final appearance of the character.

While painting color concepts and experimenting with different palettes in the sketching phase, I was listening to music, and believe it or not, the final colors of this illustration were inspired by a song. I heard the line, "Day gives way to night," and that's when the deep red and blue sparkled in my mind. If not for the song and the feedback from *ImagineFX* I'm sure the girl's hair would have ended up being pastel pink and blue (like the hair of most of my characters that I've painted digitally). It's exciting to experiment with colors that I've never used together before.

So, prepare to meet Sunset, a happy girl that's winking at you from my favorite art magazine!

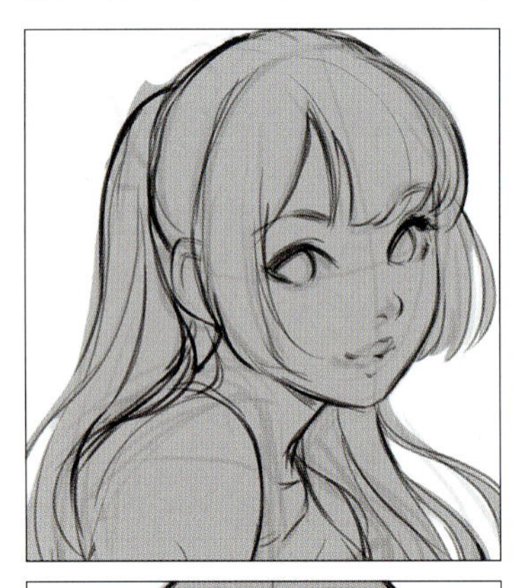
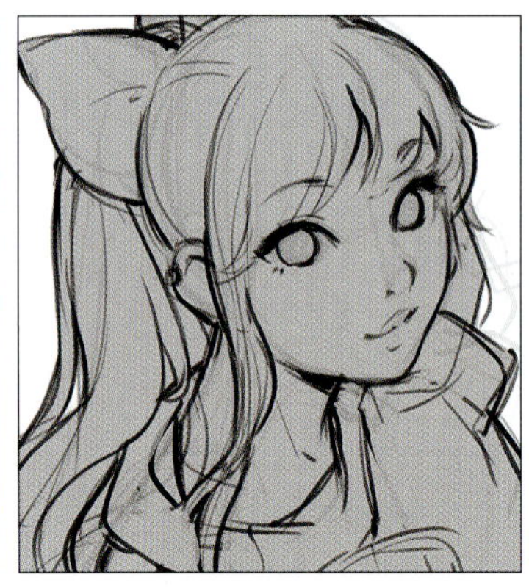
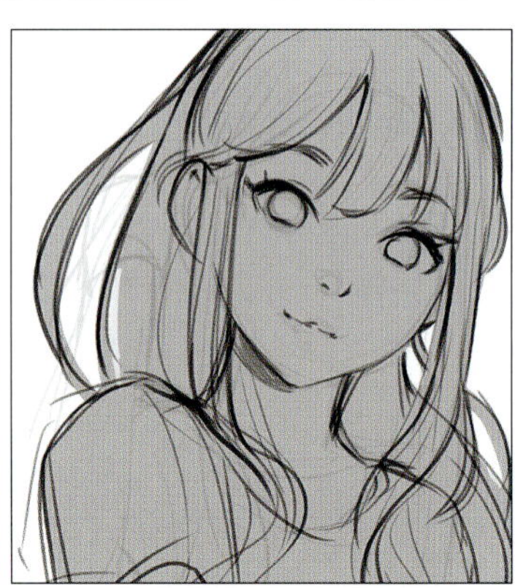
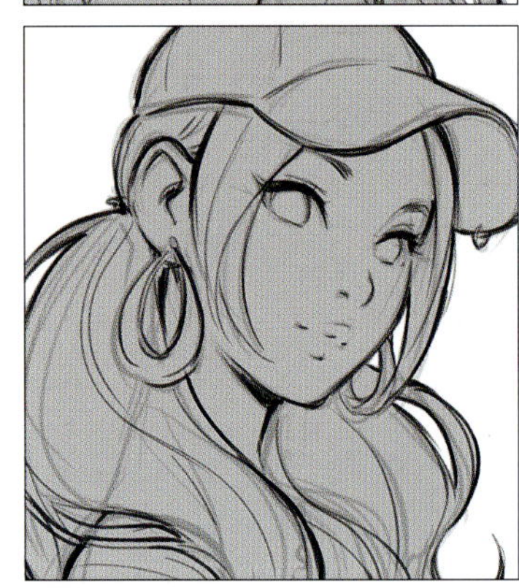
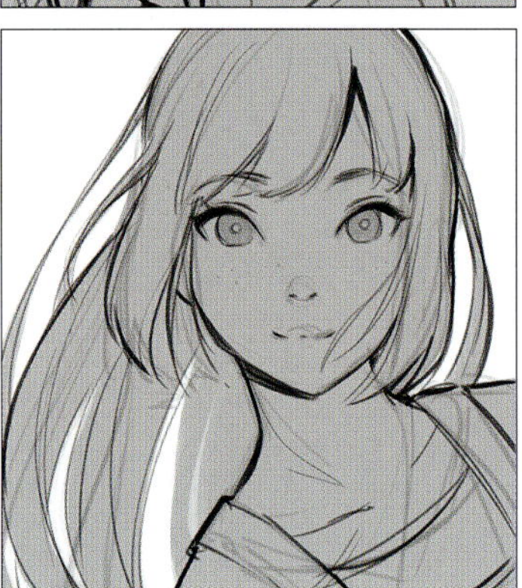
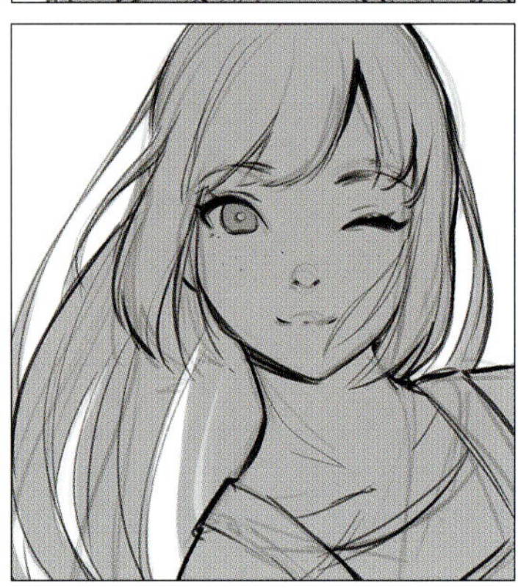

1 Generate concept sketches.

The brief I receive is pretty straightforward, with a lot of freedom for experimenting. I start by sketching some close-up shots of a woman in her twenties, making sure she's looking at the viewer and smiling. I always make the expression of the character I draw myself, so the sketching process has left me in a really good mood!

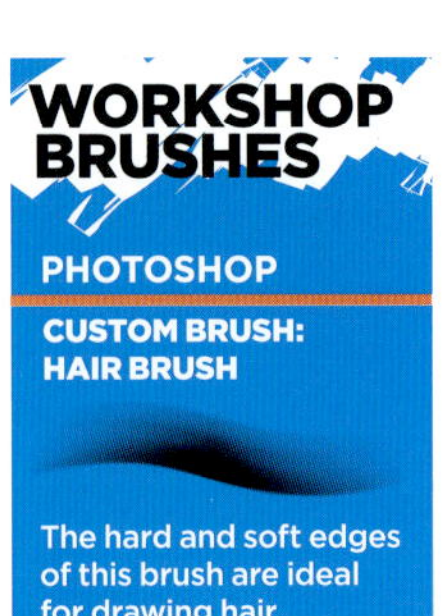

PHOTOSHOP

CUSTOM BRUSH: HAIR BRUSH

The hard and soft edges of this brush are ideal for drawing hair.

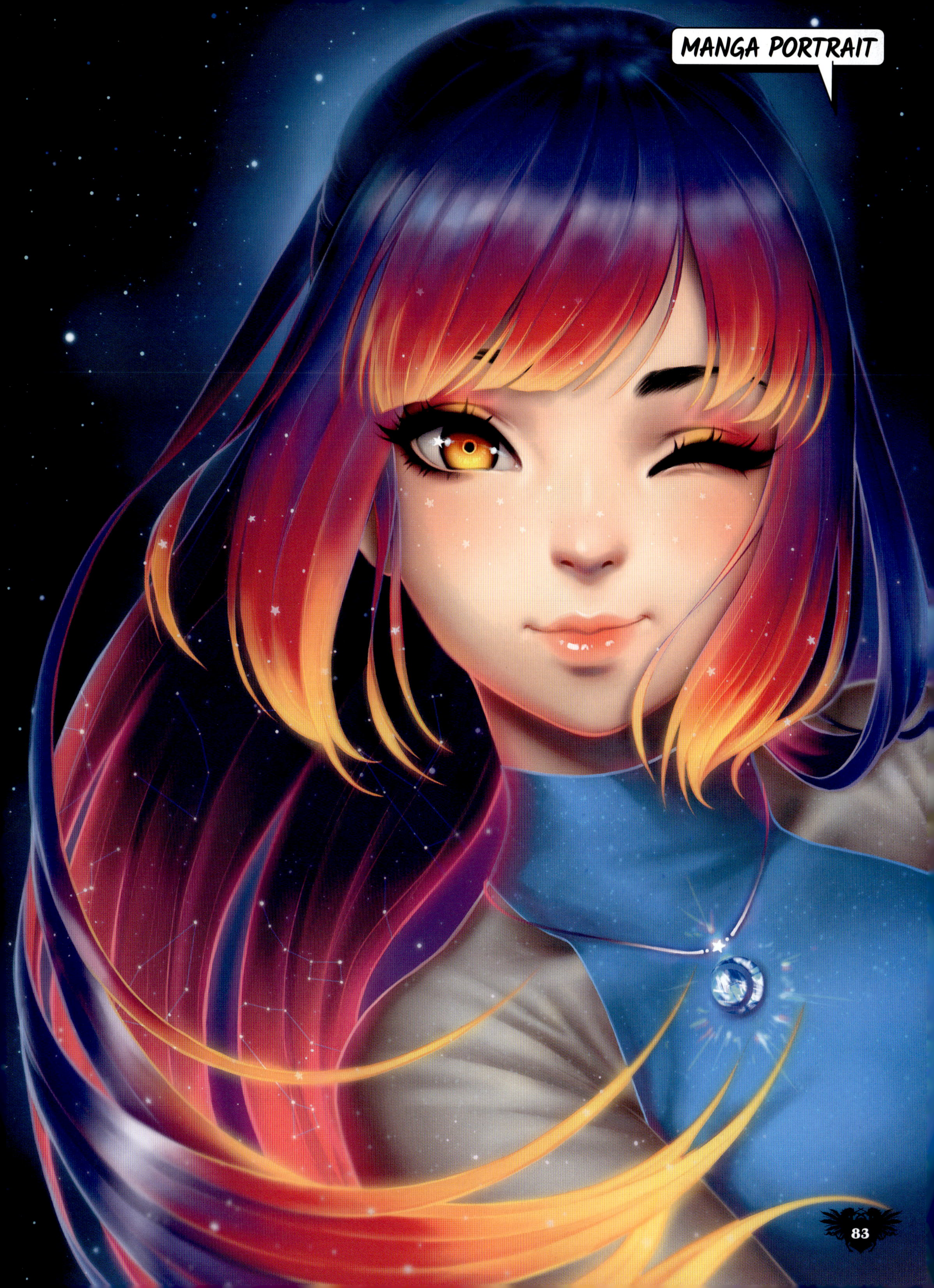
MANGA PORTRAIT

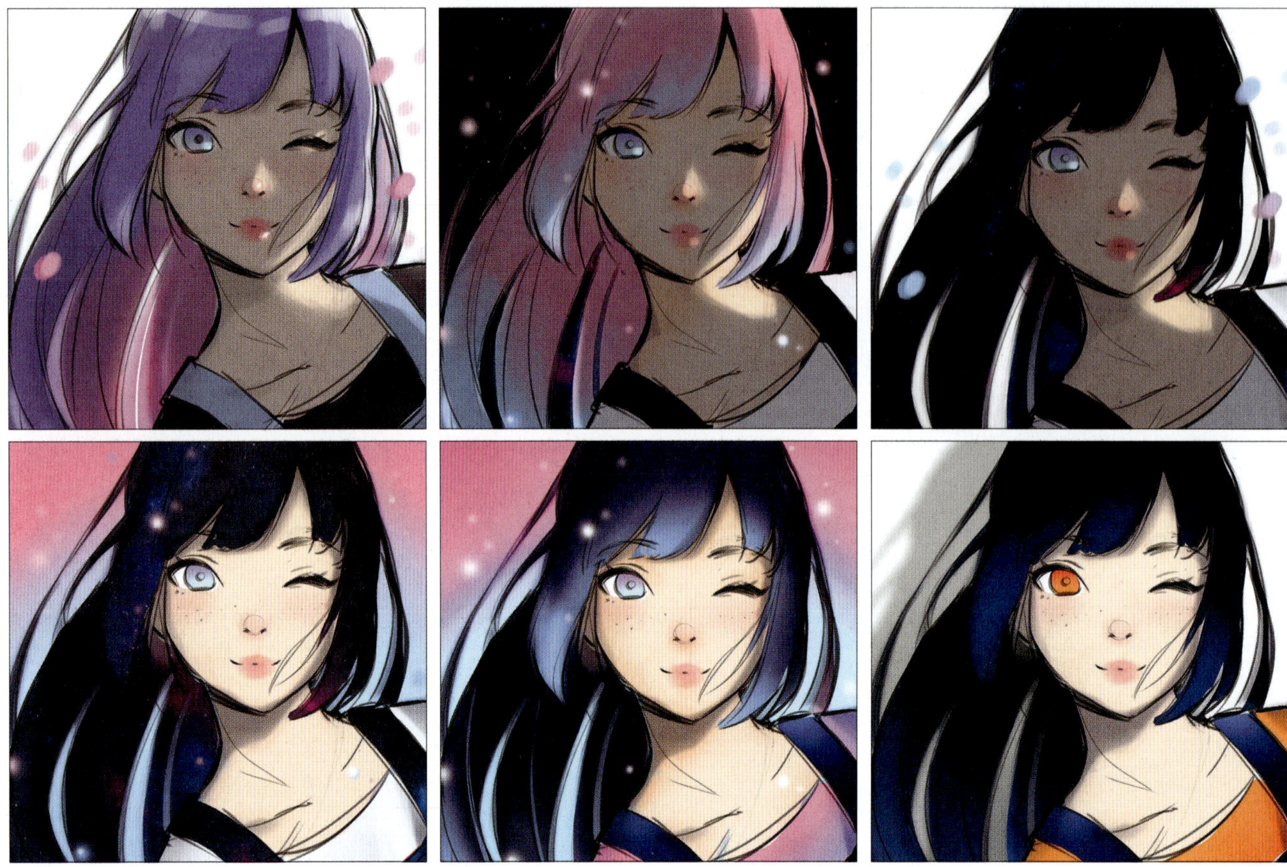

2 Apply color tests to the chosen sketch concept.

I introduce color to one of the concepts that's been chosen. Although I'm trying to be creative with the palette, and despite the brief saying "No pink," I'm sneakily trying to introduce pink combined with blue, two different light sources, and some space textures.

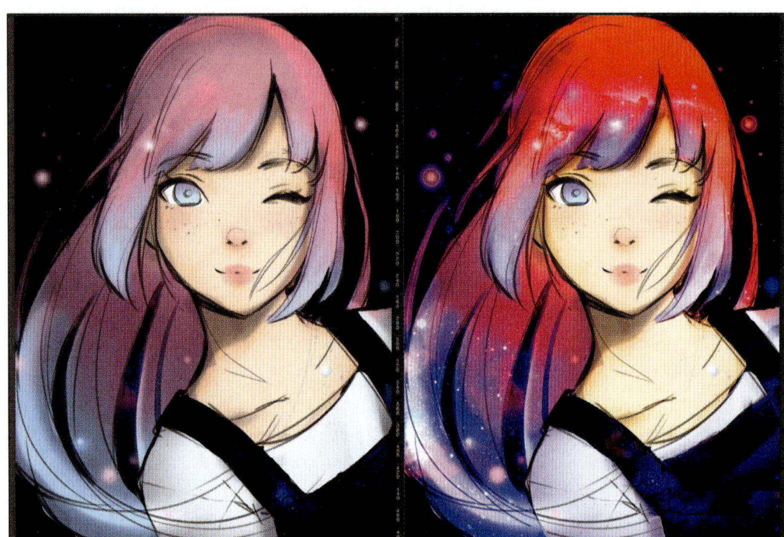

3 Act on the first round of feedback.

The scary moment is here! I receive my first feedback on the color sketches that I've sent in. It's also my first experience of having someone edit my color sketches and say what needs adjusting. The *ImagineFX* team ask me to change the pink to a more red-looking hue, add stars in the hair, and give the girl a necklace. I'm panicking just a little right now. Does this mean no more pink . . . ?

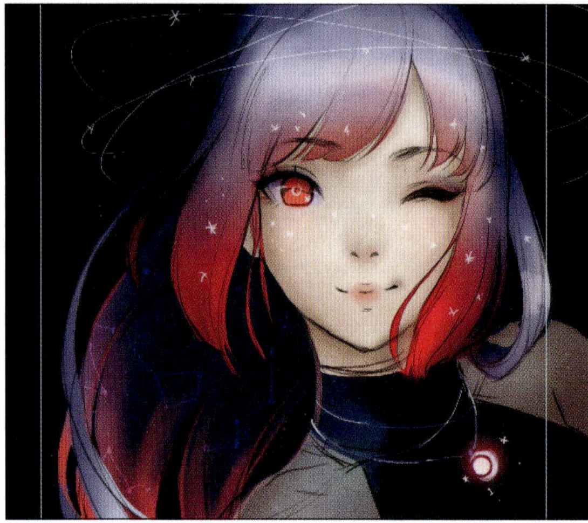

4 Forget about the pink.

I start over with new colors and a new concept for the clothes. I wasn't really happy about the request to remove the pink, but I know that I can still make this work. I paint on a larger canvas now, with extra space around the character and guides that indicate the actual crop of the cover image. I'm listening to music that keeps me relaxed and, surprisingly, also brings new color ideas!

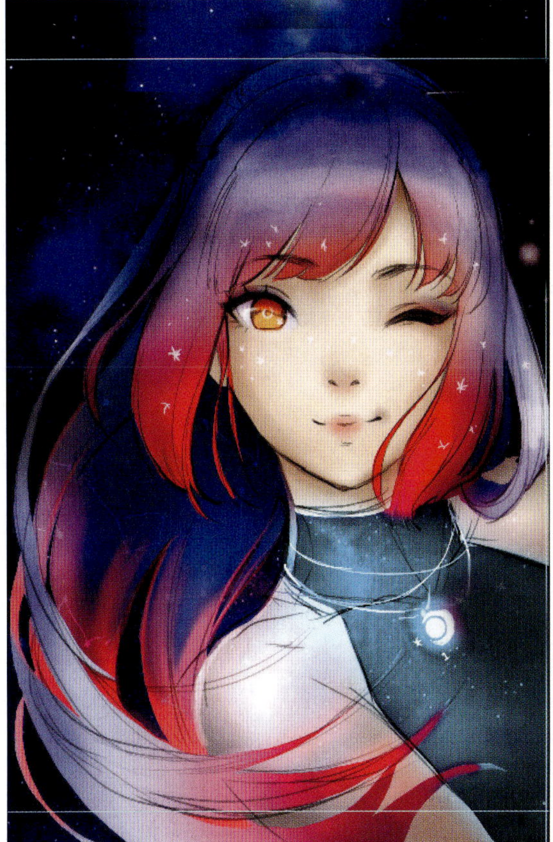

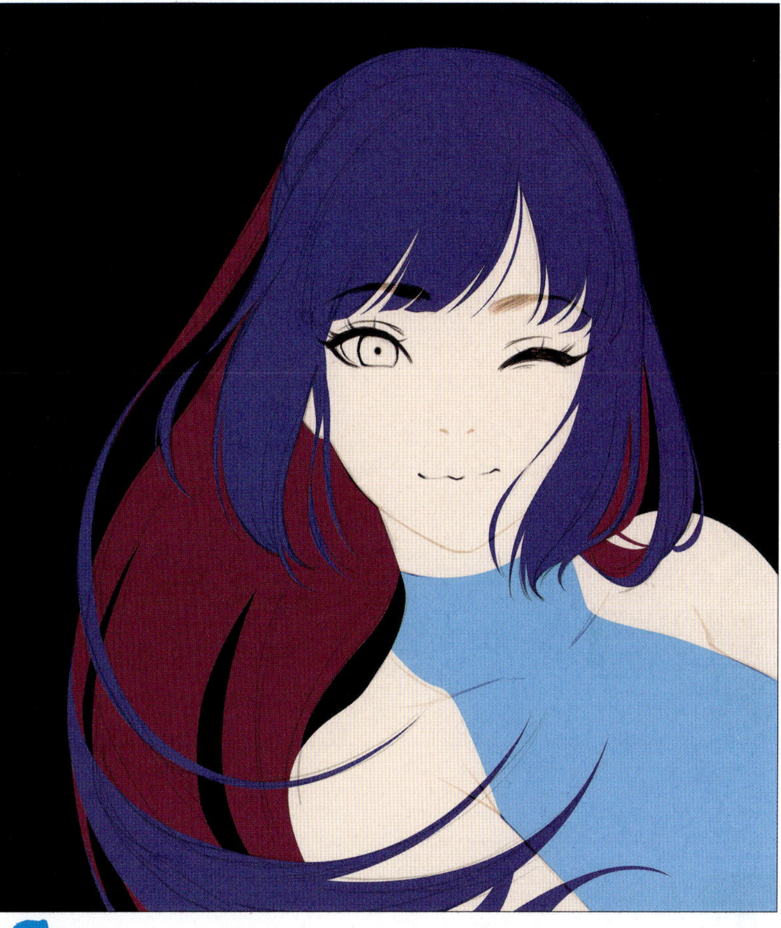

5 Get more feedback.

The new concept worked for *ImagineFX*; however, I'm asked to make some more changes. Because the painting was looking a little too dark, the team suggests brightening the dress and background, and introducing some yellow highlights in the eye. Sure! I'm much more confident on how to take the painting further now.

6 Make selections to separate out elements.

Making selections is a long and tedious process, but it's worth the effort. Some artists just paint on one or more layers, but I like to keep everything editable and easy to select. So for each element, like the skin, the hair at the front, hair at the back, and the dress, I make flat selections with the Pen tool, all on separate layers.

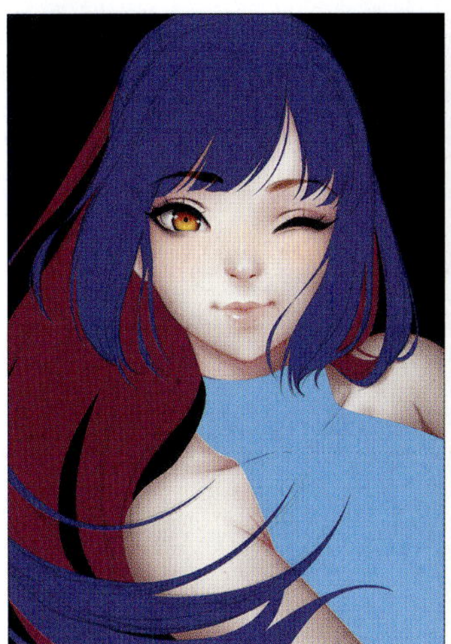

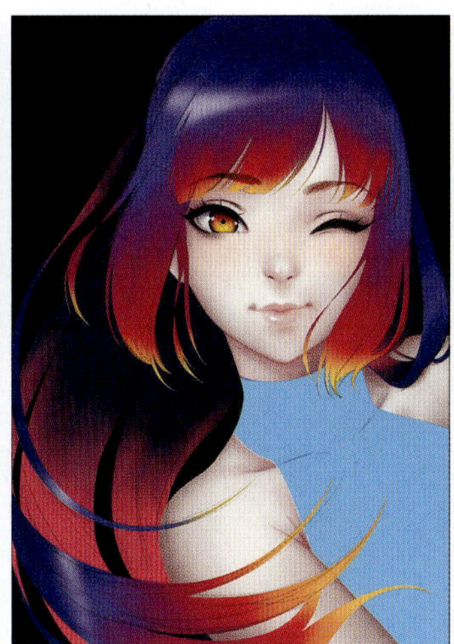

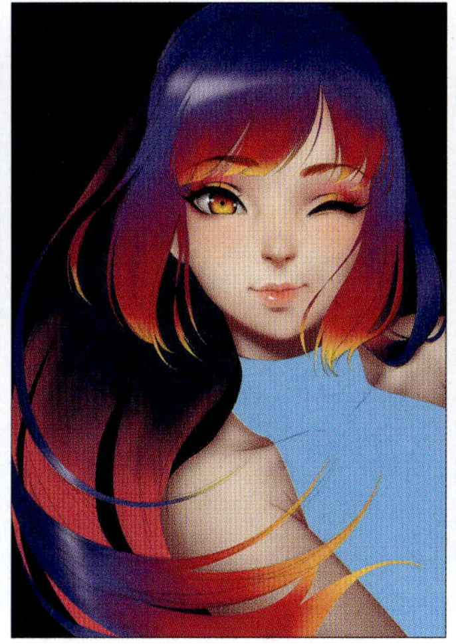

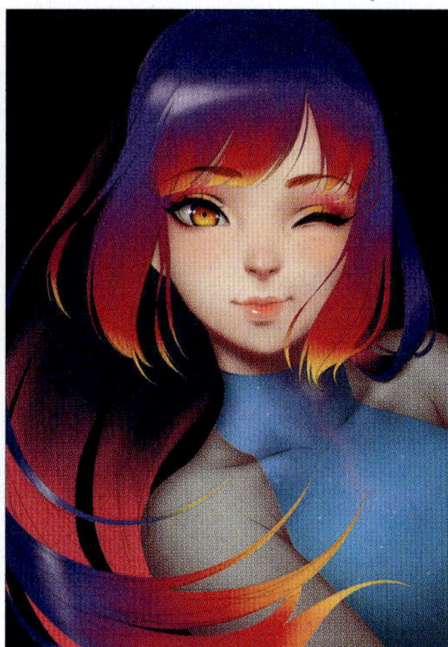

7 Paint basic colors and shade.

Once I've made a selection, I usually just lock the Transparency or create a clipping mask to the exact shape layer and then start painting. I'm adding basic colors that I want to use as a reference and then some simple shading to all of the character's elements, such as her skin or dress. This stage is more about finding the right colors than trying to make everything look perfect.

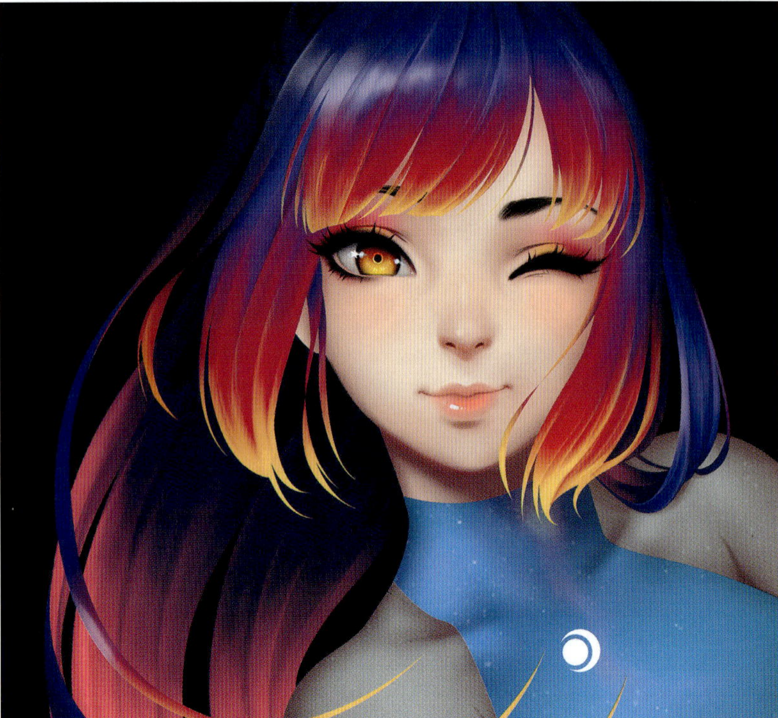

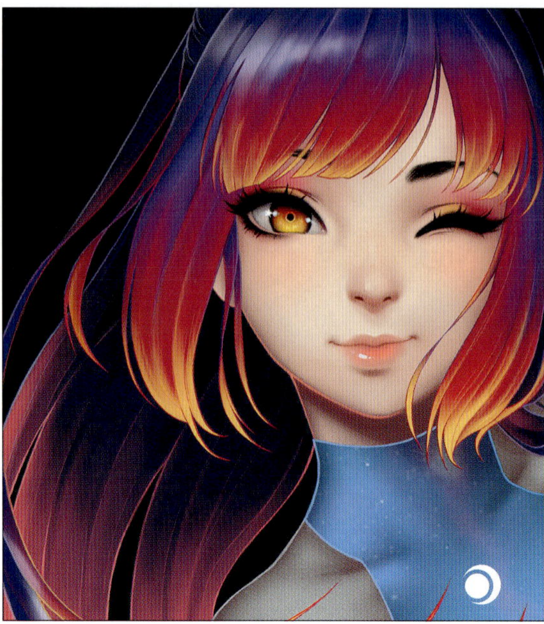

8 Paint hair texture.

Using the basic colors of the hair in the previous step, I paint up and down with my custom Hair Brush to make the strands look more like hair. As simple as it sounds, however, it takes me a few hours to paint in all those strands!

9 Create line art.

I think that a key characteristic for manga-style art is line art, so I always add it into my work at some point. Black lines would make the painting look too harsh, so I use colors that I've swatched from various places in the painting. To change the color I initially picked, I can always lock the pixels of the layer and try different ones, so there's no need to spend more time making selections.

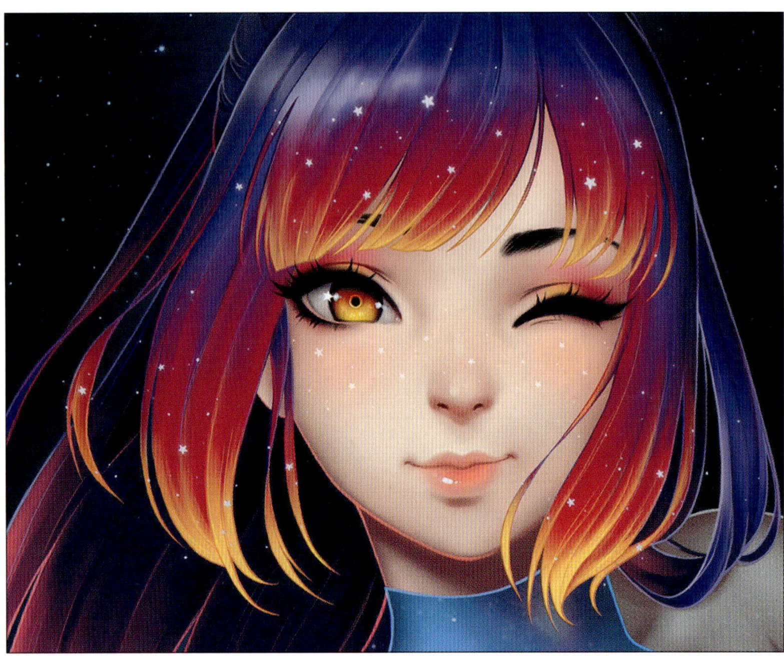

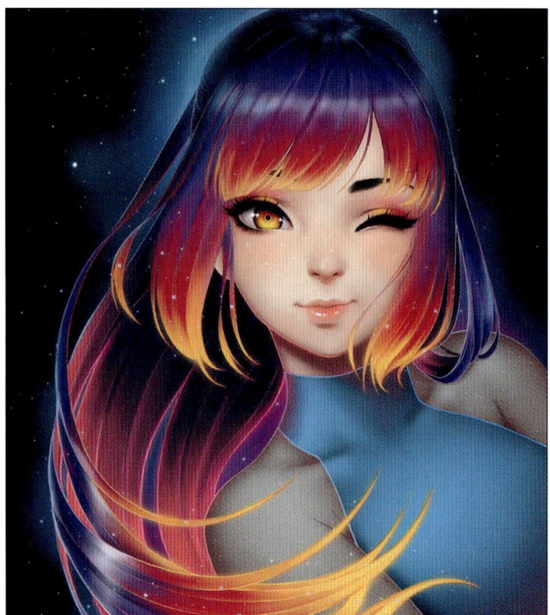

10 Paint the stars.

For stars in the background I use the brush that can be downloaded from Adobe's Creative Cloud. From the Brushes menu, click Get More Brushes. It's one of Kyle's Spatter brushes pack, called Dots 1. I adjust the Spacing and Size Jitter, add in the stars, then apply the Blur and Overlay filters, Now the stars look perfect. I paint the stars on the character's face and hair on a separate layer by hand.

11 Soften the image.

In my opinion this phase drastically changes the illustration. I no longer stick to selections, but create a new group above everything and then paint. I use a soft Round brush to soften selected edges, such as the yellow ends of the woman's hair with a color picked from exactly the same place. This makes them look like they're glowing.

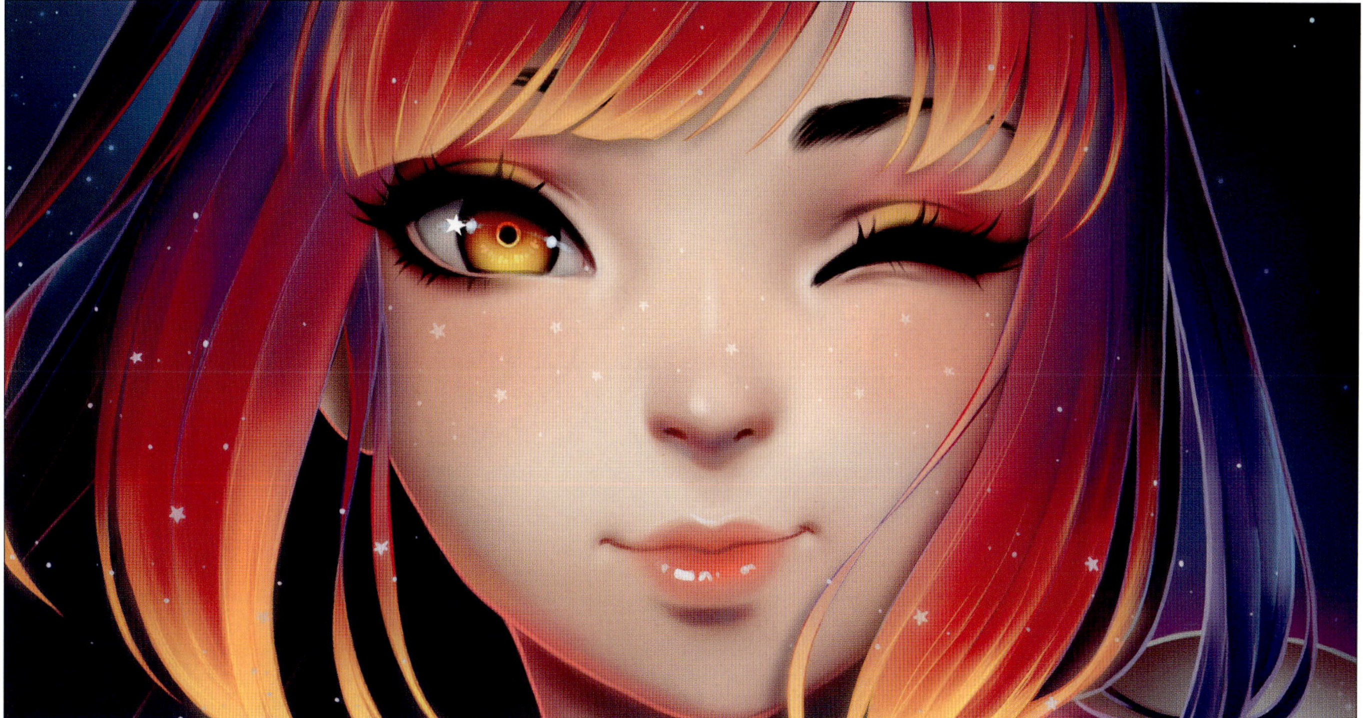

12 Introduce reflective light on the face.

With such a colorful and strong environment, glowing hair, and lots of stars, Sunset's face was looking a little flat and not part of the environment. I need to remedy this. On a Multiply layer, I add some shadows to make her look more three-dimensional, and on another one set to Normal I apply some pink and yellow on the jawline and blue on the neck, because those colors would have an effect on the shadows.

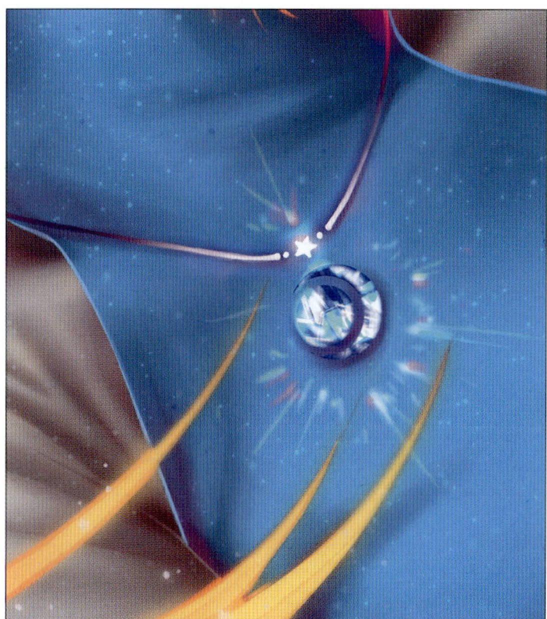

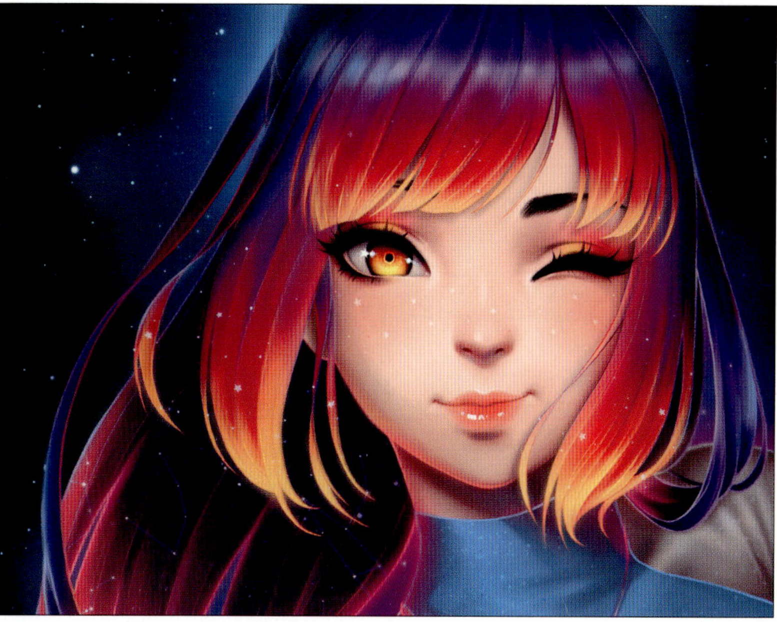

13 Design a crystal necklace.

It's time for detailing. The sleeves of Sunset's dress are missing crease lines, the dress itself receives a few brushstrokes, and then I add a diamond necklace in the shape of the sun and moon to complement her look.
I also add a few constellations to her hair to make her look even more magical.

14 Apply the finishing touches.

To finish off, my process is almost always the same. I add a Color Balance filter layer with Midtones at +3, -3, and +3, respectively, to push the reds, pinks, and blues a little further. I also flatten all layers as a copy above everything and apply a Gaussian Blur filter to it. I erase the parts that I don't want blurred, and now Sunset looks much softer and finished. Even though her hair isn't pink, I'm pleased how this painting took me on a space journey beyond my usual art frontiers!

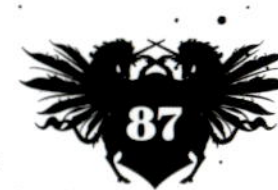

SketchUp & Photoshop

CREATE ANIME-STYLE SCENES

FeiGiap combines SketchUp's 3D-modeling tools with Photoshop coloring techniques to create an anime-style background illustration.

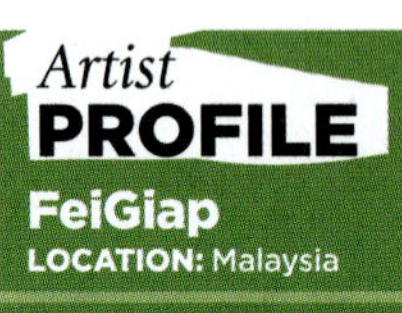

Artist PROFILE

FeiGiap

LOCATION: Malaysia

FeiGiap's the co-founder of Running Snail Studio and creative brand Loka Made. He's best known for his detailed anime-style illustration of Asian cityscapes.

https://www.deviantart.com/feigiap

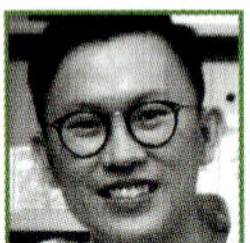

A small, cozy café in the middle of the town, surrounded by plants and trees—like a scene from a Studio Ghibli or Makoto Shinkai film. This is my initial idea as I plan an environment workshop. Here, I'll share how I use SketchUp's 3D-modeling tools to help me create an interesting background illustration. I always like to see buildings at a range of heights, with people having to use stairs to reach different levels. This makes the city look slightly different from our daily environment, which helps make it feel more interesting.

After gathering some related photo references, I'll start by sketching out the composition in Photoshop until I'm happy with the design of the scene. Then I'll move on to modeling in SketchUp. The program comes in handy when I want to draw slightly more complex buildings. It enables me to explore different camera angles and cast shadows accurately. I think it's easier to use compared to other 3D-modeling software. I build the main building structure in SketchUp and then output it as a clean line-art image.

My coloring technique is influenced by Japan 2D animation film backgrounds, like those seen in Studio Ghibli, Makoto Shinkai, and Hosoda Mamoru films. I love to study how they use color and capture light and a certain mood. In this workshop, I'll share some of my own coloring techniques and tips.

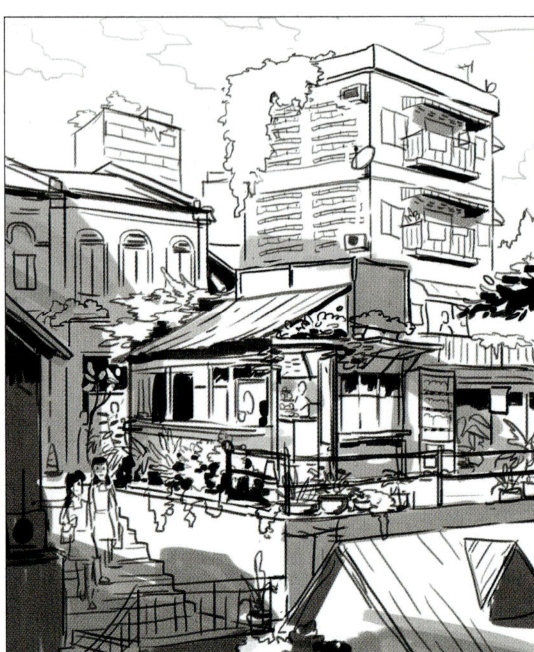

1 Make a composition sketch.

Before I start sketching I gather photo references of buildings and streets to make sure I understand the designs. I'm using my Sketch pen in Photoshop for my composition sketch. I usually keep the paper size small to avoid drawing too many details. The sketch helps me finalize the composition and plan my light and shadows.

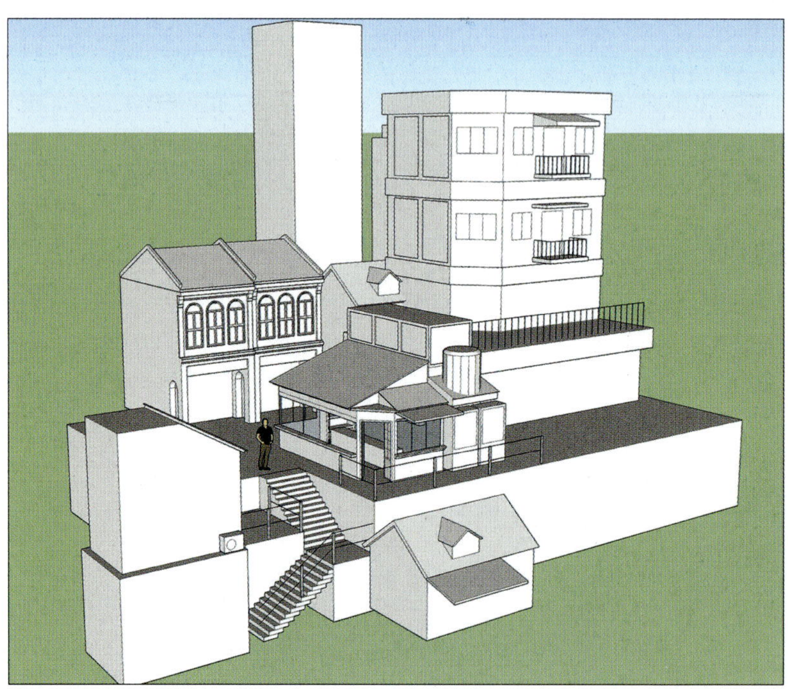

2 Model in SketchUp.

Instead of drawing the outlines in Photoshop, I'm using SketchUp to build the basic structure based on my composition sketch. Using 3D modeling can help me skip on the perspective construction process. The models I'm building here are basic, but clear enough to suggest the underlying forms of the buildings. Details such as textures and plants will be added later, during the coloring stage.

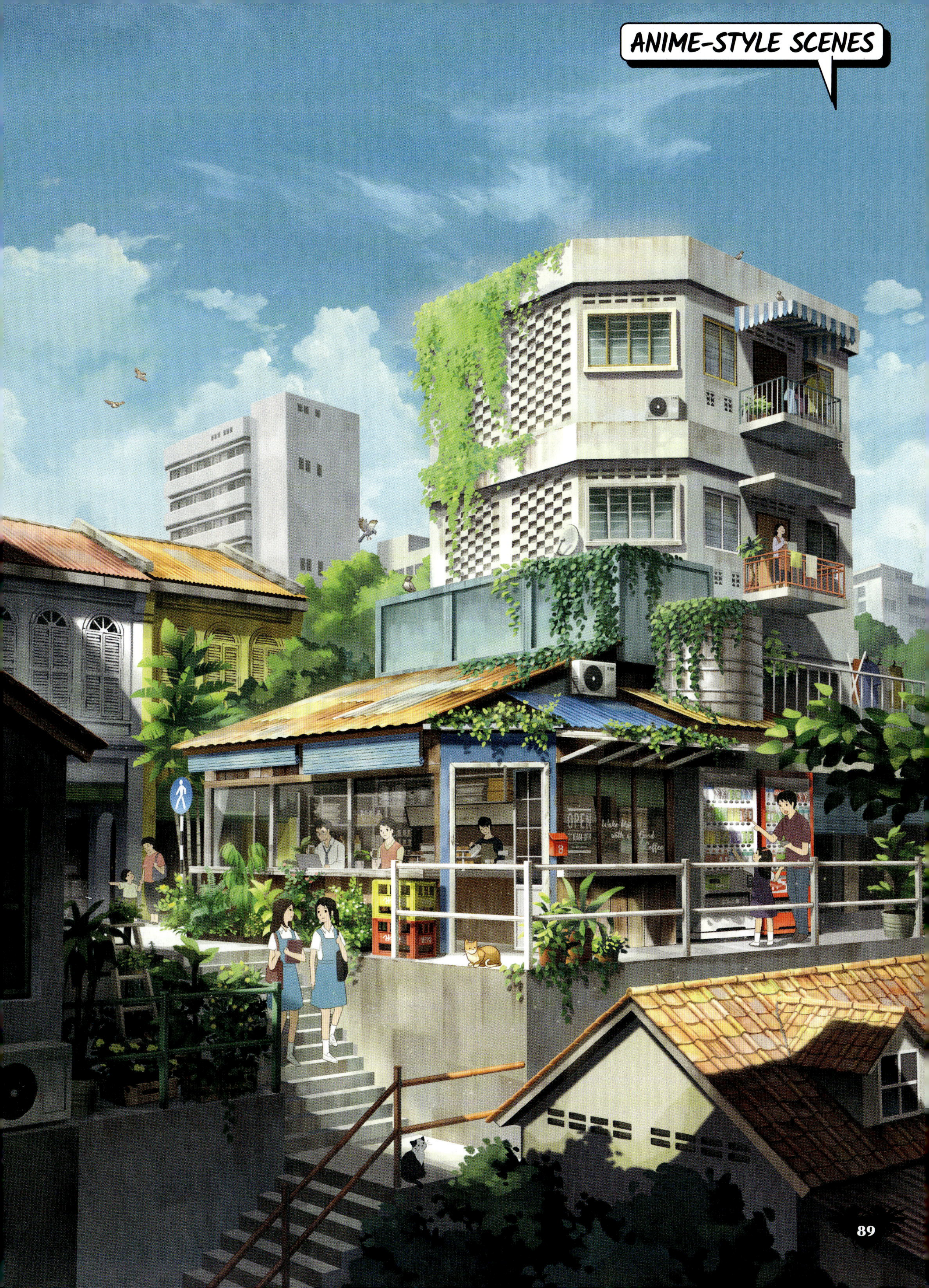
OPEN
8

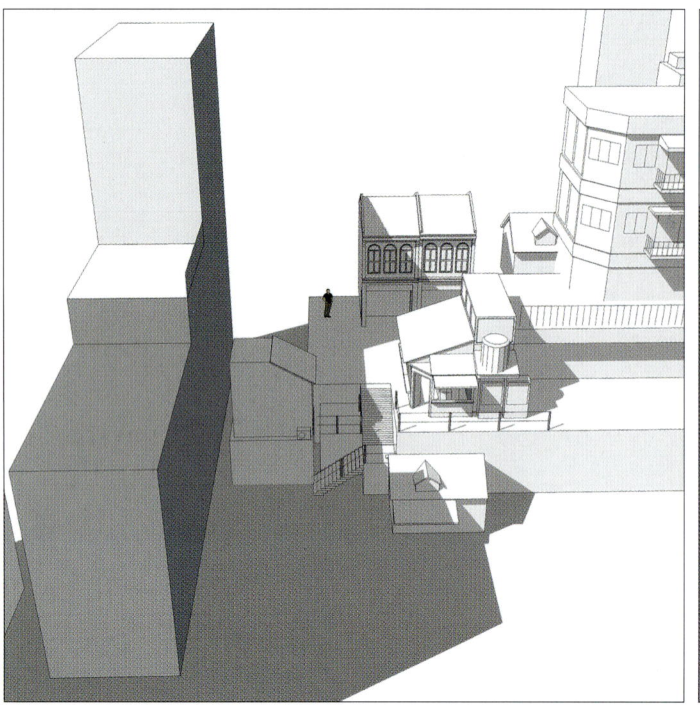

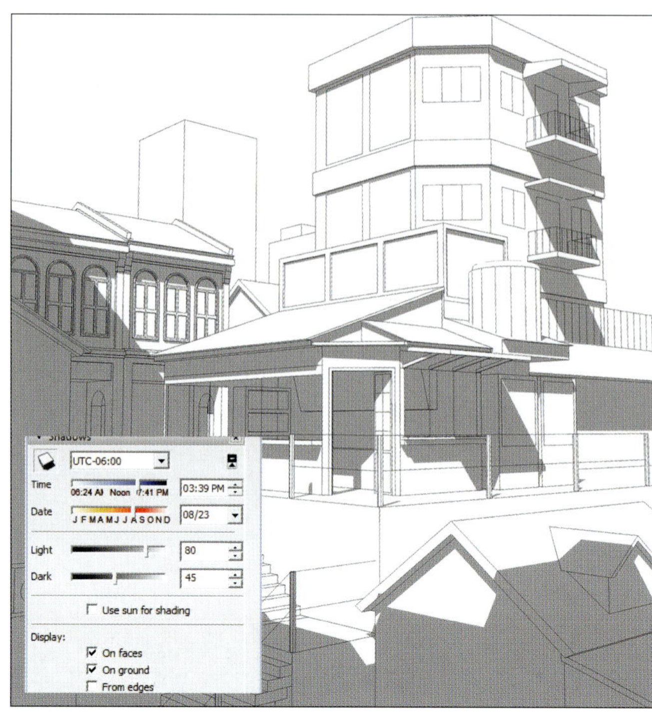

3 Cast shadows in SketchUp.

Another useful tool in SketchUp is the Shadow setting. It enables me to set different angles of light source, based on a particular timezone and time of day. To create a larger area of cast shadow, I build a high structure outside the camera and use this to cast my shadow. After this, I export the models as two different JPEGs: one with the shadow and another without.

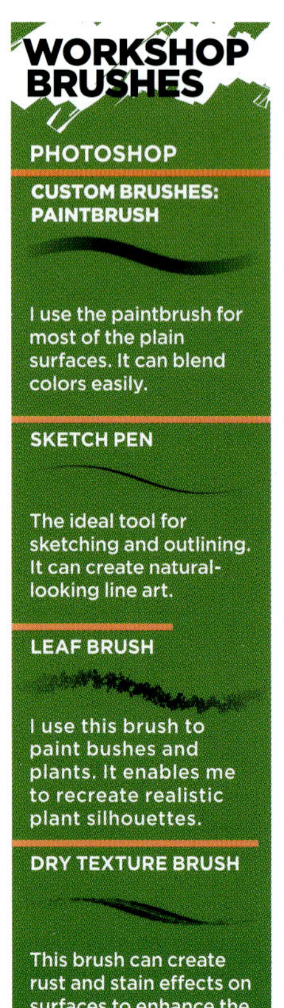

WORKSHOP BRUSHES

PHOTOSHOP

CUSTOM BRUSHES: PAINTBRUSH

I use the paintbrush for most of the plain surfaces. It can blend colors easily.

SKETCH PEN

The ideal tool for sketching and outlining. It can create natural-looking line art.

LEAF BRUSH

I use this brush to paint bushes and plants. It enables me to recreate realistic plant silhouettes.

DRY TEXTURE BRUSH

This brush can create rust and stain effects on surfaces to enhance the level of realism.

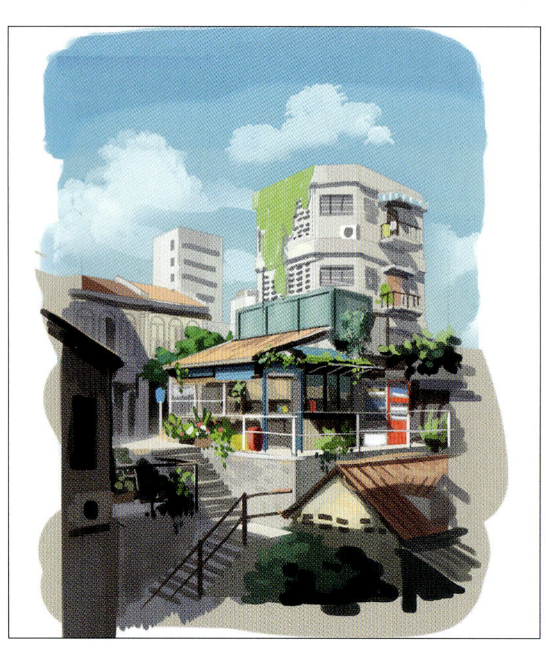

4 Color plan.

I open the modeling JPEG in Photoshop and start my color planning. Here I'll use an opaque paint-over method and again I'll work at a small size to avoid over-detailing. This stage is mainly about capturing the key colors of the background. I'll use warmer colors on light areas and cool colors on shadow areas. Tonal value is important if I'm to create an effective depth of field.

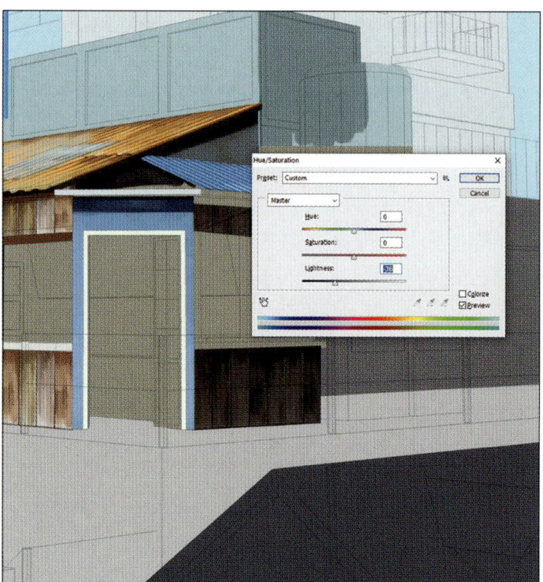

5 Generate surface textures.

I normally start my coloring on the focal point. I create plain surface textures such as wood or zinc that I can duplicate and mask on the target surface. Keep the original plain copy so that you can use it in the future. For the shadow area, I simply select the area and use Image>Adjustment>Hue/Saturation>Lightness to darken the tone. I then touch them up with a brush to make them look more natural.

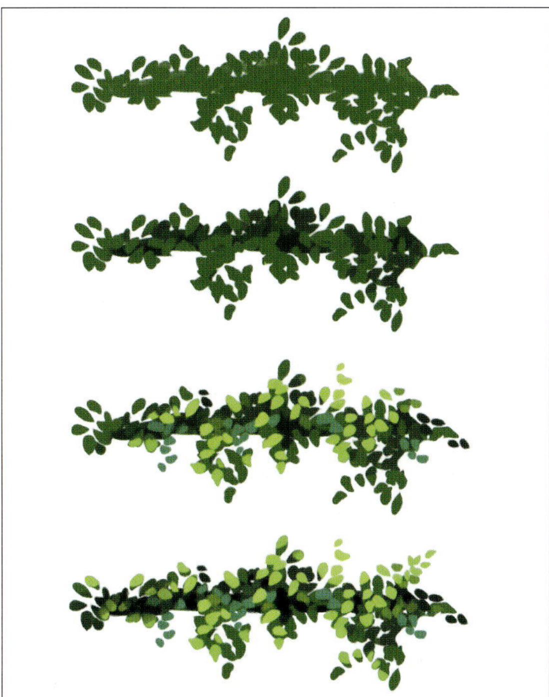

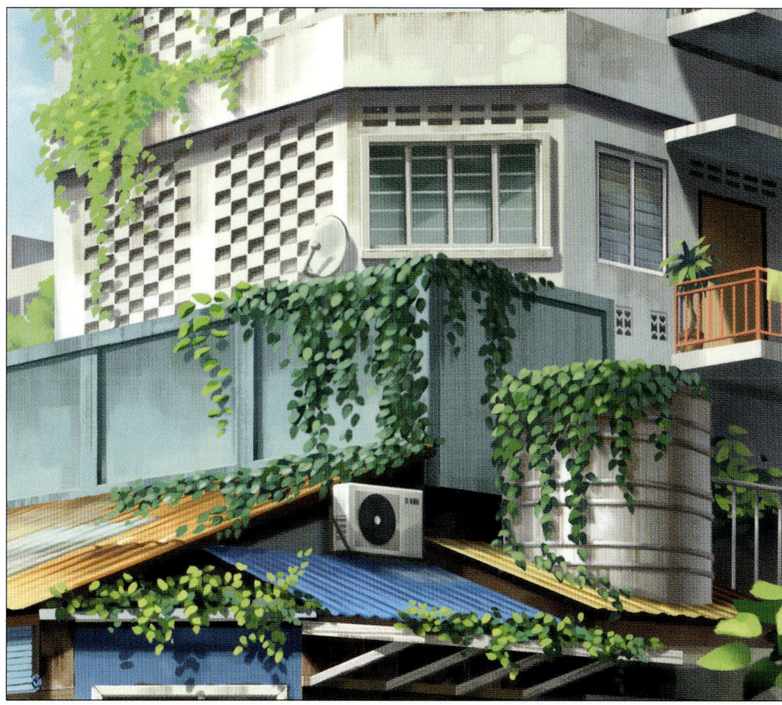

6 Paint overhanging foliage.

I want to depict the café surrounded by various plants, and my custom leaf brush tool comes in very handy for this step. I start to paint the silhouette of the foliage, then on a second layer I add a slightly darker tone and follow this with a lighter tone. Once I've achieved the basic form, I blend some parts to make it look less stiff, then paint some cast shadow between leaves so that they looks more natural.

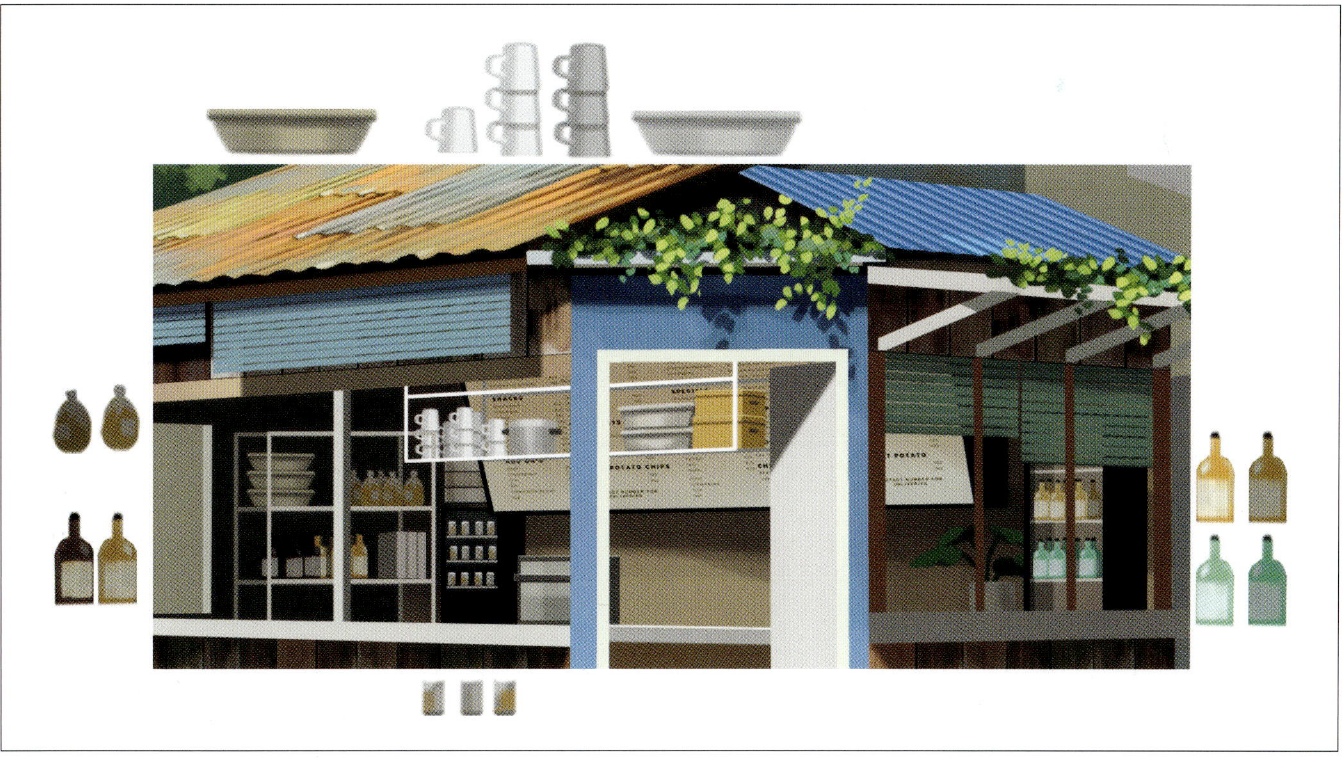

7 Populate the café's shelves with objects.

The café's interior needs to contain lots of different objects, so I create a few stock items such as mugs, drinks, and containers. Then I edit some of their colors to add variety. I place those objects on different cabinets and darken objects at the back of the café to create depth.

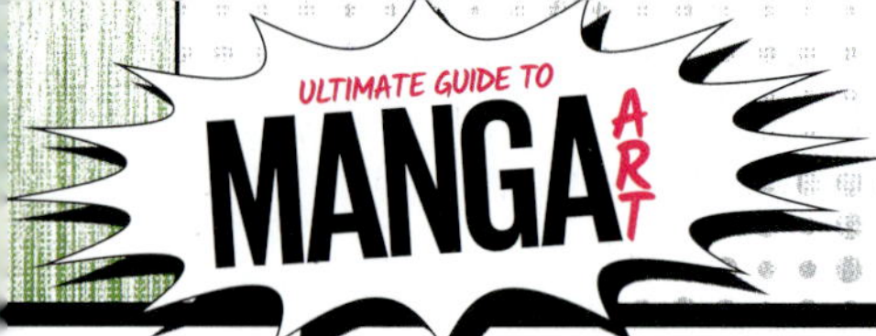

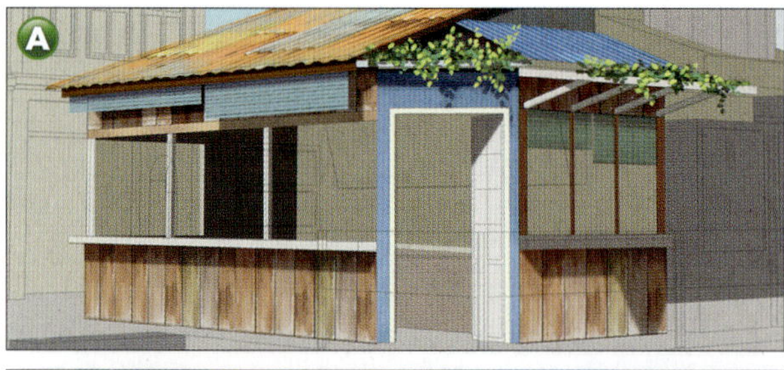

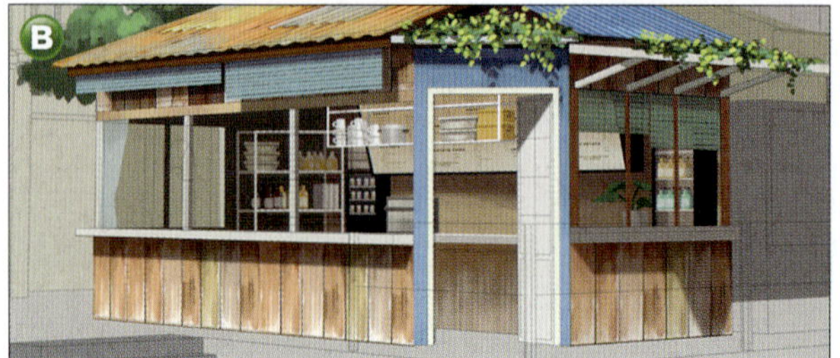

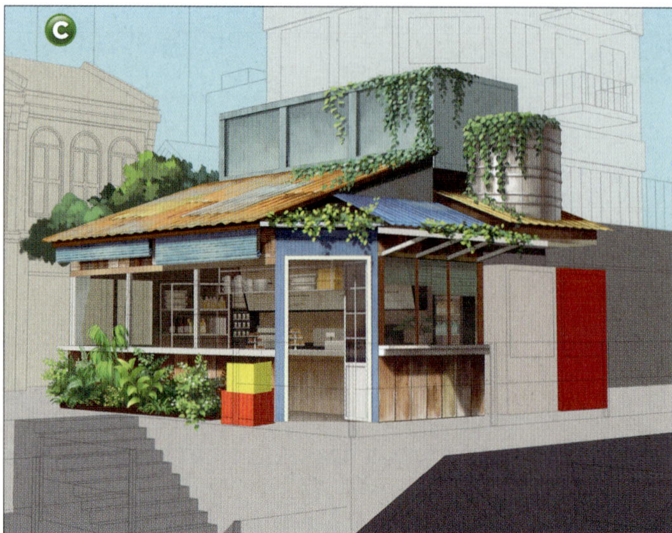

8 Detail the focal area.

I continue coloring the focal area, because the 3D outline is just the basic form **(A)**. During this stage, I refer to some photo references of café interiors so that I know what objects to add **(B)**. I also need to take care with the depth of the building. The light and shadow play an important role here, and I want to avoid the entrance and exit looking the same **(C)**. Once I'm happy with my progress here, I can continue with the rest of the background.

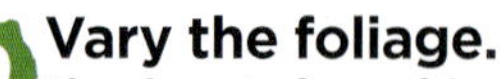

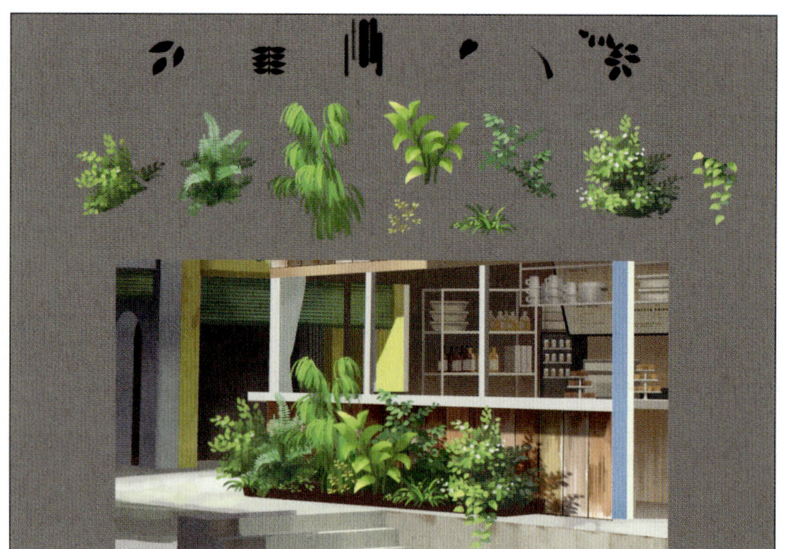

9 Vary the foliage.

The plants in front of the café are one of the most important elements in this drawing. I want them to make the building visually interesting and grab the viewer's attention, so their design needs to be more varied. I use different brushes for each of the plants to alter their leaf shapes, and adjust their color and tone slightly to highlight their differences.

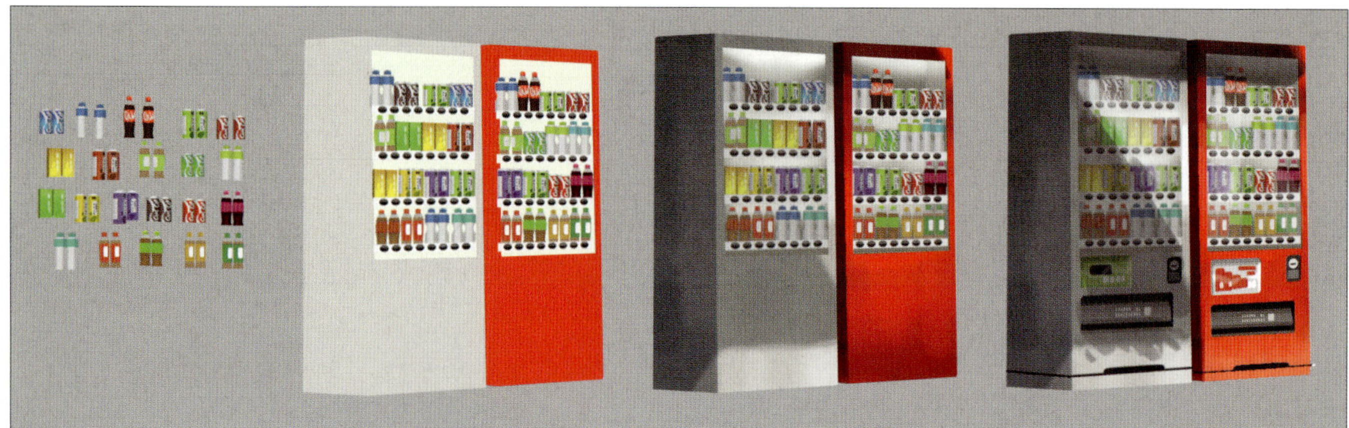

10 Fill up the vending machines and blend them into their surroundings.

One of the most challenging parts of this scene is painting the vending machines. I start by creating various can and bottle designs, and color them differently to suggest a range of drink flavors. Then I place them inside the vending machines. To create depth, I lighten the tone of the drinks and add a light effect inside the cabinet. The cast shadow on the two vending machines helps to blend them with the background.

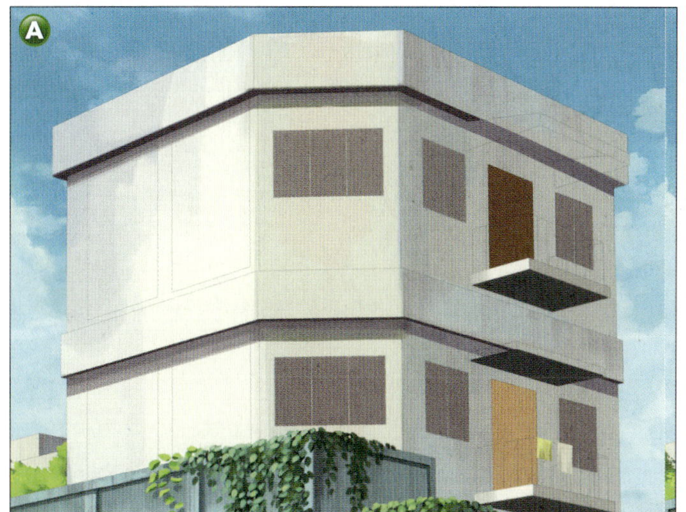

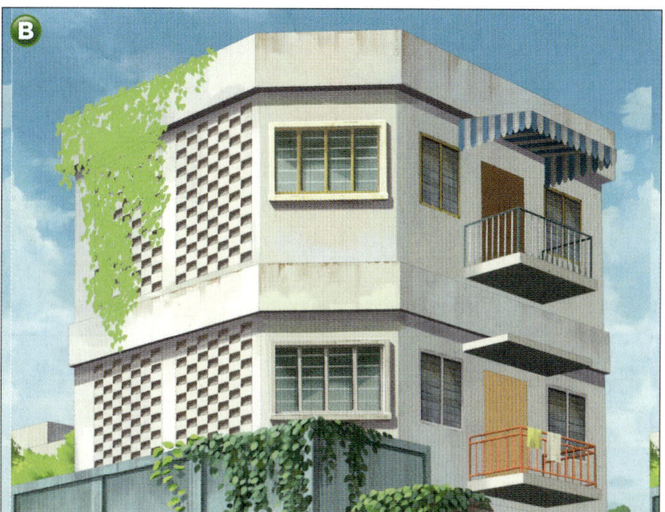

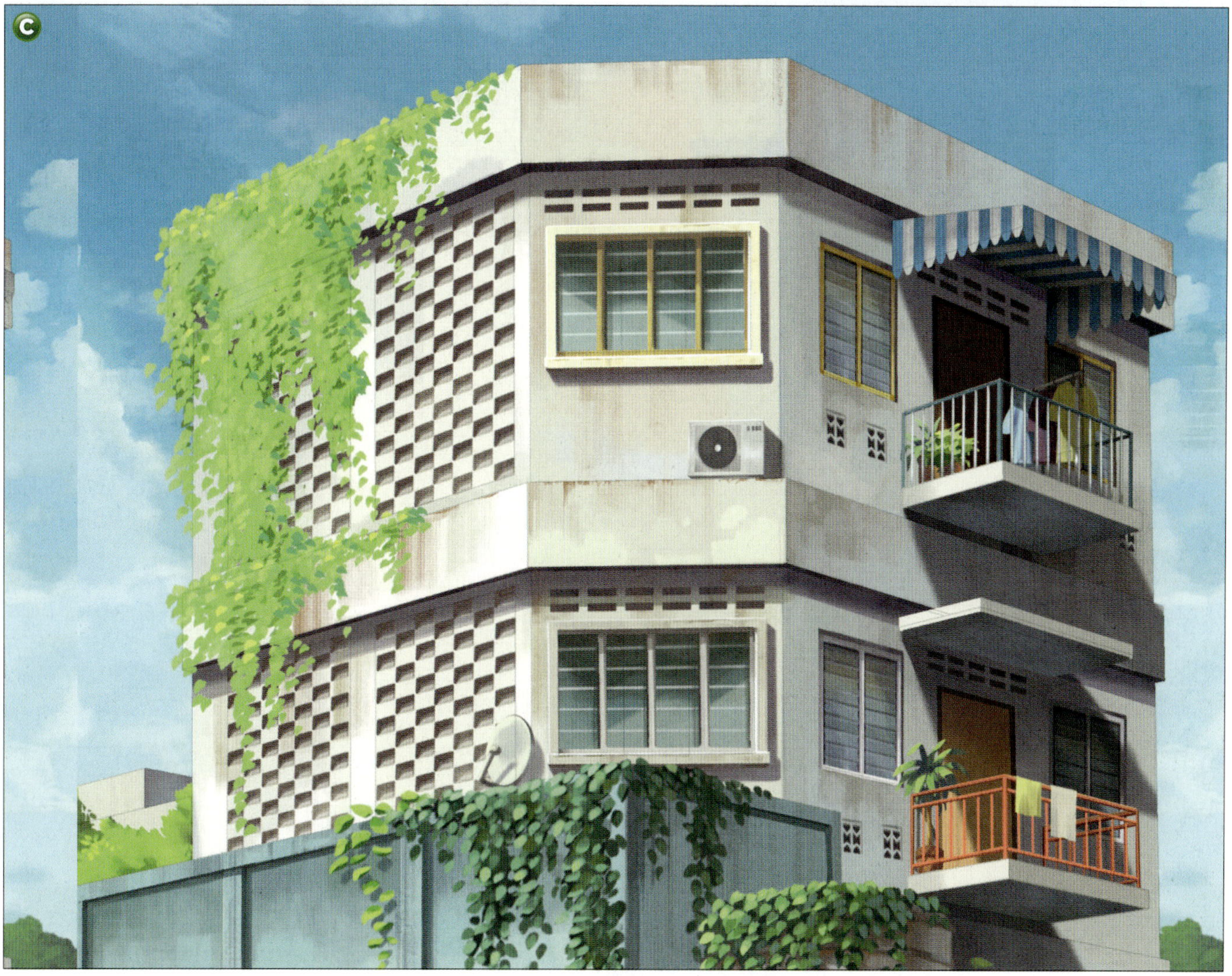

C

11 Introduce an apartment block to evoke feelings of nostalgia.
In Malaysia, there are some old three-and four-story apartments that I feel nostalgic about, so I want to put one into the background. I use the base color to define the 3D structure **(A)**. Because the building is a slight distance away from the viewer, the tonal value can be less of a contrast **(B)**. Then I add cast shadows and more details on the windows and balcony to capture that feeling of nostalgia I'm after **(C)**.

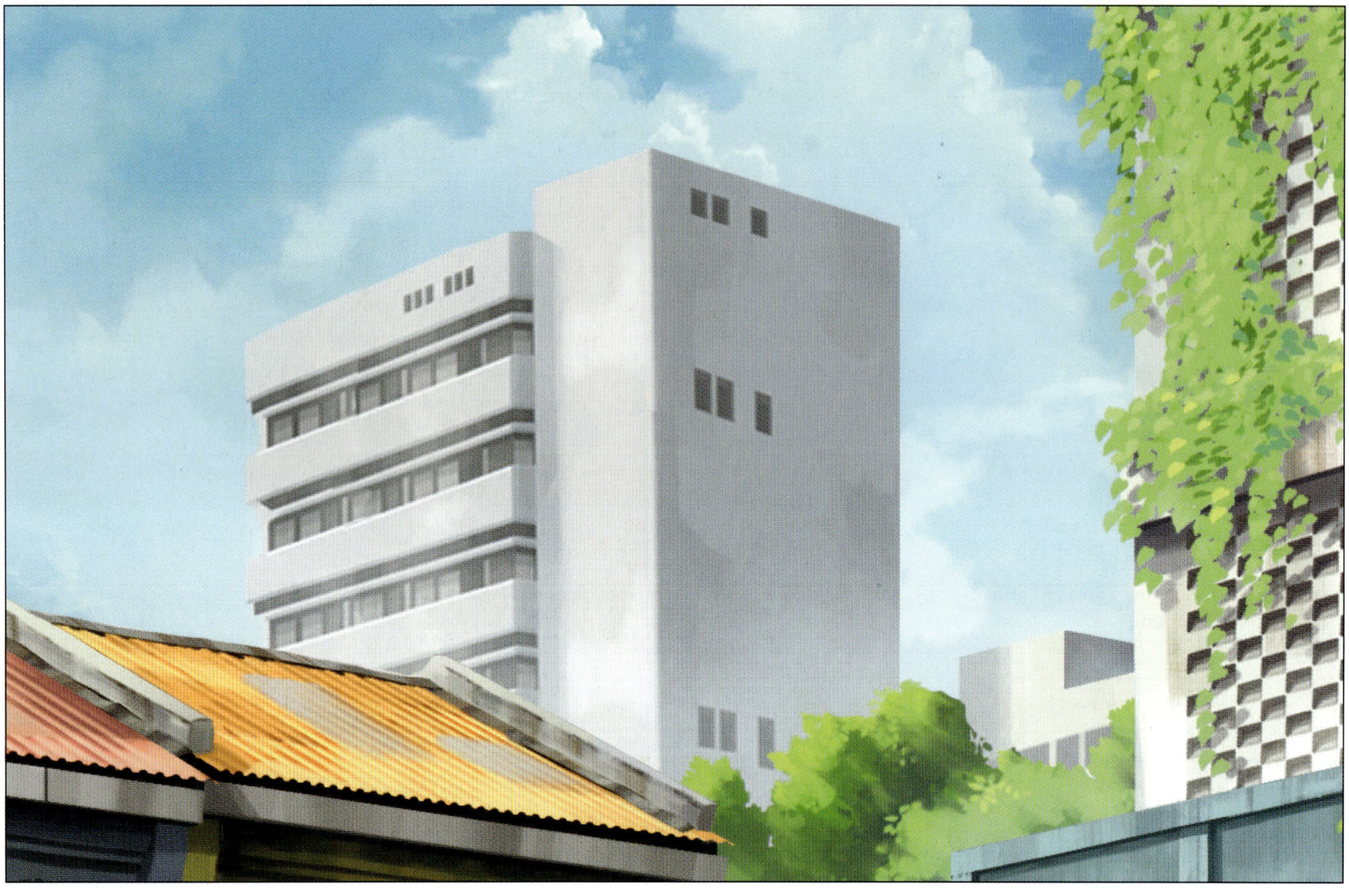

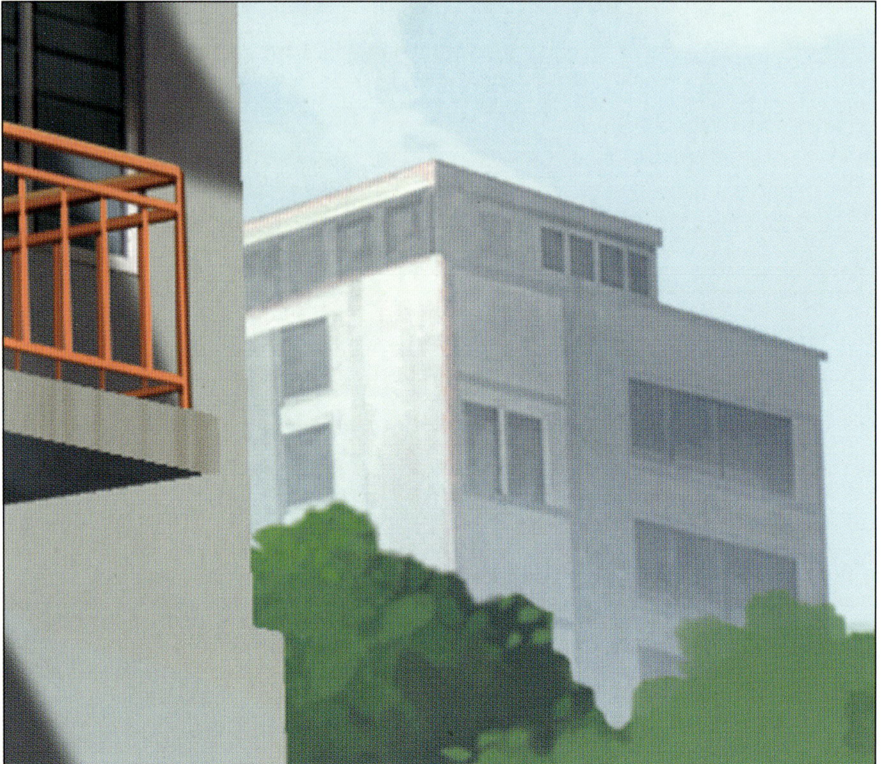

12 Paint distant buildings in the composition.

When it comes to painting background buildings, I'll blend them with the color of the sky and use less contrast tonal values without compromising the clarity of their design. Here I keep their designs simple compared to the apartment and café so that the viewer's attention remains on the focal areas. Applying a little Gaussian blur (Filter>Blur>Gaussian blur) on the background buildings will create depth of field.

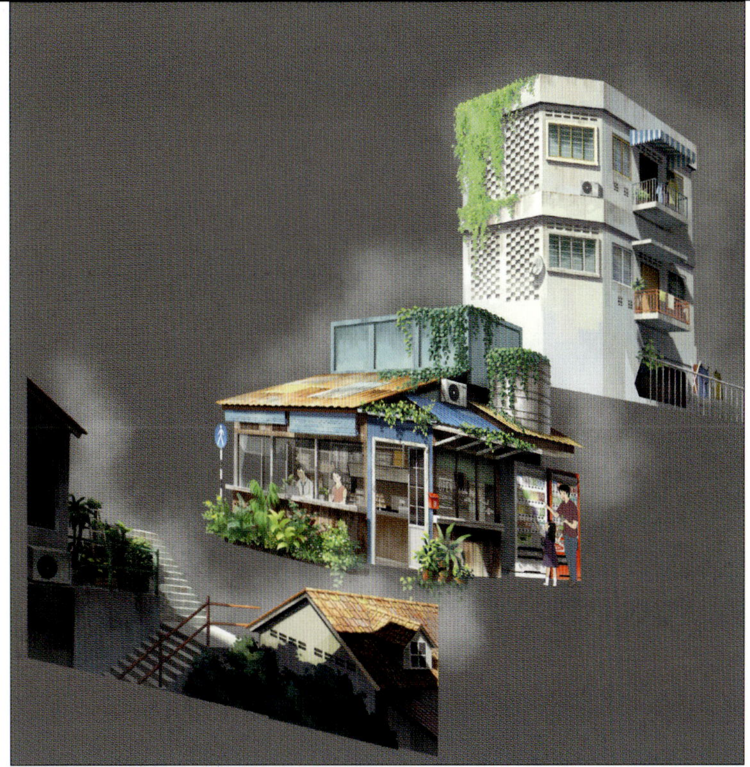

13 Generate mist between buildings and objects.

The overall coloring process is almost finished. I group my layers based on their depth distance, which helps me quickly adjust their tone by using Image>Adjustment>Levels. To enhance the depth between buildings and objects, I create a Screen layer between the group and use a soft brush to paint a mist effect. This is a common painting technique used to create anime-style backgrounds.

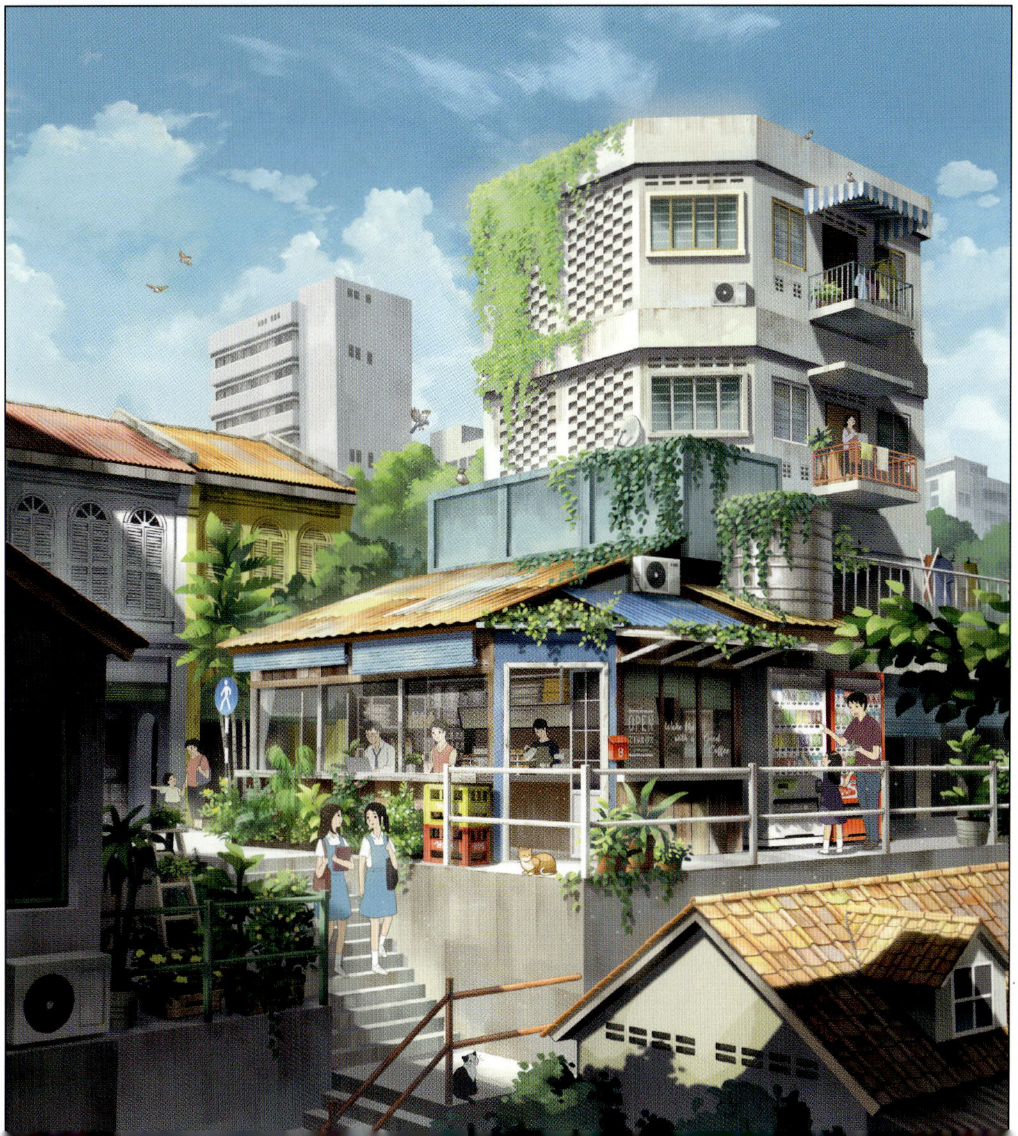

14 Add characters and final touches.

Once the background is finished, I carry out some general color and tone adjustments. To make the scenery look more lively, I get a little help from Running Snail Studio's character artist Jia Yee, who draws some characters into my artwork. I'm quite happy with the final outcome and Jia Yee's manga-style characters make this artwork looks like a screenshot from a Japanese animation. I hope you've enjoyed this workshop!

Procreate

CREATE YOUR OWN ASUKA

Learn how **Paul Kwon** (aka Zeronis) interprets a character from *Neon Genesis Evangelion*.

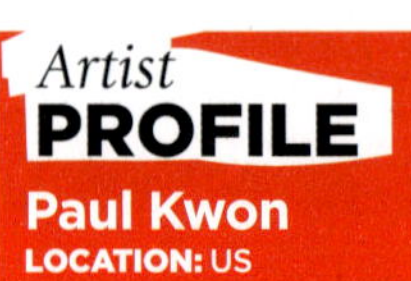

Artist PROFILE

Paul Kwon
LOCATION: US

Paul is a concept artist and illustrator. He started his career as an intern at Blizzard Entertainment, before securing a full-time job at the company. He's now a senior concept artist at Riot Games. In his spare time, he works on his own Deathverse project.
https://ifxm.ag/paul-k

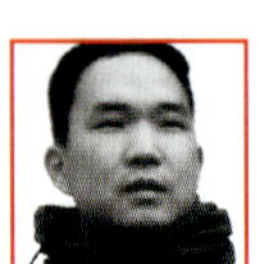

Creating character designs for living is a dream come true, especially when working on *League of Legends*. The game is chock-full of diverse and over-the-top fantasy characters, and imagining them in a completely different alternative universe is even more thrilling. That sums up my job at Riot Games as a character-concept artist developing new skins for the players.

In my spare time, I try to soak up trending visual references and expand my mental library as much as possible. From looking at amazing photographs to watching videos that tell compelling stories, to studying anime characters, mobile phone games, and of course browsing through amazing illustration and concept art online. After work, I wind down by painting fan art of characters that are either trending or are genuinely iconic in nature.

For this workshop, I'm subtly reinterpreting Asuka from the *Neon Genesis Evangelion* franchise, and give her a bit of an anime twist. I'll be using Procreate on my iPad Pro—I love this creative combo!

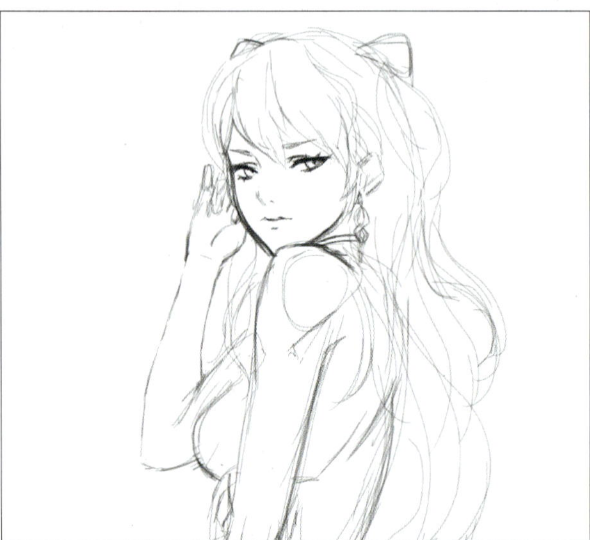

1 Keep things light while sketching.

To start, I keep the Opacity of the default Round brush pretty light to help me see where I put down the brush strokes and how they will establish the direction of the whole image. Indeed, I try to imagine what the figure will look like before putting down any strokes. This is an important skill to learn and is something that I still struggle with. I believe that comic book or manga artists are trained to do this, so this is worth bearing in mind if this is your career goal.

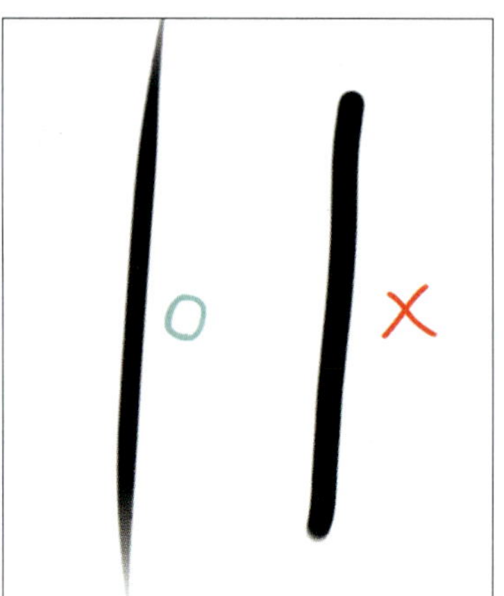

2 Finger paint.

The stroke on the left is the result of using my finger with the default Round brush. Notice the varying shape of the stroke. The Streamline brush setting keeps the strokes clean and steady, much like using a lazy mouse setting. Oddly, I can't replicate this stroke using the stylus with Pen Pressure active (right). It took time to work freely this way, but now it feels natural. I'll be using my finger to paint Asuka.

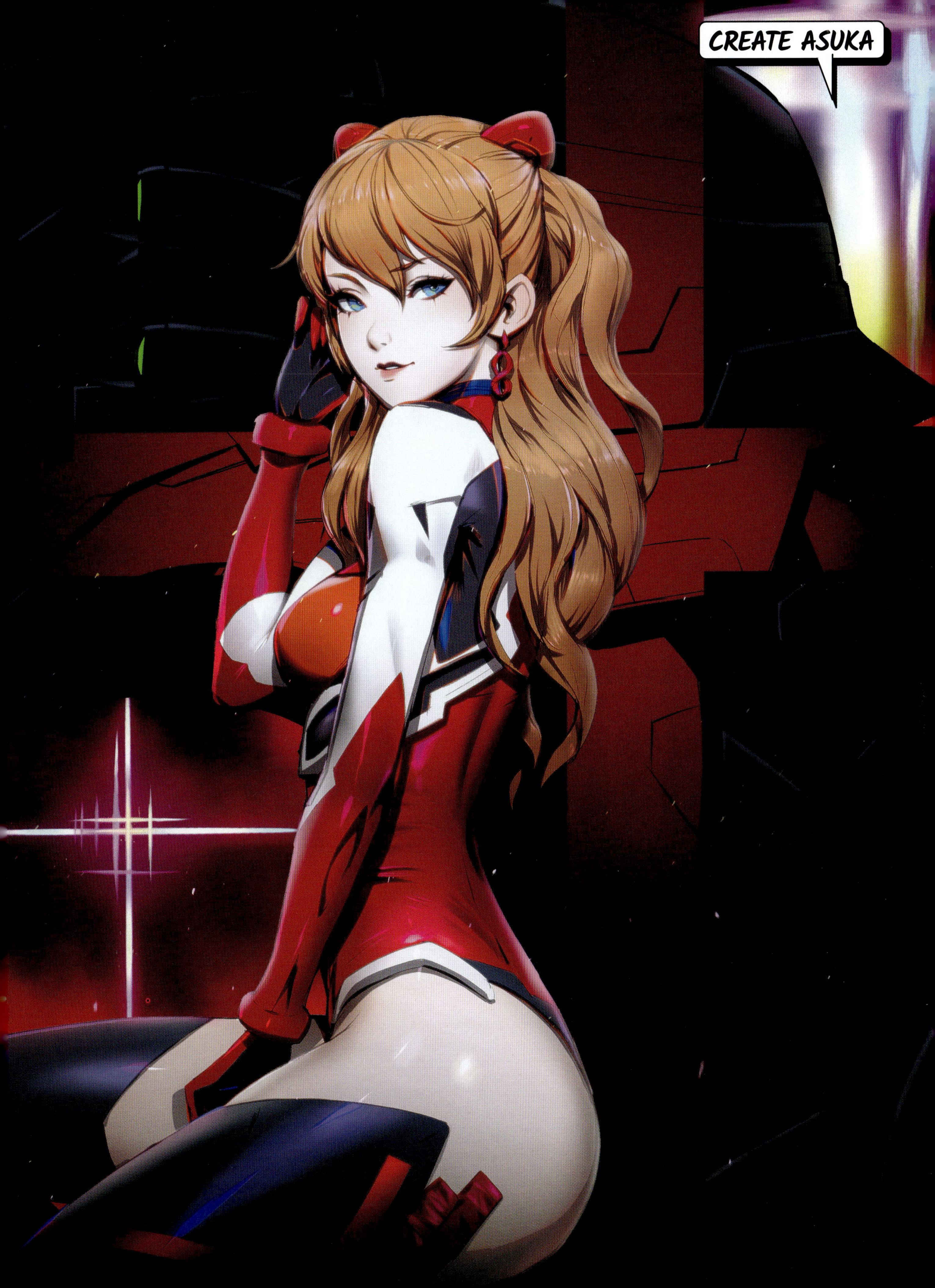
CREATE ASUKA

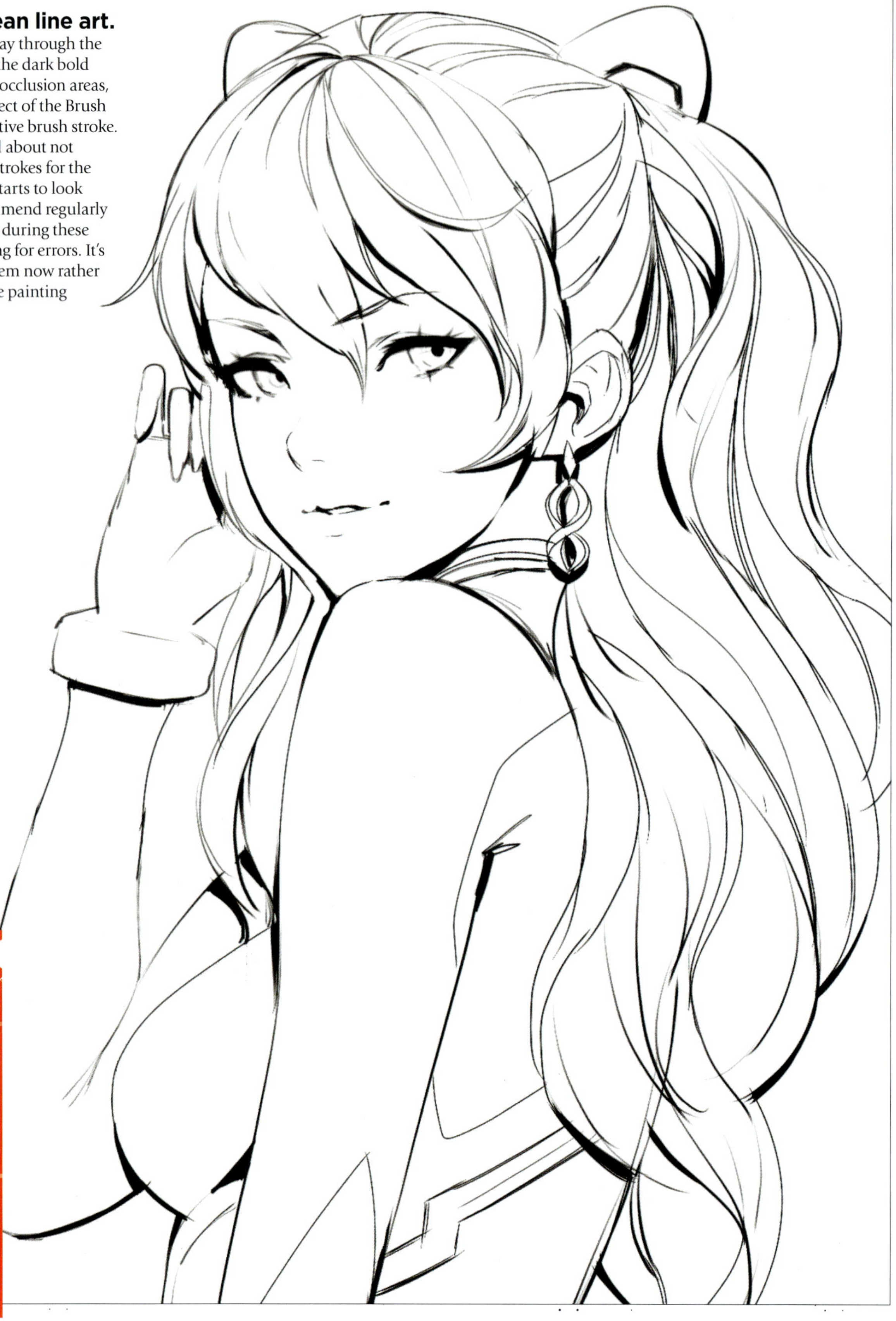

3 Make clean line art.

This is midway through the sketch process. In the dark bold lines and ambient occlusion areas, you can see the effect of the Brush pen and its distinctive brush stroke. I have to be careful about not adding too many strokes for the hair, otherwise it starts to look unnatural. I recommend regularly flipping the image during these early stages, looking for errors. It's easier to correct them now rather than later on in the painting process.

WORKSHOP BRUSHES

PROCREATE

CUSTOM BRUSHES: BRUSH PEN

I love this brush, especially without using the stylus. It creates the perfect sharp shape.

TECHNICAL PEN

I use the Technical Pen with the StreamLine setting at a mid-value for going over my lines.

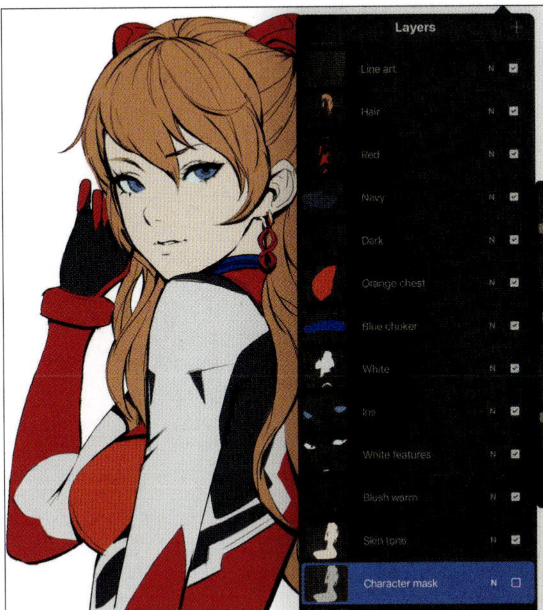

4 Mask techniques.

I use the Magic Wand equivalent tool in Procreate to select around the character, then I invert this selection to isolate the character. Next, I mask off specific parts of the character: her hair, suit, gloves, eyes, and skin. This makes it possible to apply a consistent coloring technique to the image, and enables your unique painting style to come to the fore.

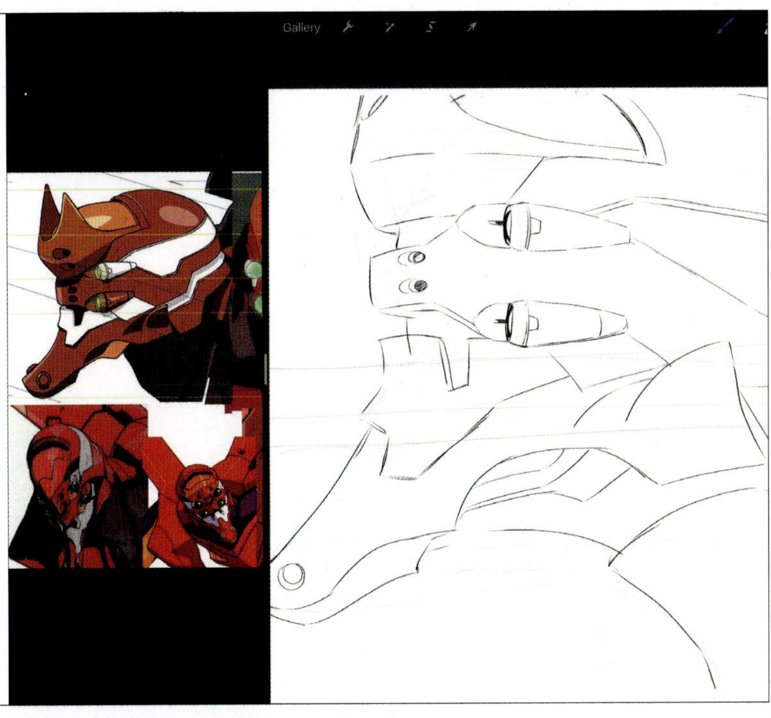

5 Customize the iPad workspace.

Here, I've split the screen to display reference material right next to the artwork—pretty handy, eh? I have reference open at all times from artworks that I've saved on to my iPad and iPhone, or from Pinterest. I also have Netflix minimized in the corner for background noise or just for listening to music.

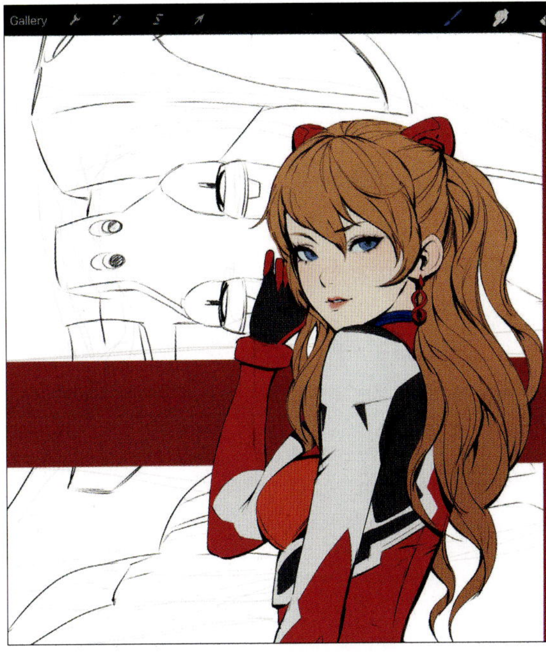

6 Start on the background.

I'm adding the Evangelion Unit in the background to create more visual interest and contrast. I roughly put down strokes to create its overall composition and look before committing to clean line art. I think it's good practice to work on the entire image at a steady pace.

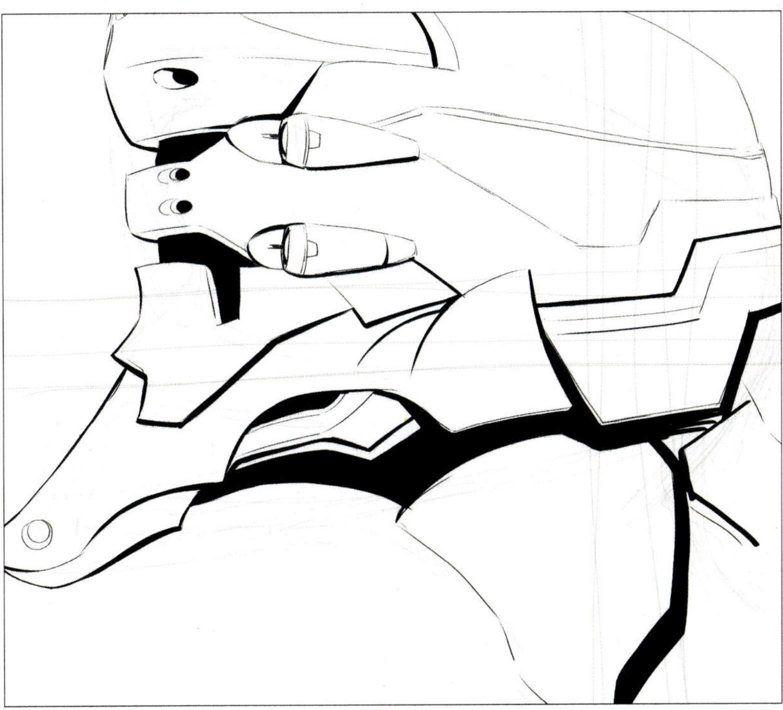

7 Create a simple yet powerful graphic shape.

Using the same Brush pen, I'm focusing on making the Eva Unit's head clear and graphically engaging. This is because its purpose is to act as a tertiary element to keep the viewer within the scene. ➤➤

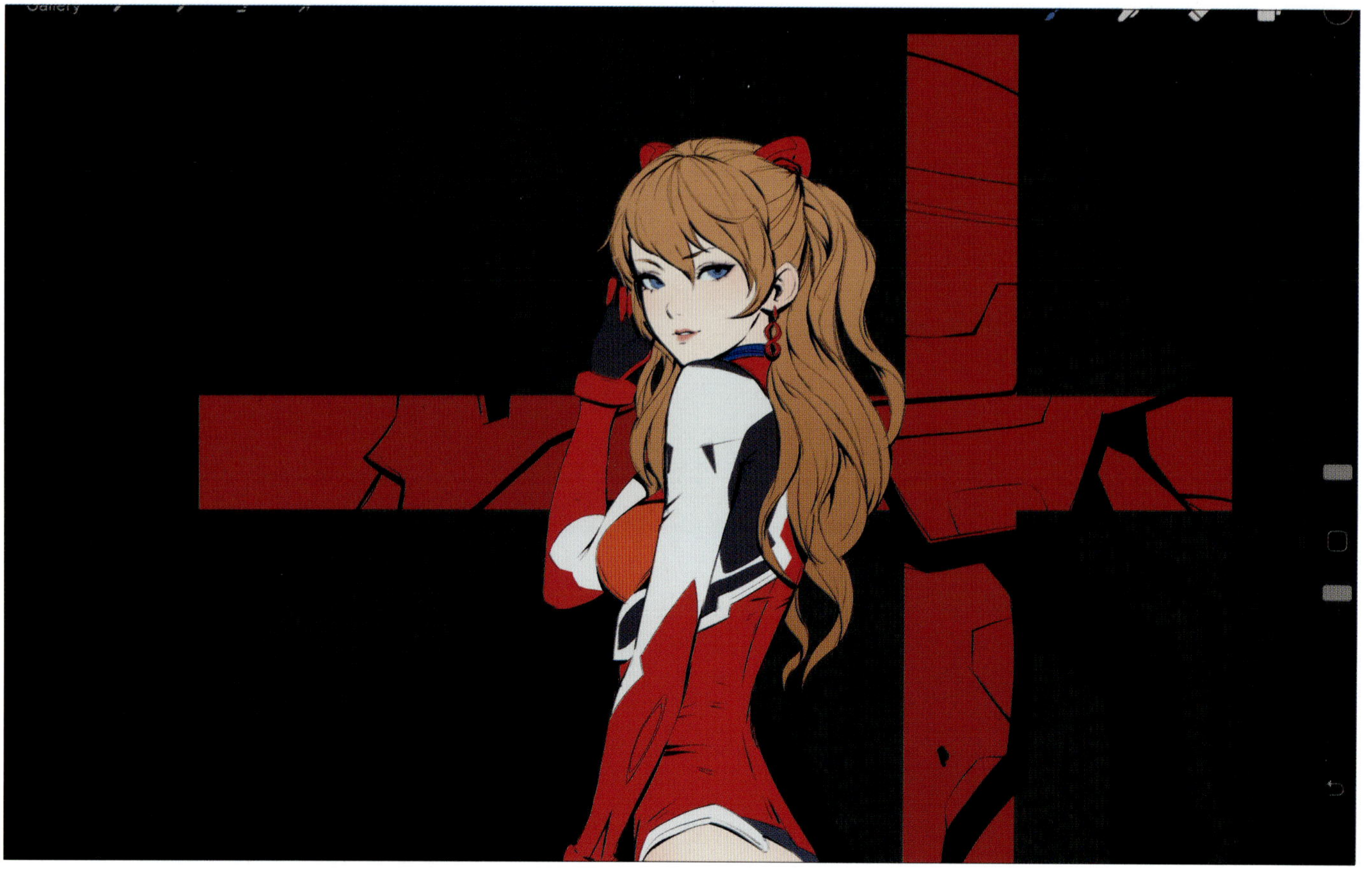

8 Accentuate the composition.

I'm exploring this composition approach, where the focal point is around the pilot's face and upper half of her body. The cross shape acts as the secondary interest behind the pilot, while Eva Unit becomes the tertiary background element blending gently into the red background.

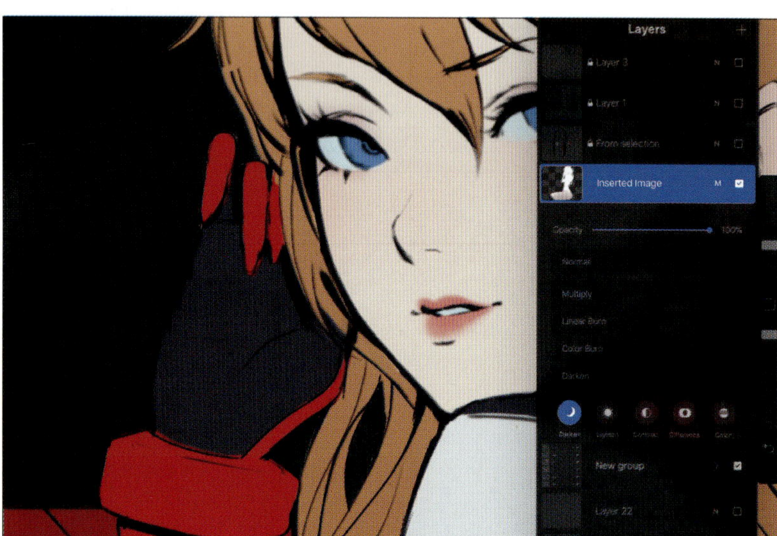

9 Use a Multiply layer for shadows.

I place the original mask of the character above all the other layers and turn it to white. I swipe two fingers and flick the layer to the right, which layer-masks it. I then change the layer type to Multiply. This enables me to add a subtle gray color without it bleeding out of the character. This is a simple process that enables you to focus on one thing at a time and gradually build up consistent shadows.

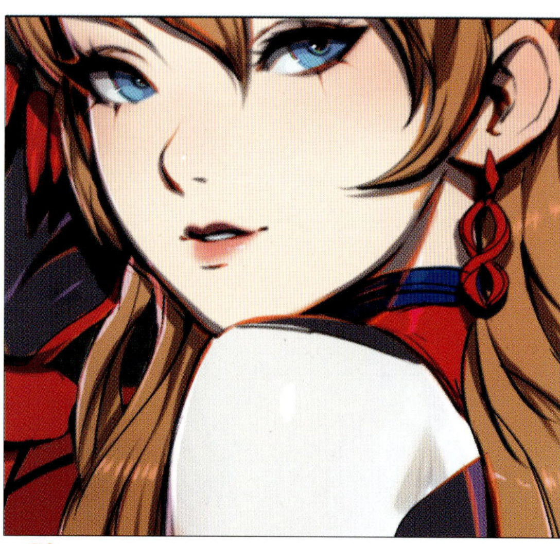

10 Paint over your lines.

After the shadows are painted over the character, I decide to experiment by adding some warm oranges over some lines, giving the character a stylized subsurface scattering appearance. This also enables me to blend the line art with the colors of the character. I'm happy with the results—it's good to try out new techniques!

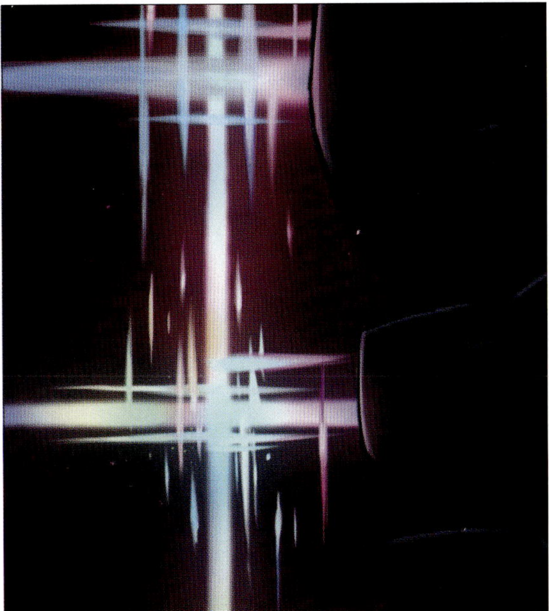

11 Add explosions.

I add some explosion shapes, which I interpret and stylize in my own way. I want to emphasize the contrast here through shapes, size, value, and color.

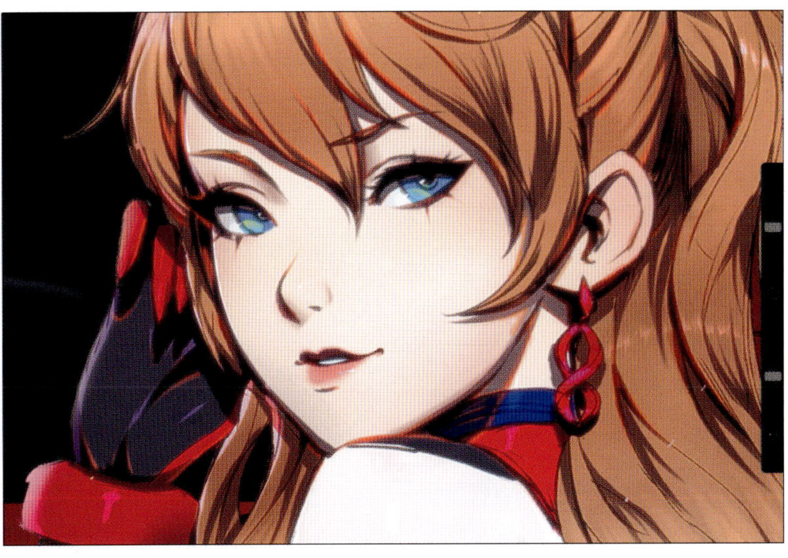

12 Apply post-processing to the character.

When the image is around 85% finished, I turn my attention to post- processing. I use blurring, sharpening, duplicating, and merging techniques, experiment with many different types of layers, and adjust the Opacity. I don't want to overdo the processing. The idea is to harmonize the values and colors, and help the image have the correct balance and pop in the focal areas. I'm trying to make Asuka blend in with the rest of the image naturally.

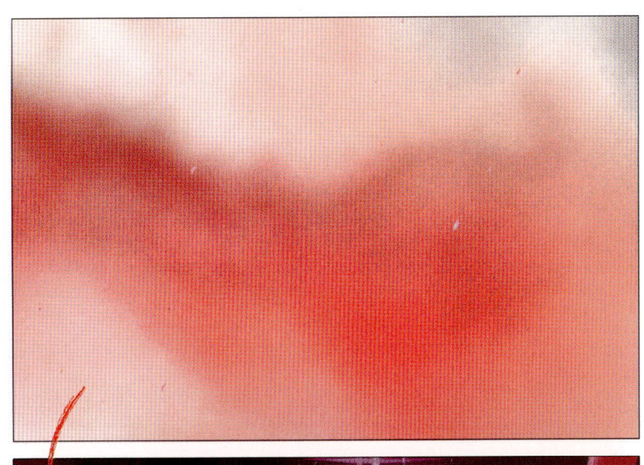

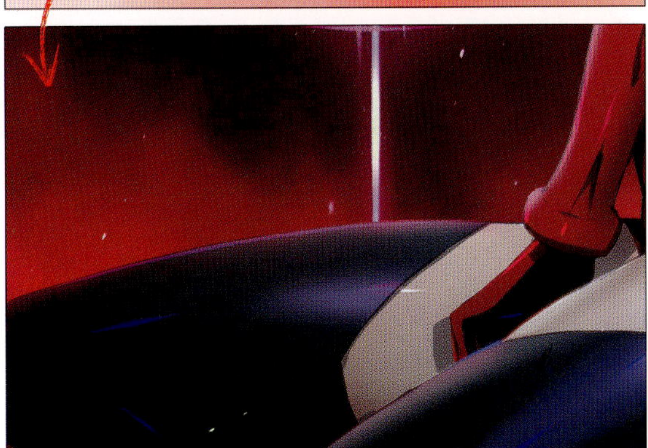

13 Add background details.

I decide to add a little more subtle details on the red background by painting in some red cloud and smoke shapes using Procreate's default Smoke brush. I also carefully apply the noise filter on many parts of the image to generate extra depth without it becoming a distraction.

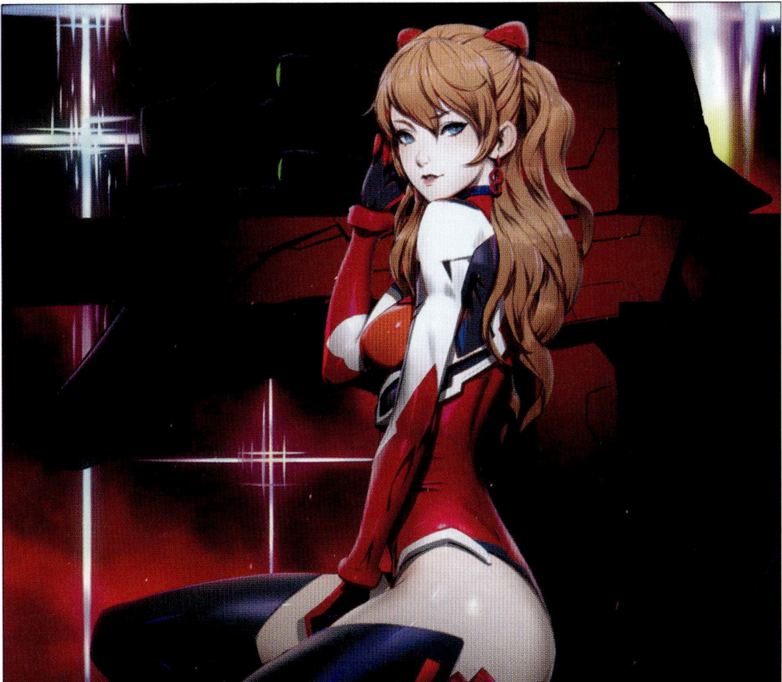

14 Run a final polish pass over the image.

This is near final, and I'm happy with how the painting's turned out. I add a lot of vignette steps to redirect the focal point to her face and upper torso. I carry out a little more color balancing using a combination of Screen, Lighten, Overlay, Color Dodge, and Add layers, bringing more vibrancy to the image's color and values. This also enables me to mask out the initial dark lines and blend everything more naturally. I also hit the edges of the character with the big soft Round brush, painting subtle rim lighting to add more three-dimensional forms to her.

Paint Tool SAI

GET BETTER AT PAINT TOOL SAI

Artist **Angela Wang** (aka awanqi) shows how to compose figures from mythology using symbology coupled with a sense of refinement.

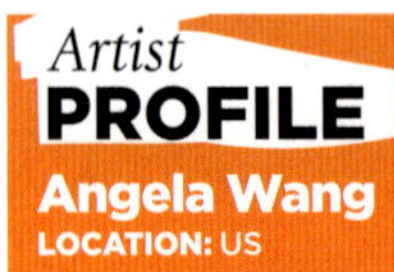

Angela Wang
LOCATION: US

Also known online as awanqi, Angela is a freelance illustrator who has a penchant for history and fantasy, and has worked for clients in publishing and comics.
www.awanqi.com

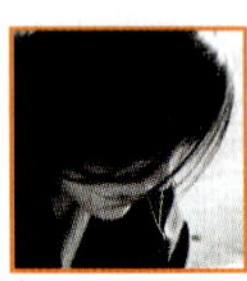

Illustration is driven by storytelling, and stories are built up with certain artistic "building blocks" such as motifs, symbolism, gestures, poses, and so on. In this workshop, I want to express the characteristics of the Greek gods Hypnos and Thanatos, using color to set the tone, lighting to direct the focus of the story, and more, all while retaining their personalities. As with many of the gods from antiquity, certain symbols are associated with each one. They're specific enough to enable the viewer to identify them using a single icon.

I'll be explaining the processes I use to create an illustration, as well as giving tips and techniques that I find useful to my artistic practice. Since many of the symbols have already been established throughout history, as an artist I'm able to use my preferences and abilities to piece together a new story from these older structures.

In my effort to create a memorable piece of art that's also recognizable to those familiar with the mythological figures, simplicity is the key to understanding what's taking place in the piece. Therefore, I've chosen to illustrate universal symbols for what each god represents. This makes my job as an artist easier, and also enables the viewer to quickly grasp the theme of my artwork.

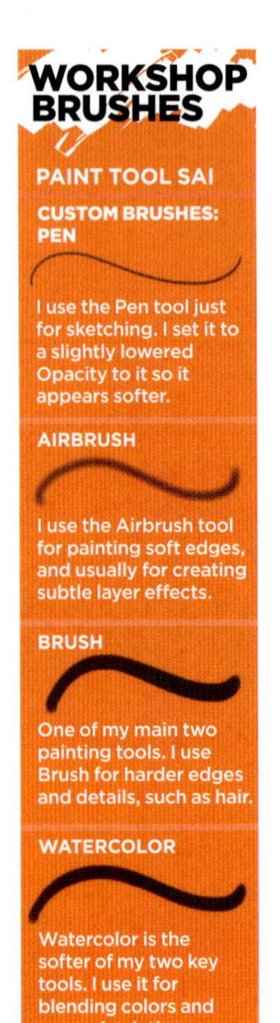

WORKSHOP BRUSHES

PAINT TOOL SAI

CUSTOM BRUSHES: PEN

I use the Pen tool just for sketching. I set it to a slightly lowered Opacity to it so it appears softer.

AIRBRUSH

I use the Airbrush tool for painting soft edges, and usually for creating subtle layer effects.

BRUSH

One of my main two painting tools. I use Brush for harder edges and details, such as hair.

WATERCOLOR

Watercolor is the softer of my two key tools. I use it for blending colors and general painting.

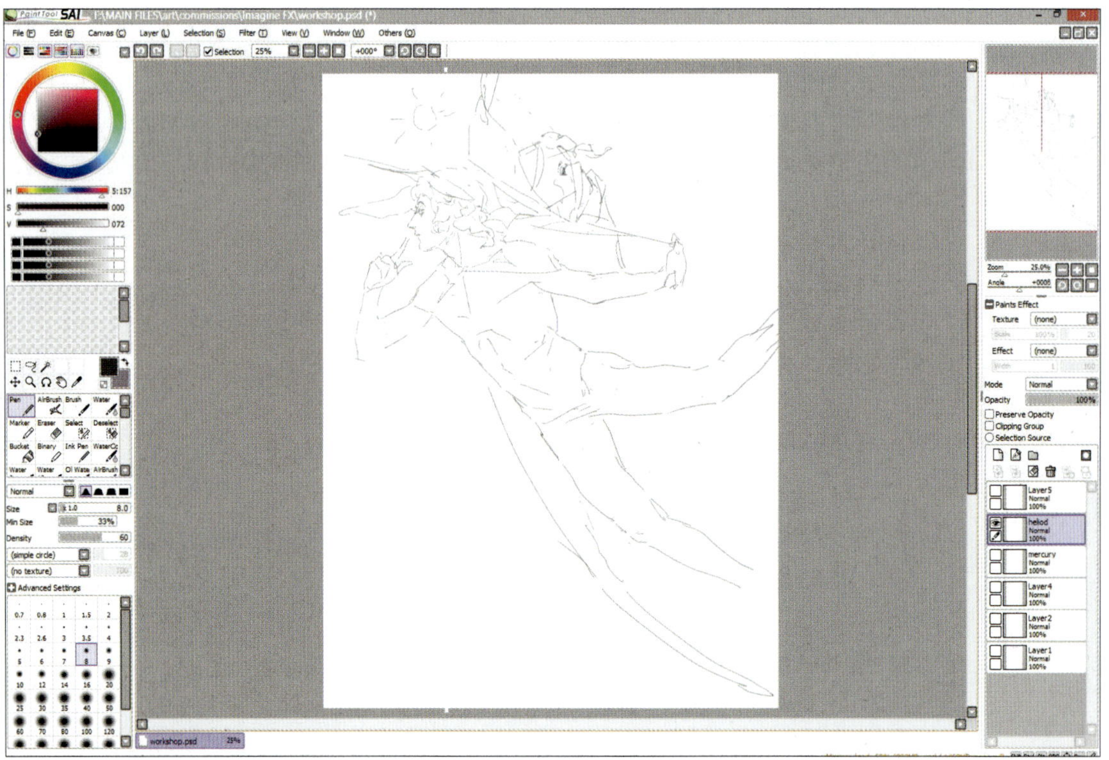

1 Test out ideas.

When coming up with a sketch, I'm less concerned with the aesthetics of neat lines. I usually start with straighter and more rigid lines that are borne out of quick movements, because I've found that this helps me to decide if I'm on the right track. I don't want to waste time guessing what I've just drawn.

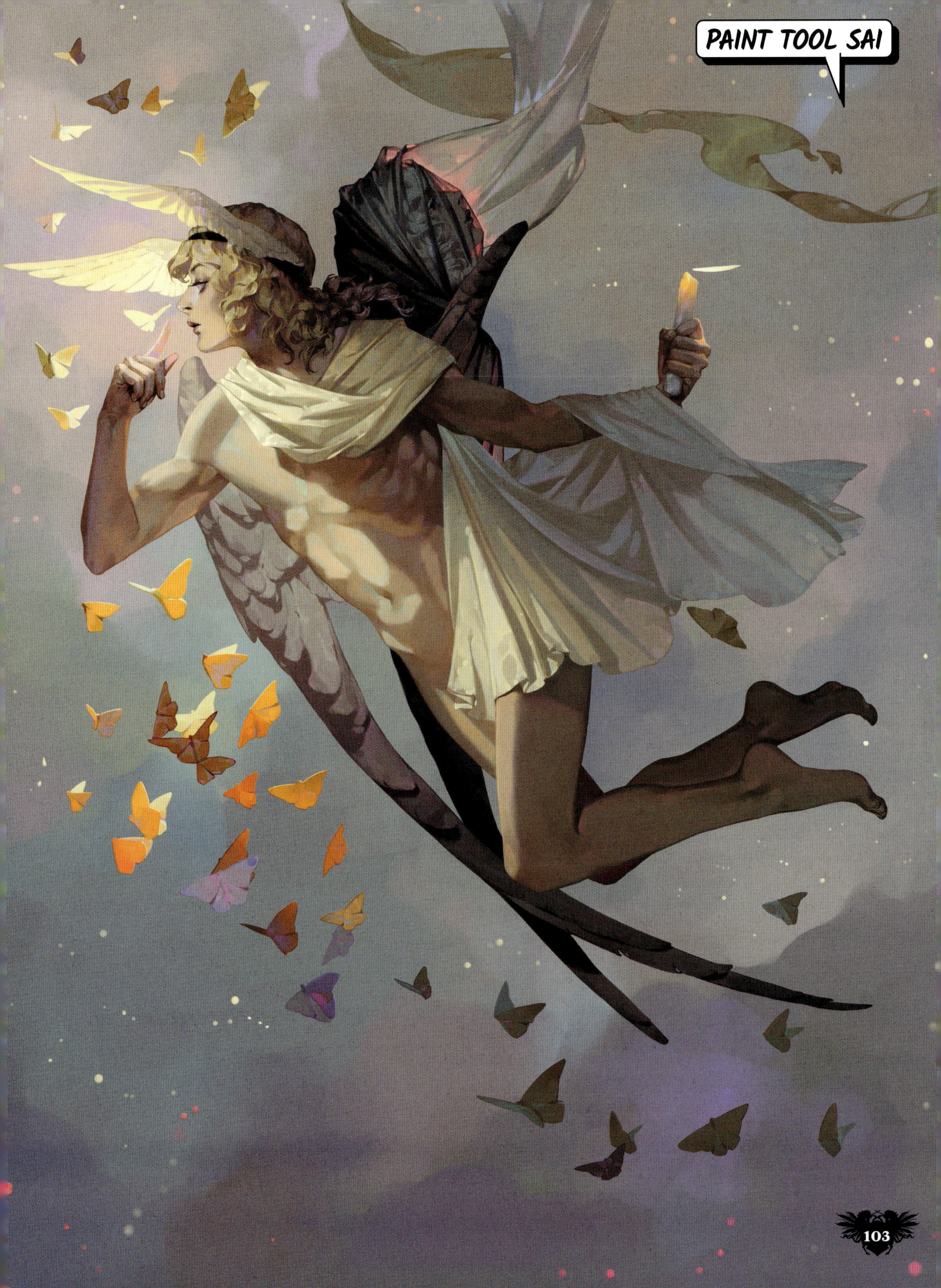
PAINT TOOL SAI

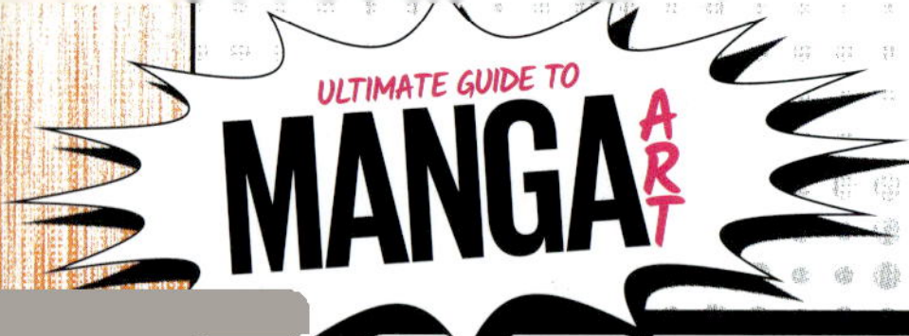

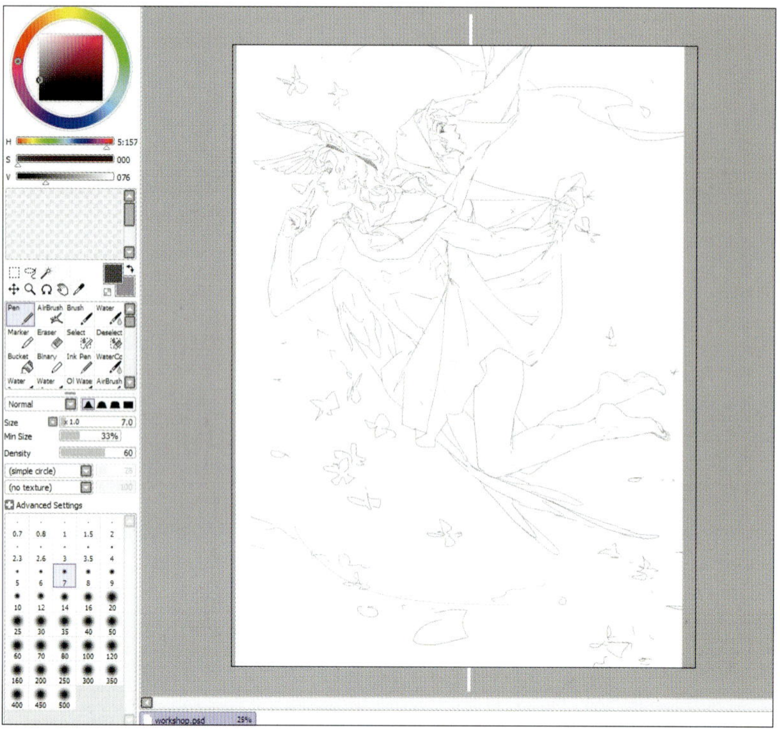

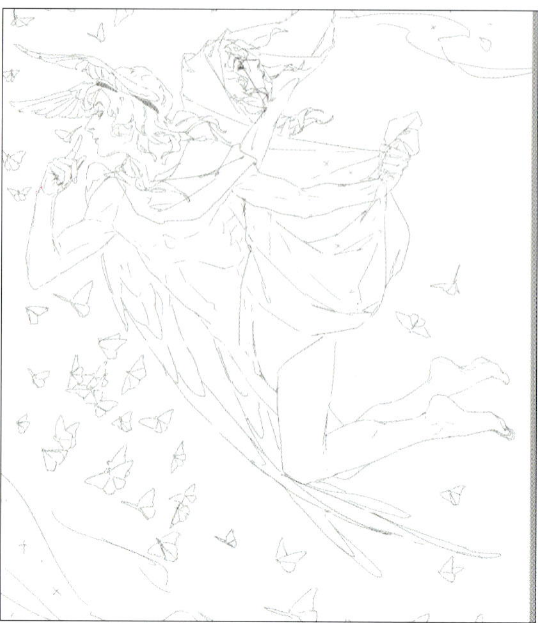

2 Refine parts of the sketch.

I'm starting to settle on the decisions I've made, which enables me to refine the more ambiguous parts of the sketch. What really gets the ball rolling is when I start detailing faces—this usually tells me that things are working out so far.

3 Get the sketch ready for painting.

I like to be neat with the sketch in the end; it makes the painting process less confusing. Once I'm happy with the results, it's time for me to fill in the base layers. Before that happens, though, my next step is to change the sketch layer to Multiply and reduce the Opacity until I can still see my sketch, but it's not overpowering the composition.

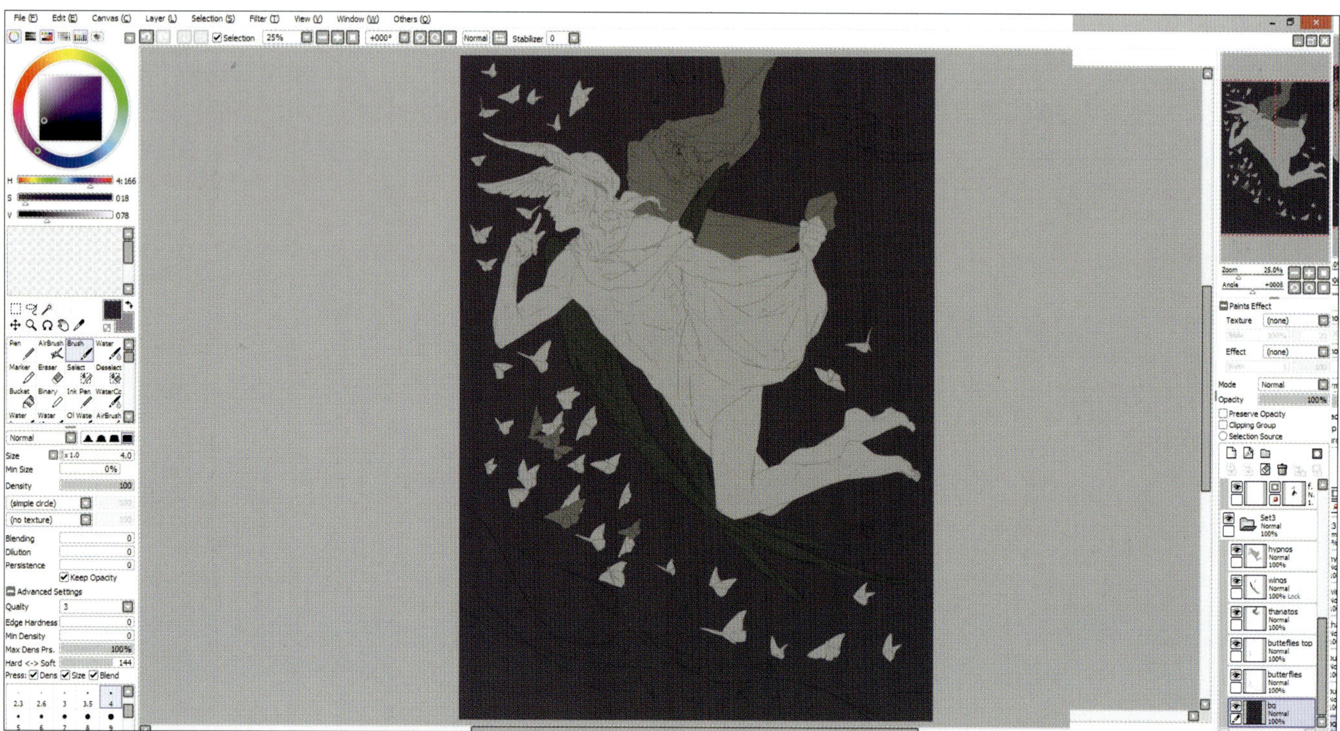

4 Fill in the base of the illustration.

Before starting the painting stage, I fill in each section with a neutral color (often shades of gray, nothing too saturated) and lock the Opacity. This enables me to paint freely, albeit roughly, without worrying about losing the shapes.

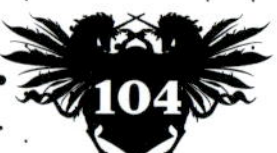

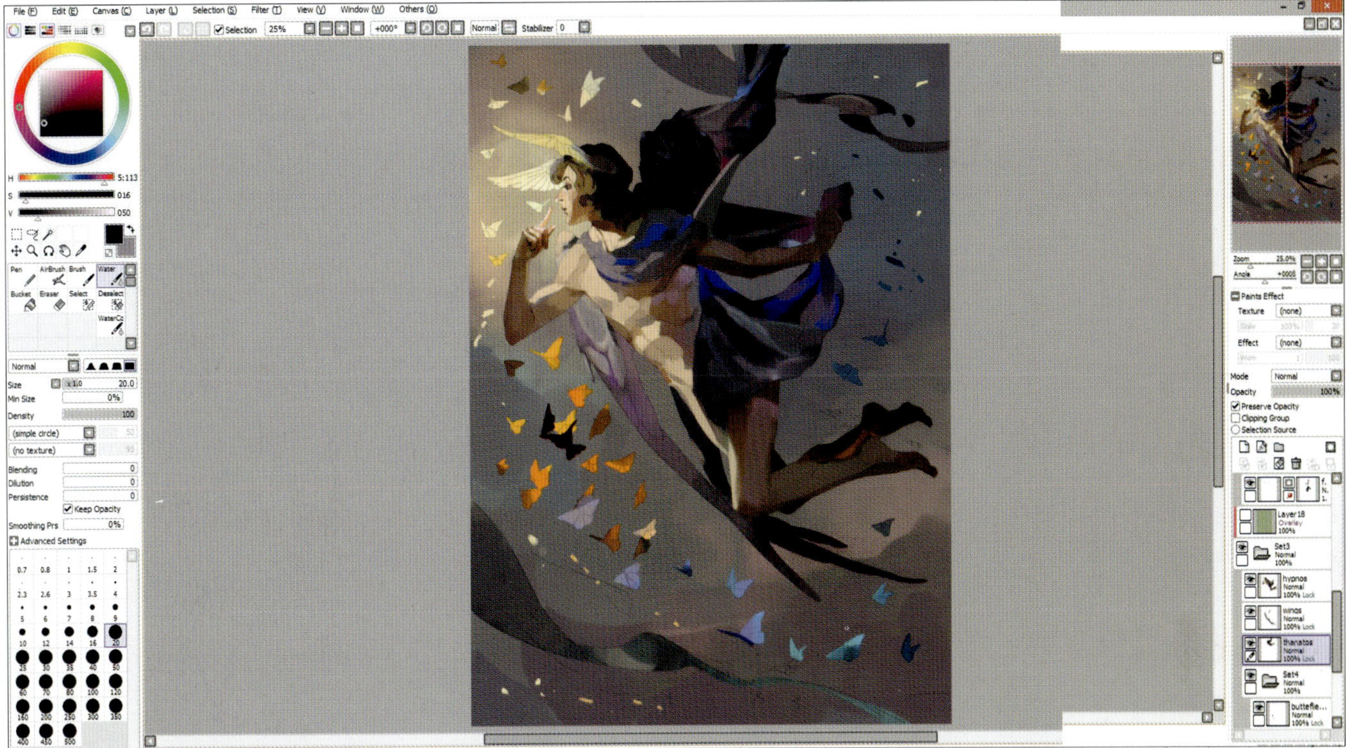

5 Establish light and color.

I'm not detailing anytime soon, which means I can go wild with colors. I usually try out different variations of value and color until I find something I like. I want the piece to have a dreamy feel, so I have blues and purples in mind as I lay down my colors.

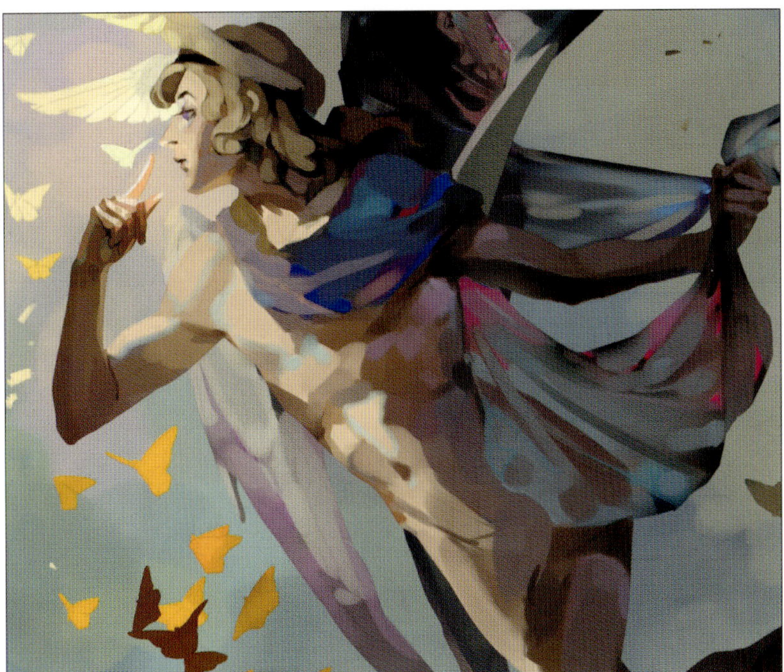

6 Start the painting process.

As I begin painting more of the details, I further reduce the sketch layer's Opacity so it's barely visible. This means I can focus on the values rather than the lines in order to establish forms. The sketch becomes more of a distraction rather than an aid as the rendering goes on, so it's always freeing to finally turn it off.

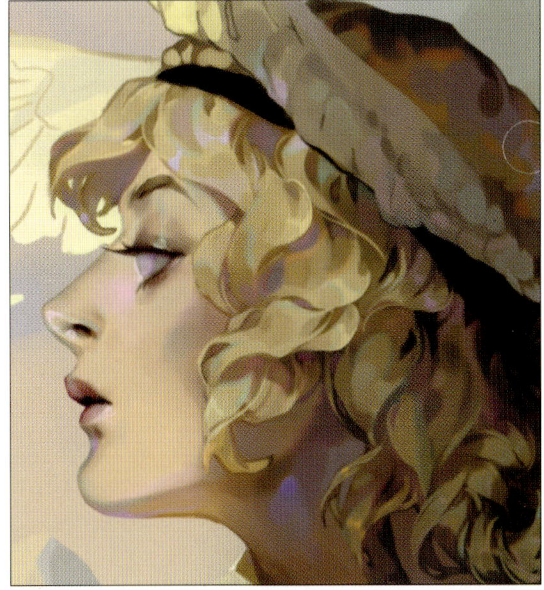

7 Go in headfirst.

I enjoy painting faces, so I always start here. This also helps me build up momentum during the creative process. Whenever I start to lose steam, I can look at the face that I've just visualized to remind myself that yes, I can actually paint. I paint with the Brush tool for harder edges and details, as well as the Watercolor tool for softening the edges where necessary.

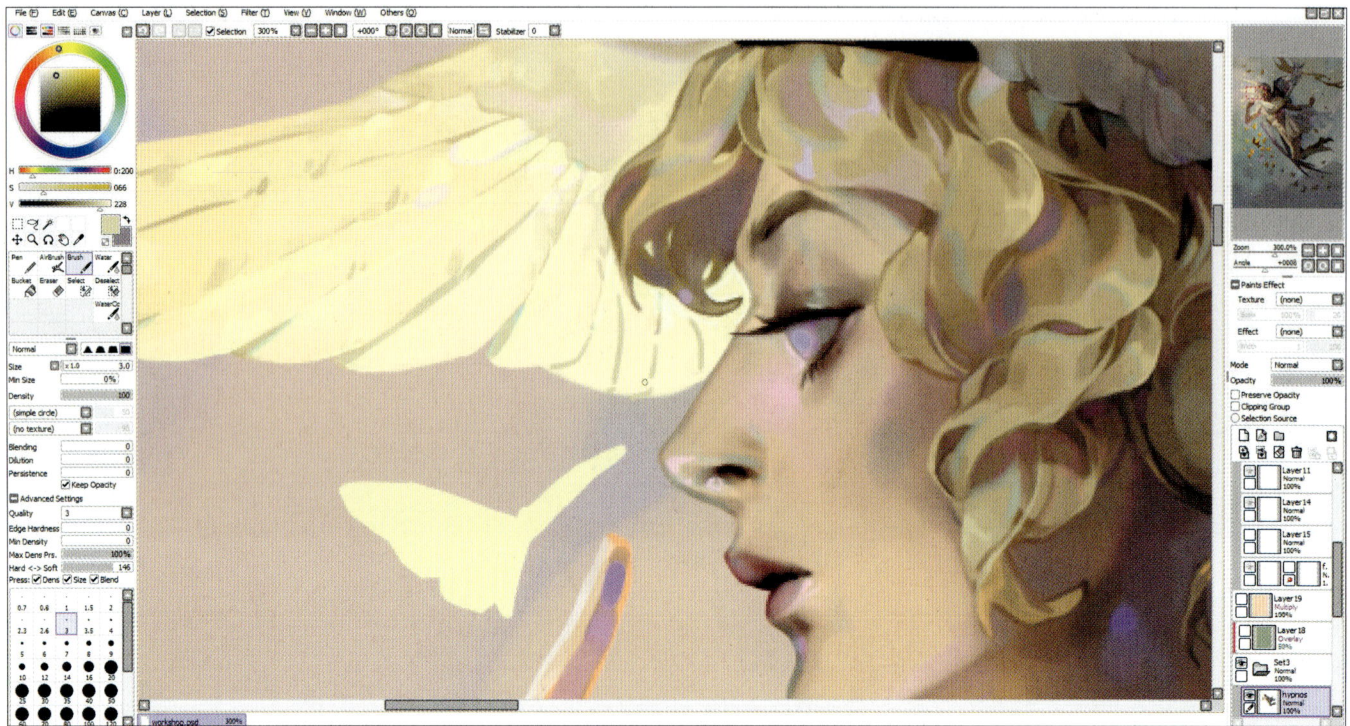

8 Work section by section.

Once one section (for example, the head) is finished, I can move onto the next. Doing so basically generates a checklist in my head on what comes next. My usual order is head, followed by the shoulders, torso, legs, and so on. I also work from the inside out, such as from the face to the hair, or from a bare arm to the fabric on top of it.

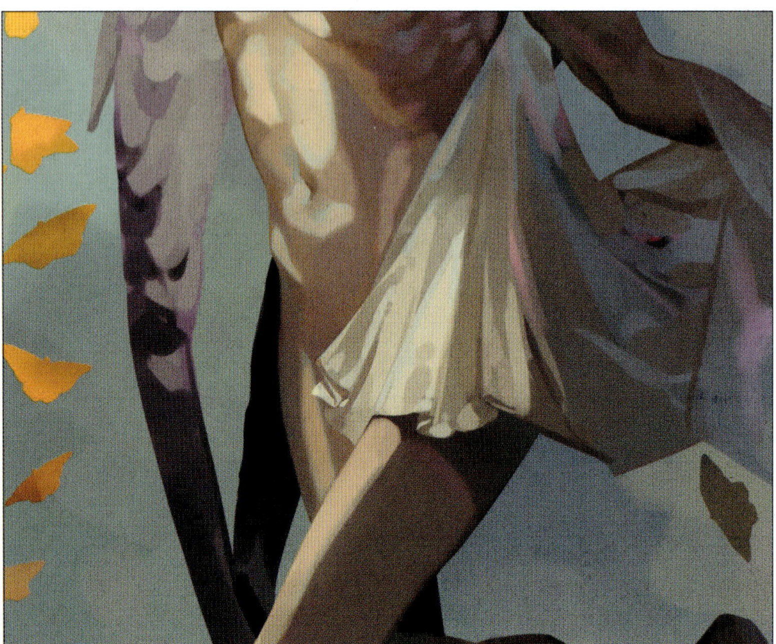

9 Render clothing and fabric.

I start loosely with the rendering before tightening it up later. This especially applies to fabric because I find it difficult to form the shapes, ruffles, and folds at first, so I spend a lot of time establishing what comes next. Because I'm working from loose to detailed, my brush usage follows in a similar manner: from Brush (hard, simple edges, and messy) to Watercolor (soft and blendable).

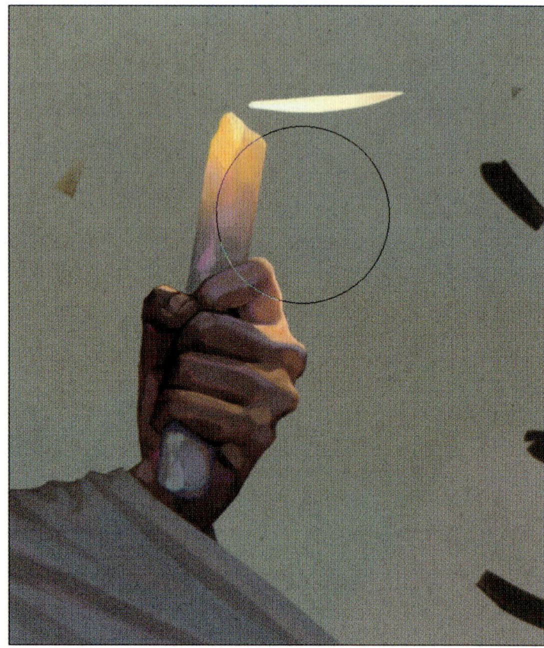

10 Make use of layer effects.

I like to use Overlay layers for glowing objects, such as the candle here. When doing so, an even and gradual spread is necessary, so I use the Airbrush tool for a super-soft placement of color. It's a small detail, but minor effects can sometimes add so much!

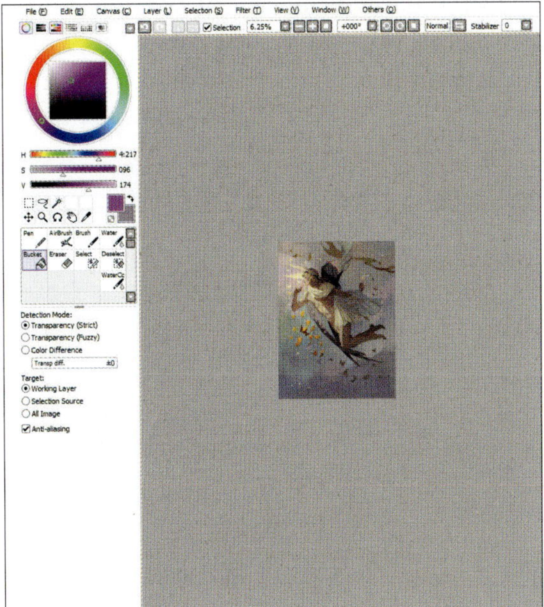

11 Zoom out.

Remember in art class when your teacher told you to step back from your artwork to see how it looks from a distance? It's the same concept here. I zoom out so the image is tiny and I can gauge the overall feel. I don't care much for the original greener background color, so I test out new colors with an Overlay layer over the background layer. It helps to see the results from afar.

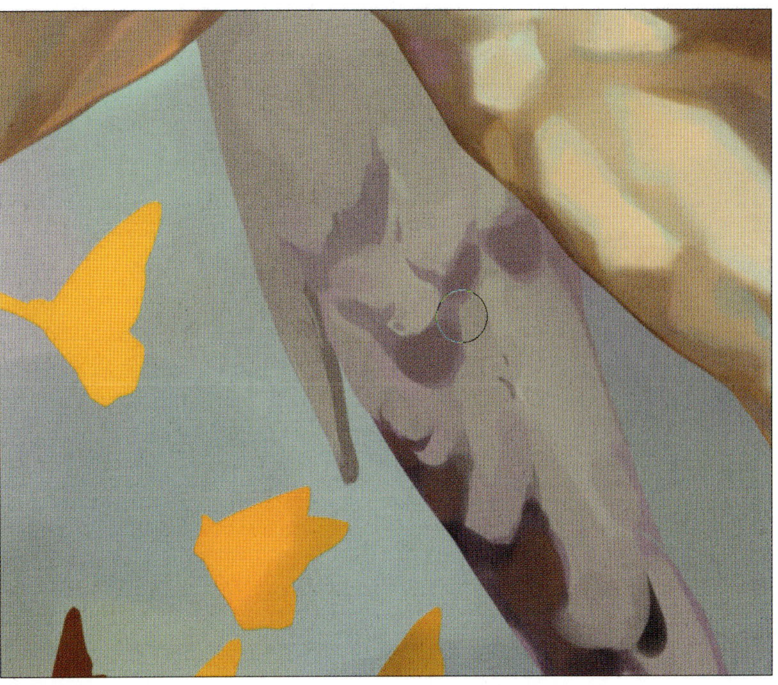

12 Paint the wings.

I find that light and shadow help shape objects that are flat, such as feathers. Using the sharper Brush tool for detailed edges and the Watercolor brush for blending and softening shadows or edges, I shape the wings with shadows first, followed by light and then details. I enjoy creating subtle color variations, so I make sure to include those at the edges where different colors or values meet.

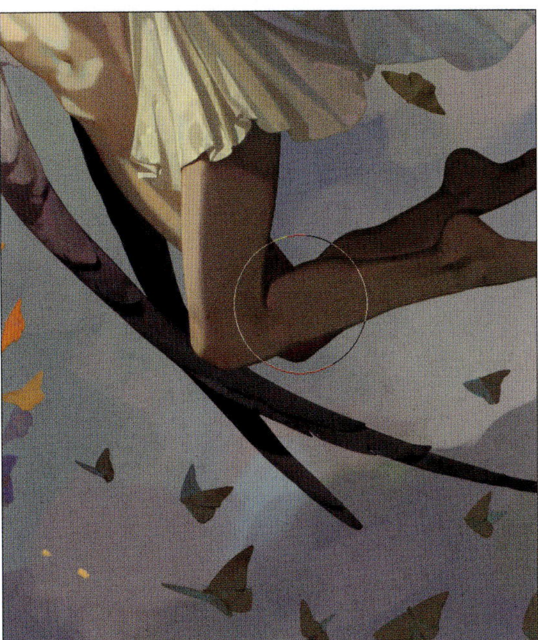

13 Make the finishing details.

As I paint the butterflies, I make sure that they either stand out against or fade out from the background. The general lighting should affect them in the same way, too, so the further they are from the light source, the darker and less colorful they become.

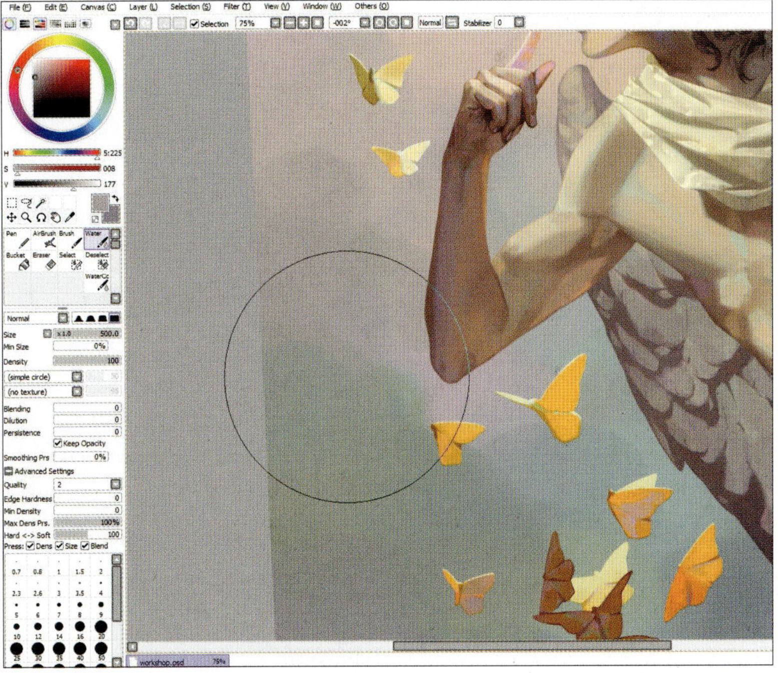

14 Refine the background.

Now I move on to the background. Because the two gods are flying, or at least floating in the air, I decide that an environment of clouds and stars is appropriate. I set the Watercolor tool at a large size and make soft marks, gradually building up the clouds to convey a sleepy, relaxing atmosphere.

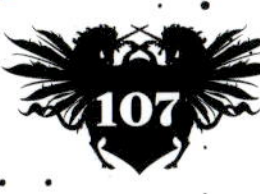

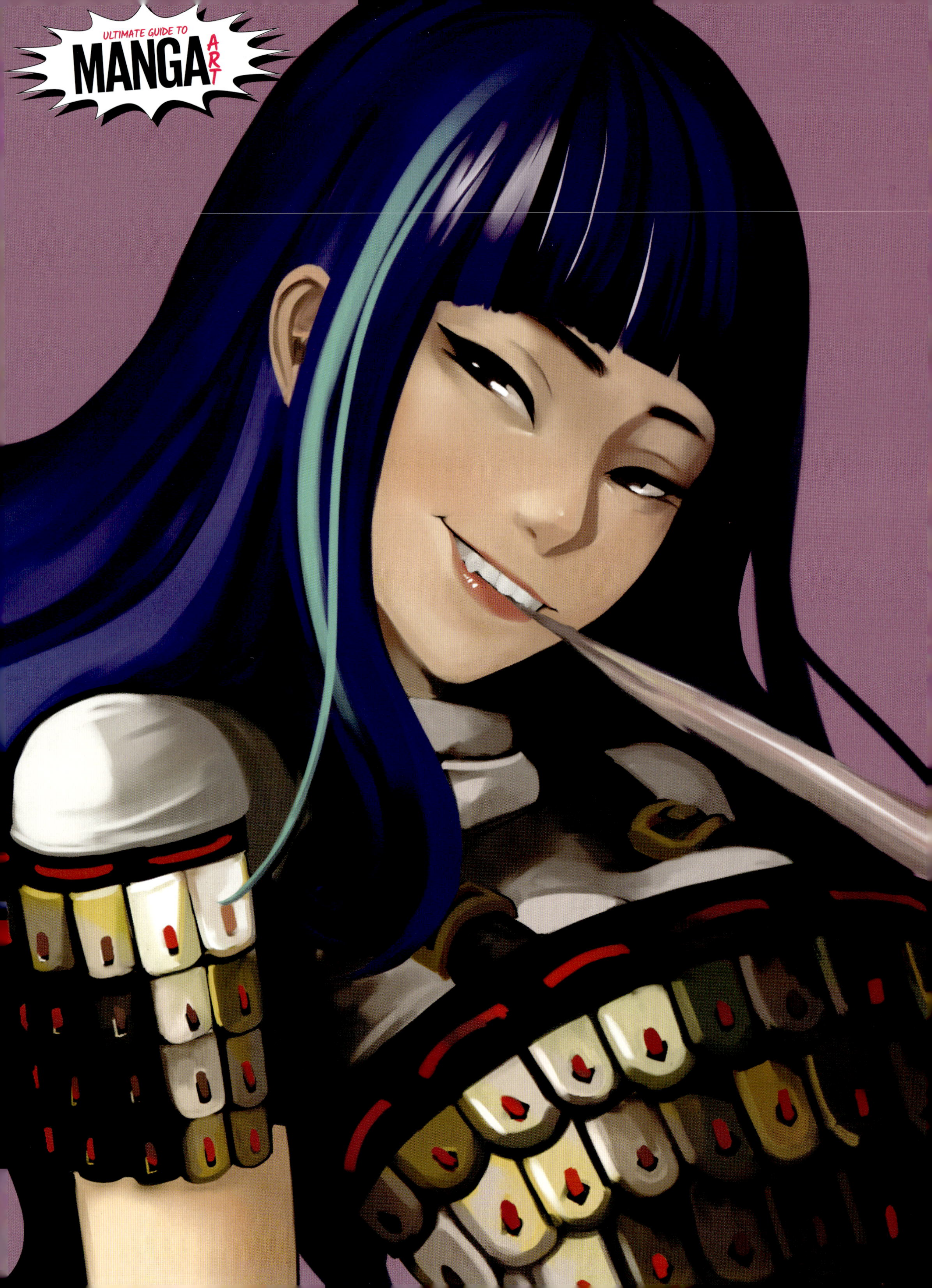
ULTIMATE GUIDE TO
MANGA ART

Artist Insight

15 TIPS ON PAINTING MANGA FACES

Collateral Damage Studios' **Zakary Lee** reveals his techniques for creating engaging manga characters, using a painting-based approach.

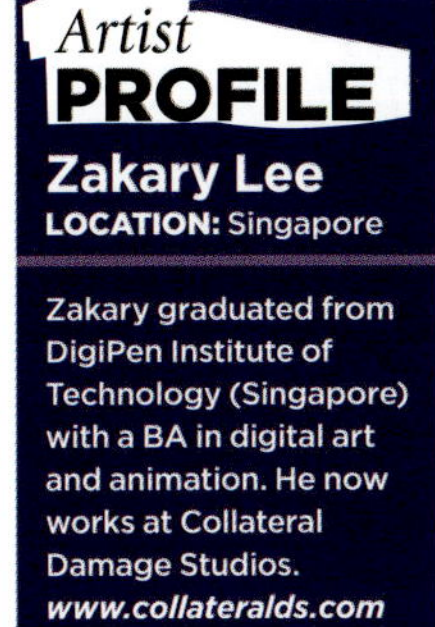

Artist **PROFILE**

Zakary Lee

LOCATION: Singapore

Zakary graduated from DigiPen Institute of Technology (Singapore) with a BA in digital art and animation. He now works at Collateral Damage Studios.

www.collateralds.com

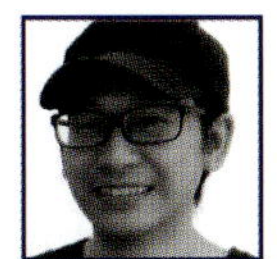

I began my drawing career by learning how to draw manga. During this time, I purchased many how-to guides for creating this distinctive art style, and discovered that the drawing methods were similar to those of western comic art. Essentially, you'd use a pencil to draw the head shape and then add lines to indicate the eye position and center of the face. Once this construction sketch is complete, the final line art is created using ink.

I followed the same drawing method when I first explored digital art with a Wacom Graphire that a friend gave to me. Yet, I couldn't get my hand-drawn line art to look right and I had to use the Pen tool. The resulting line art was clean, but it felt lifeless and lacked the energy that I would have wanted in the drawing.

After years of practice, I gradually changed my method of drawing characters. Instead of working from a sketch and then moving to line art before adding colors, I paint in grayscale, then adjust values and apply colors until I'm happy with the drawing. So here are some of my tips for drawing manga faces digitally.

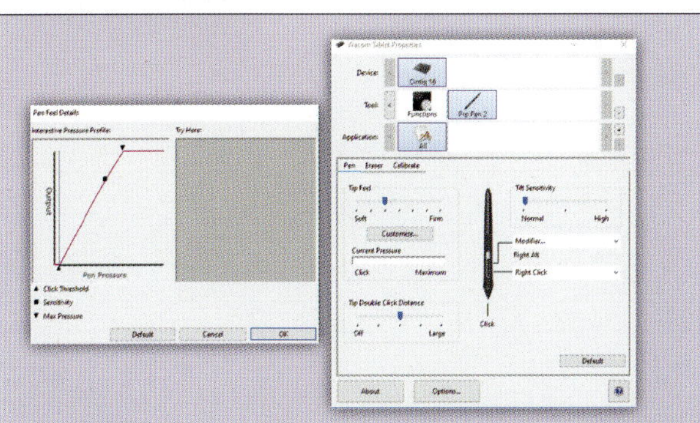

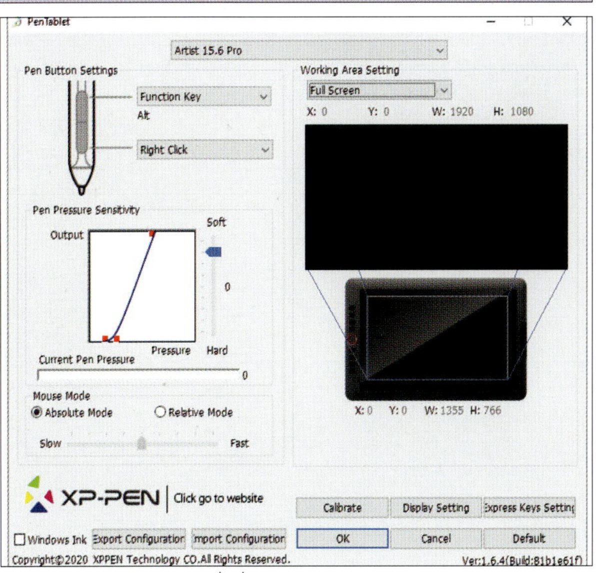

1. GET SET UP FOR DRAWING FACES.

Spend a few minutes configuring your drawing tools before you get stuck in the creative process. For example, tablets have Pen Pressure set to maximum by default. You'll have to press down hard with the pen on the tablet's surface to hit maximum output. Drawing with the maximum Pressure and Threshold settings can result in wobbly lines. By adjusting my Pressure Threshold and reducing the maximum output Threshold to about 60% of the Pressure, I can create steady lines without worrying about making my lines look consistent. For Wacom products, this setting is accessed through Wacom Tablet Properties, while for XP-PEN products access the PenWin/Mac driver.

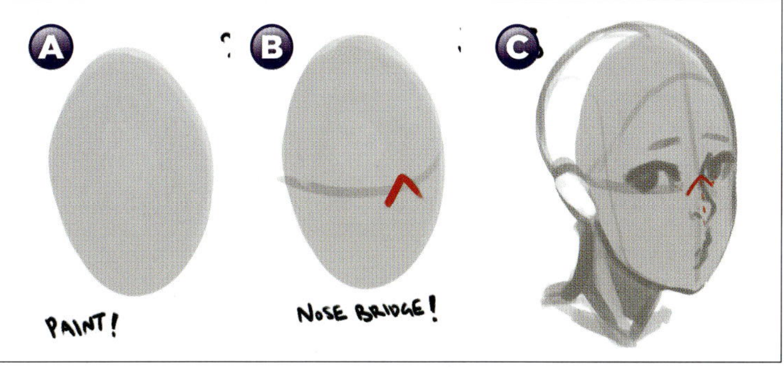

2. USE AN ARROW TO PLACE KEY FACIAL FEATURES.

After blocking out the head (**A**) I decide which direction the character is facing. Treating the head as a 3D shape, I draw a horizontal line that curves along the surface. When I draw this line, I bear in mind whether the head is tilted upwards or downwards, or facing left or right. To fix the direction of the head, I'll draw an upward-pointing arrow (**B**). This helps me locate where the nose bridge meets the root of the nose. Once this key location of the face has been identified, I can quickly paint and sketch in the centerline for the face, eyes, eyebrows, mouth, and chin (**C**). ➻

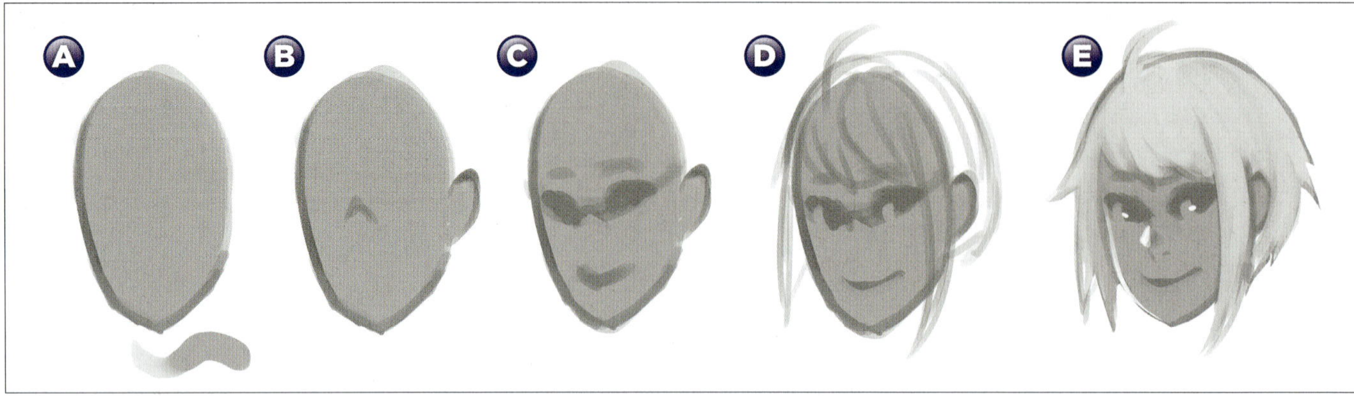

3. USE A PAINTING APPROACH WHEN SKETCHING HEADS.

I paint my sketch instead of drawing it with fine lines (**A**). I use a big brush with about 60–80% values to block in the head (**B**). Next, using a darker value, I'll outline the head and paint key features (**C**). I'll fine-tune the expression of the mouth and eyes by color-picking the gray tone and painting over the line (**D**). Finally, I'll refine the hair to get a sense of its shape, painting over lines to achieve the shape that I want (**E**).

> “The key expressive features of the human face comprise the mouth, eyebrows, and eyes.”
>
> —Zakary Lee

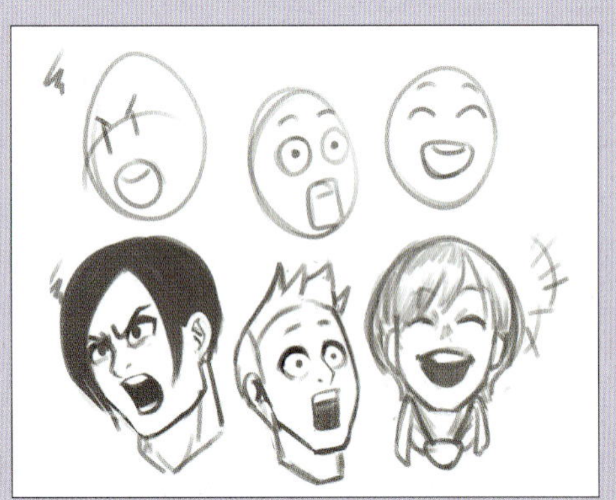

4. CAPTURE EXPRESSIONS IN CARTOON SKETCHES.

The key expressive features of the human face comprise the mouth, eyebrows, and eyes. When I draw a figure that has a particular emotion, I'll first doodle a cartoonlike image of the expression that I have in mind. After this sketch is complete, I'll try to pick out certain facial aspects within the expression. Is the mouth open? Are the teeth clenched? What do the eyebrows look like in the simple expression? I'll take note of those features and keep them in mind while I draw a refined version of the character's design on top of the initial sketch.

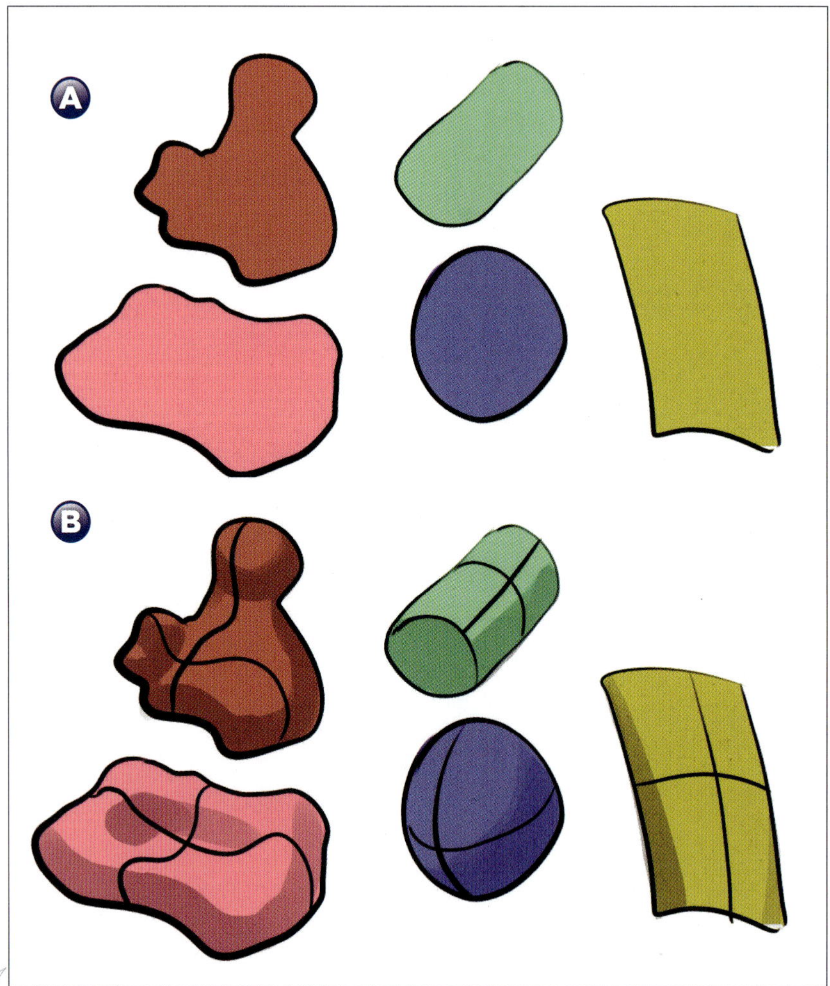

5. DRAW FORMS AND DESIGN WITH SHAPES.

Here are a collection of shapes (**A**). Drawing a line across these shapes will give a sense of depth to the object, turning it into a 3D form (**B**). After sketching the shape design, I think of them as forms so that I can shade according to the direction of light in the composition. This is good practice when drawing different-shaped heads.

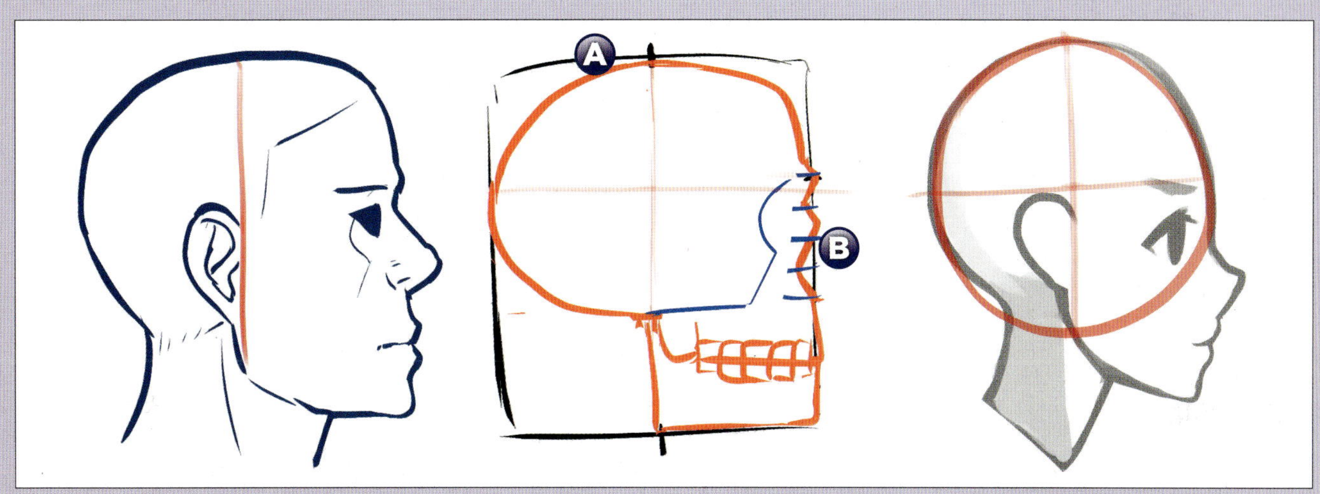

6. MAKE HEAD MEASUREMENTS.

Manga characters tend to have exaggerated features such as big eyes and tiny noses, but I feel that the profile of the skull should still be consistent with the measurements of the human skull. Above is a simplified drawing of a skull, with the braincase (**A**) and the facial bones (**B**) in proportion to each other. Compare this to a more "manga" head, and you can see that the proportions are pretty similar. The ears still sit on the vertical half of the braincase, while the brow line lies on the horizontal half of the braincase.

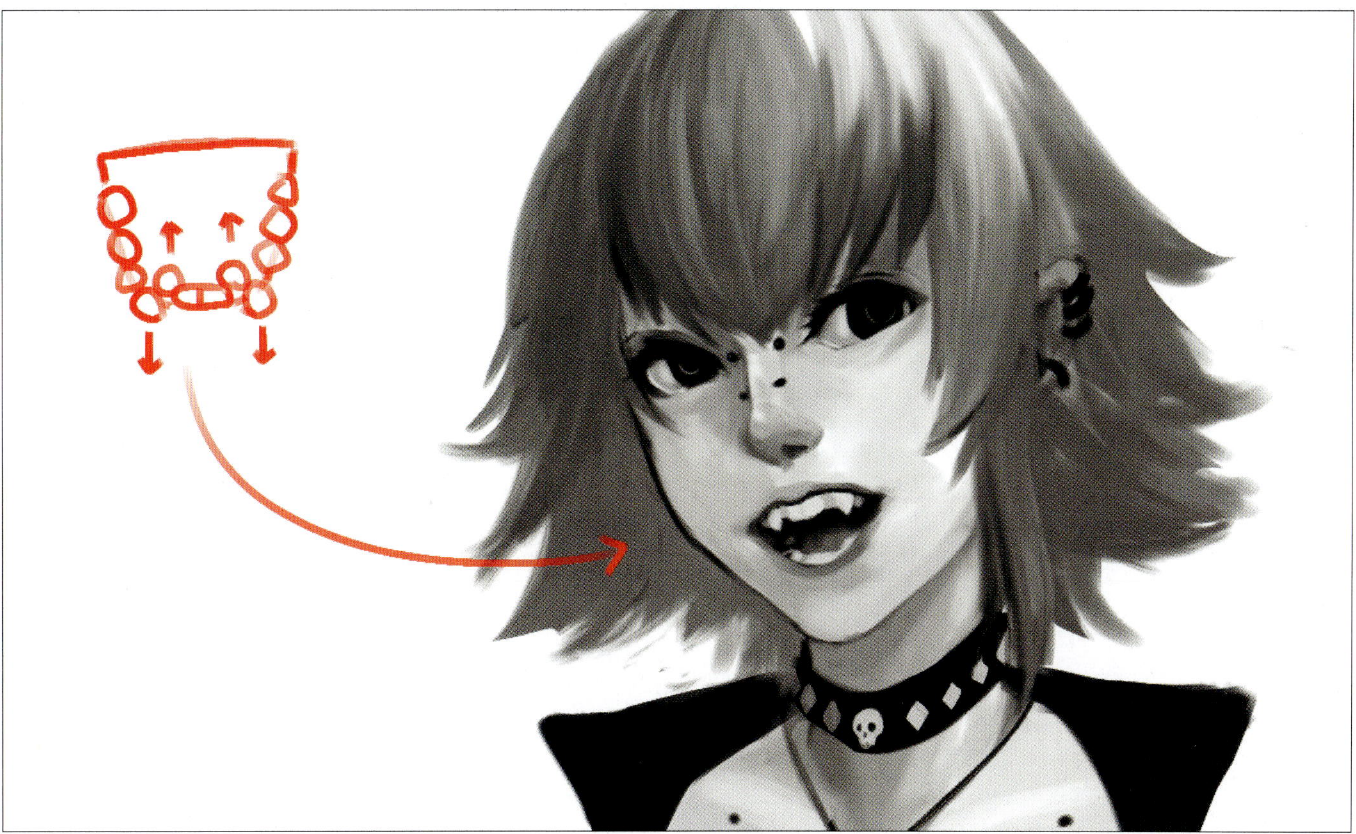

7. DRAW IMPERFECT TEETH.

Teeth are one of the things that I really like to draw, and I don't usually draw perfectly straight teeth. Some manga or anime characters have "cute little fangs" that give them a sense of unconventional cuteness. I incorporate this look into some of my characters, although I'll mix things up by painting crooked teeth, some teeth that are pushed to the back, and canine teeth that are pushed to the front. ➸

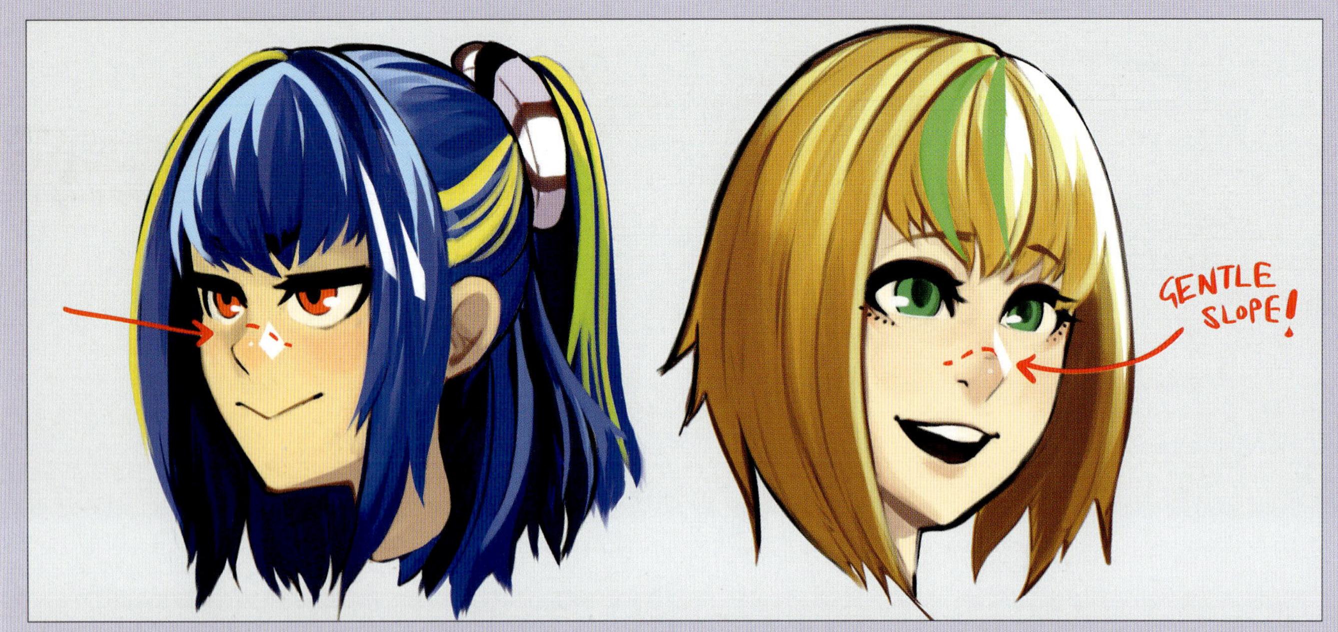

8. USE LIGHT OR SHADOW TO INDICATE THE NOSE BRIDGE INSTEAD OF A LINE.
The nose bridge area of the face is actually a slope, and the protrusion would be less pronounced on a manga-styled character. Instead of drawing a hard line to indicate the nose bridge, I use the shadow or highlights with a sharp edge alongside the nose, which highlights the form of the nose bridge.

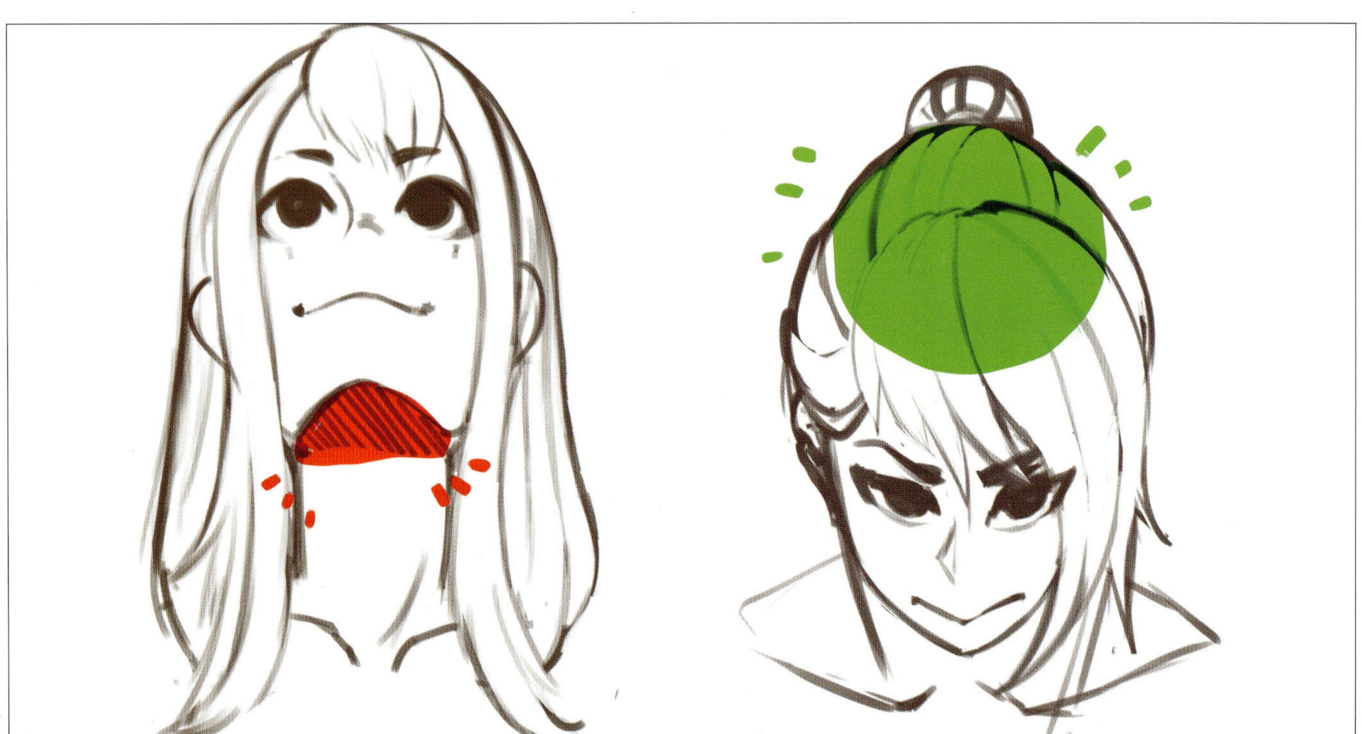

9. DRAW FRONTAL HEAD TILTS.
Try visualizing the head tilt from the profile view. Using a circle and a box, I can visualize what the head tilt will look like from the side. I draw vertical lines extending from key features such as the chin, center of the braincase, ears, and the top of the head. This enables me to see what I'll need to paint when attempting to draw the head from the front. Above are examples of a manga character's head tilted up and down. Remember to draw the underside of the jaw when drawing a tilted-up head, and the crown when drawing a head that's tilted down.

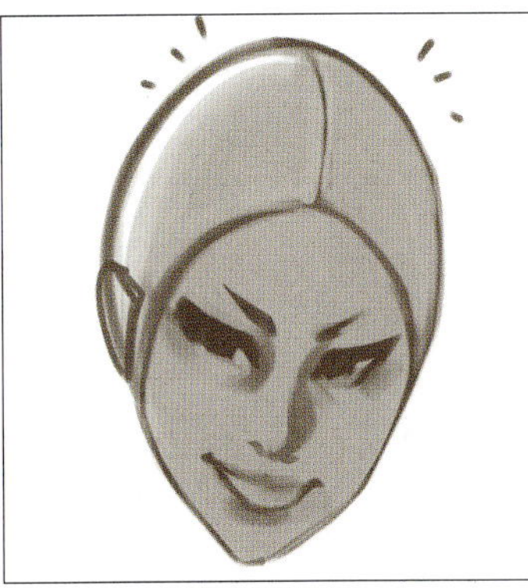

10. USE A SWIMMING CAP FOR HEAD ANGLES.

Drawing a swimming cap can help you determine the angle of the head. Visualize a swimming cap with a seam in the middle, and put that on your character. By covering all your character's hair and ears, you can now focus on drawing the facial features. Furthermore, you can use the cap's edge as the hairline, and because swimming caps cover the ears, I can draw the ears behind this edge with confidence, thus placing them in the right position.

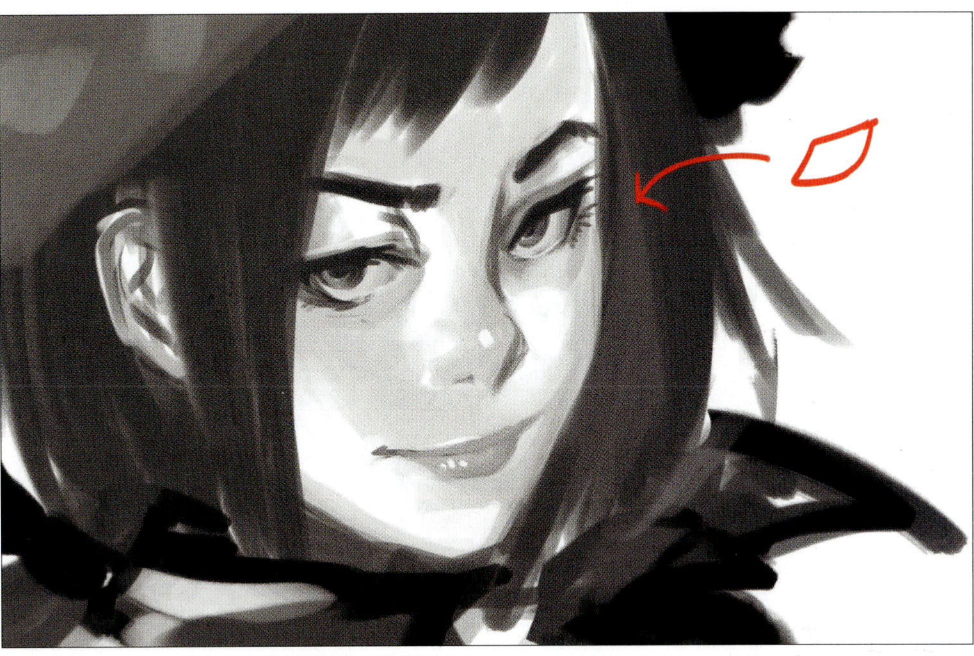

11. KEEP THE DRAWING OF THE EYES SIMPLE.

The curvature of the eyeball makes it complicated to draw at an angle and symmetrically, so keeping it simple will improve your skill at drawing realistic eyes quickly and relatively easily. Furthermore, take note of the shape of your character's eyes. Does the eye have an inward or downward tilt? Is the iris normally small or large? These will help you sketch your character's eyes at more complex angles.

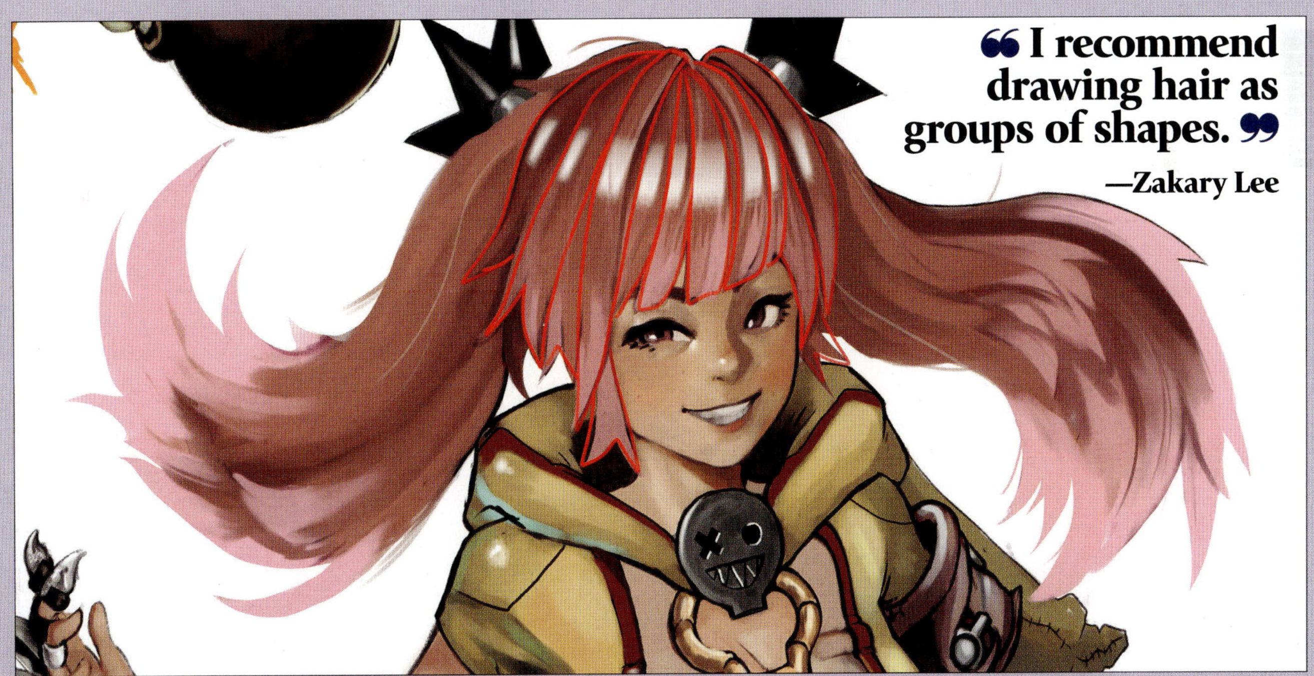

> “I recommend drawing hair as groups of shapes.”
> —Zakary Lee

12. DRAW HAIR IN CLUMPS.

You don't have to draw every single strand of hair. Instead, I recommend drawing hair as groups of shapes. Start with big shapes such as the bangs, back of the head, and any ponytails or pigtails that the character might have. Break those big shapes down into medium-size shapes and then into smaller clumps of hair. You can then add single strands of hair afterwards for added detail.

13. TECHNIQUES FOR PAINTING EYES

Discover how to ensure your characters' eyes are, well, eye-catching!

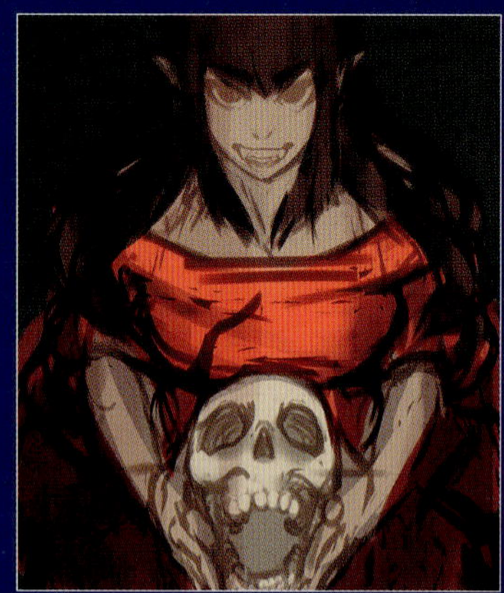

A Start with a flat color for the iris.

When sketching and drawing the eyes, paint the whole iris as a flat color. It can be the same color as your sketch brush. Painting the whole iris during the sketch phase will help make the sizes of both irises consistent with each other. It also makes it easier to compare and check whether both irises are the same size or not.

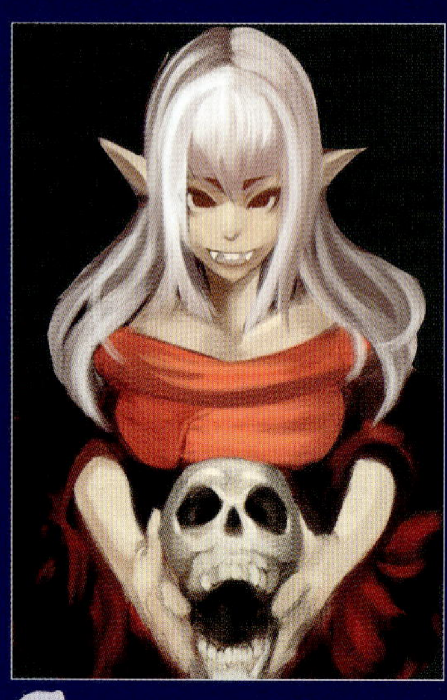

B Use the eyes to explain the lighting.

During the painting process, I'll spend a little time rendering the upper and lower eyelids. Because the eye socket is concave in shape and the light source is coming from an upwards direction, I paint the upper eyelids in a dark value and the lower eyelids in a lighter value.

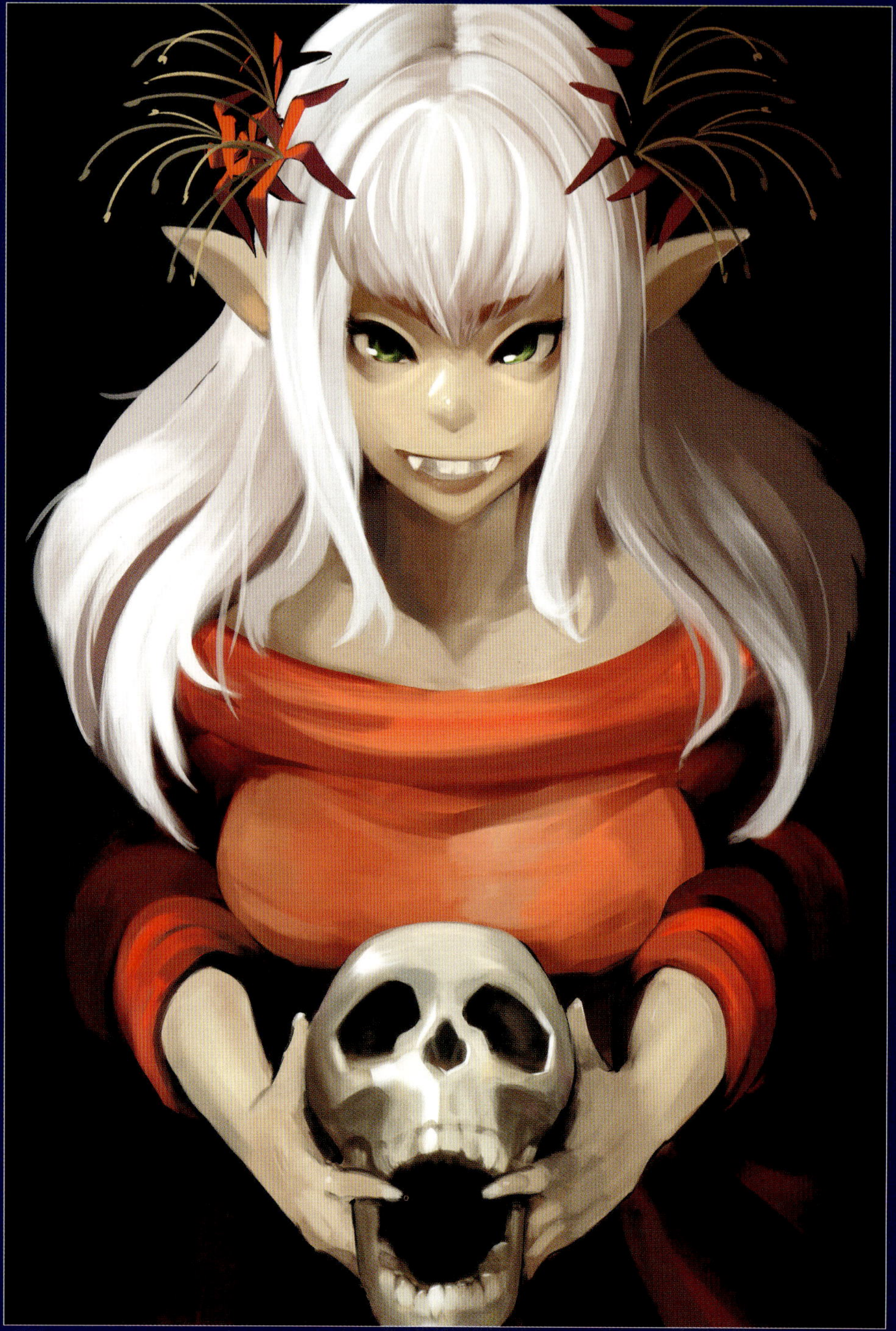

C Pick an iris color that's based on the rest of the composition.

Finally, I return to detailing the iris. I'll take a look at the overall picture and colors that I've used and then decide what color the iris of the character should be. Because the painting features predominantly red colors, I decide to go with a green color for the eyes. I also save my white value for the very end, applying a little highlight to the eyes.

14. USE SHAPES IN YOUR CHARACTER DESIGNS.
Whenever I've run into a brick wall when attempting to design an original outfit for a character, my solution is to duplicate a character's head a few times and then doodle whatever shape that comes to my mind alongside each one. So I'll focus on a single shape—a crescent or triangle, say—and then design a costume which resembles that shape. This method works with hairstyles, too.

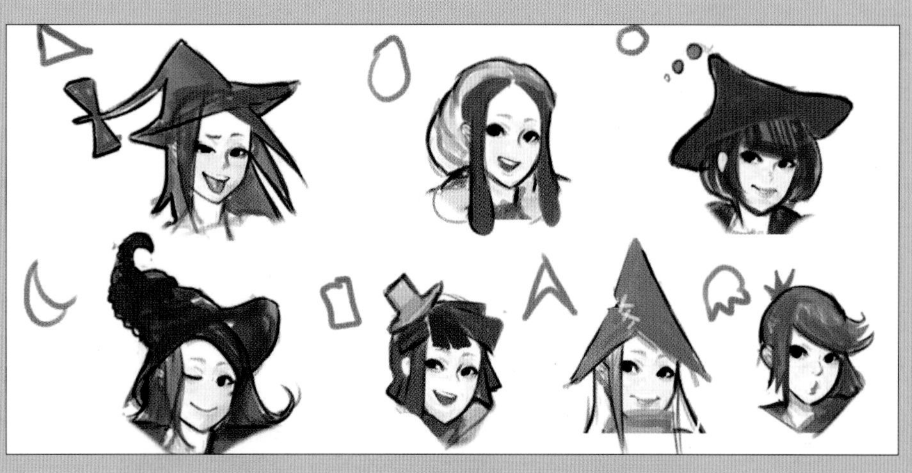

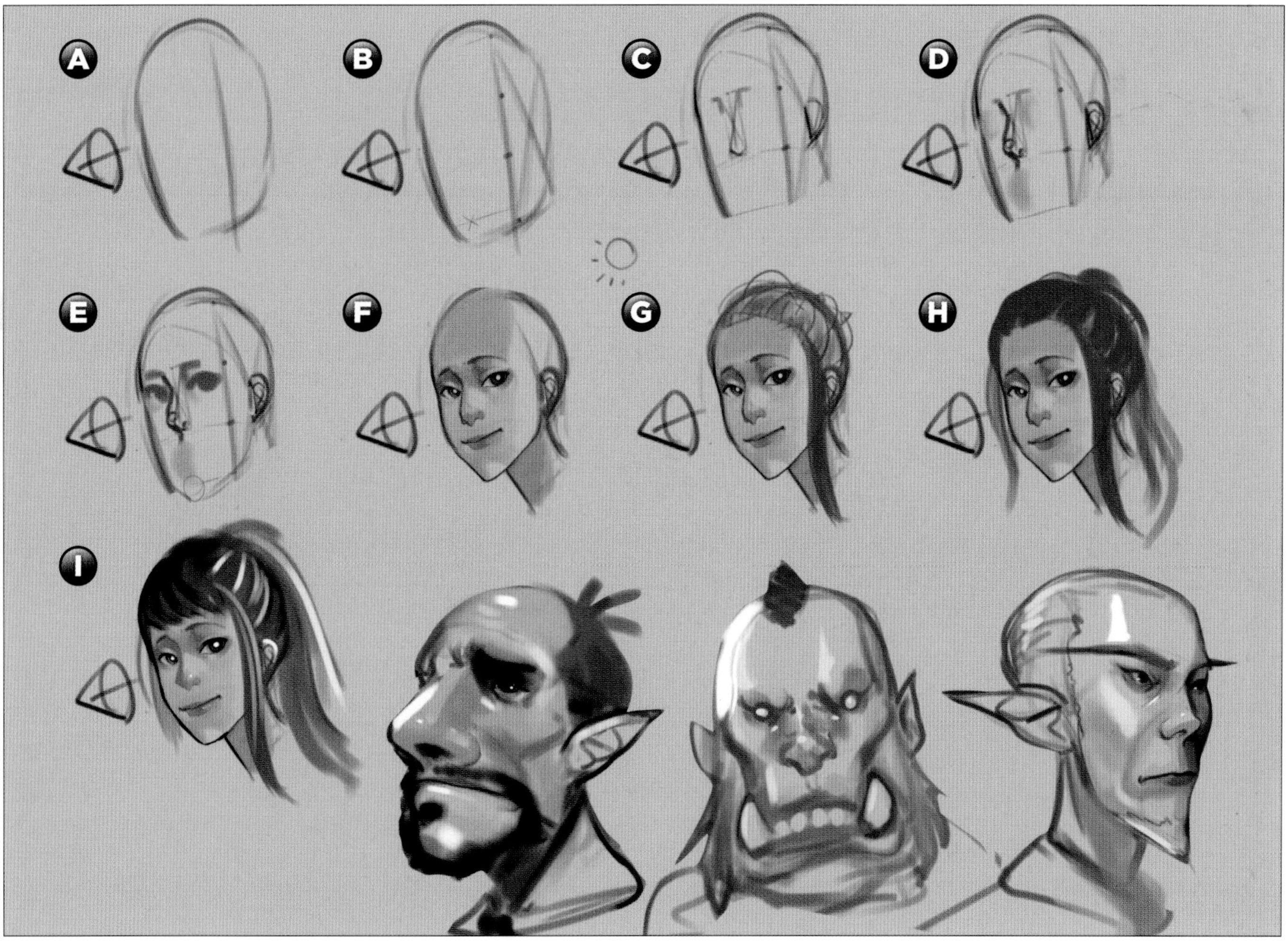

15. TRY DIFFERENT METHODS TO SUIT YOUR ART.
Above is a method of constructing the head with a rounded-edge box instead of the traditional egg shape (**A**)-(**I**). I also use the same method to draw three fantasy characters. I skew and manipulate the human skull proportions to fit fantastical characters. Make the eyes smaller, the jaw bigger, or even enlarge the nose. You can use different construction methods to either draw people in a similar style or draw different styled characters, all using the same construction method. It's all about finding the form of the subject that you're drawing. There are many methods of constructing heads; I would suggest testing and trying every one of them that you can find out there! Find a method that suits your art, or develop one for yourself.

Artist insight

15 TIPS FOR BETTER CHARACTER ART

Artists from Singapore's **Collateral Damage Studios** walk you through the key steps of creating and refining your manga characters.

As Japanese animation grew in popularity, artists around the world started taking up the general basics of the art form and making it their own. We've all seen many outstanding works of art with clear manga influence that originated outside of Japan.

Collateral Damage Studios (CDS) is an illustration studio from Singapore. We employ some of the best manga art talents in Singapore to produce an extensive portfolio of manga art. Beyond just providing key visuals for anime conventions or mascot designs for video games, our artists enjoy creating character art and stories to call their own.

For the aspiring artist wanting to create your own character, it can be tempting to just follow the manga template wholesale. It's important to note that basic art and storytelling fundamentals are still necessary in the creation of good manga art.

Here, three CDS artists will share their expertise and experience when it comes to creating and refining manga character art. From how to clean up your character sketches, picking the right colors, and how to craft a story for them, there's plenty to incorporate into your own manga workflow.

ADVICE ON CLEANING UP YOUR SKETCHES WITH LOW ZI RONG

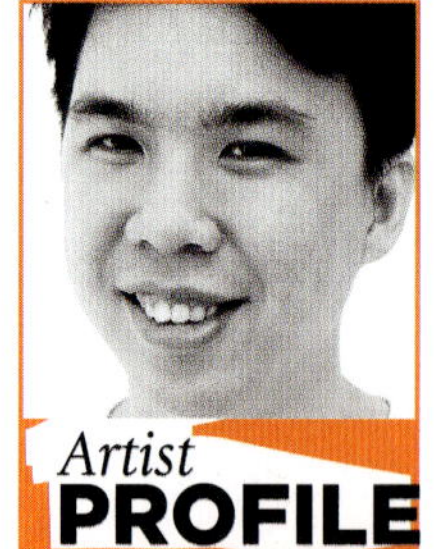

Artist **PROFILE**

Low Zi Rong
LOCATION: Singapore

As the resident character designer for CDS, Low is best known for his anime mascot design for Internet Explorer and Anime Festival Asia. He's also an accomplished animation director for the viral IE anime short.
https://ifxm.ag/low-zr

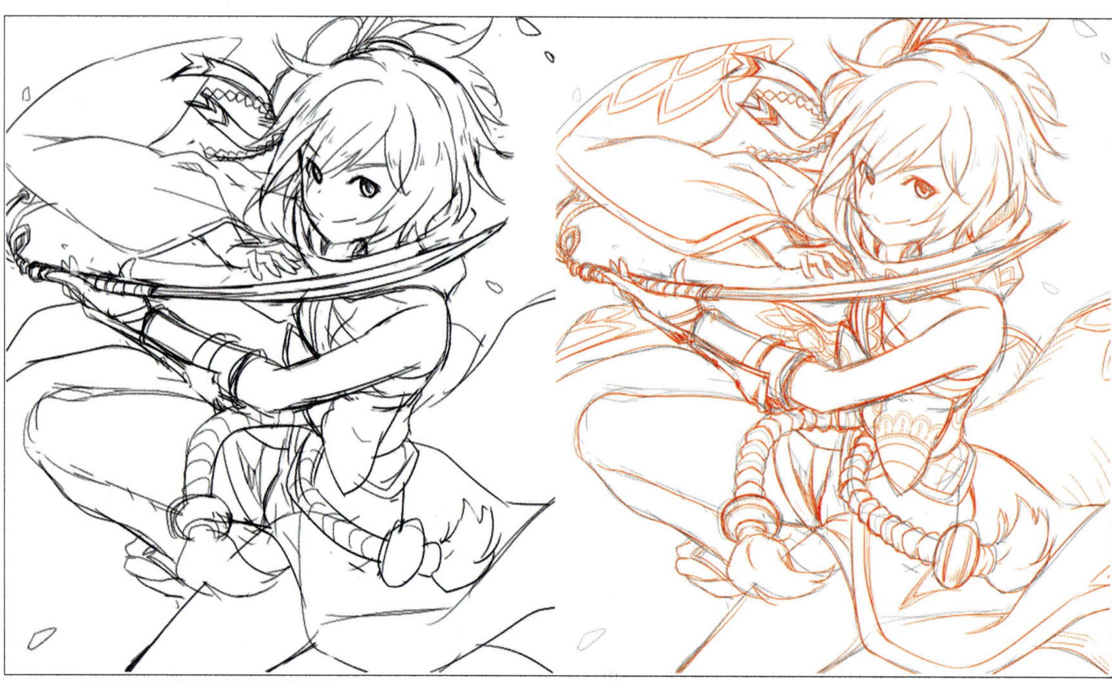

1. TIGHTEN UP YOUR ROUGHS.

I usually start with a rough sketch, working out the pose and the flow of the other objects such as the costume and hair. Then, I'll take a quick second pass to refine parts of the picture and add more details that can aid in my line-work process later. If you're working on a single layer, it can be easy to accidently erase portions of the original sketch when you're zoomed in and focused on adding details, resulting in the overall composition being altered. I recommend using a new layer to flesh out the details, while keeping the original composition on another layer for easy reference.

2. DIFFERENTIATE LAYERS WITH COLOR.
I find it useful to change the color of my pencil before cleaning up the sketch. Even if you reduce the opacity of the sketch layer during the cleanup stage, unwanted lines that are overlooked might be mistaken for lines from the original sketch. Changing the color of the sketch to another color can make the distinction between the sketch layer and cleanup layer more obvious, and reduce stray lines when cleaning up. Using colors to highlight different areas that you might want to separate into layers also serves as a visual reminder when lining them.

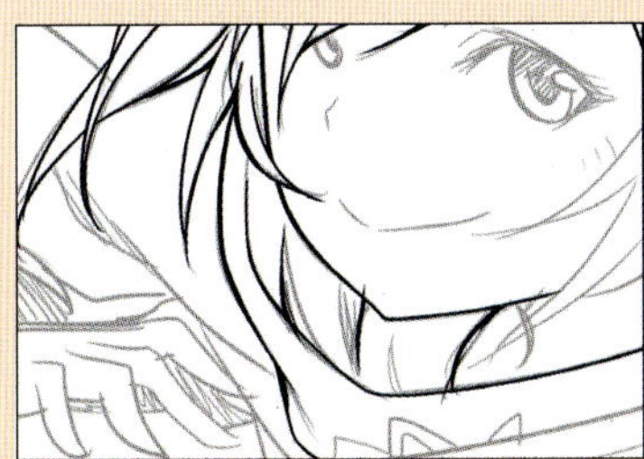

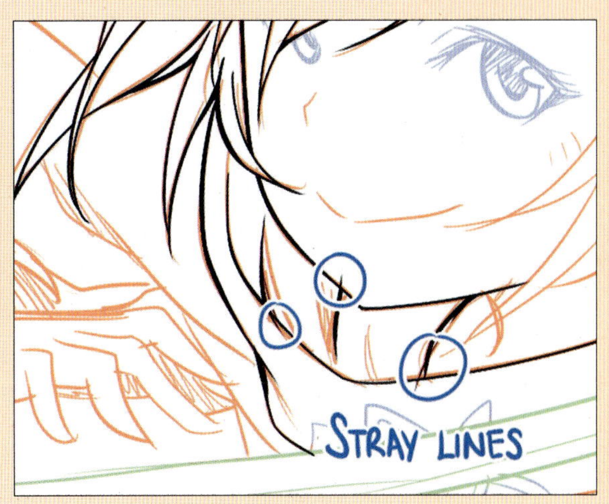

> I find it useful to change the color of my pencil before cleaning up the sketch.
> —Low Zi Rong

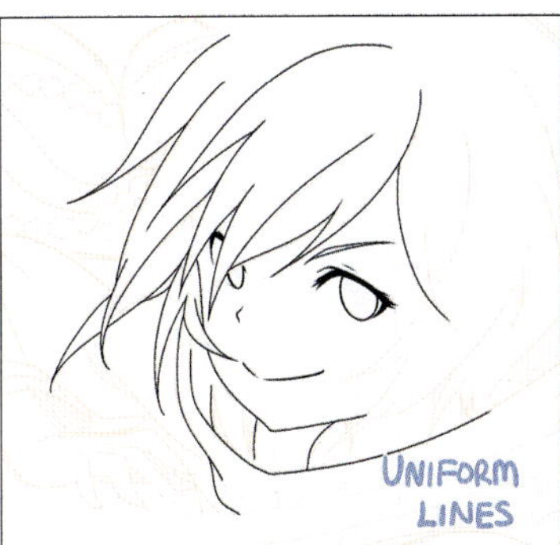

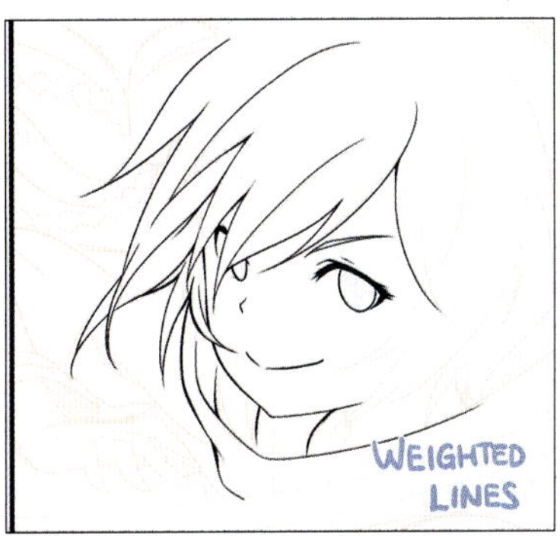

3. ADD WEIGHT TO YOUR LINES.
Apart from certain art styles or production requirements, giving your lines different thicknesses adds depth to your drawing. In general, drawing thinner lines of elements closer to the light source and thicker lines for those further away can make your art pop. One example when it's not necessary to add weight to your lines is for animation production, is when production time is limited and the consistency of lines between frames is more important.

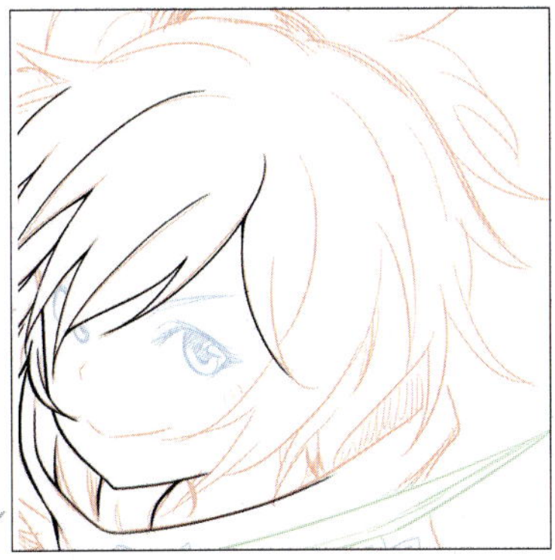

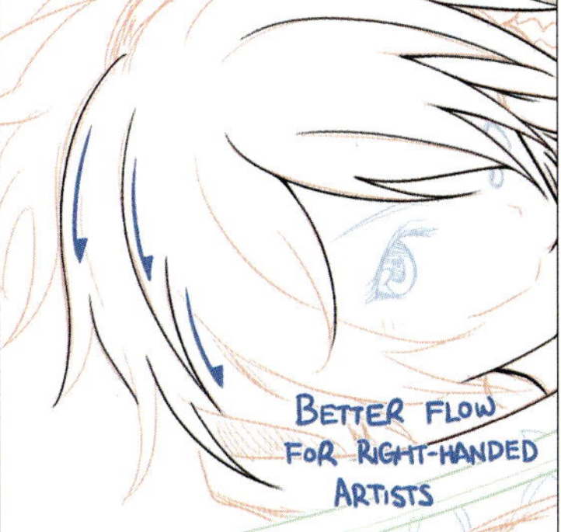

4. ROTATE AND FLIP THE CANVAS.
To achieve clean and smooth-flowing lines, it's usually better to clean up curves correctly in a single stroke. Most painting software enables you to rotate and flip the canvas freely to adjust the angle at which you tackle those curves. Flipping the canvas as you draw is also a good way to check the balance of the image if you've been staring at your artwork for too long.

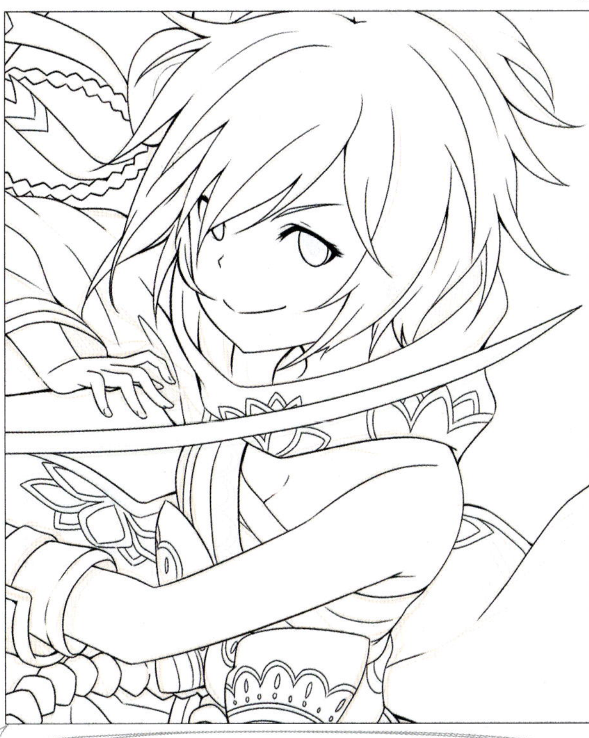

5. CHECK THE DEVELOPING ARTWORK.
As mentioned earlier, during cleanup we tend to zoom in and focus on the finer details of the artwork. We end up taking localized decisions on how certain strokes would be cleaned without bearing in mind context of the whole image. This might result in, for example, a well-drawn hand that's clearly out of proportion when compared to the rest of the body. Therefore, it's important to zoom out occasionally to check everything's still on track as you clean up your sketch.

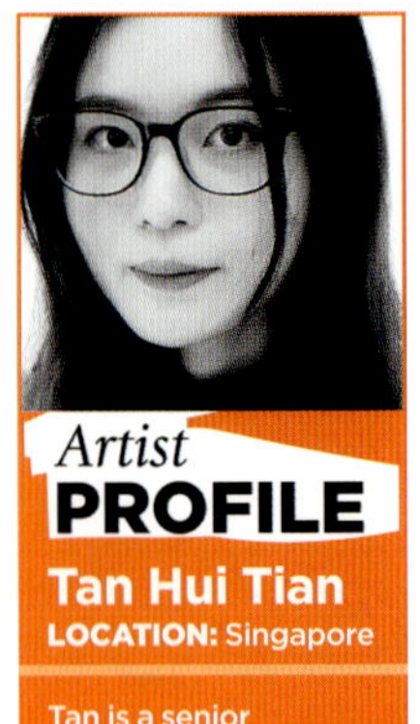

Artist
PROFILE

Tan Hui Tian
LOCATION: Singapore

Tan is a senior illustrator with CDS. She comes from a graphic design background, and her work emphasizes a strong design sense.
https://ifxm.ag/tan-ht

APPLY **TAN HUI TIAN'S** *COLOR THEORY TIPS TO YOUR FIGURES.*

1. GO BEYOND COLOR THEORY.

Colors convey mood and meaning, and you can use them to direct or misdirect the audience. At its most effective, just the color palette can bring to mind the object. It also serves as a bond when different objects share the same palette, such as the historical significance of the red, blue, and white stripes in Pan-Slavic flags. Beyond basic color theory, the science of colors, and its everyday usage can be useful information. For instance, knowing that in European culture, royalty is represented by purple, while in India, deep red and ochre symbolize grandeur and wealth, can be useful in creating culturally specific characters.

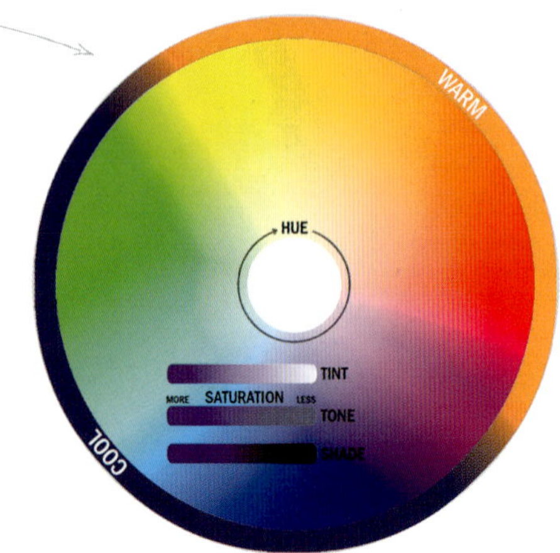

2. CONSIDER THE CONCEPT.

When I create a character design, form follows function. A hierarchy of information applies to color design, too. Areas of high contrast will attract more focus, and bright colors can indicate narrative significance. I try to go from a macro overview before tackling details. Here, the characters are twins working as bodyguards. They share a black, green, and white palette, but also have spots of pink or cyan to differentiate them. I also try to ensure that no other in-universe characters have a similar palette. The narrative theme is dark, and therefore the general color palette reflects that and is muted.

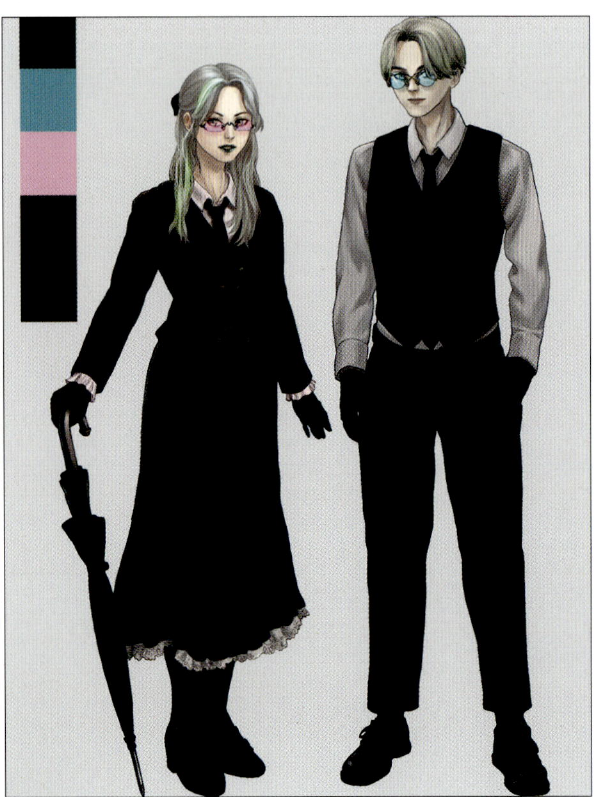

3. BUILD A PALETTE.

I use tools like Adobe Kuler and ColorLovers for inspiration—you can use Kuler to create a palette from an existing image. Before deciding on a palette, explore options with a character color sheet (usually with flat colors). Also, keep in mind the usage and context of the image. If, say, it's meant as a final asset in an environment, make sure it contrasts against the main environmental colors. I tend to use a neutral white light for shading, so that it's easy to adjust the character art in different lighting conditions afterwards.

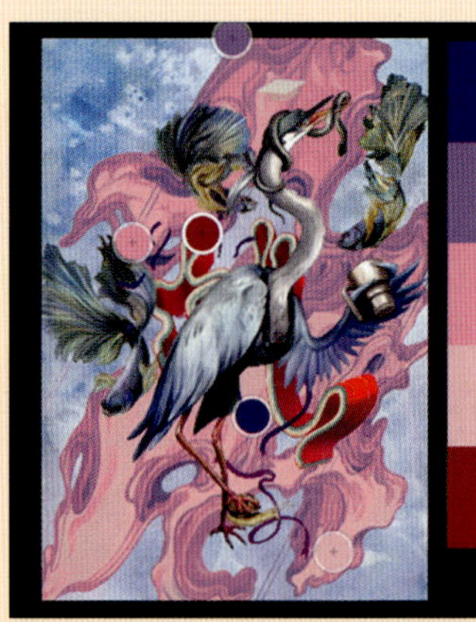

> **"Before settling on a palette, explore options with a character color sheet."**
> **—Tan Hui Tian**

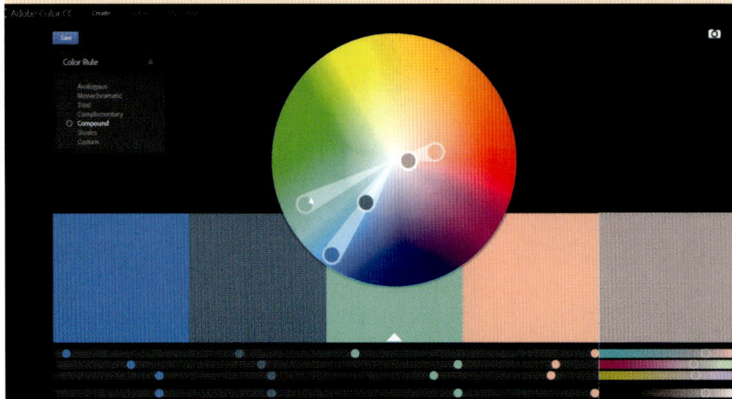

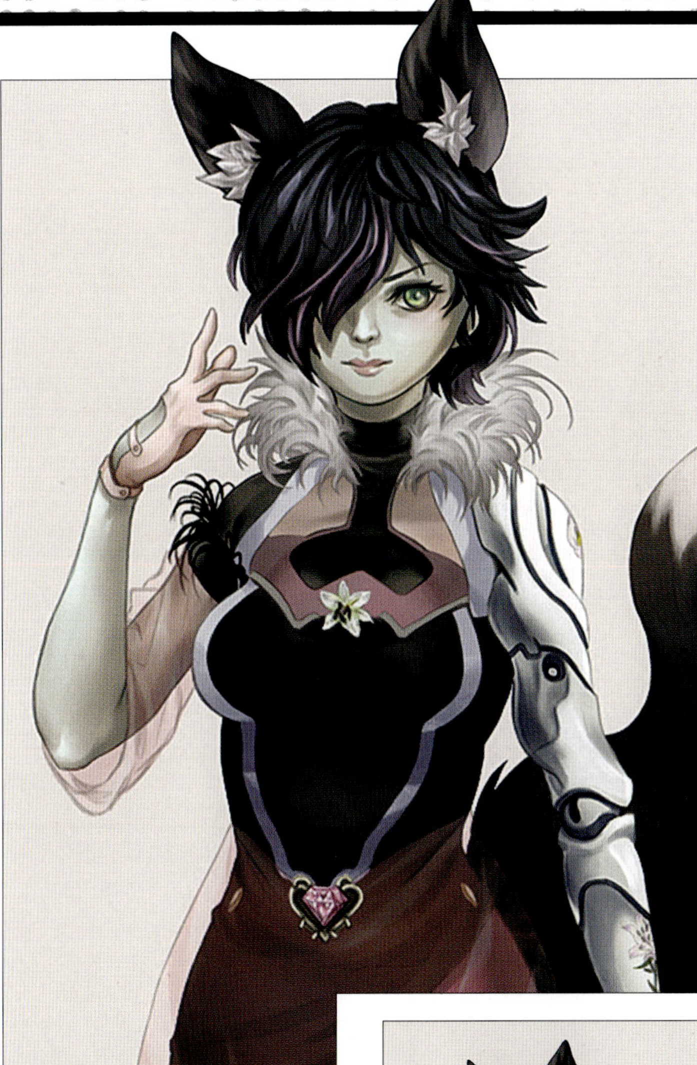

4. CONSIDER COLOR SYMBOLISM.

People perceive colors differently (think of viewers who might suffer from chromophobia or experience color blindness). But there are general meanings and physiological effects associated with colors. For instance, I tend to avoid fully saturated colors such as CMYK magenta, because it gives me a headache! There are some exceptions when a "pop" aesthetic may be preferred. In my example, the character is a heiress who's revealed to be the main villain of the game towards the end. Her smaller stature and weak body makes her an unexpected villain, but the impression of vulnerability is further enforced with a predominantly pink-and-white palette, which signifies innocence. Whereas, the impression of inner darkness is supported by the presence of a darker palette.

5. HOW TO CHANGE YOUR COLORS

Tips for colorizing elements that are already rendered.

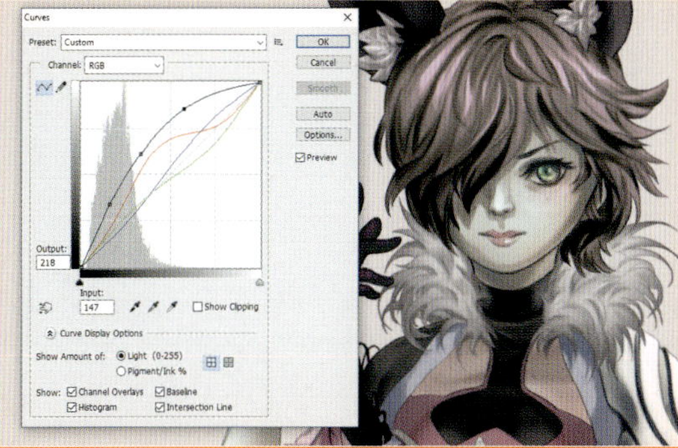

A Separate out elements.

Make sure all the different parts of the character are on individual layers for ease of editing. If I want to change a character's hair from black to pink for instance, I'll use Photoshop's Curve tool to brighten it first.

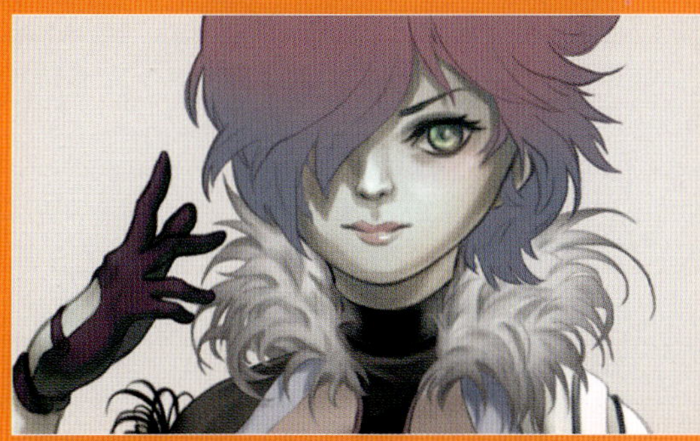

B Try out different hair looks.

To do a gradient color on her hair, Ctrl-select the hair layer, and then place a solid gradient on a new layer. Duplicate the gradient layer multiple times, and play around with Color, Overlay, and Screen blending modes.

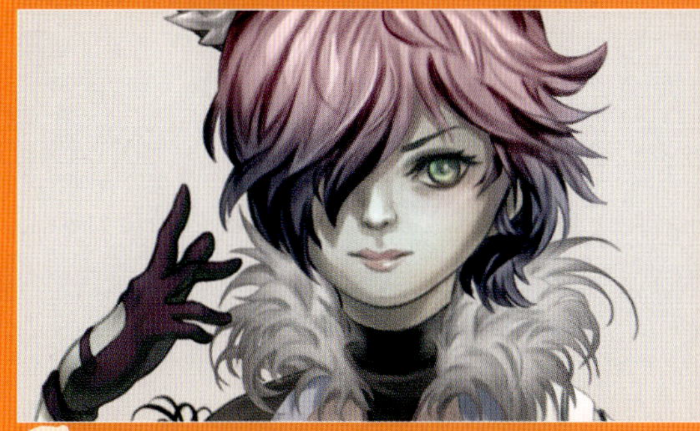

C Making adjustments by hand.

I use Color Balance, as well as a separate layer set in Screen mode, to finalize the color change. Sometimes, when there isn't enough tonal information for the color change, I'll paint them in as needed.

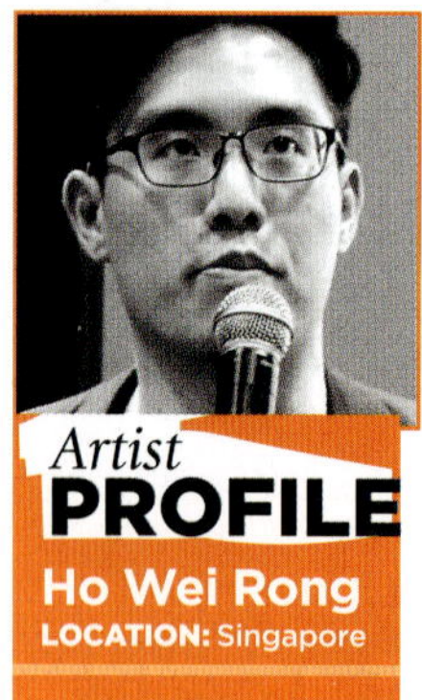

Artist
PROFILE

Ho Wei Rong
LOCATION: Singapore

Self-published webcomic artist Ho Wei Rong has spent the past decade developing and researching comic processes, which he has used to bring his debut webcomic, *ExCo*.
https://ifxm.ag/ex-co

DEVELOP A STORY FOR YOUR CHARACTER WITH HO WEI RONG.

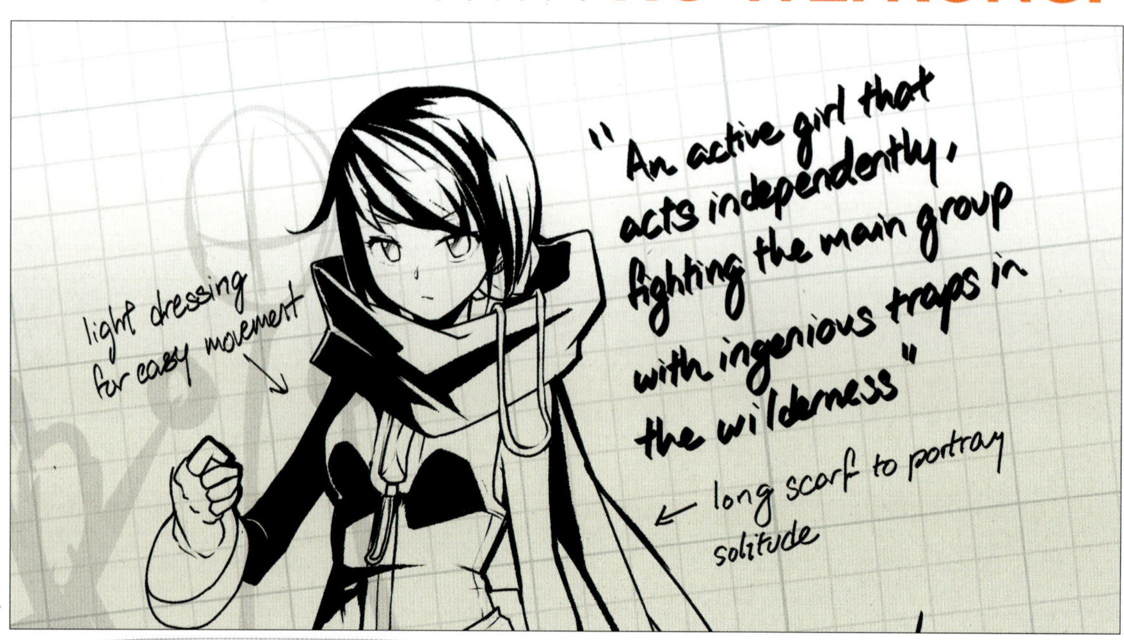

1. CREATE A FOCUS: THE ONE-LINER.

The key to creating a good character story is to have a strong center to build your story around—the selling point that your readers can instantly recognize. It should be easily described in one succinct line. I use this one-liner to provide direction from which I develop the rest of my character's story. Something as simple as "a girl with a love of stationery and humanity thrust into circumstances beyond herself," can be enough to form the base of your character's story.

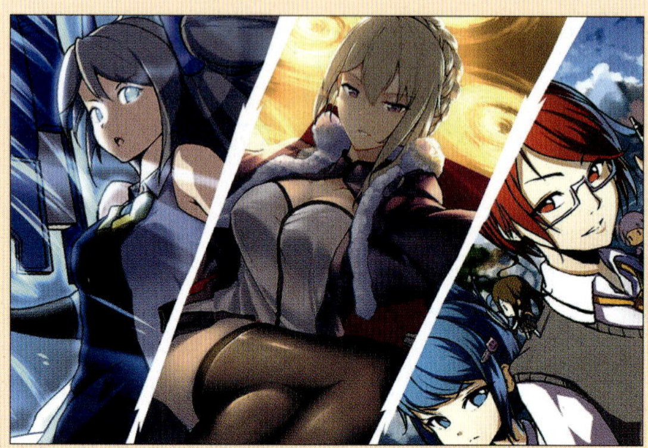

2. COLOR-CODE.

When differentiating characters, the quickest and most visible way to do so is by the use of colors. Colors can tell a story on their own, whether through the meaning of individual hues, or the relationship between certain colors. I use purple for a character with royal poise and wit, and red for a go-getter type with a childish lilt. And the contrast between red and blue enables me to create a story of contrasting opinion and values.

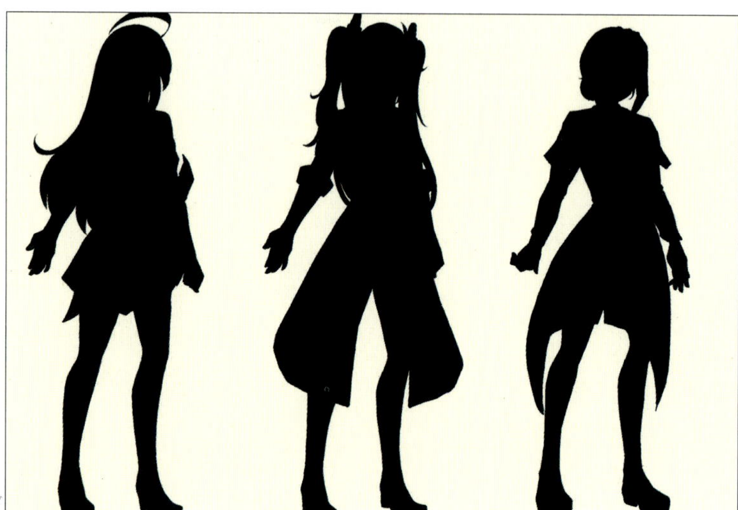

3. CREATE A DISTINCT SILHOUETTE.

Bodies come in all shapes and sizes in western comics. However, for manga, most body types and sizes fall within the same general categories, only differentiated by gender. In trying to create a distinct silhouette within the stricter rules of manga, I often fall back on two specific areas: hairstyle and unique design elements. I use contrasting hairstyles for my different characters, which allows for the variation in silhouette demanded for distinction. Where available, I also add unique shapes and objects to my clothing design to further set the silhouettes apart.

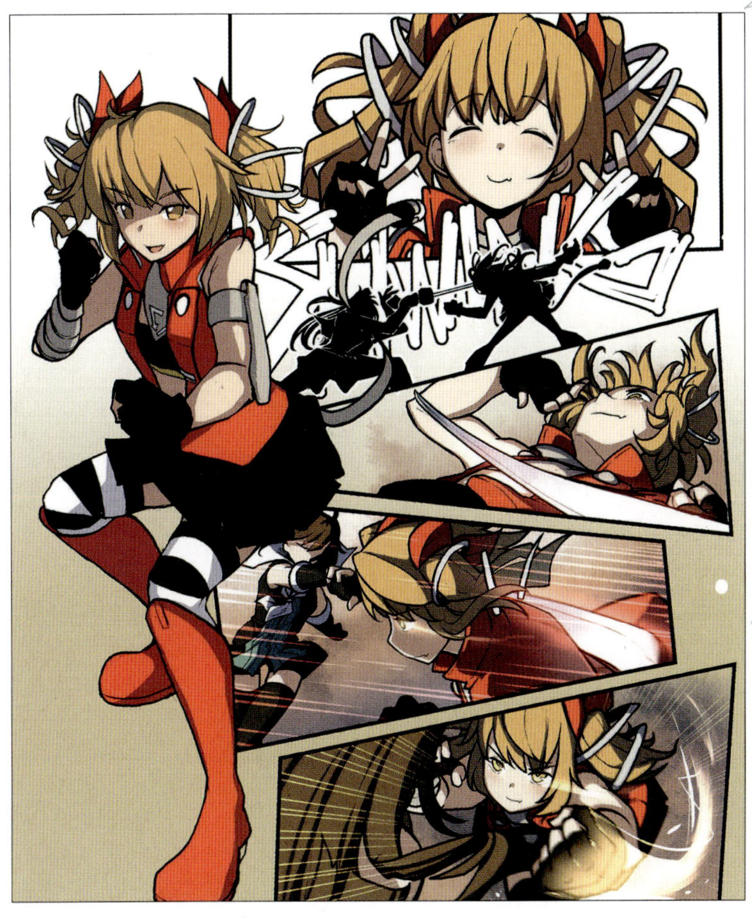

4. TELL A STORY THROUGH THE USE OF STRONG VISUALS.

When introducing a character, it's important that both their personality and abilities are displayed within the first few frames. To that end, in battle comics I ensure that their introductions enable them to fight an enemy.

I use this approach to establish the character's verbal tics and choice of actions, as well as the powers and capability that they're able to display. For a comic set in everyday life, I use a mundane daily task or scene for the same function, showing how the character approaches a problem that would be immediately familiar to the readers.

> **"When introducing a character, it's important that both their personality and abilities are displayed within the first few frames."**
>
> **—Ho Wei Rong**

5. BEGIN WITH AN END IN MIND.

It's relatively easy to create a character's personality and traits. What isn't easy is creating a role for the character. I begin this task by deciding what purpose this character will play in my overall storyline. I use something vague, but directional, like "background character in the second arc," or "mid-stage villain boss for the hero's first battle." This influences my choice of colors, elements, and extravagance of design. After all, a throwaway character who appears in the background of two chapters will be much more subdued in design than one who has a major role in the hero's development.

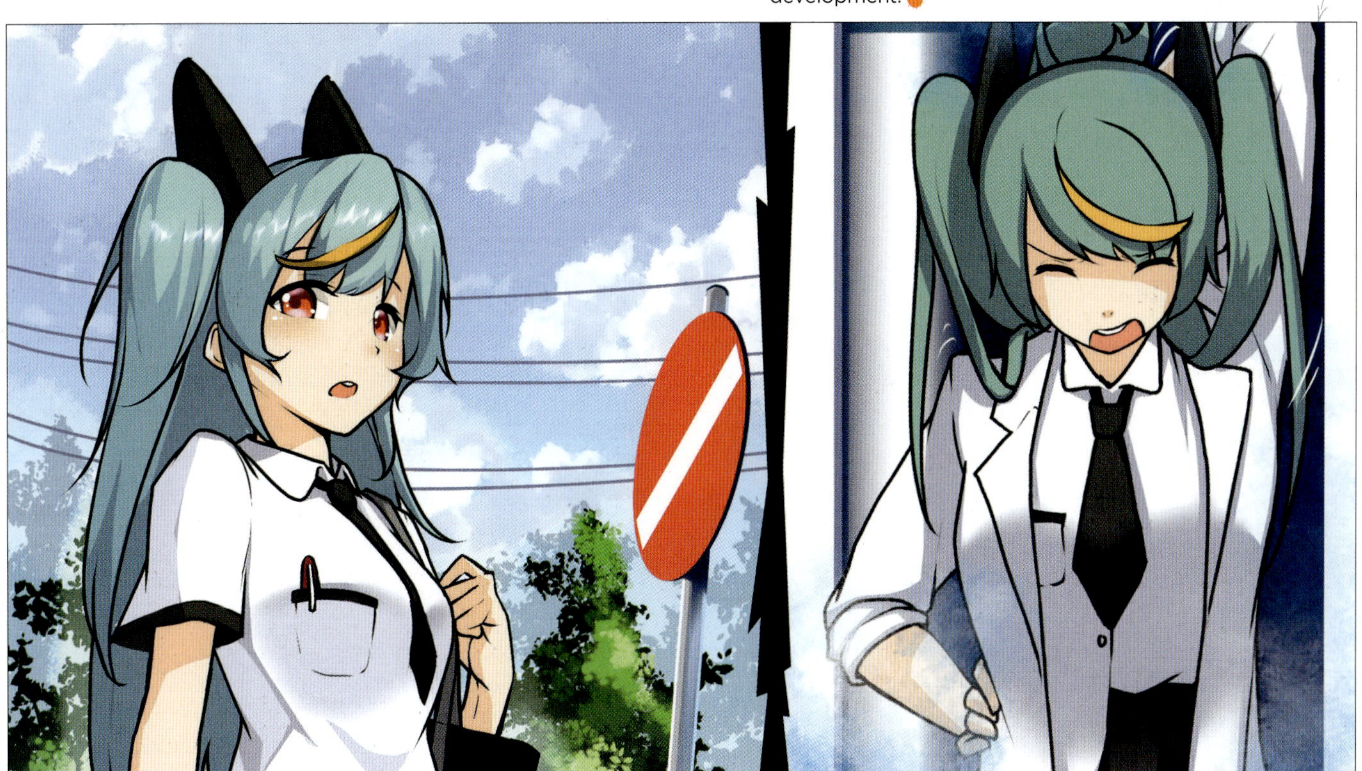

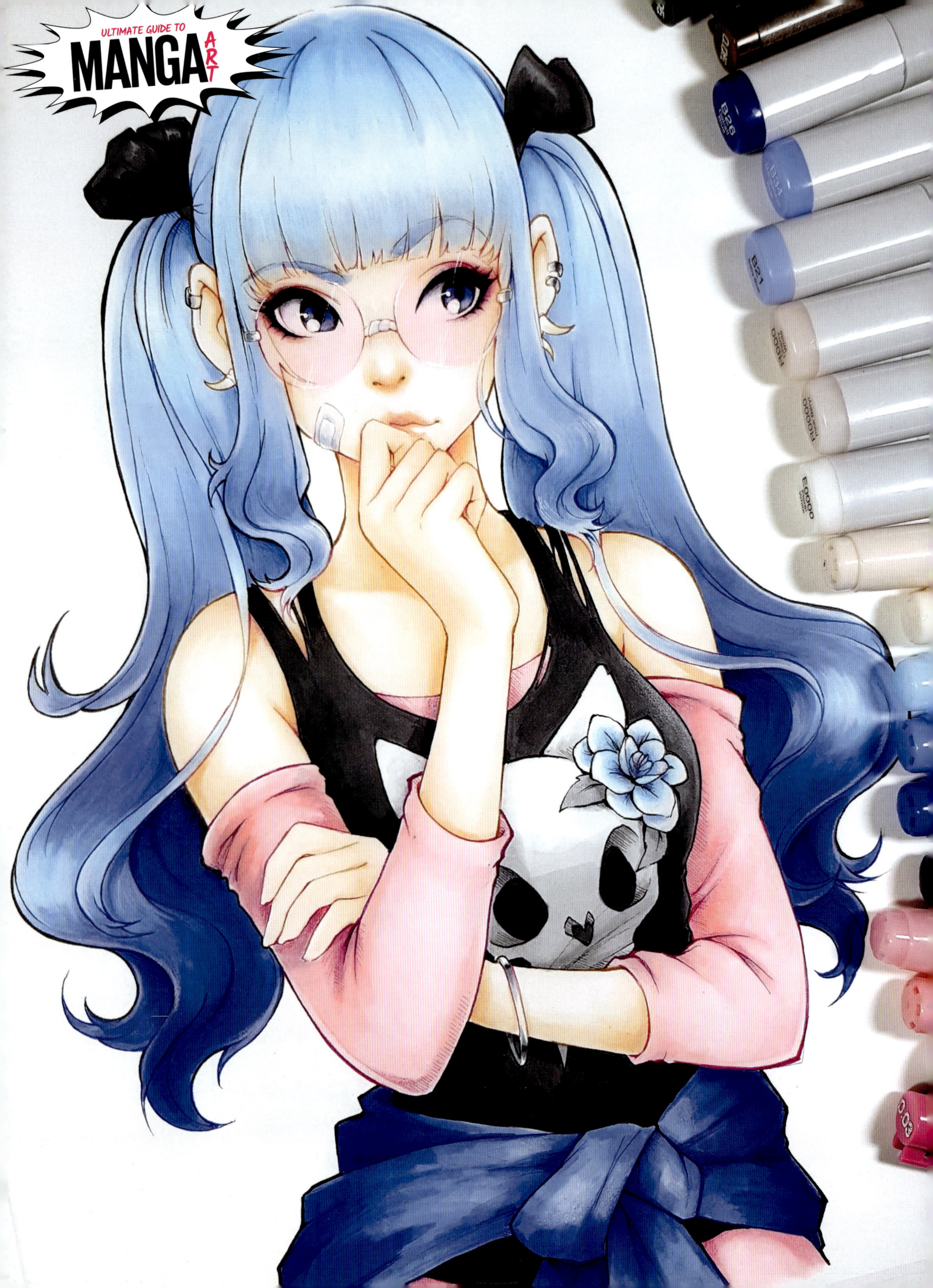
ULTIMATE GUIDE TO
MANGA ART
B26
B34
B21
E000
R0000
E0000
0.03

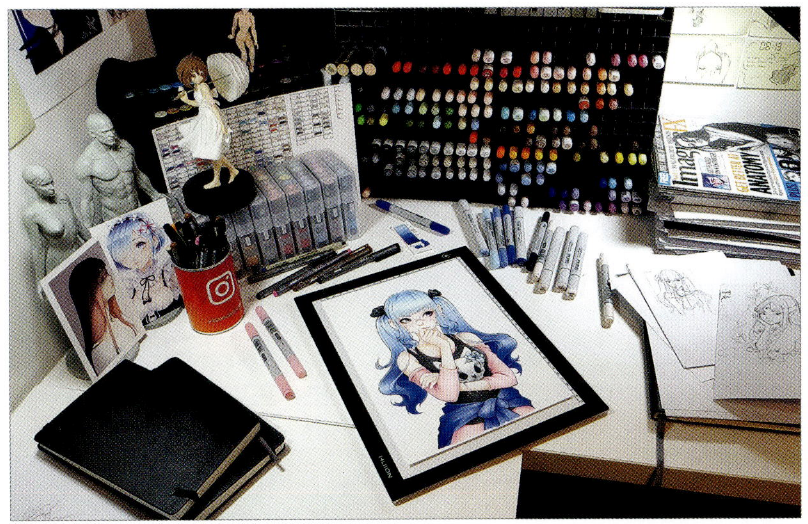

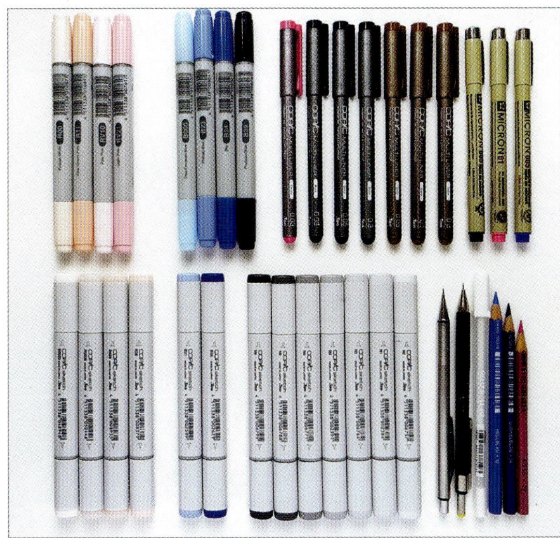

CHARACTER DESIGN IN COPIC MARKERS

Discover how ASIA LADOWSKA expertly blends pencils and markers to create an original manga character whose innocent appearance belies a nefarious streak.

Copic Markers appeared on my radar almost two years ago and I haven't looked back since. It was around the time I started my Instagram page, and my followers could see how the collection of five markers was growing slowly and how much could be achieved with just a few pens. I often limit my usage of markers; a few colors can create refreshing works, while using too many can have the opposite effect.

I'm proud and happy to be able to inspire over one million followers with my daily drawings. Working in the office and studying during the day, I know how hard it is to find the energy and motivation to draw after work or school, but I try to tell everyone to never give up their passions. I started out by spending a few minutes every evening on sketching, but the joy that finished image brings me is so strong that these days, I can spend the whole night drawing without noticing!

For this workshop, I challenged myself to come up with a simple character design, mostly to focus on and demonstrate how I use Copic Markers, but don't be deceived! The character and the pose may be simple, but I equipped this girl with accessories and details that add to her personality. At first glance, she may look innocent and harmless, but then you notice a faint smile and one lifted eyebrow complemented by a little patch on her jaw, a sabre-cat-skull design on her top, and clawlike earrings. Then you realize that she's up to no good. Blue colors calm the painting and pink glasses add to a dreamlike atmosphere.

The palette is limited to three main colors: blue, black, and pink. If you look closely, they not only work well together, but they're also composed in harmony wherever I've added them to the paper.

Each color is featured in no more than three elements: blue (hair, blouse, and rose); pink (glasses, sleeves, and material at the bottom of the page); black (her top and the two ribbons tying her twin ponytails). This adds rhythm and harmony to the painting.

Follow the step-by-step breakdown and learn how I combine markers and pencils in this limited color palette to create a range of shades and tones in a harmonious image.

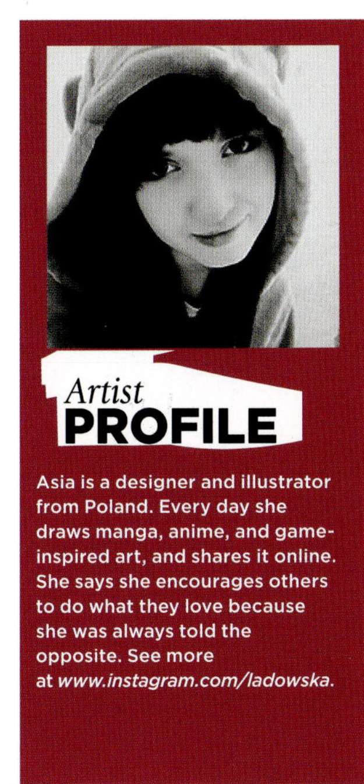

Artist **PROFILE**

Asia is a designer and illustrator from Poland. Every day she draws manga, anime, and game-inspired art, and shares it online. She says she encourages others to do what they love because she was always told the opposite. See more at *www.instagram.com/ladowska*.

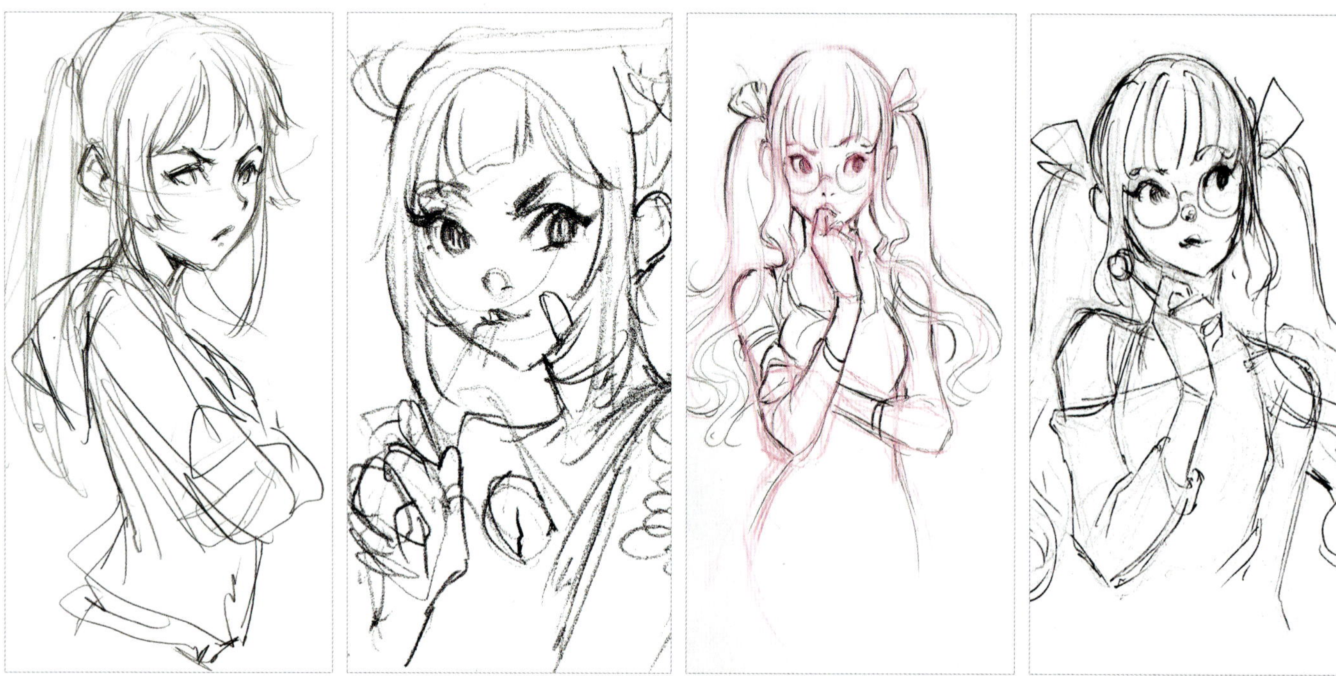

1 Sketch the day away.

It's okay to spend time developing ideas—sketching them out for a while before developing a final drawing. On a good day, it can take five minutes to draw what I want, when hours of labor won't bring the same fresh and satisfying result. Take your time and keep sketches loose.

MATERIALS

PAPER

- Canson Moulin du Roy, 300gsm, hot pressed watercolor paper, cheap printer paper for sketching

PENCILS

- Mechanical pencils with black and colored leads. Black, 0.35mm (HB) and 0.5mm (2B); Pink, Uni NanoDia 0.5mm (HB)

MARKERS

- Copic Sketch and Ciao Markers: E0000, R0000, R000, R00, R11, R30, RV10, RV21, B000, B21, B24, B23, B26, B39, N0, N1, N2, N3, N4, N6, and N8

MULTILINERS

- Copic and Sakura Micron in various colors and thicknesses: 0.03, 0.05, 0.1, 0.3—sepia, black, pink, and blue

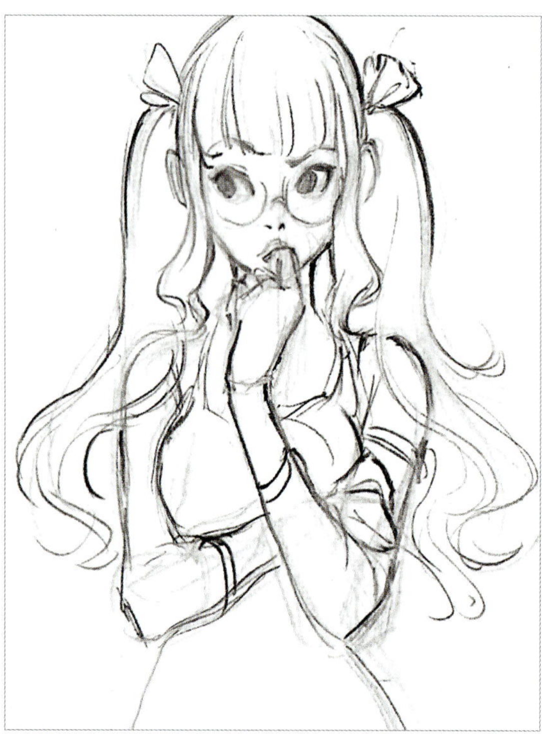

2 Incorporate different media.

Hello, Photoshop! At this stage, I'd usually choose my favorite messy sketch, scan, and open it in Photoshop. Here, I change the image to black and white and make use of the Liquify tool. Flipping it horizontally reveals some mistakes in the drawing.

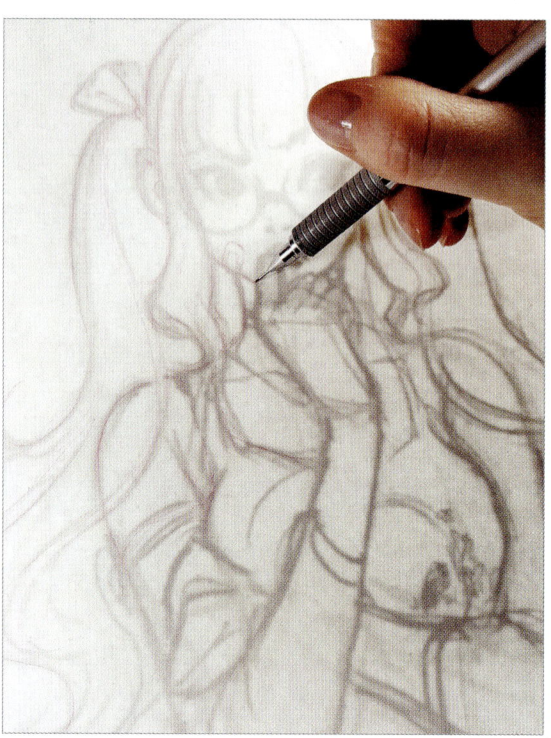

3 Size matters!

My sketches are tiny because it's easier to control the character's proportions. It also stops me from adding a lot of details at the beginning of the process. I scale the design to A4 size and print out to then transfer to a smooth watercolor paper using a light box.

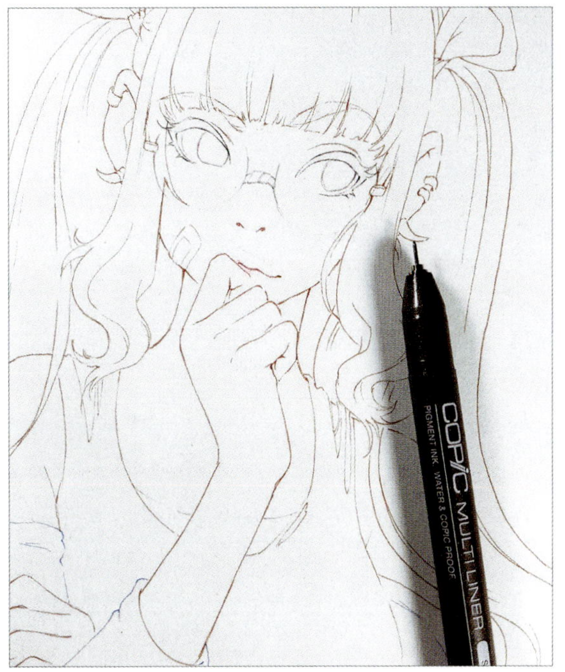

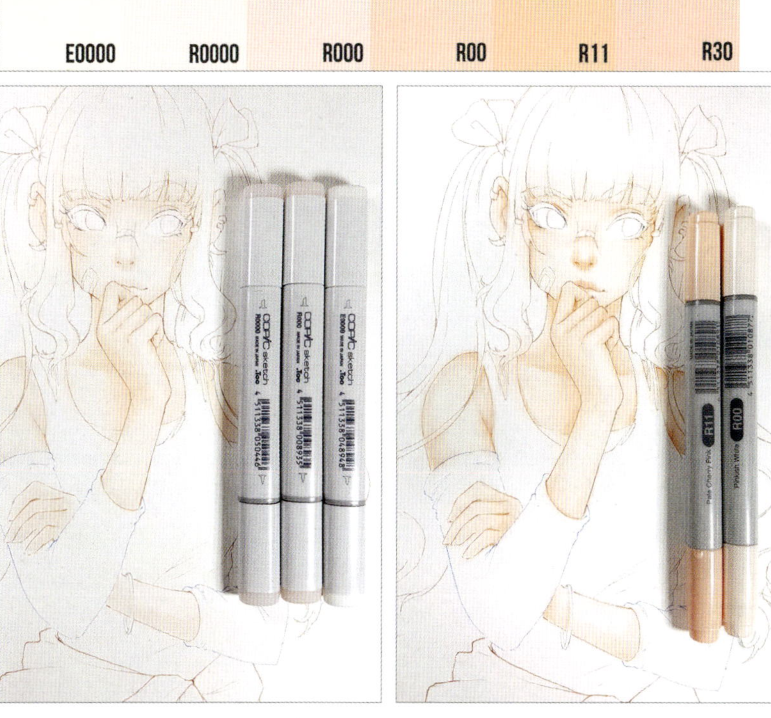

4 Add the first layer of ink.

Before inking, I make some tweaks and add details with pencil, and then put down a thin line mostly with the Sepia Copic Multiliner. Sepia is a safe choice because almost all other colors can cover it in the second stage of inking. Note that ink fades when used with markers, so there's no need to overwork the line art at this stage.

5 Build the color.

Alcohol markers tend to pick up ink that's already on the paper, so it's best to start from the lightest parts of the composition and build up darker colors gradually. The tip will always find a chance to pick up dark ink and create smudges. Bearing this in mind, I start coloring the skin first.

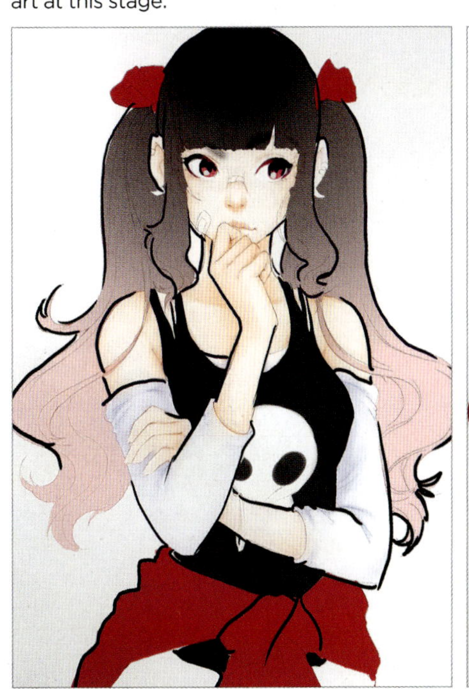

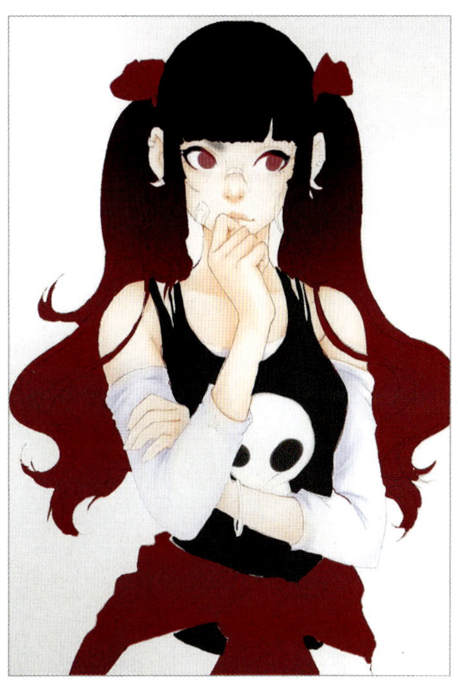

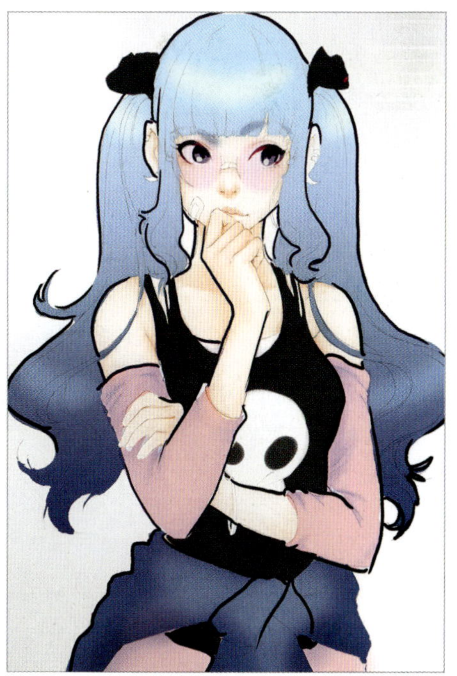

6 Decide on the color palette.

Photoshop comes in handy again! Digital software makes it easy for me to try out a range of possibilities and color combinations, to the degree where I almost decide to use the colors I don't have as markers! When I'm working out a color palette, I try digital coloring first or draw little five-minute thumbnails on paper and color them in traditionally. In the end I settle on the blue-pink-black palette.

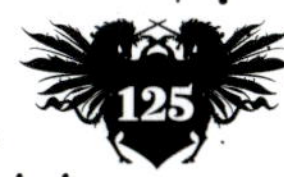

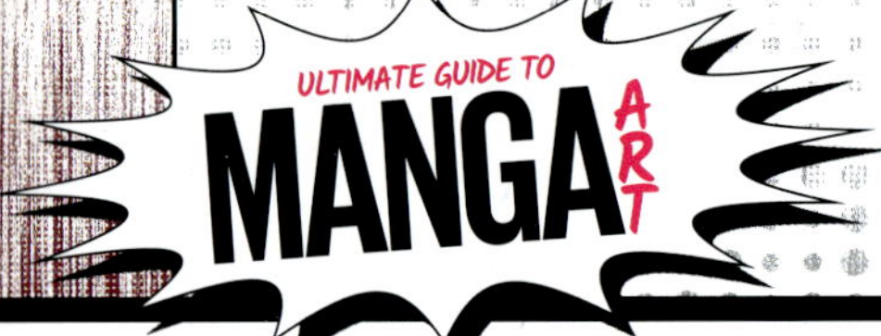

B000

B21

B24

B23

B26

B39

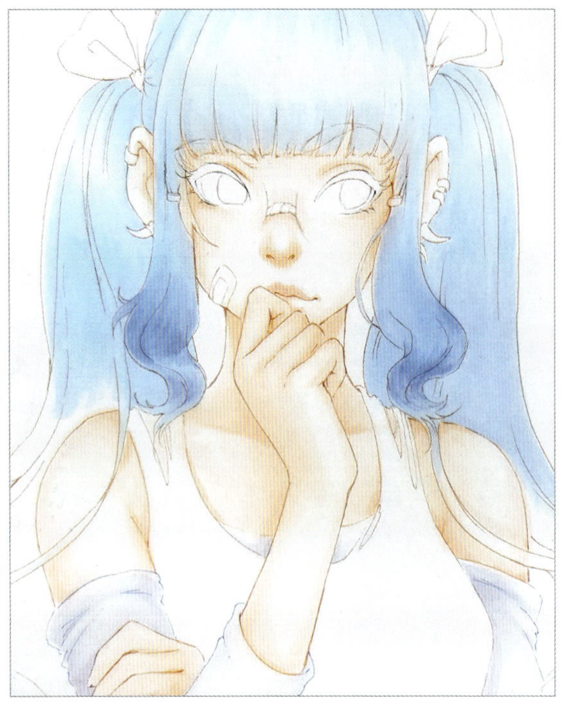

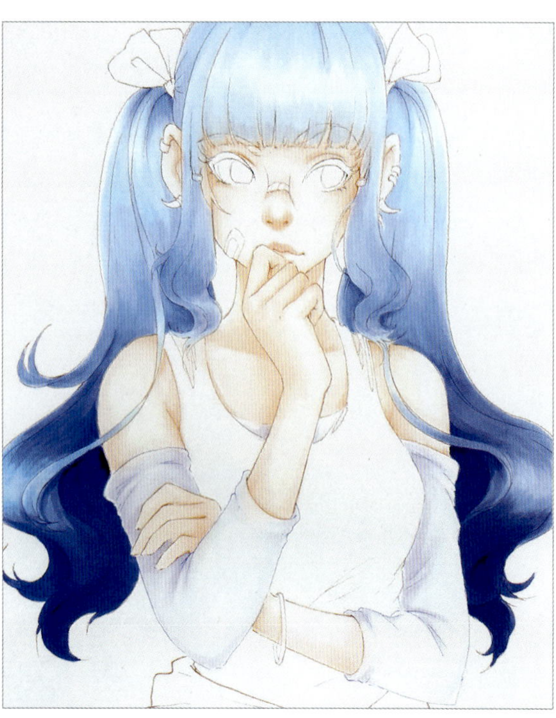

7 Color the character's hair.

I love using vibrant gradient colors to paint hair! Copic markers can blend seamlessly, and to achieve this, I regularly switch between markers, using a lighter color to create smooth blends. It takes some patience, but it's worth it. I would recommend blending your markers while the ink is still wet.

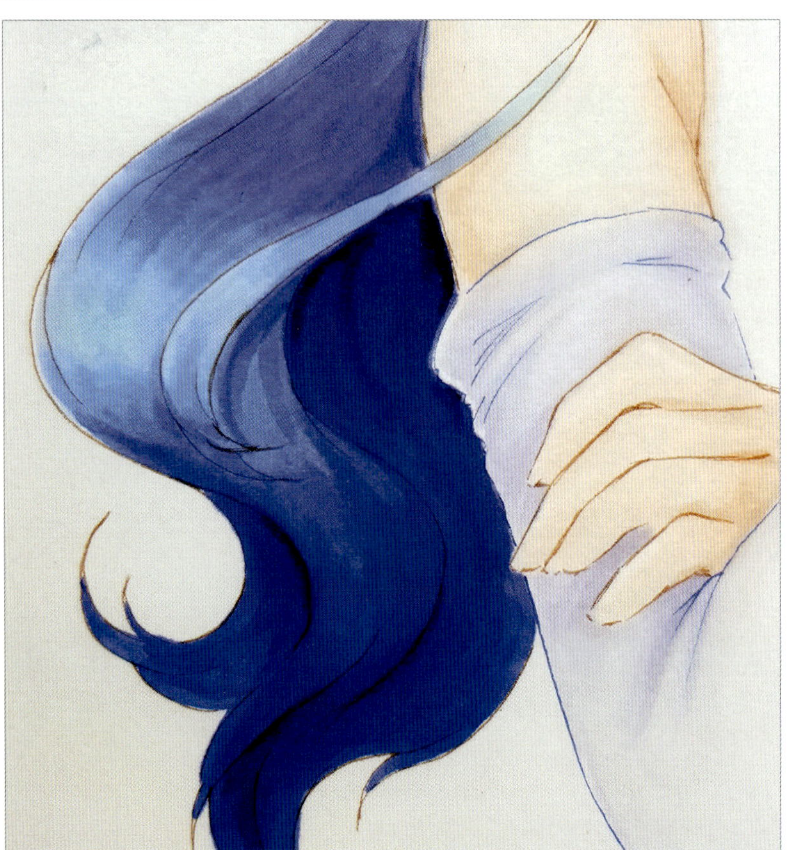

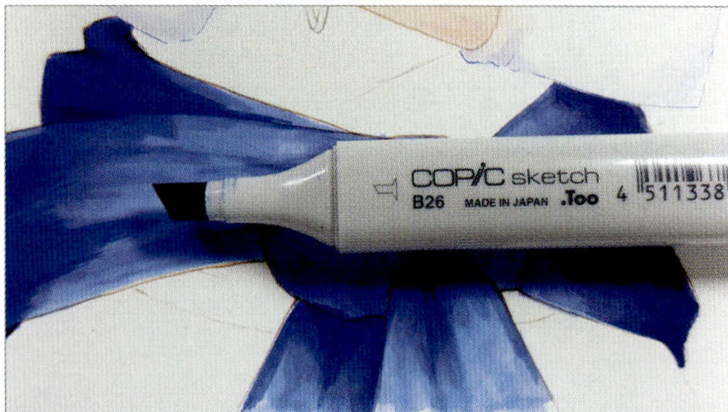

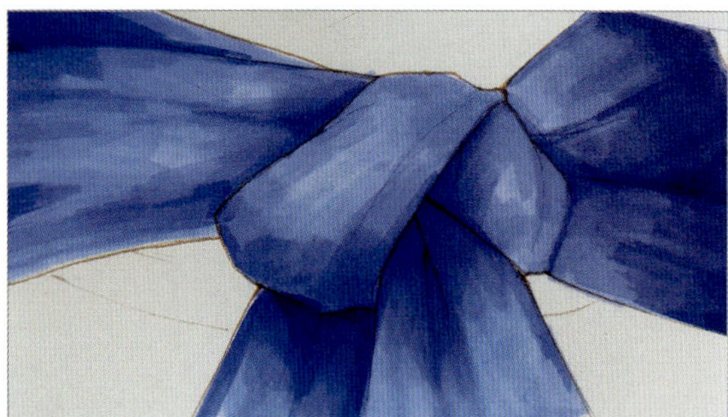

8 Discover the magic of Copic blending.

I'm using the same colors for both the hair and the blouse tied around her waist. I use the side with a brush nib for her hair, which enables me to blend softly. For the blouse, I use the broad nib of the markers to create a realistic material look. Using markers with different tips makes it possible to create a range of textures.

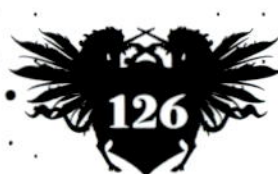

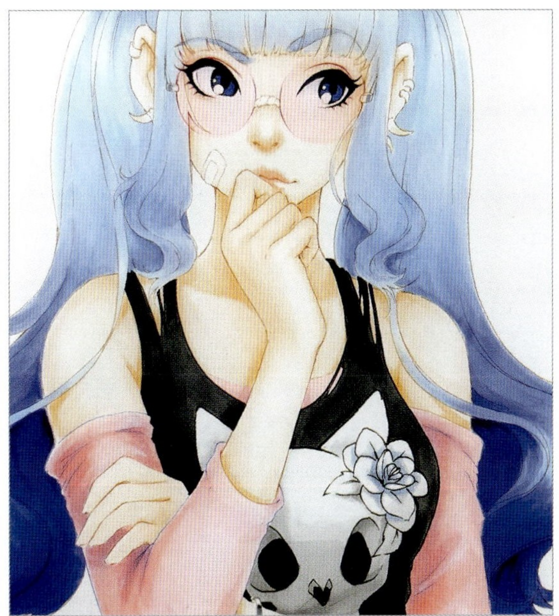

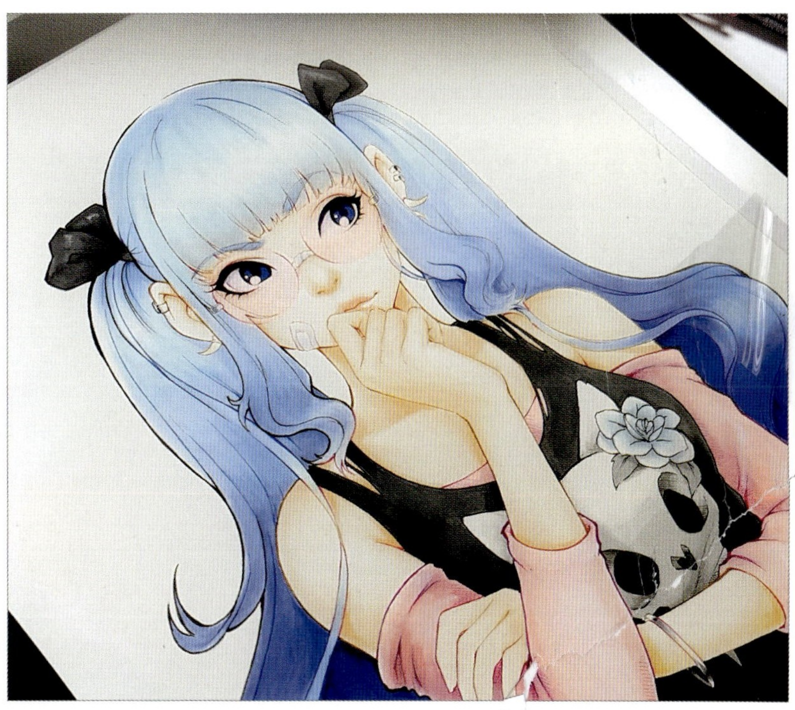

9 Design accessories.

This is the fun part of the process. Her top shows a cute sabre-toothed cat's skull with cat ears. Adding a flower makes the cat look cute and complements my color composition, which was missing a blue accent. Her glasses, earrings, patch on her jaw, and bows all come together to create a dangerously sweet character!

10 Add a second layer of ink.

Now I apply a second layer of line work, using various colors of multiliners. Varying the line thickness keeps things interesting. The first layer has already faded with the amount of alcohol and ink involved. Time to bring it back!

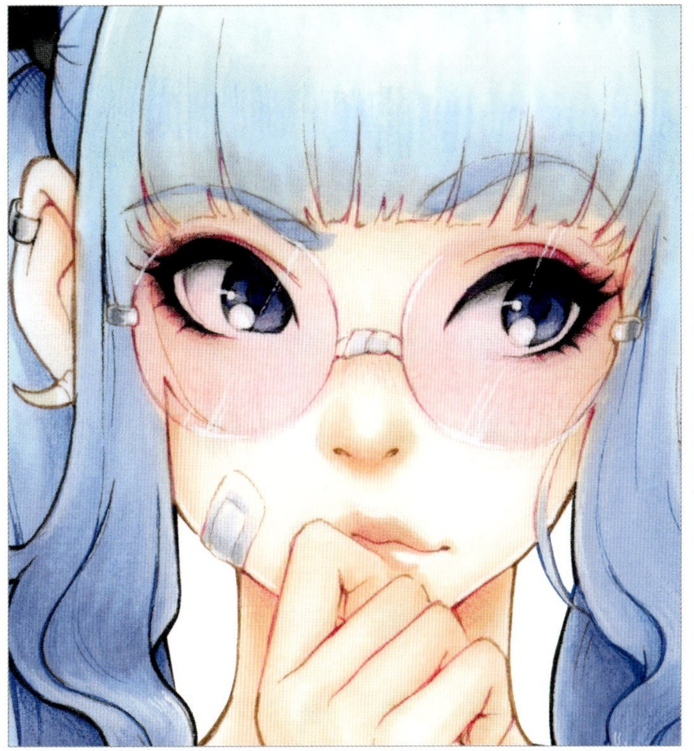

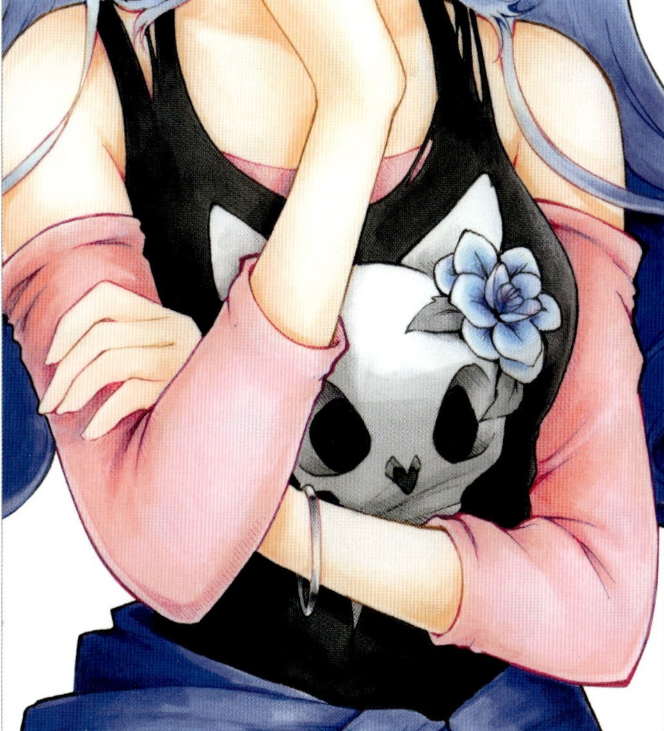

11 Put the final touches on the character.

I use colored pencils to make barely noticeable changes to the drawing, such as deepening the shadows and adding a blush to the character's cheeks. Colored pencils complement markers well and can cover small imperfections and uneven blending.

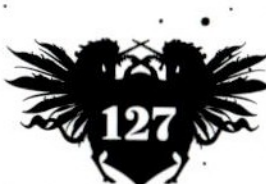

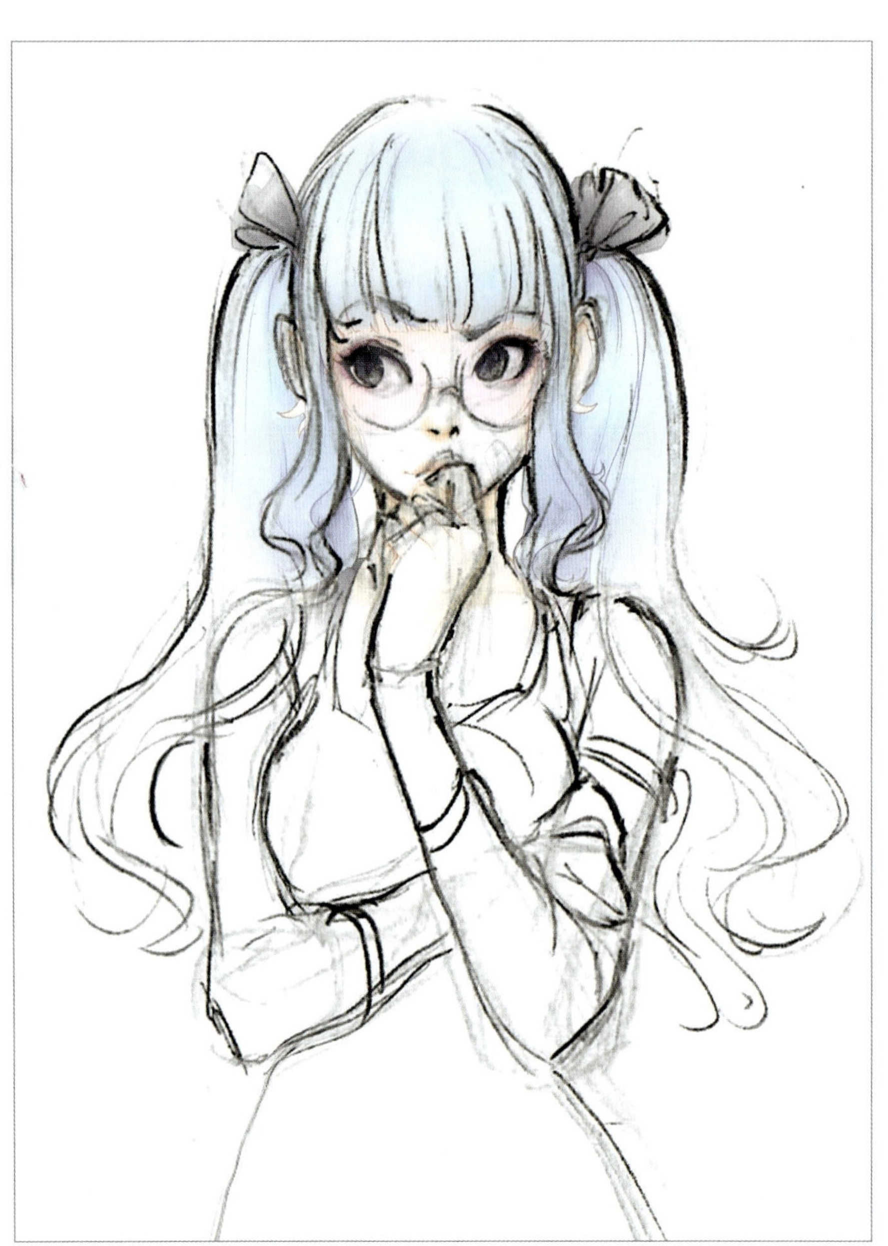